myFocus INTERVENTION

LEVEL

A

Pearson

Glenview, Illinois Boston, Massachusetts
Chandler, Arizona New York, New York

Pearson Education, Inc. 330 Hudson Street, New York, NY 10013

Pearson

ISBN-13: 978-0-328-99390-1
ISBN-10: 0-328-99390-5
3 19

PART 1: FOUNDATIONAL SKILLS

PRINT CONCEPTS

PHONOLOGICAL AWARENESS

PHONICS, MORPHOLOGY, AND SPELLING

VOCABULARY

PART 2: READING, WRITING, AND LANGUAGE

READING LITERATURE

READING INFORMATIONAL TEXT

WRITING

LANGUAGE AND CONVENTIONS

INQUIRY AND RESEARCH

myFocus Intervention Program Overview

Targeted, Flexible Intervention

myFocus Intervention is designed to help teachers target and address students' intervention needs, whether students require minor or intensive remediation. *myFocus Intervention* can be used either as a companion to *myView* or as a separate, standalone intervention.

Components

The *myFocus Intervention* system has three components. All components are available online at PearsonRealize.com.

myFocus Intervention
Teacher Resource Guide
Available in print and online

myFocus Reader
Available in print and online

myFocus Reader
Teaching Support
Available online

myFocus Intervention Teacher Resource Guide

Targeted instruction focuses on development of skills and strategies to help students achieve on-grade-level expectations. The lessons are tied to national and state English Language Arts standards. Lessons can be used flexibly, based on students' differing instructional needs and rates of mastery.

Discrete skills are scaffolded into small, manageable minilessons for thorough coverage, focused practice, and built-in progress monitoring. Data-driven assessments after sets of related lessons allow teachers to monitor students' progress efficiently and effectively.

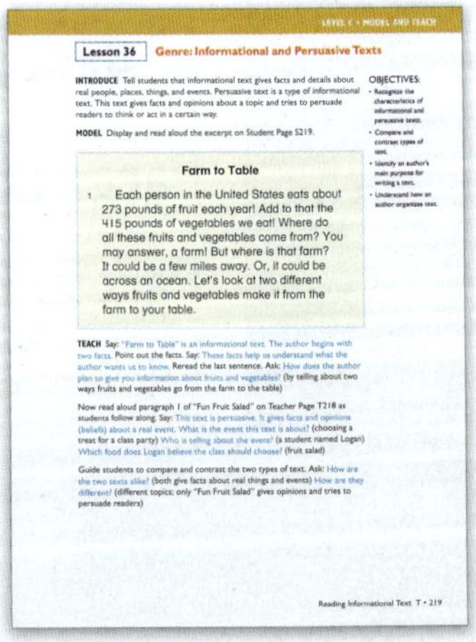
Lesson 36 Genre: Informational and Persuasive Texts

INTRODUCE Tell students that informational text gives facts and details about real people, places, things, and events. Persuasive text is a type of informational text. This text gives facts and opinions about a topic and tries to persuade readers to think or act in a certain way.

MODEL Display and read aloud the excerpt on Student Page S219.

Farm to Table

1 Each person in the United States eats about 273 pounds of fruit each year! Add to that the 415 pounds of vegetables we eat! Where do all these fruits and vegetables come from? You may answer, a farm! But where is that farm? It could be a few miles away. Or, it could be across an ocean. Let's look at two different ways fruits and vegetables make it from the farm to your table.

TEACH Say: "Farm to Table" is an informational text. The author begins with two facts. Point out the facts. Say: These facts help us understand what the author wants us to know. Reread the last sentence. Ask: How does the author plan to give you information about fruits and vegetables? (by telling about two ways fruits and vegetables go from the farm to the table)

Now read aloud paragraph 1 of "Fun Fruit Salad" on Teacher Page T218 as students follow along. Say: This text is persuasive. It gives facts and opinions (beliefs) about a real event. What is the event this text is about? (choosing a treat for a class party) Who is telling about the event? (a student named Logan) Which food does Logan believe the class should choose? (fruit salad)

Guide students to compare and contrast the two types of text. Ask: How are the two texts alike? (both give facts about real things and events) How are they different? (different topics; only "Fun Fruit Salad" gives opinions and tries to persuade readers)

OBJECTIVES:
- Recognize the characteristics of informational and persuasive texts.
- Compare and contrast types of text.
- Identify an author's main purpose for writing a text.
- Understand how an author organizes text.

Reading Informational Text T • 219

myFocus Reader The *myFocus Readers* are based on the work of Elfrieda "Freddy" H. Hiebert. Dr. Hiebert's work has proven that struggling readers can engage in complex thinking, but they may lack basic foundational skills in English. The texts are carefully crafted to include an appropriate balance of text complexity and vocabulary frequency.

The selections in *myFocus Reader* expose students to a variety of genres. Nonfiction texts tie to science and social studies concepts. All texts build students' academic vocabulary and comprehension of increasingly complex texts.

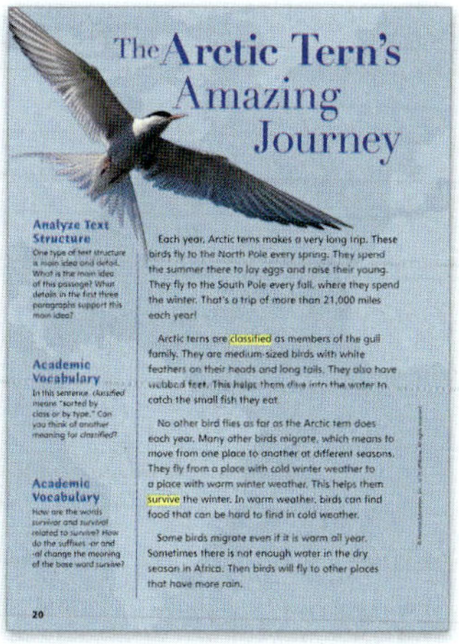
The Arctic Tern's Amazing Journey

Analyze Text Structure
One type of text structure is main idea and detail. What is the main idea of this passage? What details in the first three paragraphs support this main idea?

Each year, Arctic terns makes a very long trip. These birds fly to the North Pole every spring. They spend the summer there to lay eggs and raise their young. They fly to the South Pole every fall, where they spend the winter. That's a trip of more than 21,000 miles each year!

Academic Vocabulary
In this sentence, *classified* means "sorted by class or by type." Can you think of another meaning for *classified*?

Arctic terns are classified as members of the gull family. They are medium-sized birds with white feathers on their heads and long tails. They also have webbed feet. This helps them dive into the water to catch the small fish they eat.

Academic Vocabulary
How are the words *survivor* and *survival* related to *survive*? How do the suffixes *-or* and *-al* change the meaning of the base word *survive*?

No other bird flies as far as the Arctic tern does each year. Many other birds migrate, which means to move from one place to another at different seasons. They fly from a place with cold winter weather to a place with warm winter weather. This helps them survive the winter. In warm weather, birds can find food that can be hard to find in cold weather.

Some birds migrate even if it is warm all year. Sometimes there is not enough water in the dry season in Africa. Then birds will fly to other places that have more rain.

20

***myFocus Reader* Teaching Support** Teaching support is designed to be used with small groups of students. Instruction integrates foundational skills with comprehension and vocabulary skills and strategies. Instruction also engages students in meaningful conversation about selections in their *myFocus Reader* and how they compare to other texts students have read.

myFocus Reader Teaching Support engages students in a First Read of the text that focuses on skill and strategy development and in a Second Read that focuses on deepening comprehension by exploring the big idea of the text and making connections to other texts and to students' experiences.

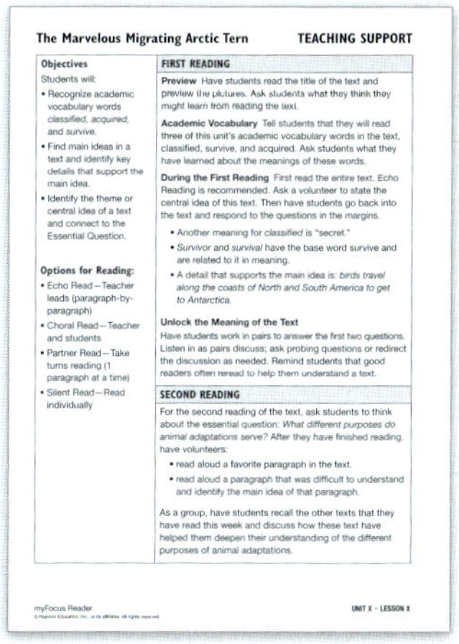
The Marvelous Migrating Arctic Tern **TEACHING SUPPORT**

Objectives	FIRST READING
Students will: • Recognize academic vocabulary words *classified, acquired,* and *survive.* • Find main ideas in a text and identify key details that support the main idea. • Identify the theme or central idea of a text and connect to the Essential Question. **Options for Reading:** • Echo Read—Teacher leads (paragraph-by-paragraph) • Choral Read—Teacher and students • Partner Read—Take turns reading (1 paragraph at a time) • Silent Read—Read individually	**Preview** Have students read the title of the text and preview the pictures. Ask students what they think they might learn from reading the text. **Academic Vocabulary** Tell students that they will read three of this unit's academic vocabulary words in the text, classified, survive, and acquired. Ask students what they have learned about the meanings of these words. **During the First Reading** First read the entire text. Echo Reading is recommended. Ask a volunteer to state the central idea of this text. Then have students go back into the text and respond to the questions in the margins. • Another meaning for *classified* is "secret." • *Survivor* and *survival* have the base word survive and are related to it in meaning. • A detail that supports the main idea is: *birds travel along the coasts of North and South America to get to Antarctica.* **Unlock the Meaning of the Text** Have students work in pairs to answer the first two questions. Listen in as pairs discuss; ask probing questions or redirect the discussion as needed. Remind students that good readers often reread to help them understand a text. **SECOND READING** For the second reading of the text, ask students to think about the essential question: *What different purposes do animal adaptations serve?* After they have finished reading, have volunteers: • read aloud a favorite paragraph in the text. • read aloud a paragraph that was difficult to understand and identify the main idea of that paragraph. As a group, have students recall the other texts that they have read this week and discuss how these text have helped them deepen their understanding of the different purposes of animal adaptations.

myFocus Reader UNIT X • LESSON X

myFocus Intervention Teacher Resource Guide

Comprehensive Intervention Coverage in Two Parts

myFocus Intervention offers lessons that cover the spectrum of students' intervention needs, from foundational skills to reading literature, reading informational text, writing, and language

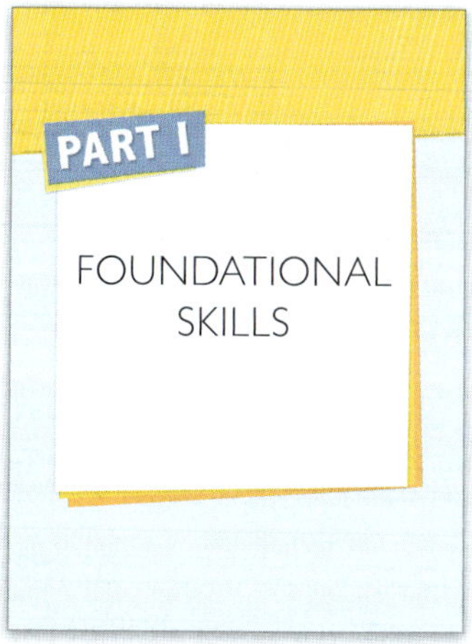

Key Elements of Reading Intervention Lessons

Part 1: Foundational Skills Focus The first part of *myFocus Intervention* focuses on Foundational Skills, as identified in national and state English Language Arts standards, and provides in-depth instruction, practice, and assessment in Print Concepts; Phonological Awareness; Phonics, Morphology, and Spelling; Fluency; and Vocabulary.

Teacher Pages

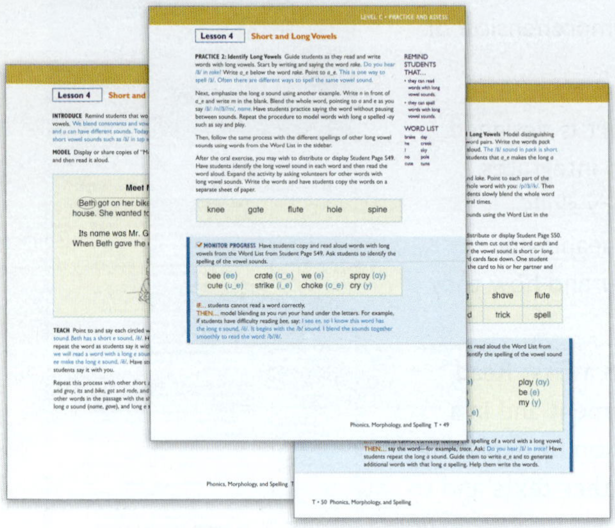

Student Pages

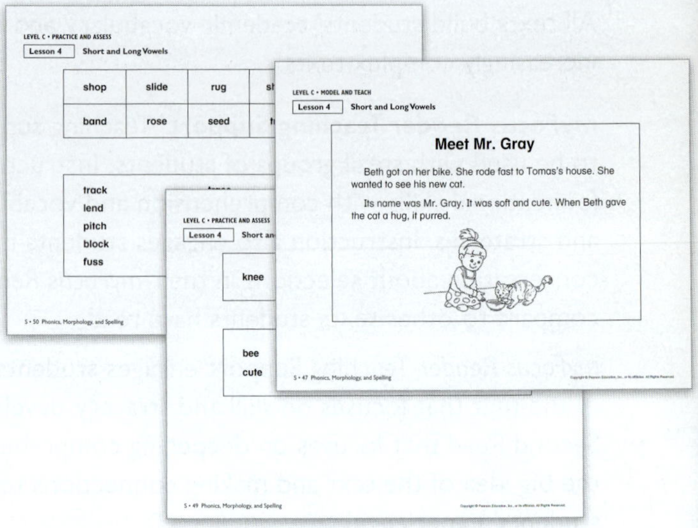

Part 2: Reading, Writing, and Language Focus The second part of *myFocus Intervention* focuses on national and state standards for Reading Literature, Reading Informational Text, Writing, and Language and Conventions.

Teacher Pages

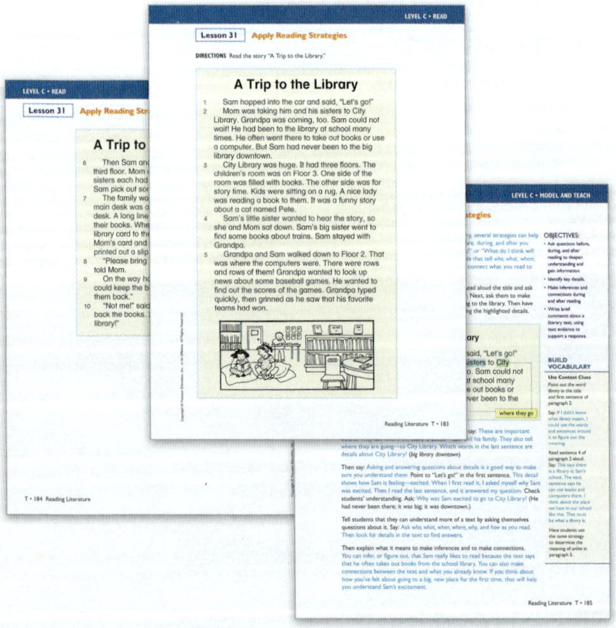

Student Pages

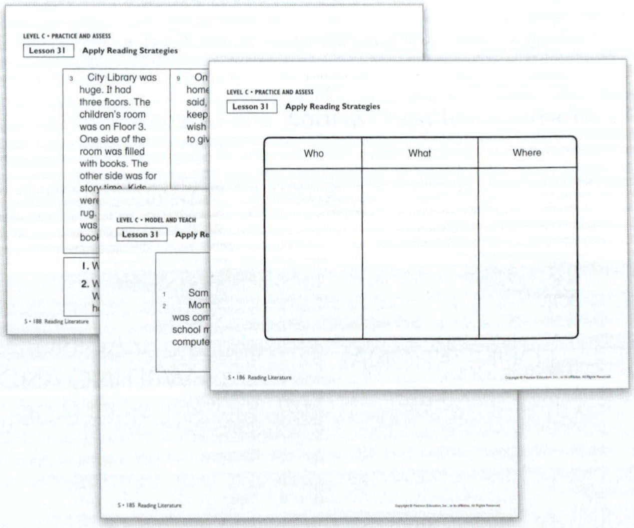

myFocus Intervention Lesson Overview

Teacher Pages

Format and Features

- Easy-to-use, consistent format
- Designed for flexible use
- Guided and independent practice in each lesson
- Progress monitoring at every step to ensure mastery
- Key objectives based on national and state English Language Arts standards

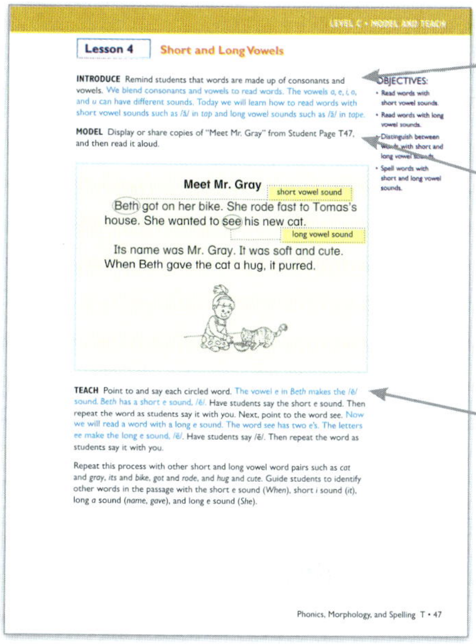

LEVEL C • MODEL AND TEACH

Lesson 4 Short and Long Vowels

INTRODUCE Remind students that words are made up of consonants and vowels. We blend consonants and vowels to read words. The vowels *a, e, i, o,* and *u* can have different sounds. Today we will learn how to read words with short vowel sounds such as /ă/ in *tap* and long vowel sounds such as /ā/ in *tape.*

MODEL Display or share copies of "Meet Mr. Gray" from Student Page T47, and then read it aloud.

OBJECTIVES:
- Read words with short vowel sounds.
- Read words with long vowel sounds.
- Distinguish between words with short and long vowel sounds.
- Spell words with short and long vowel sounds.

Meet Mr. Gray

short vowel sound

Beth got on her bike. She rode fast to Tomas's house. She wanted to see his new cat.

long vowel sound

Its name was Mr. Gray. It was soft and cute. When Beth gave the cat a hug, it purred.

TEACH Point to and say each circled word. The vowel *e* in *Beth* makes the /ĕ/ sound. *Beth* has a short *e* sound, /ĕ/. Have students say the short *e* sound. Then repeat the word as students say it with you. Next, point to the word see. Now we will read a word with a long *e* sound. The word see has two e's. The letters ee make the long e sound, /ē/. Have students say /ē/. Then repeat the word as students say it with you.

Repeat this process with other short and long vowel word pairs such as *cat* and *gray*, *its* and *bike*, *got* and *rode*, and *hug* and *cute*. Guide students to identify other words in the passage with the short e sound (*When*), short *i* sound (*it*), long *a* sound (*name, gave*), and long e sound (*She*).

Phonics, Morphology, and Spelling T • 47

INTRODUCE section identifies and defines the skill.

MODEL section and passage help teachers model the skill in context.

TEACH section allows teachers to explain, expand on, and clarify the initial skill instruction.

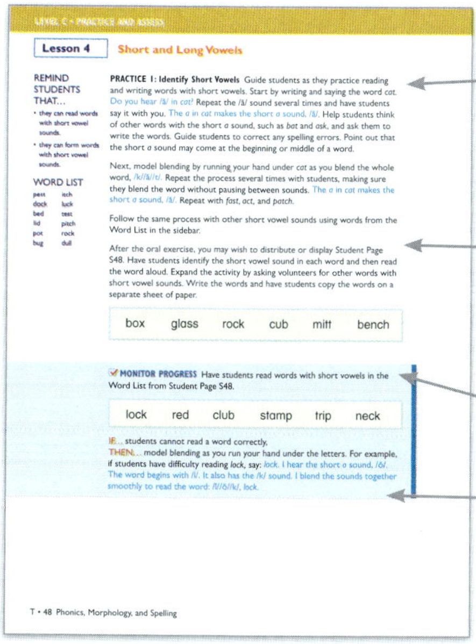

LEVEL C • PRACTICE AND ASSESS

Lesson 4 Short and Long Vowels

REMIND STUDENTS THAT...
- they can read words with short vowel sounds.
- they can form words with short vowel sounds.

WORD LIST

pest	itch
dock	luck
bed	test
lid	pitch
pot	rock
bug	dull

PRACTICE 1: Identify Short Vowels Guide students as they practice reading and writing words with short vowels. Start by writing and saying the word *cat.* Do you hear /ă/ in *cat*? Repeat the /ă/ sound several times and have students say it with you. The *a* in *cat* makes the short *a* sound, /ă/. Help students think of other words with the short *a* sound, such as *bat* and *ask*, and ask them to write the words. Guide students to correct any spelling errors. Point out that the short *a* sound may come at the beginning or middle of a word.

Next, model blending by running your hand under *cat* as you blend the whole word, /k//ă//t/. Repeat the process several times with students, making sure they blend the word without pausing between sounds. The *a* in *cat* makes the short *a* sound, /ă/. Repeat with *fast*, *act*, and *patch.*

Follow the same process with other short vowel sounds using words from the Word List in the sidebar.

After the oral exercise, you may wish to distribute or display Student Page S48. Have students identify the short vowel sound in each word and then read the word aloud. Expand the activity by asking volunteers for other words with short vowel sounds. Write the words and have students copy the words on a separate sheet of paper.

box glass rock cub mitt bench

✔ **MONITOR PROGRESS** Have students read words with short vowels in the Word List from Student Page S48.

lock red club stamp trip neck

IF... students cannot read a word correctly,
THEN... model blending as you run your hand under the letters. For example, if students have difficulty reading *lock*, say: *lock*. I hear the short *o* sound, /ŏ/. The word begins with /l/. It also has the /k/ sound. I blend the sounds together smoothly to read the word: /l//ŏ//k/, *lock.*

T • 48 Phonics, Morphology, and Spelling

Guided practice helps students develop skills.

Routines, passages, and examples are included at point of use.

Monitor Progress helps teachers quickly assess student proficiency and determine next steps.

Student Pages

Projectable and Printable Pages The models, passages, examples, and graphic organizers on Teacher Lesson Pages are also included as student-facing pages. Student Pages can be projected digitally for group work. They can also be printed so students have their own copies for reading and writing.

Model and Teach Each Model and Teach passage also appears as a Student Page. Students can follow along as the teacher reads the passage aloud, noting how the focused skill is introduced in context. As students gain reading proficiency, they can use the passages for repeated readings as well as for comprehension practice.

Student Pages allow students to follow along, read, and annotate the model passage.

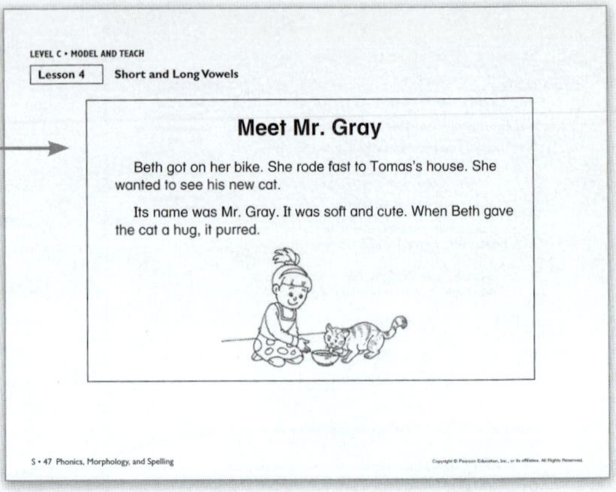
LEVEL C • MODEL AND TEACH

Lesson 4 Short and Long Vowels

Meet Mr. Gray

Beth got on her bike. She rode fast to Tomas's house. She wanted to see his new cat.

Its name was Mr. Gray. It was soft and cute. When Beth gave the cat a hug, it purred.

S • 47 Phonics, Morphology, and Spelling

Practice and Assess Practice and Assess passages, examples, and graphic organizers also appear as Student Pages. Students use these pages—whether displayed for the group or as individual handouts—to practice the skills and demonstrate independent mastery.

Student Pages allow students to engage in the lesson through a variety of whole-group, small-group, and individual work that supports learning.

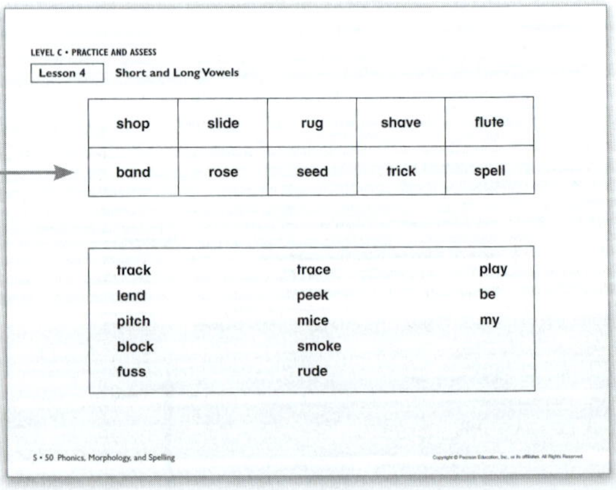
LEVEL C • PRACTICE AND ASSESS

Lesson 4 Short and Long Vowels

shop	slide	rug	shave	flute
band	rose	seed	trick	spell

track	trace	play
lend	peek	be
pitch	mice	my
block	smoke	
fuss	rude	

S • 50 Phonics, Morphology, and Spelling

Read Passages and Build Vocabulary

Read Passages All Reading Literature and Reading Informational Text close reading lessons are preceded by a two-page reading passage. Teachers can read these passages aloud and give students copies to follow along or read and reread on their own. The Read passages offer a variety of brief texts on engaging, grade-appropriate literary, science and technology, and social studies topics, and they give students opportunities to apply close reading skills. Students are encouraged to annotate their copies of the passages as they analyze details and interact with the text and illustrations.

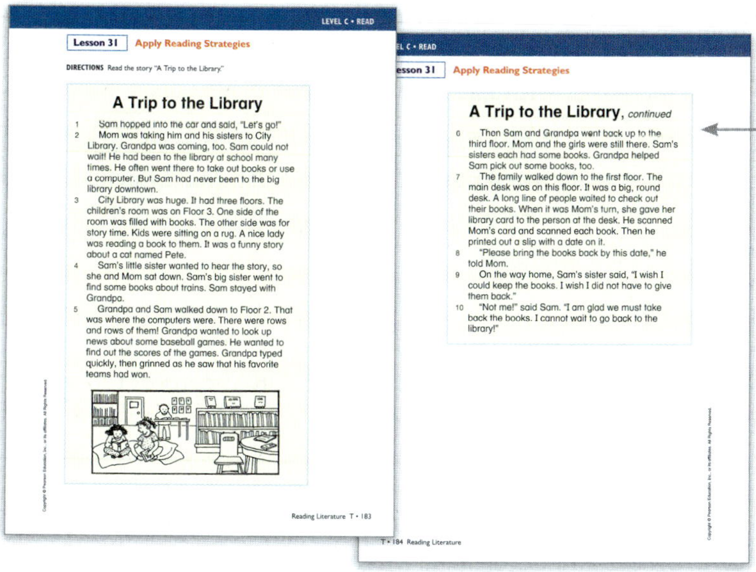

LEVEL C • READ

Lesson 31 Apply Reading Strategies

DIRECTIONS Read the story "A Trip to the Library."

A Trip to the Library

1 Sam hopped into the car and said, "Let's go!"

2 Mom was taking him and his sisters to City Library. Grandpa was coming, too. Sam could not wait! He had been to the library at school many times. He often went there to take out books or use a computer. But Sam had never been to the big library downtown.

3 City Library was huge. It had three floors. The children's room was on Floor 3. One side of the room was filled with books. The other side was for story time. Kids were sitting on a rug. A nice lady was reading a book to them. It was a funny story about a cat named Pete.

4 Sam's little sister wanted to hear the story, so she and Mom sat down. Sam's big sister went to find some books about trains. Sam stayed with Grandpa.

5 Grandpa and Sam walked down to Floor 2. That was where the computers were. There were rows and rows of them! Grandpa wanted to look up news about some baseball games. He wanted to find out the scores of the games. Grandpa typed quickly, then grinned as he saw that his favorite teams had won.

Reading Literature T • 183

Lesson 31 Apply Reading Strategies

A Trip to the Library, *continued*

6 Then Sam and Grandpa went back up to the third floor. Mom and the girls were still there. Sam's sisters each had some books. Grandpa helped Sam pick out some books, too.

7 The family walked down to the first floor. The main desk was on this floor. It was a big, round desk. A long line of people waited to check out their books. When it was Mom's turn, she gave her library card to the person at the desk. He scanned Mom's card and scanned each book. Then he printed out a slip with a date on it.

8 "Please bring the books back by this date," he told Mom.

9 On the way home, Sam's sister said, "I wish I could keep the books. I wish I did not have to give them back."

10 "Not me!" said Sam. "I am glad we must take back the books. I cannot wait to go back to the library!"

T • 184 Reading Literature

Read passages help students engage with longer texts to practice close reading.

Build Vocabulary In most Reading Literature and Reading Informational Text close reading lessons, the Model and Teach section includes a brief Build Vocabulary feature. The feature gives students targeted practice with strategies to help determine the meaning of words and phrases in context. After a Think Aloud, students demonstrate how to determine the meaning of a new word or phrase in context by applying the strategy on their own.

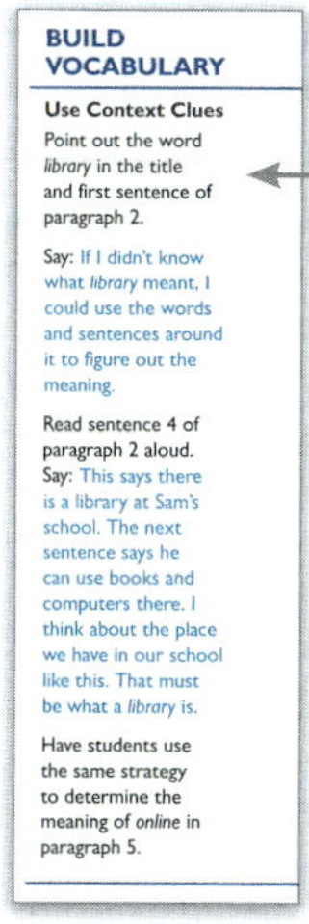

BUILD VOCABULARY

Use Context Clues

Point out the word *library* in the title and first sentence of paragraph 2.

Say: If I didn't know what *library* meant, I could use the words and sentences around it to figure out the meaning.

Read sentence 4 of paragraph 2 aloud.

Say: This says there is a library at Sam's school. The next sentence says he can use books and computers there. I think about the place we have in our school like this. That must be what a *library* is.

Have students use the same strategy to determine the meaning of *online* in paragraph 5.

Build Vocabulary features introduce vocabulary strategies, model the strategy, and have students apply it independently.

Formative Assessment

Monitor Progress and Checkpoint Assessments Ongoing formative assessment guides intervention and ensures that struggling readers master the skills they need to learn without spending time on the skills they already know. Within the *myFocus Intervention* program, formative assessment opportunities are quick, efficient, and data-driven. Formative assessment occurs within each Practice minilesson (Monitor Progress and Independent Practice) and after a series of related lessons within a strand (Checkpoint Assessments). For effective assessment, use these steps.

1. **Identify individual intervention needs.** Without intervention focused precisely on each student's needs, the gap between students performing at and below level often increases with each grade.
   - For the youngest students or those struggling with discrete skills, teachers may be able to identify specific weaknesses. Teachers use the Checkpoint Assessments to determine precise gaps in skills development and to ensure that intervention is focused and effective.
   - For students with broad gaps in multiple skill areas or those who are performing well below grade level, teachers are advised to use a research-based diagnostic assessment tool, such as Pearson's DRA®2, to determine students' full reading-intervention needs accurately.
2. **Monitor progress quickly and frequently.** As teachers work through intervention lessons with students, they use the Monitor Progress activities to check students' progress and determine whether each student should advance or whether reteaching is needed. If students continuously struggle with the Monitor Progress and Independent Practice formative assessments, teachers can adjust the pace of the intervention (see p. T24).
3. **Check that students are retaining and developing knowledge.** Teachers use the Checkpoint Assessments to guide pacing and determine intervention entry and exit points.
   - As students develop skills across multiple lessons, teachers use the Checkpoint Assessments to ensure that students have retained the skills and can apply them in new and diverse contexts. Checkpoint Assessment data help teachers determine when to review skills, adjust instruction and pacing as needed, and gauge intervention exit points.
   - For any level and intensity of intervention, the Checkpoint Assessments offer a quick way to determine key skills proficiency.

Monitor Progress Monitor Progress assessment occurs after each minilesson. The final minilesson culminates in Independent Practice, in which students demonstrate what they have learned independently.

IF.../THEN... directives guide intervention based on Monitor Progress results.

> **MONITOR PROGRESS** Have students copy and read aloud words with long vowels from the Word List from Student Page S49. Ask students to identify the spelling of the vowel sounds.
>
> | | | | |
> |---|---|---|---|
> | bee (ee) | crate (a_e) | we (e) | spray (ay) |
> | cute (u_e) | strike (i_e) | choke (o_e) | cry (y) |
>
> IF... students cannot read a word correctly,
> THEN... model blending as you run your hand under the letters. For example, if students have difficulty reading *bee*, say: I see ee, so I know this word has the long e sound, /ē/. It begins with the /b/ sound. I blend the sounds together smoothly to read the word: /b//ē/.

Checkpoint Assessments Two-page Checkpoint Assessments occur after similar lessons within a strand. Assessment instructions, scoring, and remediation options are included with each Checkpoint Assessment.

Scoring instructions help teachers assess students' mastery of skills and shape future instruction.

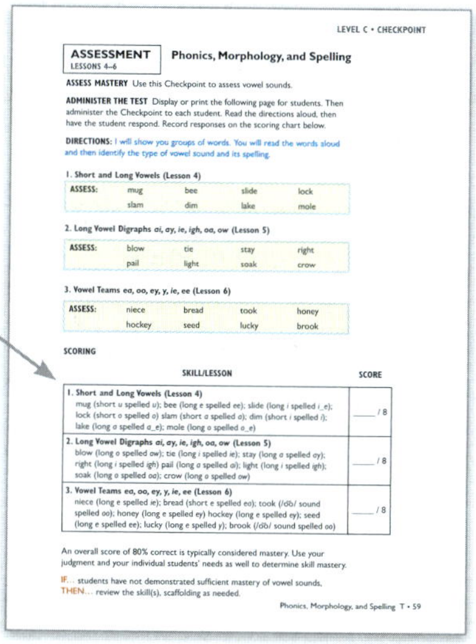
LEVEL C • CHECKPOINT

ASSESSMENT LESSONS 4–6 **Phonics, Morphology, and Spelling**

ASSESS MASTERY Use this Checkpoint to assess vowel sounds.

ADMINISTER THE TEST Display or print the following page for students. Then administer the Checkpoint to each student. Read the directions aloud, then have the student respond. Record responses on the scoring chart below.

DIRECTIONS: I will show you groups of words. You will read the words aloud and then identify the type of vowel sound and its spelling.

1. Short and Long Vowels (Lesson 4)

ASSESS:	mug	bee	slide	lock
	slam	dim	lake	mole

2. Long Vowel Digraphs *ai, ay, ie, igh, oa, ow* (Lesson 5)

ASSESS:	blow	tie	stay	right
	pail	light	soak	crow

3. Vowel Teams *ea, oo, ey, y, ie, ee* (Lesson 6)

ASSESS:	niece	bread	took	honey
	hockey	seed	lucky	brook

SCORING

SKILL/LESSON	SCORE
1. Short and Long Vowels (Lesson 4) mug (short *u* spelled *u*); bee (long *e* spelled *ee*); slide (long *i* spelled *i_e*); lock (short *o* spelled *o*) slam (short *a* spelled *a*); dim (short *i* spelled *i*); lake (long *a* spelled *a_e*); mole (long *o* spelled *o_e*)	___ / 8
2. Long Vowel Digraphs *ai, ay, ie, igh, oa, ow* (Lesson 5) blow (long *o* spelled *ow*); tie (long *i* spelled *ie*); stay (long *a* spelled *ay*); right (long *i* spelled *igh*) pail (long *a* spelled *ai*); light (long *i* spelled *igh*); soak (long *o* spelled *oa*); crow (long *o* spelled *ow*)	___ / 8
3. Vowel Teams *ea, oo, ey, y, ie, ee* (Lesson 6) niece (long e spelled *ie*); bread (short e spelled *ea*); took (/o͝o/ sound spelled *oo*); honey (long e spelled *ey*) hockey (long e spelled *ey*); seed (long e spelled ee); lucky (long e spelled *y*); brook (/o͝o/ sound spelled *oo*)	___ / 8

An overall score of 80% correct is typically considered mastery. Use your judgment and your individual students' needs as well to determine skill mastery.

IF... students have not demonstrated sufficient mastery of vowel sounds,
THEN... review the skill(s), scaffolding as needed.

Phonics, Morphology, and Spelling T • 59

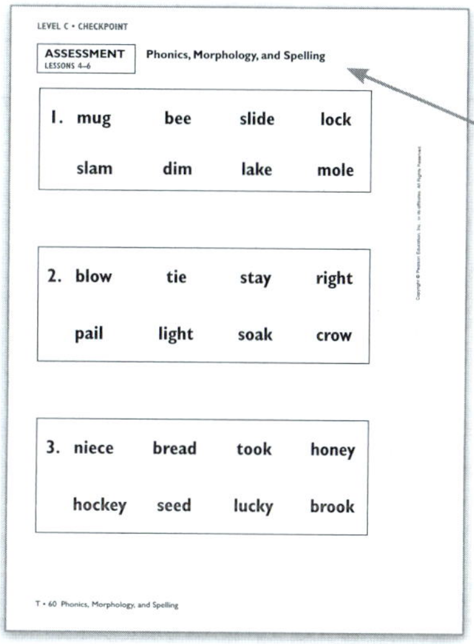
LEVEL C • CHECKPOINT

ASSESSMENT LESSONS 4–6 **Phonics, Morphology, and Spelling**

1.	**mug**	**bee**	**slide**	**lock**
	slam	**dim**	**lake**	**mole**

2.	**blow**	**tie**	**stay**	**right**
	pail	**light**	**soak**	**crow**

3.	**niece**	**bread**	**took**	**honey**
	hockey	**seed**	**lucky**	**brook**

T • 60 Phonics, Morphology, and Spelling

Short, targeted assessments determine students' proficiency across multiple lessons of instruction.

Skills Overview

Foundational Skills Trace

In Part 1, the *myFocus Intervention* program provides a clear sequence of discrete lessons that cover the full range of Foundational Skills, as identified in national and state standards, that are critical to reading success. Students' intervention needs vary widely. Many students require differing levels of intervention in particular skill areas, and teachers may need to reteach or introduce skills that are typically taught well below a student's current grade level.

The Foundational Skills Trace shows when concepts are introduced in the program as well as how they develop and expand across grades. At a glance, teachers can see the prerequisite skills students need to learn prior to addressing grade-level standards. Teachers can then determine entry points and customize an intervention path to focus on skills a student has not yet mastered, while avoiding reteaching skills the student may already know.

The skill strands vary by grade level. Use a student's current grade-level proficiency to begin determining intervention needs. Then use the skill strands to determine main areas for foundational skills intervention and identify skills and skill concepts requiring review or in-depth instruction. Students struggling with phonics and fluency may require intervention in basic Print Concepts and Phonological Awareness (Grade K and 1 skills, which *myFocus Intervention* presents in Levels A, B, and C) to substantively improve their literacy. Use the skills trace on the next few pages to identify grade-level expectations for foundational skills and to gauge grade-level proficiency.

	LEVEL					
FOUNDATIONAL SKILLS STRAND	**Level A** (Grade K)	**Level B** (Grade 1)	**Level C** (Grade 2)	**Level D** (Grade 3)	**Level E** (Grade 4)	**Level F** (Grade 5)
Print Concepts	•					
Phonological Awareness	•	•	•			
Phonics, Morphology, and Spelling	•	•	•	•	•	•
Fluency		•	•	•	•	•
Vocabulary	•	•	•	•	•	•

Focus on Decoding Follow each horizontal skill concept band to the left to determine prerequisite skills. For example, if a student struggles with Lesson 1, *Identify and Produce Rhyme and Alliteration,* for Level B Phonological Awareness, begin intervention instruction with Level A Phonological Awareness, Lesson 6, or, if needed, with Level A, Lesson 5.

Levels A, B, C (Grades K, 1, 2)
Print Concepts and Phonological Awareness

STRAND AND TOPIC	LEVEL A (GRADE K)					LEVEL B (GRADE 1)					LEVEL C (GRADE 2)
Print Concepts											
Features of Print	L1 Books, Sentences, and Words	L2 Understand Words and Sentences									
Alphabetic Code	L3 Learn the Letters in the Alphabet 1	L4 Learn the Letters in the Alphabet 2									
Phonological Awareness											
Rhyme	L5 Identify Rhyming Words and Alliteration	L6 Produce Rhyming Words and Alliteration				L1 Identify and Produce Rhyme and Alliteration					L1 Identify and Produce Rhyming Words and Alliteration
Syllables	L7 Blend and Count Syllables in Spoken Words	L8 Segment and Count Syllables in Spoken Words									
Onset and Rime	L9 Blend Onset and Rime	L10 Segment Onset and Rime									
Initial, Final, and Medial Sounds	L11 Identify Same and Different Initial Sounds	L12 Identify Same and Different Final Sounds	L13 Identify Same and Different Medial Sounds	L14 Isolate Initial, Final, and Medial Sounds		L6 Isolate Initial, Final, and Medial Sounds in Single-Syllable Words					
Adding, Substituting, and Changing Phonemes	L15 Add Initial Phonemes	L16 Add Final Phonemes	L17 Delete or Change Initial Phonemes	L18 Delete or Change Final Phonemes	L19 Change Medial Phonemes						L3 Add, Change, Remove, and Manipulate Phonemes
Blending and Segmenting	L20 Blend and Segment Two to Three Phonemes into Words					L7 Segment and Blend Sounds	L8 Blend and Segment Three- and Four-Phoneme Words	L9 Blend, Segment, and Count Five or More Phonemes	L10 *r*-Controlled Vowels	L11 Consonant Digraphs	
Short Vowel Sounds						L2 Identify Short Vowels					
Long Vowel Sounds						L3 Identify Long Vowels	L4 Review Short and Long Vowel Sounds	L5 Distinguish Short and Long Vowel Sounds			L2 Distinguish Long and Short Vowel Sounds
More Vowel Sounds						L12 Diphthongs and Variants	L13 Schwa /ə/ Sound				

All Print Concepts and Phonological Awareness skills are covered in Levels A, B, and C (Grades K, 1, and 2).

Level A (Grade K)
Phonics, Morphology, and Spelling; Fluency; Vocabulary

STRAND AND TOPIC	LEVEL A (GRADE K)				
Phonics, Morphology, and Spelling					
Consonants: Sounds and Graphemes	L21 Connect Sound and Letter: Consonants 1	L22 Connect Sound and Letter: Consonants 2	L23 Connect Sound and Letter: Consonants 3	L24 Spelling: Soft Consonant Sounds	L32 Consonant Blends
Vowels: Sounds and Graphemes (Short Vowels)	L25 Short *a*	L26 Short *i*	L27 Short *o*	L28 Short *e*	L29 Short *u*
Vowels: Sounds and Graphemes (Long Vowels)	L30 Long *a, i,* and o	L31 Long *e* and *u*			
Vowels: Sounds and Graphemes (Vowel Teams and Patterns)					
High-Frequency Words	L33 High-Frequency Words 1	L34 High-Frequency Words 2	L35 High-Frequency Words 3		
Decoding (Segmenting and Blending)					
Syllable Patterns					
Prefixes, Suffixes, and Inflectional Endings					
Irregular Spellings					
Fluency					
Oral Reading (Accuracy and Rate)					
Oral Reading (Expression)					
Vocabulary					
Vocabulary (References)					
Vocabulary (Context Clues)	L36 Define Unfamiliar Words				
Vocabulary (More Strategies)	L37 Sort Words into Categories				

Level B (Grade 1)

Phonics, Morphology, and Spelling; Fluency; Vocabulary

STRAND AND TOPIC	LEVEL B (GRADE 1)				
Phonics, Morphology, and Spelling					
Consonants: Sounds and Graphemes	L16 Consonant Digraphs *sh, th, ph, gh*	L17 Consonant Digraphs and Trigraphs *ch, tch, wh*	L18 Consonant Digraphs and Trigraphs *dge, ng, nk, ck*	L19 Silent Consonant Patterns *kn, wr, mb*	
Vowels: Sounds and Graphemes (Short Vowels)					
Vowels: Sounds and Graphemes (Long Vowels)	L20 Long Vowels and the Silent *e* Rule	L21 Long Vowel Patterns • Long *e, o,* and *i* (Spelled *e, o, i*) • Long *i* (Spelled *y* and *igh*) • Long *e* (Spelled *y*)	L22 Vowel Teams *ee, ea, ai, ay, oa, ow*		
Vowels: Sounds and Graphemes (Vowel Teams and Patterns)	L26 Diphthongs and Vowel Patterns				
High-Frequency Words	L30 Read and Spell High-Frequency Words 1	L31 Read and Spell High-Frequency Words 2			
Decoding (Segmenting and Blending)	L14 Decode Regularly Spelled VC and CVC Words	L15 Decode Words: Initial and Final Blends • Initial Blends • Final Blends • Three-Letter Initial Blends	L28 Compound Words and Contractions		
Syllable Patterns	L23 Understand Syllables • Count Syllables • Closed Syllables • Open Syllables	L24 Syllable Patterns • VC/CV and V/CCV • V/CV • VC/V	L25 Syllable Patterns: *r*-Controlled Vowels		
Prefixes, Suffixes, and Inflectional Endings	L27 Inflected Endings • *-s, -es* • *-ed* • *-ing*	L29 Prefixes and Suffixes			
Irregular Spellings					
Fluency					
Oral Reading (Accuracy and Rate)	L35 Fluency: Read Accurately	L36 Fluency: Read with Appropriate Rate			
Oral Reading (Expression)	L37 Read with Appropriate Expression				
Vocabulary					
Vocabulary (References)	L32 Use a Dictionary and Glossary				
Vocabulary (Context Clues)	L33 Use Context Clues: Definition				
Vocabulary (More Strategies)	L34 Word Categories				

Level C (Grade 2)
Phonics, Morphology, and Spelling; Fluency; Vocabulary

STRAND AND TOPIC	LEVEL C (GRADE 2)				
Phonics, Morphology, and Spelling					
Consonants: Sounds and Graphemes	L17 Blends, Digraphs, and Trigraphs				
Vowels: Sounds and Graphemes (Short Vowels)					
Vowels: Sounds and Graphemes (Long Vowels)	L4 Short and Long Vowels	L5 Long Vowel Digraphs *ai, ay, ie, igh, oa, ow*			
Vowels: Sounds and Graphemes (Vowel Teams and Patterns)	L6 Vowel Teams *ea, oo, ey, y, ie, ee*	L7 Vowel Teams *oo, ew, ue, ui*	L8 Vowel Patterns with *aw, au, al, wa, augh, ough*	L9 Diphthongs	
High-Frequency Words	L18 Read and Spell High-Frequency Words				
Decoding (Segmenting and Blending)	L15 Compound Words, Contractions, and Abbreviations				
Syllable Patterns	L10 Syllable Patterns • Syllable Types • C + *-le* • VCCCV	L11 Syllable Patterns: Long Vowels in Open and Closed Syllables			
Prefixes, Suffixes, and Inflectional Endings	L12 Words with Prefixes	L13 Words with Suffixes	L14 Words with Inflected Endings • *-s, -es, -ed, -ing* • *-er, -est* • *Spelling Changes*		
Irregular Spellings	L16 Silent Consonants • *kn* • *gn, mn* • *st, rh*				
Fluency					
Oral Reading (Accuracy and Rate)	L24 Read Accurately with Appropriate Rate	L25 Use Punctuation Cues for Appropriate Phrasing			
Oral Reading (Expression)	L26 Read with Appropriate Expression				
Vocabulary					
Vocabulary (References)	L19 Determine the Meanings of Unfamiliar Words				
Vocabulary (Context Clues)	L20 Use Context Clues: Synonyms and Antonyms				
Vocabulary (More Strategies)	L21 Understand Multiple-Meaning Words	L23 Comparatives and Superlatives	L23 Words with Affixes		

Level D (Grade 3)

Phonics, Morphology, and Spelling; Fluency; Vocabulary

STRAND AND TOPIC	LEVEL D (GRADE 3)				
Phonics, Morphology, and Spelling					
Consonants: Sounds and Graphemes					
Vowels: Sounds and Graphemes (Short Vowels)					
Vowels: Sounds and Graphemes (Long Vowels)					
Vowels: Sounds and Graphemes (Vowel Teams and Patterns)	L5 Vowel Patterns				
High-Frequency Words	L12 Read and Spell High-Frequency Words				
Decoding (Segmenting and Blending)	L3 Multisyllable Words	L4 Compound Words • Compounds • Spelling Compounds • Compounds with Longer Word Parts			
Syllable Patterns	L6 Syllable Patterns				
Prefixes, Suffixes, and Inflected Endings	L1 Prefixes and Suffixes • Isolate Prefixes • Isolate Suffixes • Determine Meaning of Affixes	L2 Words with Latin Suffixes • *-able* • *-er, -or, -ist* • *-ment, -ty, -ity*	L8 Adding Endings • Endings *-ed, -ing*: Double Final Consonant • Endings *-er, -est* • *-ed, -ing*: Drop Final *e*	L9 More Endings and Irregular Plurals • Ending *-es:* Spelling Change *y* to *i* • Ending *-ed:* Spelling Change *y* to *i* • Irregular Plurals	
Irregular Spellings	L7 Plurals • Plural *-s* • Plural *-es* • Plural *f* or *fe* to *v*	L9 (see above)	L10 Contractions • Contractions *n't, 'm* • Contractions *'s, 'd* • Contractions *'re, 've, 'll*	L11 Possessives and Abbreviations • Singular Possessives • Plural Possessives • Abbreviations	
Fluency					
Oral Reading (Accuracy and Rate)	L17 Read Accurately with Appropriate Rate	L18 Use Punctuation Cues for Appropriate Phrasing			
Oral Reading (Expression)	L19 Read with Appropriate Expression				
Vocabulary					
Vocabulary (References)					
Vocabulary (Context Clues)	L13 Use Context Clues				
Vocabulary (More Strategies)	L14 Determine the Meanings of Unfamiliar Words	L15 Greek and Latin Word Parts and Affixes	L16 Homophones, Homographs, Synonyms, and Antonyms		

Focus on Fluency and Comprehension Use each horizontal skill concept band to the left to determine prerequisite skills. Grade-level standards for students at Level E (Grade 4) and Level F (Grade 5) shift from decoding text to reading fluently and comprehending text. If students need intervention with print concepts, sound-letter correspondences, or basic phonics concepts, see the Level E lessons listed below as well as skills in Levels A–D (Grades K–3) to guide instruction.

Level E (Grade 4)
Phonics, Morphology, and Spelling; Fluency; Vocabulary

STRAND AND TOPIC	LEVEL E (GRADE 4)					
Phonics, Morphology, and Spelling						
Decoding	L1 Regular and Irregular Plurals	L2 Vowel Patterns	L3 Syllable Patterns	L4 Prefixes and Suffixes	L5 Decode Compound Words	L6 Decode Words Using Roots
Fluency						
Comprehension (Purpose and Understanding)	* See Part 2 (Reading, Writing, and Language)					
Comprehension (Literature)						
Comprehension (Informational Text)						
Comprehension (Vocabulary/ Meaning)						
Oral Reading (Accuracy and Rate)	L13 Accuracy and Rate					
Oral Reading (Appropriate Phrasing/ Punctuation Cues)	L14 Appropriate Phrasing and Punctuation Cues					
Oral Reading (Expression and Intonation)	L15 Expression and Intonation					
Overall Fluency						
Vocabulary (Context Clues)	L8 Use Context Clues 1	L9 Use Context Clues 2	L10 Understand Multiple-Meaning Words and Homophones			
Vocabulary						
Vocabulary (Word Relationships)						
Vocabulary (Greek and Latin Affixes and Roots)	L12 Greek and Latin Roots					
Vocabulary (Affixes and Roots)	L11 Words with Affixes					
Vocabulary (References)	L7 Determine the Meanings of Unfamiliar Words					

Writing Skills Trace

STRAND AND TOPIC	LESSONS BY LEVEL					
	LEVEL A (GRADE K)	LEVEL B (GRADE 1)	LEVEL C (GRADE 2)	LEVEL D (GRADE 3)	LEVEL E (GRADE 4)	LEVEL F (GRADE 5)
Text Types	L56 Write Text: Narrative and Informational	L58 Write Narrative Text	L48 Write Narrative Text	L47 Write Narrative Text	L43 Write Narrative Text	L39 Write Narrative Text
		L59 Write Informational Text and Correspondence	L49 Write Informational Text and Correspondence	L48 Write Informational Text	L44 Write Informational Text	L40 Write Informational Text
				L49 Write Argumentative Text	L45 Write Argumentative Text	L41 Write Argumentative Text
				L50 Write Correspondence	L46 Write Correspondence	L42 Write Correspondence
Plan and Develop Writing	L53 Ask and Answer Questions About a Prompt	L55 Use a Prompt to Identify a Writing Topic	L44 Plan and Develop Writing	L43 Analyze a Prompt	L39 Plan Your Writing	L34 Plan Response to a Prompt
			L45 Draft: Develop Ideas and Use Structure	L44 Plan and Draft a Piece of Writing	L40 Draft Your Writing	L35 Use Clear Organization
Inquiry and Research	L54 Use a Topic to Recall and Gather Information	L56 Gather Information About a Topic and Draft	L55 Inquiry and Research	L57 Inquiry and Research	L52 Inquiry and Research	L48 Inquiry and Research
	L60 Inquiry and Research	L64 Inquiry and Research				
Strengthen and Revise Writing	L55 Revise and Edit	L57 Add Specific Details to Support Ideas	L46 Revise Writing	L45 Revise Organization in a Piece of Writing	L41 Link Ideas with Transitions	L36 Strengthen Opening and Concluding Statements
			L47 Edit and Publish Writing	L46 Revise and Edit	L42 Revise and Edit for Clarity and Precision	L37 Revise, Edit, and Rewrite
						L38 Expand, Combine, and Reduce Sentences for Style and Effect

Detailed instruction on and practice with narrative, informational, and argumentative writing modes are covered within most lessons.

Language and Conventions Skills Trace

STRAND AND TOPIC	LESSONS BY LEVEL					
	LEVEL A (GRADE K)	LEVEL B (GRADE 1)	LEVEL C (GRADE 2)	LEVEL D (GRADE 3)	LEVEL E (GRADE 4)	LEVEL F (GRADE 5)
Grammar and Usage	L57 Understand Nouns, Verbs, and Prepositions	L61 Nouns and Pronouns	L50 Complete Sentences with Subject-Verb Agreement	L51 Understand Subject-Verb and Pronoun-Antecedent Agreement	L47 Sentences	L43 Complete Sentences with Subject-Verb Agreement
	L58 Understand Pronouns and Adjectives	L62 Adjectives, Adverbs, and Prepositions	L51 Understand Nouns, Verbs, and Pronouns	L52 Understand Coordinating and Subordinating Conjunctions	L48 Nouns and Verbs	L44 Nouns, Pronouns, and Verbs
		L63 Subject-Verb Agreement	L52 Adjectives, Adverbs, and Conjunctions	L53 Nouns and Verbs	L49 Adjectives and Adverbs	L45 Adjectives and Adverbs
				L54 Pronouns and Prepositions	L50 Pronouns, Prepositions, and Conjunctions	L46 Prepositions, Prepositional Phrases, and Conjunctions
				L55 Adjectives and Adverbs		
Capitalization, Punctuation, and Spelling	L59 Capitalize and Punctuate Sentences	L60 Produce and Expand Sentences	L53 Contractions and Possessives	L56 Capitalization and Punctuation	L51 Capitalization and Punctuation	L47 Use Capitalization and Punctuation
			L54 Capitalization and Punctuation			

Intervention and Your Students

myFocus Intervention includes the common threads of effective reading intervention programs: a focus on planning, pacing, and adapting to students' needs; supportive activities to build language, fluency, and home-school connections; and a current research base on proven intervention philosophy and practice.

Planning

myFocus Intervention offers a consistent lesson format to make instruction, practice, and assessment during intervention clear and easy to use. Student models, activities, routines, and assessments are provided at point of use and follow a gradual-release model. The pace of the lessons is naturally dependent on the needs of each student. The chart below provides a suggested pacing for lessons, many of which might typically take about one week.

Weekly Lesson Plan

DAY 1	MODEL AND TEACH	**INTRODUCE** ("I do")	• Introduce general concept or skill to students.
		MODEL ("I do")	• Identify the skill in context, through an annotated reading model. • Reinforce that the foundational skills are intrinsic to overall reading fluency. • Model fluency through regular read-alouds. • Give repeated practice with decodable, developmentally appropriate text.
		TEACH ("I do")	• Explain the skill in context. • Teach the skill explicitly.
DAY 2	PRACTICE AND ASSESS	**PRACTICE 1** ("We do")	• Guide practice of the most basic aspects of the skill through reteaching and routines. • Display or distribute Student Pages to give students guided practice.
		MONITOR PROGRESS ("We do")	• Assess students' progress. • Review or reteach as needed.
DAY 3		**PRACTICE 2** ("We do")	• Guide practice of intermediate aspects of the skill through reteaching and routines. • Display or distribute Student Pages to give students guided practice.
		MONITOR PROGRESS ("We do")	• Assess students' progress. • Review or reteach as needed.
DAY 4		**PRACTICE 3** ("We do")	• Guide practice of the most difficult aspects of the skill through reteaching and routines. • Display or distribute Student Pages to give students guided practice.
		INDEPENDENT PRACTICE ("You do")	• Assess students' independent progress. • Review or reteach as needed. • Move on to next lesson.

Pacing

myFocus Intervention is intended to be used in addition to the core curriculum and may be used in a variety of ways. The lesson format is consistent but adaptive and easy to implement. It can be flexibly used both for students needing brief, targeted intervention for particular skills and for students requiring broader and more intensive intervention across strands and even across multiple grade levels. Teachers can focus on intervention lessons that complement and reinforce grade-level instruction taught in their core curriculum. Alternatively, they may focus on reviewing (or introducing) prerequisite skills from earlier grades needed for students to approach and achieve grade-level reading expectations.

Customizing Intervention Models Teachers can adapt the program in ways that best fit the intervention needs of their students, adjusting for the percentage of students in class requiring intervention and the resources available in their classroom, school, and district. The models below offer several ways to use *myFocus Intervention.*

Intervention Models

- **One-on-one intervention**
- **Small groups (outside of class)**
- **Small groups (in class)**

Level of Intervention Needed (LOW → HIGH)			
HIGH	One-on-One Extensive Intervention (classroom teacher)		One-on-One Intervention (literacy specialists/aides)
		Small Groups (groups organized by intervention needs of students)	
LOW	Small Groups (in class to reteach/review core instruction)		Small Groups (before or after class to reteach/review core instruction)
	Number of Students Requiring Intervention LOW →		HIGH

Adapting to Students' Needs

myFocus Intervention follows a consistent format, but the sequence and number of lessons in the program are not prescriptive. Intervention should be quick and efficient, targeted to the skills and concepts that are proving barriers to grade-level reading proficiency. If a straightforward concept is introduced and quickly mastered in a session or two, teachers should move on. On the other hand, some lessons may require several sessions for instruction, modeling, and to practice skills before students will show mastery. The number of sessions, their duration, and the intervention model used should be tailored to students' needs. For example, students needing intensive intervention may require 30-minute daily sessions for instruction, practice, and progress monitoring. For students needing minimal intervention, two to three 30-minute small-group sessions may be enough to teach the concept and provide sufficient guided practice and assessment.

Customizing Intervention As students' proficiency improves, teachers may wish to have students focus on only the second or third minilesson after concepts are taught and modeled. The goal is to make intervention as quick and efficient as possible. Pacing should be adapted as students' skill level increases.

Intensive Intervention

- 30-minute sessions of daily instruction one-on-one or in small groups

Moderate Intervention

- 30-minute sessions, 2–3 times/week, one-on-one or in small groups

Minimal Intervention

- 30-minute sessions, 2–3 times/week, stations in class
- 30-minute sessions, 2–3 times/week, in small groups, to preteach or reteach

IF... students continue to struggle, THEN... adjust pacing by

1. determining gaps in knowledge and teaching prerequisite skills.
2. increasing number of sessions per week.
3. decreasing the number of students in sessions.

IF... students improve quickly, THEN... adjust pacing by

1. using the Checkpoint Assessments to gauge student mastery, teaching entire lessons only if needed.
2. decreasing the number of sessions per week.
3. increasing the number of students in sessions.

Building Language

Vocabulary As students' reading proficiency develops, they encounter increasingly sophisticated texts with more precise, nuanced, and complex vocabulary. Vocabulary can be a barrier for struggling students who may have limited exposure to new words, both in quantity and in complexity. By Grade 3 or 4, students begin to encounter large numbers of new words in each subject area. As a result, students' vocabulary gains (or deficits) are multiplied.

Focus on Academic Vocabulary In Grades K–2, students focus on decoding texts with basic words they typically already know (e.g., *child, house*). As students learn more about content areas, they learn domain-specific words (e.g., *polygon, chrysalis*). These words are usually unfamiliar words that are often explicitly taught as vocabulary. National and state English Language Arts standards, however, place a particular emphasis on academic vocabulary, or "words that characterize written and especially academic text—but are not so common in everyday conversation."[1] Unlike domain-specific vocabulary, academic vocabulary appears in all types of texts: informational texts (*relative, vary, accumulate*), technical writing (*itemize, structure*), and literary texts (*unfortunate, dignified, stroll*). These words require particular instructional attention because they are often abstract, vital to comprehension, useful across multiple contexts, and important in communicating meanings or insights.

In most cases, texts will have more words than can be taught, and teachers will need to decide which words to focus on. To understand complex texts, students need to be able to generate the meanings of new words based on their knowledge about how words work in English.[2] To this end, teachers can aim to teach words that have high utility across multiple texts and content areas and around which students can make connections to other related words. They can ask questions of students that help them understand nuances in meaning, such as

1. If you encountered a bear on a hike, would you be more likely to *stroll, saunter,* or *sprint* away? Model what each of these actions looks like.
2. If you wanted to compliment your aunt's bright new outfit, which word might you use? Which words would you avoid? *brassy, bold, gaudy, striking*
3. Would you rather be in a conversation in which people were *bantering* or *squabbling*?

---

1. Beck, I. L., M. G. McKeown, and L. Kucan. 2008. *Creating Robust Vocabulary: Frequently Asked Questions and Extended Examples.* New York: Guilford.

2. Hiebert, E. H., and P. David Pearson. 2014. *Generative Vocabulary Instruction.* New York: Pearson Education.

Building Fluency

Reading fluency is inextricably linked to reading comprehension. As students develop fluency, or automaticity with decoding, they are able to focus more attention on comprehension, or understanding the meaning of a text. Repeated readings of the same text help students develop automaticity, and this technique is emphasized throughout *myFocus Intervention*. As teachers gauge students' fluency, they should keep in mind that comprehension is the true goal of automaticity in decoding and proficiency in oral reading.

Mastering Full Alphabet Decoding To develop fluency, students must first develop full alphabetic knowledge and be proficient in full alphabet decoding. Students who use only the first and last parts of a word to identify it are using partial alphabetic decoding. Students who only partially decode may seem to read fluently and quickly at first, but they will struggle as texts become more complex and include more unfamiliar words (and fewer visual cues). Students who partially decode should be encouraged to slow down and fully decode each word, focusing on improving accuracy as opposed to rate. As students achieve full alphabetic decoding, their rate will improve as well.

Miscue Analysis Once students are capable of independently reading passages, teachers can use miscue analysis to diagnose students' reading proficiency. To perform a miscue analysis, give the student an unfamiliar passage to read aloud. As the student reads, mark the following types of errors on your own copy of the passage. Log students' miscues to determine areas in which they need additional review and support.

Miscue	Explanation	Example	Analysis
correction	Student corrects error without prompting.	I even saw a fox! was/saw	Self correcting is a good strategy, but check that the student is not reading too quickly.
omission	Student leaves out a word(s).	I saw a (bat) fly and a kangaroo jump.	Check that the student is not reading too quickly. Omission may also signal that sight-word recognition is weak.
insertion	Student inserts a word(s) that isn't in the text.	We went to the zoo. too I saw a bat fly ^ and a kangaroo jump.	The student may be reading too quickly. Check that insertions do not detract from meaning.

Miscue	Explanation	Example	Analysis
repetition	Student repeats a word or section of text.	I saw a bat fly and a kangaroo jump.	Repetition of a word or phrase often means the student is struggling to comprehend meaning.
reversal	Student reverses order of the print (e.g., saying "of" instead of "for").	I heard a duck quack.	Check for reversals that change the meaning. The student may need to slow down.
substitution	Student reads a different word from the one in the text.	We went (want) to the zoo.	The student may not understand the word. Check whether the substituted word is logical or simply a guess. Focus on full alphabet decoding.

How to Measure Fluency Reading passages are differentiated to cover a range of reading levels within a classroom.

LEVEL/GRADE	MINILESSON	WCPM
A (Grade K)	N/A	N/A
B (Grade 1)	1	Choral read
B (Grade 1)	2	20–35
B (Grade 1)	3	35–50
C (Grade 2)	1	50–65
C (Grade 2)	2	65–80
C (Grade 2)	3	80–95
D (Grade 3)	1	70–85
D (Grade 3)	2	85–100
D (Grade 3)	3	100–115
E (Grades 4)	1	95–105
E (Grades 4)	2	105–115
E (Grades 4)	3	115–125
F (Grade 5)	1	110–120
F (Grade 5)	2	120–130
F (Grade 5)	3	130–140

Adapted from Hasbrouck, Jan, and Gerald Tindal. 2005. "Oral Reading Fluency: 90 Years of Measurement." Web. 3 August 2015. http://eric.ed.gov/?id=ED531458.

Teachers can use the following routine with students individually or in student pairs. It is important to emphasize that learning to read fluently takes practice and that doing repeated readings and keeping track of reading times helps students see how their reading improves with practice. The goal of fluency practice is not to read fast, but to read accurately, at an appropriate rate, and with expression. Automaticity with print enables students to devote more mental energy to comprehension.

1. Introduce Timed Repeated Readings Tell students that today they will read a passage multiple times. Each time they read, they (or you) will keep track of how many words they read correctly in one minute. Say that you will time their reading for one minute. They will underline any words they don't know as they read. When the time is up, students will draw a line after the last word they read.

2. Measure Fluency After one minute, tell students that it is time to figure out how many words they read correctly. Show them how to use the numbers at the right of the passage to identify the total number of words they read. Then have them count the words they underlined. To figure out how many words they read correctly, tell students to take the total number of words they read and subtract the number of underlined words. For example, if their total is 65 words and they underlined 5 words, they will subtract 5 from 65. That means they read 60 words correct per minute (60 WCPM). Have students read the same selection three times and record their best score on their charts.

3. Track Progress Use the chart below to track fluency and especially to show students how repeated readings and practice in general improve their scores.

Fluency Progress Chart

Name ______________________________

150																														
145																														
140																														
135																														
130																														
125																														
120																														
115																														
110																														
105																														
100																														
95																														
90																														
85																														
80																														
75																														
70																														
65																														
60																														
55																														
	1	2	3	4	5	6	7	8	9	10	11	12	13	14	15	16	17	18	19	20	21	22	23	24	25	26	27	28	29	30

Building a Home-School Connection

Successful intervention is dependent on regular communication between teachers and students' parents or guardians. Sharing learning goals and expectations as well as any potential concerns is critical. Through clear, consistent, and regular communication, teachers can outline how they are working with students in class and what additional intervention instruction will address gaps in learning. They can share which techniques are most effective with each student and offer suggestions for how to expand learning gains to engage students outside the classroom. When teachers share clear expectations and regular progress updates, parents and guardians better reinforce their student's learning while also offering their own questions and observations to guide further instruction. Shared knowledge is empowering; it gives parents and guardians more leverage as advocates for and contributors to their student's learning, both in recognizing and addressing concerns and in developing curious, enthusiastic, and motivated learners.

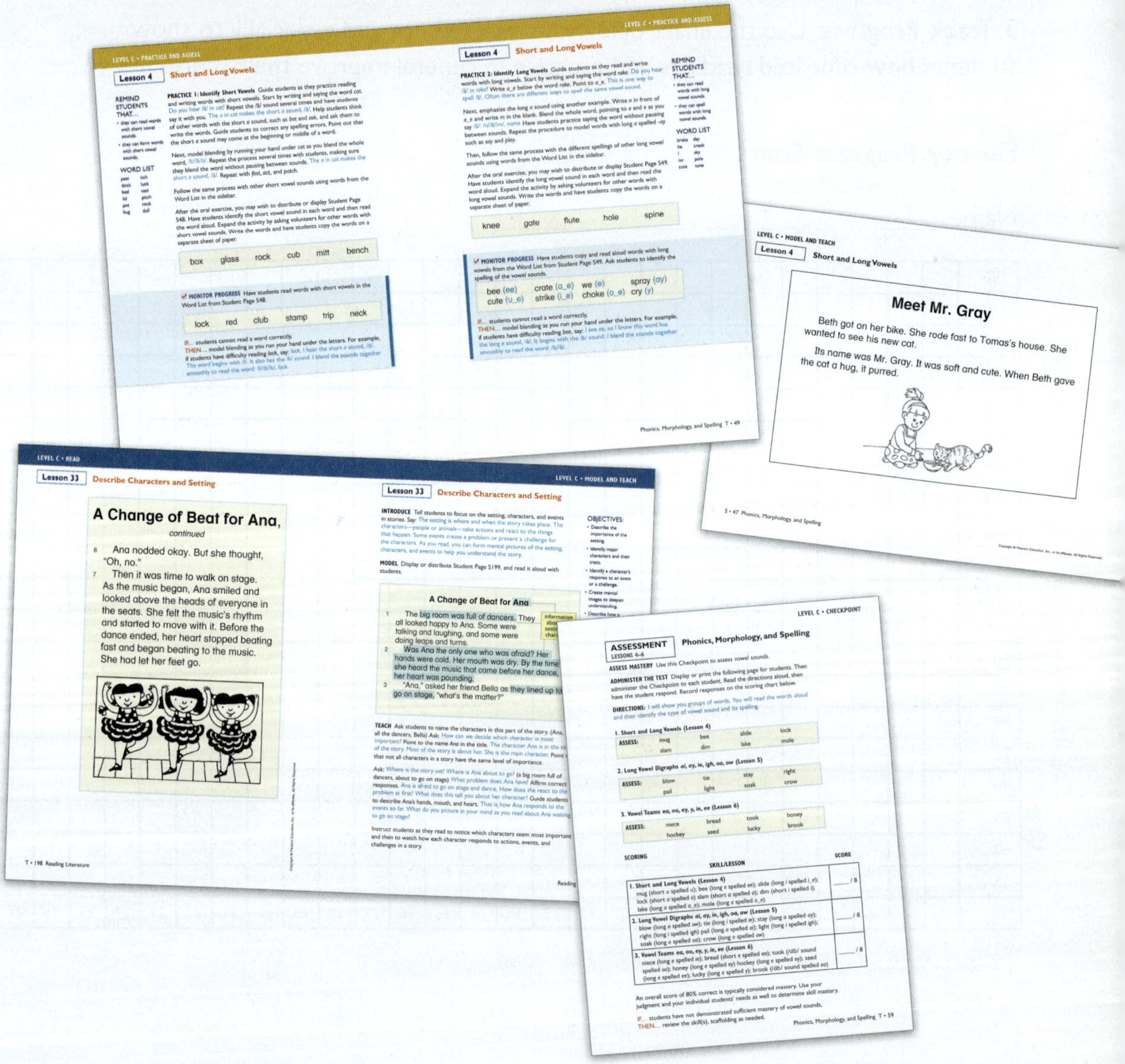

Understanding the Research Base

Effective, targeted intervention is research based in best-practices instruction. The more teachers understand the reasons for particular skills and strategies, the more effective they can be in facilitating student mastery of critical learning goals.

Developing a Research-Based Approach According to the Common Core State Standards, "no set of grade-specific standards can fully reflect the great variety in abilities, needs, learning rates, and achievement levels of students in any given classroom." Instead of being an isolated measure of grade-level proficiency, standards should be used as markers along the path to college and career readiness. The way students learn to read and develop critical thinking skills depends on many different factors, including age, primary language, cultural heritage, and experiences (*FirstSchool* 2014). To address the needs of all students, a curriculum must be flexible. The skill sequence should be progressive but integrated, with each grade's skills building on previous grade-level instruction. The sequence for each grade makes connections and prerequisites among skills clear, within and across grades, to make scaffolding and targeted intervention appropriately flexible and efficient.

To facilitate skills mastery, research supports a gradual release of responsibility. Teachers model first, and then they guide practice. Eventually students work in groups and then independently (Frey and Fisher 2011). This approach matches the common "I do it," "We do it," "You do it together," and "You do it alone" model for lessons (Fisher and Frey 2014).

Teaching Skills in Context Engaging and motivating context allows for effective reading instruction (Shanahan et al. 2010). When a skill is presented in context, students know exactly why they need to practice that particular skill and how that skill fits into general reading proficiency. Context, therefore, gives students a real-world example of the skill in practice and motivates students to engage in the lesson. All lessons in the program include a model passage or stimulus to anchor the lesson. This modeling reinforces the fact that literacy skills are in service to mastery of real-world texts and tasks.

Using Formative Assessment to Guide Intervention Instruction
Teachers use assessment to set goals for students, monitor progress toward those goals, give feedback on that progress, and adjust teaching as needed (Allal 2010). By observing how students respond to this ongoing formative assessment, teachers can adjust or focus activities in each lesson. Research shows that effective formative assessment strives to answer the questions *Where am I going? Where am I now?* and *Where to next?* (Frey and Fisher 2011). By answering these questions, students know exactly why they are being assessed, what skills they need to address to improve, and what skills they will need for future classroom work.

Understanding the Research Base: Bibliography

Allal, Linda. 2010. "Assessment and the Regulation of Learning." Penelope Peterson, Eva Baker, and Barry McGaw (Eds.), *International Encyclopedia of Education Vol. 3* (3rd ed.), 348–352. Oxford: Elsevier.

California Department of Education. 2014. *ELA/ELD Framework.* Sacramento, California: California Department of Education. Ch. 1, 33–34; Ch. 3, 39–40; Ch. 4; Ch. 5; Ch. 12, 16.

FirstSchool: Transforming PreK–3rd Grade for African American, Latino, and Low-Income Children. Ed. Ritchie, Sharon, and Laura Gutmann. 2014. New York: Teachers College Press.

Fisher, Douglas, and Nancy Frey. 2014. *Better Learning Through Structured Teaching: A Framework for the Gradual Release of Responsibility (Second Ed).* Alexandria, VA: ASCD.

Frey, Nancy, and Douglas Fisher. 2011. *The Formative Assessment Action Plan: Practical Steps to More Successful Teaching and Learning.* Alexandria, VA: ASCD.

Hudson, Roxanne. 2011. "Fluency Problems: When, Why, and How to Intervene." Rollanda E. O'Connor and Patricia F. Vadasy (Eds.), *Handbook of Reading Interventions,* 169–197. New York: Guilford.

National Association for the Education of Young Children. 2009. *Developmentally Appropriate Practice in Early Childhood Programs Serving Children from Birth Through Age 8.* Washington, D.C.: National Association for the Education of Young Children. 5–6.

National Governors Association Center for Best Practices and Council of Chief State School Officers. 2010. *Common Core State Standards for English Language Arts and Literacy in History/Social Studies, Science, and Technical Subjects.* Washington, DC: Authors. 6.

Shanahan, Timothy, K. Callison, C. Carriere, N. K. Duke, P. D. Pearson, C. Schatschneider, and J. Torgesen. 2010. *Improving Reading Comprehension in Kindergarten Through 3rd Grade: A Practice Guide* (NCEE 2010-4038). Washington, DC: National Center for Education Evaluation and Regional Assistance, Institute of Education Sciences, U.S. Department of Education.

PART I

FOUNDATIONAL SKILLS

Lesson 1 Books, Sentences, and Words

INTRODUCE Explain that language is spoken and written. Tell students that they can learn how to read written language by following words from left to right, top to bottom, and page by page.

MODEL Ask students to watch your finger move along the text as you read the passage from Student Page S33. Move your finger from left to right, just beneath each word. At the end of a line, move your finger back to the left and down to the next line to continue modeling.

Before the Storm

Liz went outside to put her toys away.
Then Liz felt water.
She jumped.
She ran to the house as the rain came.

LEFT → RIGHT

Read left to right.

TEACH After you read the passage once, move your finger under the first line of text again. My finger moves from left to right. We read from left to right. Then read the passage again and move your finger under each word as you read. My finger moves down after the end of a line. When we read, we read from left to right and from top to bottom. When you reach the bottom of a page, go to the top left of the next page. Demonstrate these movements again.

Use a classroom book as you continue teaching. Hold up a book and read the title aloud as you move your finger under the words. The front cover of a book always shows the title. This is the front cover. Turn the book over. This is the back cover. Often it is blank. Turn back to the front cover. Model opening the book. We hold a book right side up and open it like this. Close the book, then open it again and have students make the same motion with their hands or with a book of their own. When we are ready to read, we open the book. The first page inside the cover is the title page. It shows the title just like the cover does. Read the title aloud again.

OBJECTIVES:

- Recognize that spoken words are written in groups of letters.
- Understand that English print is read left to right, top to bottom, and page by page.
- Understand how to hold a book right side up and how to turn the pages.
- Identify the front cover, back cover, and title page of a book.

Lesson 1 Books, Sentences, and Words

REMIND STUDENTS THAT ...

- spoken words are represented by groups of letters.
- text is read from left to right.
- readers hold a book right side up.
- a book has a front cover, a back cover, and a title page.

PRACTICE 1 Tell students you are going to show them how to find words in a sentence. Write out or display the following sample sentence from Student Page S34.

> Bees live in hives.

Explain that a word is a group of letters and that in a written sentence words are separated by spaces. Say: Bees is the first word. *Live* is the second word. *Bees* and *live* are separated by a space. Now point out the other words in this sentence. Pause for students to point out each word. Offer corrective feedback as needed.

Next, tell students you will help them read words in a sentence. You found the words in the sentence. To read the sentence, I read each word, starting on the left. I read each word until I get to the last word on the right.

Write or display the following sample sentences from Student Page S34.

> 1. Bees like flowers.
> 2. Bees make honey.
> 3. Liz likes to eat honey.

Have volunteers circle the words in the sentences and then draw arrows under the sentences to show in which direction the sentences should be read.

Next, have students hold a book right side up. As you say each book part, have students point to the appropriate part on their own books and repeat the name after you: front cover; back cover; title page. Have students set their books down and turn the pages as they would if they were reading it.

☑ **MONITOR PROGRESS** Have students look at the following sentence from Student Page S34.

> Honey can be good for you.

Have students circle each word in the sentence. Then ask them to draw an arrow to show in which direction the sentence should be read.

IF... students have difficulty identifying words,
THEN... model the correct response by circling each word in the sentence.

Lesson 1 Books, Sentences, and Words

PRACTICE 2 Remind students that words are made up of letters and that we read words from left to right. Write or display the following sample paragraph from Student Page S35.

> Liz and Ann are sisters.
> They like to play.
> Liz likes bees.
> Ann does not!

Point to the first word in the first sample sentence. I start reading words from the left. Where should I go to continue reading? Pause for students to respond. Yes, I should read from left to right. Where should I go when I get to the end of a line? Yes, I should go to the next line below it, starting at the left.

Ask volunteers to point out the direction in which each sentence should be read. Have students draw an arrow to indicate the correct direction.

Hold up a book right side up. Ask a volunteer to come up and point to the title on the front cover. Ask another volunteer to come up and move his or her finger in the correct direction under the title. Then repeat the exercise with the book's title page.

REMIND STUDENTS THAT ...

- spoken words are written in groups of letters.
- text is read from left to right and top to bottom.
- readers hold a book right side up.
- a book has a front cover, a back cover, and a title page.

✓ **MONITOR PROGRESS** Distribute the following passage from Student Page S35 and ask: In which direction do you read the passage? Draw an arrow under each line to show how you read the passage.

> Liz has a brother named Jon.
> Jon likes to climb trees.
> Liz also likes to climb trees.
> Both Liz and Jon like bees.

IF... students have difficulty with directionality,
THEN... model the correct process by rereading each sample sentence and moving your finger under each word as you read. Have students repeat the sentence after you, using their finger to show directionality as they say the words with you.

Lesson 1 Books, Sentences, and Words

REMIND STUDENTS THAT ...

- spoken words are written in print by groups of letters.
- words are read from left to right, top to bottom, and page by page.
- readers hold a book right side up.
- a book has a front cover, a back cover, and a title page.

PRACTICE 3 Tell students they will learn how to read written words. Display the following passage from Student Page S36.

> **The Monster**
>
> One day, Jon was in the woods.
> He saw a big egg.
> He took it home.
> A baby monster came out!
> Jon told his mother.
> They put it in a basket.

Read aloud the title of the story. Where should I start reading this story? Pause for students to respond. Yes, I should read starting from the left, at the top of the text. I will read the words from left to right. Read the passage to the end of the first line, underlining each word with your finger. Where do I read next? Pause for students to respond. Yes, I should read the next line down, starting from the left. Continue reading aloud to the end of the passage, modeling directionality with your finger as you read.

Open a classroom book and have a student volunteer demonstrate directionality by moving a finger across the page. Invite other students to demonstrate holding a book right side up; to identify the front cover, back cover, and title page; and to show how to turn the pages of a book.

☑ **INDEPENDENT PRACTICE** Have individuals choose a classroom book and open to the first page with words. Then ask the following questions: Where should you start reading? Where should you go after you get to the end of the first line? Where should you go after you get to the end of the first page?

IF... students have difficulty determining basic print concepts,
THEN... model the correct process by moving your finger under the text, emphasizing your movements from left to right and top to bottom.

Before the Storm

Liz went outside to put her toys away.
Then Liz felt water.
She jumped.
She ran to the house as the rain came.

LEFT → RIGHT

Lesson 1 **Books, Sentences, and Words**

Bees live in hives.

1. Bees like flowers.

2. Bees make honey.

3. Liz likes to eat honey.

Honey can be good for you.

Lesson 1 Books, Sentences, and Words

Liz and Ann are sisters.
They like to play.
Liz likes bees.
Ann does not!

Liz has a brother named Jon.
Jon likes to climb trees.
Liz also likes to climb trees.
Both Liz and Jon like bees.

The Monster

One day, Jon was in the woods.
He saw a big egg.
He took it home.
A baby monster came out!
Jon told his mother.
They put it in a basket.

Lesson 2 Understand Words and Sentences

INTRODUCE Remind students that they have looked at words on the pages of books. Hold up a book that is open to a page with a short sentence. Words are groups of letters. Point to the individual words, from left to right. We read words from left to right. We read words together to understand what is written. Sweep your hand from left to right as you read the words.

MODEL Display or share copies of the passage "A Winning Team" from Student Page S37. Read the first line aloud. Repeat the sentence, pausing after each word. A sentence is a group of words. The words are separated by spaces. This sentence has three words. Point to each word. The words are made of letters.

Point to the first letter of the first word, *Kim*. This is one letter. It is just part of this word. Point to the *i* and the *m* in turn. Here is another letter. And here is the last letter. This word is made up of 1-2-3 letters. And I know that this word is done because there's a space after it.

A Winning Team

Kim runs fast.
So does Sam.
I run fast too.
We are on a team.
Our team races.
We win a lot.

TEACH A sentence says something or asks a question. These sentences tell about a team. Point to the first sentence and say: Let's count the words in this sentence. Raise a finger, starting with the thumb, as you say the sentence. *Kim runs fast.* I raised one finger for *Kim,* one finger for *runs,* and one finger for *fast.* Repeat the sentence, pointing to one finger for each word. How many words does this sentence have? Yes, the sentence has three words. Follow the same procedure with the remaining sentences. Ask students to tell you how many words are in the sentence, and affirm correct answers.

Now point to several individual letters in the passage. Each time, say: Is this a letter or a word? That's right, this is a letter. Then ask several volunteers to choose a word and tell how many letters are in it. Sum up: Each word is made up of letters. A group of words makes a sentence.

OBJECTIVES:

- Understand that sentences are made of words.
- Understand that words are made of letters.
- Distinguish between letters and words.
- Segment and count words in spoken sentences.

Lesson 2 Understand Words and Sentences

REMIND STUDENTS THAT ...

- they can recognize the difference between a letter and a word.
- words are groups of letters that are separated by spaces.

PRACTICE I Tell students that you are going to show them how to find written words. Say: *We run fast.* How many words did you hear? I will say the sentence again: *We run fast.* Repeat the sentence and hold up a finger, starting with the thumb, for each word. There are three words in this sentence: We (pause and point to your thumb) run (pause and point to the next finger) fast (point to the third finger).

Display or write out the sentence from Student Page S38. Point to *We*. We is the first word. It has two letters. There is a space after the last letter. Repeat with *run* (*run* is the next word; it has three letters; there is a space after the last letter) and *fast* (*fast* is another word; it has four letters).

We run fast.

Display or share the following sentences from Student Page S38. Have volunteers circle the individual words in each sentence. When they are done, point to each sentence and ask: How many words do we see in this sentence? Affirm correct answers.

Two teams race.
Our team wins.
We run home.

MONITOR PROGRESS Have students circle each word in the following sentence from Student Page S38. Have them count the words and tell you how many words are in the sentence.

Sam and Kim go home.

IF... students have difficulty isolating words,
THEN... point to the spaces between words and say: A space comes between each word. Then, model counting the words.

Lesson 2 Understand Words and Sentences

PRACTICE 2 Tell students you are going to help them find words in sentences and that later they will count the words.

Display the sentence from Student Page S39. Let's start by listening for words in sentences. We'll raise one finger for each word that we hear. Raise your thumb first.

Listen closely: *Sam runs.* We raise a thumb for *Sam* and we raise the next finger for *runs.* Now let's see how the sentence looks on a page. Repeat the sentence as you display it or write it on the board.

> Sam runs.

Read the sentence, raising your thumb for *Sam* and the next finger for *runs.* Point to your thumb, say: *Sam*, and then point to the printed word *Sam.* Point to your finger, say: *runs*, and then point to the written word *runs.* How many words do you see? **(2)**

Then write or display the following sample sentences from Student Page S39.

> Kim runs past Sam.
> Sam yells.
> Kim runs faster.
> Kim gets home first.

Have students point to the separate words in each sentence and tell you how many words there are.

REMIND STUDENTS THAT ...

- words are separated by spaces in print.

MONITOR PROGRESS Distribute the following sentences from Student Page S39 and ask: Which sentences have two words? Have students point to sentences with two words. Repeat for the sentences with three words and four words.

> Kim ate lunch.
> Sam rested.
> Sam slept.
> Sam woke up hungry.

IF... students miscount words in sentences,
THEN... point to the first sentence. I can use the number of spaces to help me count the words. *Kim, space, ate, space, lunch. Kim ate lunch.* There are three words in this sentence. Repeat as needed.

Lesson 2 Understand Words and Sentences

REMIND STUDENTS THAT ...

- they can count the words in a printed sentence.

PRACTICE 3 Help students learn the segmenting procedure. Begin with a spoken sentence from Student Page S40. I will say a sentence. Listen carefully for the different words: *Our school has teams.* Now watch my hand as I say the sentence again. I will raise a finger for each word, starting with my thumb. Raise a finger for each word as you repeat the sentence. How many words did I say? Yes, I said four words.

> Our school has teams.
> Teams work hard.
> I am on two teams.

Display the sample sentences from Student Page S40. Remind students that words are separated by spaces in printed text. Point to the first sentence and say: You know that this sentence has four words. How many words do the other sentences have? Point to each sentence and invite students to respond. After completing the list once, ask for volunteers to point to the sentence with three words, the sentence with four words, and the sentence with five words.

☑ **INDEPENDENT PRACTICE** Show students the sentence list from Student Page S40. Have them silently count the words in each sentence.

> Kim and Sam and I are on a team.
> Bo is also on our team.
> We race other teams.
> When we win, we are happy.
> When we lose, we cheer for the other team.

IF... students miscount the words,
THEN... model counting orally while pointing to each word in the sentence.

Lesson 2 **Understand Words and Sentences**

A Winning Team

Kim runs fast.
So does Sam.
I run fast too.
We are on a team.
Our team races.
We win a lot.

Lesson 2 Understand Words and Sentences

We run fast.

Two teams race.
Our team wins.
We run home.

Sam and Kim go home.

Lesson 2 **Understand Words and Sentences**

Sam runs.

Kim runs past Sam.
Sam yells.
Kim runs faster.
Kim gets home first.

Kim ate lunch.
Sam rested.
Sam slept.
Sam woke up hungry.

Lesson 2 Understand Words and Sentences

Our school has teams.
Teams work hard.
I am on two teams.

Kim and Sam and I are on a team.
Bo is also on our team.
We race other teams.
When we win, we are happy.
When we lose, we cheer for the other team.

ASSESSMENT
LESSONS 1–2

Print Concepts

ASSESS MASTERY Use this Checkpoint to assess students' mastery of book, sentence, and word recognition.

ADMINISTER THE TEST Administer the Checkpoint orally to each student. Provide a classroom book to each student and give each student a copy of the next page. Instruct students as follows.

1. Books, Sentences, and Words (Lesson 1)
I will ask you about books. First, hold up the book. Now, point to the front cover. Now, show me the back cover. Place the book in front of you and open it to the title page. Finally, show me how you turn the pages to read the book.

Now, I will ask you about words in sentences. Look at the sentence on the sheet I handed out. Show me the way to read it. For example, you can move your hand to show me how to read the sentence.

ASSESS: Cats are fun pets.

2. Understand Words and Sentences (Lesson 2)
Look at the sentence and tell me how many words you see. You may count the words silently or out loud. You may also point to each word you see.

ASSESS: The big dog sat.

SCORING

SKILL/LESSON	SCORE
1. Books, Sentences, and Words (Lesson 1) • Identify front cover, back cover, and title page of book. • Hold book right side up and turn pages correctly. • Read sentence left to right. Cats are fun pets. ⟶	 Y N Y N Y N
2. Understand Words and Sentences (Lesson 2) The big dog sat. (4 words)	_____ / 4

An overall score of 80% correct is typically considered mastery. Use your judgment and your individual students' needs as well to determine skill mastery.

IF... students score below the benchmark,
THEN... review those discrete skills, going back to the lessons to reteach and scaffold as needed.

ASSESSMENT
LESSONS 1–2

Print Concepts

Cats are fun pets.

The big dog sat.

Lesson 3 Learn the Letters in the Alphabet I

INTRODUCE Explain that every word is made of letters. Letters are used to spell sounds. Letters can be written as uppercase or lowercase. In this lesson, we'll learn how to look for and write letters. Sing the alphabet song with students.

MODEL Display the passage "At the Zoo" or share copies of Student Page S43 with students. Read it aloud. Say: The words in this passage use every letter in the alphabet.

At the Zoo

We went to the zoo.
I saw a bat fly and a kangaroo jump.
I heard a duck quack.
I even saw a fox!

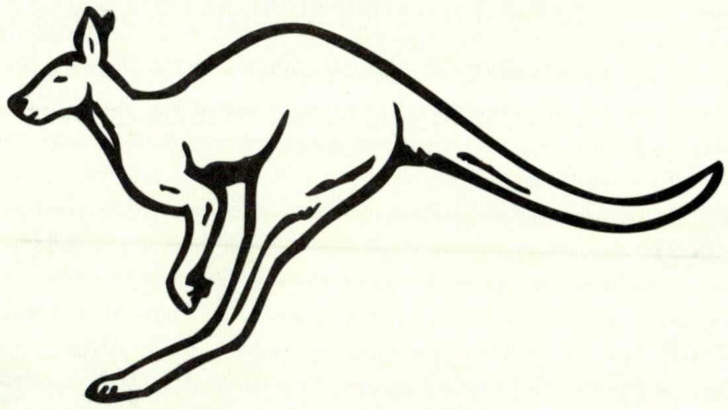

TEACH Display a large alphabet chart with both upper- and lowercase letters. Say the name of each letter, and then help students locate all the lowercase letters in the passage. For example, say: This is a lowercase letter *a*. Do you see *a* in the passage? Circle the letters as you identify them. *At* starts with *a*. The *a* in *At* is uppercase. *A* sounds like /a/. Point to the letter. What is the name of this letter? *A*.

OBJECTIVES:

- Recognize all letters.
- Identify letters in words.
- Print all letters.

Lesson 3 Learn the Letters in the Alphabet I

REMIND STUDENTS THAT ...

- they can recognize the letters *a* and *b*.
- they can identify the letters *a* and *b* in words.
- they can print the letters *a* and *b*.

PRACTICE 1: Recognize Letters *a* and *b* Display or distribute the letter cards from Student Page S44. Follow the routine to teach each letter. You may wish to cut the letters out to create separate picture cards.

Routine

1. Display the letter. Model how to write upper- and lowercase *a* on the board. For example, say: This is uppercase *A*. This is lowercase *a*.

2. Name the letter. What is the name of this letter? Yes; *a*.

3. Identify the letter. Point to the apple card. What is this? Pause for responses. Yes, an apple. What letter does *apple* start with? Have students circle the letter and say it aloud. Yes, it's the letter *a*. *Apple* starts with *a*.

4. Write the letter. Model writing lowercase *a*. Have students print lowercase *a* several times. Then model writing uppercase *A* and have students print it several times.

5. Extend practice. Extend practice by having students write the letter *a* on several sticky notes and then attach them to any objects in the room that begin with *a*.

Aa	Bb
 apple	 ball

Repeat the routine for the remaining letter.

MONITOR PROGRESS Display the sentence from Student Page S44. Have individuals identify all instances of each letter taught. Check that students can print each letter independently.

A girl named Barbara has the bat.

IF... students misidentify or confuse any letters,
THEN... review key steps in the routine, and provide additional practice.

Lesson 3 Learn the Letters in the Alphabet I

PRACTICE 2: Recognize Letters *c* and *d* Display or distribute the letter cards from Student Page S45. Follow the routine to teach each letter. You may wish to cut the letters out to create separate picture cards.

Routine

1. Display the letter.	Model how to write upper- and lowercase *c* on the board. For example, say: This is uppercase *C*. This is lowercase *c*.
2. Name the letter.	What is the name of this letter? Yes; *c*.
3. Identify the letter.	Point to the cat card. What is this? Pause for responses. Yes, a cat. What letter does *cat* start with? Have students circle the letter and say it aloud. Yes, it's the letter *c*. *Cat* starts with *c*.
4. Write the letter.	Model writing lowercase *c*. Have students print lowercase *c* several times. Then model writing uppercase *C* and have students print it several times.
5. Extend practice.	Have students find examples of the letter *c* in words around the room, including students' names, signs, and objects.

REMIND STUDENTS THAT ...

- they can recognize the letters *c* and *d*.
- they can identify the letters *c* and *d* in words.
- they can print the letters *c* and *d*.

Cc	Dd

cat	dog

Repeat the routine for the remaining letter. Call attention to letters that are easily confused, such as *b* and *d*. Give students extra practice distinguishing and writing these letters.

☑ **MONITOR PROGRESS** Display the sentence from Student Page S45. Have individuals identify all instances of each letter taught. Check that students can print each letter independently.

The ice made Doug cold.

IF... students struggle to write particular letters,
THEN... model again how to write the letter and give students additional practice writing both the letter and new words containing it.

Lesson 3 Learn the Letters in the Alphabet I

REMIND STUDENTS THAT ...

- they can recognize the letters e and *f*.
- they can identify the letters e and *f* in words.
- they can print the letters e and *f*.

PRACTICE 3: Recognize Letters e and *f* Display or distribute the letter cards from Student Page S46. Follow the routine to teach each letter. You may wish to cut the letters out to create separate picture cards.

Routine

1. Display the letter. Model how to write upper- and lowercase e on the board. For example, say: This is uppercase *E*. This is lowercase e.

2. Name the letter. What is the name of this letter? Yes; e.

3. Identify the letter. Point to the egg card. What is this? Pause for responses. Yes, an egg. What letter does egg start with? Have students circle the letter and say it aloud. Yes, it's the letter e. *Egg* starts with e.

4. Write the letter. Model writing lowercase e. Have students print lowercase e several times. Then model writing uppercase *E* and have students print it several times.

5. Extend practice. Have students choose a classroom book and then find and copy two words that begin with or include the letter e.

Ee	Ff

egg	fish

Repeat the routine for the remaining letter. Call attention to letters that are easily confused, such as *E* and *F*. Give students extra practice distinguishing and writing these letters.

☑ **MONITOR PROGRESS** Display the sentence from Student Page S46. Have individuals identify all instances of each letter taught. Check that students can print each letter independently.

Every fly likes fresh food.

IF... students misidentify or confuse any letters,
THEN... review key steps in the routine, and have students practice writing additional words with those letters.

Lesson 3 Learn the Letters in the Alphabet I

PRACTICE 4: Recognize Letters *g* and *h* Display or distribute the letter cards from Student Page S47. Follow the routine to teach each letter. You may wish to cut the letters out to create separate picture cards.

Routine

1. Display the letter. Model how to write upper- and lowercase *g* on the board. For example, say: This is uppercase *G*. This is lowercase *g*.

2. Name the letter. What is the name of this letter? Yes; *g*.

3. Identify the letter. Point to the guitar card. What is this? Pause for responses. Yes, a guitar. What letter does *guitar* start with? Have students circle the letter and say it aloud. Yes, it's the letter *g*. *Guitar* starts with *g*.

4. Write the letter. Model writing lowercase *g*. Have students print lowercase *g* several times. Then model writing uppercase *G* and have students print it several times.

5. Extend practice. Have students make their own picture cards by drawing a letter on each card and then finding or drawing a picture of something that begins with the letter.

Gg	Hh

guitar	hat

Repeat the routine for the remaining letter. Call attention to letters that students may find difficult, such as *C* and *G*. Give students extra practice distinguishing and writing these letters.

✓ MONITOR PROGRESS Display the sentence from Student Page S47. Have individuals identify all instances of each letter taught. Check that students can print each letter independently.

That is great, Hugh!

IF… students struggle to identify particular letters,
THEN… model again how to identify the letters in several words and give students additional writing practice.

REMIND STUDENTS THAT …

- they can recognize the letters *g* and *h*.
- they can identify the letters *g* and *h* in words.
- they can print the letters *g* and *h*.

Lesson 3 Learn the Letters in the Alphabet I

REMIND STUDENTS THAT ...

- they can recognize the letters *i* and *j*.
- they can identify the letters *i* and *j* in words.
- they can print the letters *i* and *j*.

PRACTICE 5: Recognize Letters *i* and *j* Display or distribute the letter cards from Student Page S48. Follow the routine to teach each letter. You may wish to cut the letters out to create separate picture cards.

Routine

1. Display the letter. Model how to write upper- and lowercase *i* on the board. For example, say: This is uppercase *I*. This is lowercase *i*.

2. Name the letter. What is the name of this letter? Yes; *i*.

3. Identify the letter. Point to the igloo card. What is this? Pause for responses. Yes, it is an igloo. What letter does *igloo* start with? Have students circle the letter and say it aloud. Yes, it's the letter *i*. *Igloo* starts with *i*.

4. Write the letter. Model writing lowercase *i*. Have students print lowercase *i* several times. Then model writing uppercase *I* and have students print it several times.

5. Extend practice. Have students create an alphabet book, using a marker to write and decorate each letter on its own page. Later, have them open to a page and trace the letter with a finger.

Ii	Jj
 igloo	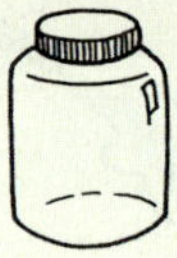 jar

Repeat the routine for the remaining letter. Note that lowercase *i* and *j* are easily confused. Give students ample practice distinguishing and writing these letters.

☑ **MONITOR PROGRESS** Display the sentence from Student Page S48. Have individuals identify all instances of each letter taught. Check that students can print each letter independently.

I told Ji I was just too tired.

IF... students misidentify or confuse any letters,
THEN... review key steps in the routine, and have students practice writing additional words with those letters.

Lesson 3 Learn the Letters in the Alphabet I

PRACTICE 6: Recognize Letters *k* and *l* Display or distribute the letter cards from Student Page S49. Follow the routine to teach each letter. You may wish to cut the letters out to create separate picture cards.

Routine

1. Display the letter.	Model how to write upper- and lowercase *k* on the board. For example, say: This is uppercase *K*. This is lowercase *k*.
2. Name the letter.	What is the name of this letter? Yes; *k*.
3. Identify the letter.	Point to the key card. What is this? Pause for responses. Yes, a key. What letter does *key* start with? Have students circle the letter and say it aloud. Yes, it's the letter *k*. *Key* starts with *k*.
4. Write the letter.	Model writing lowercase *k*. Have students print lowercase *k* several times. Then model writing uppercase *K* and have students print it several times.
5. Extend practice.	Have students choose a classroom book and then find and copy two words that include the letter *k*.

REMIND STUDENTS THAT . . .

- they can recognize the letters *k* and *l*.
- they can identify the letters *k* and *l* in words.
- they can print the letters *k* and *l*.

Kk	Ll
 key	 lion

Repeat the routine for the remaining letter. Call attention to letters that are easily confused, such as lowercase *i* and uppercase *I*. Give students extra practice distinguishing and writing these letters.

MONITOR PROGRESS Display the sentence from Student Page S49. Have individuals identify all instances of each letter taught. Check that students can print each letter independently.

King Luis lost his kite.

IF... students misidentify or confuse any letters,
THEN... review key steps in the routine, and have students practice writing additional words with those letters.

Lesson 3 Learn the Letters in the Alphabet 1

REMIND STUDENTS THAT …

- they can recognize the letters *m* and *n*.
- they can identify the letters *m* and *n* in words.
- they can print the letters *m* and *n*.

PRACTICE 7: Recognize Letters *m* and *n* Display or distribute the letter cards from Student Page S50. Follow the routine to teach each letter. You may wish to cut the letters out to create separate picture cards.

Routine

1. Display the letter.	Model how to write upper- and lowercase *m* on the board. For example, say: This is uppercase *M*. This is lowercase *m*.
2. Name the letter.	What is the name of this letter? Yes; *m*.
3. Identify the letter.	Point to the monkey card. What is this? Pause for responses. Yes, a monkey. What letter does *monkey* start with? Have students circle the letter and say it aloud. Yes, it's the letter *m*. *Monkey* starts with *m*.
4. Write the letter.	Model writing lowercase *m*. Have students print lowercase *m* several times. Then model writing uppercase *M* and have students print it several times.
5. Extend practice.	Have students write the letter *m* on a clean sheet of paper. Ask them to think of words that begin with the sound /m/. As they name each word, ask them to draw a picture of the word.

Mm	Nn
 monkey	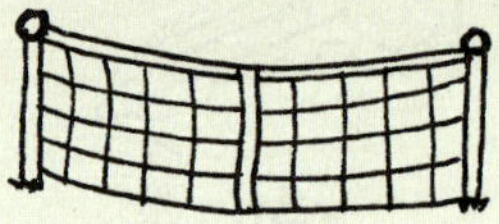 net

Repeat the routine for the remaining letter. Note that students may find it difficult to distinguish lowercase *m* and *n*. Give students ample practice distinguishing and writing these letters.

☑ **MONITOR PROGRESS** Display the sentence from Student Page S50. Have individuals identify all instances of each letter taught. Check that students can print each letter independently.

Miss Lin makes banana nut muffins.

IF… students struggle to identify particular letters,
THEN… model again how to identify the letters in several words and give students additional writing practice.

At the Zoo

We went to the zoo.
I saw a bat fly and a kangaroo jump.
I heard a duck quack.
I even saw a fox!

Lesson 3 Learn the Letters in the Alphabet I

Aa	Bb

apple	ball

A girl named Barbara has the bat.

Lesson 3 Learn the Letters in the Alphabet I

Cc	Dd

cat	dog

The ice made Doug cold.

Lesson 3 Learn the Letters in the Alphabet I

Ee	Ff

egg	fish

Every fly likes fresh food.

Lesson 3 Learn the Letters in the Alphabet I

Gg	Hh

guitar	hat

That is great, Hugh!

Lesson 3 **Learn the Letters in the Alphabet I**

Ii	Jj
 igloo	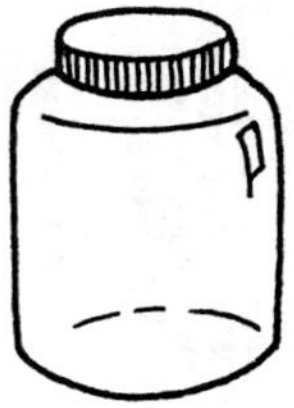 jar

I told Ji I was just too tired.

Lesson 3 Learn the Letters in the Alphabet I

Kk	Ll
 key	 lion

King Luis lost his kite.

Lesson 3 Learn the Letters in the Alphabet I

Mm	Nn
 monkey	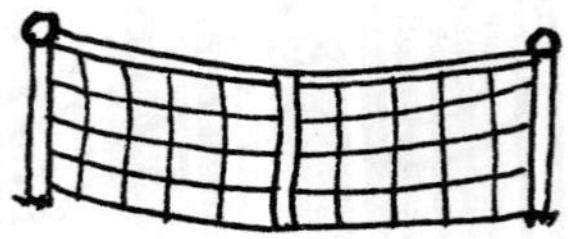 net

Miss Lin makes banana nut muffins.

Lesson 4 Learn the Letters in the Alphabet 2

RF.K.1.d Recognize and name all upper- and lowercase letters of the alphabet.

OBJECTIVES:

- Recognize all letters.
- Identify letters in words.
- Print all letters.

INTRODUCE Explain that every word is made of letters. Letters are used to spell sounds. Letters can be written as uppercase or lowercase. In this lesson, we'll learn how to look for and write letters. Sing the alphabet song with students.

MODEL Display the following passage "Indoors" or share copies of Student Page S51. Read it aloud. Say: The words in this passage use every letter in the alphabet.

Indoors

We fly through the rain.
Quick, indoors!
Remove our boots.
Unzip the wet parkas.
Change into pajamas.
How exciting!

TEACH Display a large alphabet chart with both upper- and lowercase letters. Say the name of each letter, and then help students locate all the letters in the passage. For example, say: This is a capital letter *R*. This is a lowercase letter *r*. Do you see *R*s in the passage? Circle the letters as you identify them. *Remove* starts with *r*. *R* sounds like /r/. Point to the letter. What is the name of this letter? *R*.

Lesson 4 Learn the Letters in the Alphabet 2

REMIND STUDENTS THAT …

- they can recognize the letters *o* and *p*.
- they can identify the letters *o* and *p* in words.
- they can print the letters *o* and *p*.

PRACTICE 1: Recognize Letters *o* and *p* Display or distribute the letter cards from Student Page S52. Follow the routine to teach each letter. You may wish to cut the letters out to create separate picture cards.

Routine

1. Display the letter. Model how to write upper- and lowercase *o* on the board. For example, say: This is uppercase *O*. This is lowercase *o*.

2. Name the letter. What is the name of this letter? Yes; *o*.

3. Identify the letter. Point to the otter card. What is this? Pause for responses. Yes, an otter. What letter does *otter* start with? Have students circle the letter and say it aloud. Yes, it's the letter *o*. *Otter* starts with *o*.

4. Write the letter. Model writing lowercase *o*. Have students print lowercase *o* several times. Then model writing uppercase *O* and have students print it several times.

5. Extend practice. Extend practice by having students find examples of the letter *o* in words around the room, including students' names, signs, and objects.

Oo	Pp
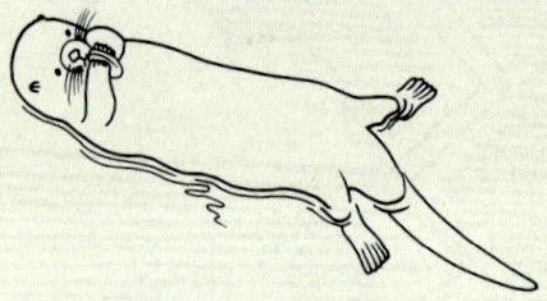	
otter	pie

Repeat the routine for the remaining letter. Call attention to letters that are easily confused, such as *b* and *p*. Give students extra practice distinguishing and writing these letters.

☑ **MONITOR PROGRESS** Display the sentence from Student Page S52. Have individuals identify all instances of each letter taught. Check that students can print each letter independently.

Open the present now, Pat.

IF… students misidentify or confuse any letters,
THEN… review key steps in the routine, and provide additional practice.

Lesson 4 Learn the Letters in the Alphabet 2

PRACTICE 2: Recognize Letters *q* and *r* Display or distribute the letter cards from Student Page S53. Follow the routine to teach each letter. You may wish to cut the letters out to create separate picture cards.

Routine

1. Display the letter. Model how to write upper- and lowercase *q* on the board. For example, say: This is uppercase *Q*. This is lowercase *q*.

2. Name the letter. What is the name of this letter? Yes; *q*.

3. Identify the letter. Point to the queen card. What is this? Pause for responses. Yes, a queen. What letter does *queen* start with? Have students circle the letter and say it aloud. Yes, it's the letter *q*. *Queen* starts with *q*.

4. Write the letter. Model writing lowercase *q*. Have students print lowercase *q* several times. Then model writing uppercase *Q* and have students print it several times.

5. Extend practice. Have students make picture cards. Have them draw the letter *Q* on a card. Say several words that begin with *q* (*quilt, quarter*) and have students draw one of the words on their card. Then help them write the word on the card.

REMIND STUDENTS THAT ...

- they can recognize the letters *q* and *r*.
- they can identify the letters *q* and *r* in words.
- they can print the letters *q* and *r*.

Qq	Rr

queen	rock

Repeat the routine for the remaining letter. Call attention to letters that students may find difficult, such as *p* and *q*. Give students extra practice distinguishing and writing these letters.

☑ **MONITOR PROGRESS** Display the sentence from Student Page S53. Have individuals identify all instances of each letter taught. Check that students can print each letter independently.

Red quilts are quite warm.

IF... students struggle to write particular letters,
THEN... model again and give students additional practice writing the letter and new words containing it.

Lesson 4 Learn the Letters in the Alphabet 2

REMIND STUDENTS THAT ...

- they can recognize the letters *s* and *t*.
- they can identify the letters *s* and *t* in words.
- they can print the letters *s* and *t*.

PRACTICE 3: Recognize Letters s and t Display or distribute the letter cards from Student Page S54. Follow the routine to teach each letter. You may wish to cut the letters out to create separate picture cards.

Routine

1. Display the letter.	Model how to write upper- and lowercase s on the board. For example, say: This is uppercase S. This is lowercase s.
2. Name the letter.	What is the name of this letter? Yes; s.
3. Identify the letter.	Point to the sun card. What is this? Pause for responses. Yes, the sun. What letter does *sun* start with? Have students circle the letter and say it aloud. Yes, it's the letter s. *Sun* starts with s.
4. Write the letter.	Model writing lowercase s. Have students print lowercase s several times. Then model writing uppercase S and have students print it several times.
5. Extend practice.	Have students find examples of the letter s in words around the room, including students' names, signs, and objects.

Ss	Tt
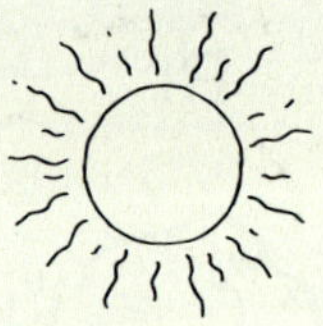 sun	 tiger

Repeat the routine for the remaining letter. Call attention to letters that are easily confused, such as *t* and *f*. Give students extra practice distinguishing and writing these letters.

☑ **MONITOR PROGRESS** Display the sentence from Student Page S54. Have individuals identify all instances of each letter taught. Check that students can print each letter independently.

Sis eats toast.

IF... students misidentify or confuse any letters,
THEN... review key steps in the routine, and have students practice writing additional words with those letters.

Lesson 4 Learn the Letters in the Alphabet 2

PRACTICE 4: Recognize Letters *u* and *v* Display or distribute the letter cards from Student Page S55. Follow the routine to teach each letter. You may wish to cut the letters out to create separate picture cards.

Routine

1. Display the letter.	Model how to write upper- and lowercase *u* on the board. For example, say: This is uppercase *U*. This is lowercase *u*.
2. Name the letter.	What is the name of this letter? Yes; *u*.
3. Identify the letter.	Point to the umbrella card. What is this? Pause for responses. Yes, an umbrella. What letter does *umbrella* start with? Have students circle the letter and say it aloud. Yes, it's the letter *u*. *Umbrella* starts with *u*.
4. Write the letter.	Model writing lowercase *u*. Have students print lowercase *u* several times. Then model writing uppercase *U* and have students print it several times.
5. Extend practice.	Have students choose a classroom book and then find and copy two words that begin with or include *u*.

Uu	Vv

umbrella	volcano

Repeat the routine for the remaining letter. Call attention to letters that are easily confused, such as *u*, *v*, and *w*. Give students extra practice distinguishing and writing these letters.

REMIND STUDENTS THAT ...

- they can recognize the letters *u* and *v*.
- they can identify the letters *u* and *v* in words.
- they can print the letters *u* and *v*.

☑ **MONITOR PROGRESS** Display the sentence from Student Page S55. Have individuals identify all instances of each letter taught. Check that students can print each letter independently.

Use a very quiet voice to whisper.

IF... students struggle to identify particular letters,
THEN... model again how to identify the letters in several words and give students additional writing practice.

Lesson 4 Learn the Letters in the Alphabet 2

REMIND STUDENTS THAT ...

- they can recognize the letters *w* and *x*.
- they can identify the letters *w* and *x* in words.
- they can print the letters *w* and *x*.

PRACTICE 5: Recognize Letters *w* and *x* Display or distribute the letter cards from Student Page S56. Follow the routine to teach each letter. You may wish to cut the letters out to create separate picture cards.

Routine

1. Display the letter. Model how to write upper- and lowercase *w* on the board. For example, say: This is uppercase *W*. This is lowercase *w*.

2. Name the letter. What is the name of this letter? Yes; *w*.

3. Identify the letter. Point to the worm card. What is this? Pause for responses. Yes, a worm. What letter does *worm* start with? Have students circle the letter and say it aloud. Yes, it's the letter *w*. *Worm* starts with *w*.

4. Write the letter. Model writing lowercase *w*. Have students print lowercase *w* several times. Then model writing uppercase *W* and have students print it several times.

5. Extend practice. Have students write the letter *w* on several sticky notes and then attach them to any objects in the room that begin with or contain *w*.

Ww	Xx
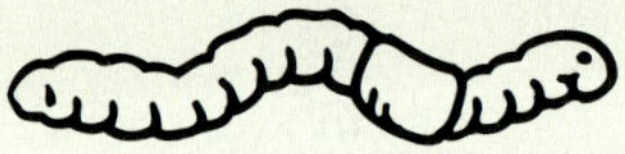	
worm	x-ray

Repeat the routine for the remaining letter. Explain that not many words begin with *x*, but *x* can be found inside words such as *exciting* and at the end of words such as *box*. Give students ample practice distinguishing and writing these letters.

MONITOR PROGRESS Display the sentence from Student Page S56. Have individuals identify all instances of each letter taught. Check that students can print each letter independently.

We drink extra water when we exercise.

IF... students misidentify or confuse any letters,
THEN... review key steps in the routine, and have students practice writing additional words with those letters.

Lesson 4 Learn the Letters in the Alphabet 2

PRACTICE 6: Recognize Letters y and z Display or distribute the letter cards from Student Page S57. Follow the routine to teach each letter. You may wish to cut the letters out to create separate picture cards.

Routine

1. Display the letter. Model how to write upper- and lowercase *y* on the board. For example, say: This is uppercase *Y*. This is lowercase *y*.

2. Name the letter. What is the name of this letter? Yes; *y*.

3. Identify the letter. Point to the yo-yo card. What is this? Pause for responses. Yes, a yo-yo. What letter does *yo-yo* start with? Have students circle the letter and say it aloud. Yes, it's the letter *y*. *Yo-yo* starts with *y*.

4. Write the letter. Model writing lowercase *y*. Have students print lowercase *y* several times. Then model writing uppercase *Y* and have students print it several times.

5. Extend practice. Have students find examples of the letter *y* in words around the room, including students' names, signs, and objects as well as in books.

Yy	Zz
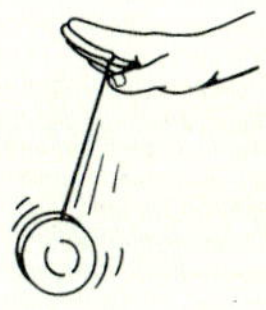 yo-yo	 zebra

Repeat the routine for the remaining letter. Call attention to letters that students might find difficult, such as lowercase *z* and *s*. Give students extra practice distinguishing and writing these letters.

MONITOR PROGRESS Display the sentence from Student Page S57. Have individuals identify all instances of each letter taught. Check that students can print each letter independently.

Did you see the zebra at the zoo yet?

IF... students misidentify or confuse any letters,
THEN... review key steps in the routine, and have students practice writing additional words with those letters.

REMIND STUDENTS THAT ...

- they can recognize the letters *y* and *z*.
- they can identify the letters *y* and *z* in words.
- they can print the letters *y* and *z*.

Lesson 4 Learn the Letters in the Alphabet 2

REMIND STUDENTS THAT ...

- they can recognize the letters in the alphabet.
- they can identify letters in words.
- they can print each letter.

PRACTICE 7: Review Follow the routine to review any letter. You may wish to cut out letters to create new picture cards.

Routine

1. Display the letter. Model how to write upper- and lowercase letters on the board. For example, say: This is uppercase *M*. This is lowercase *m*.

2. Name the letter. Point to the letter. What is the name of this letter? Yes; *m*. The name of this letter is *m*.

3. Identify the letter. Point to a card or an object with a name beginning with *m*. What is this? Pause for responses. Yes, a mouth. The beginning sound is /m/. What letter does *mouth* start with? Have students say the name of the letter aloud. Yes, it's the letter *m*. *Mouth* starts with *m*.

4. Write the letter. Model writing upper- and lowercase *m*. Have students print both letters several times.

5. Extend practice. Have students continue developing their own alphabet books. Turn to the page with the letter. Ask for examples of words that begin with that letter. Have students draw pictures of new words that begin with the letter, and then help students write the words.

For additional practice, have students print each letter and write words that begin with that letter.

☑ **INDEPENDENT PRACTICE** Display the illustration from Student Pages S58. Have individuals identify the letter being reviewed. Check that students can print the upper- and lowercase letters independently.

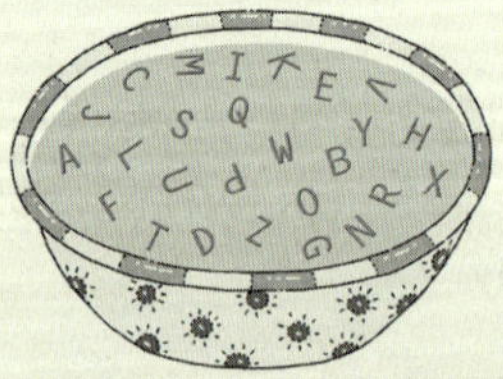

IF... students struggle to identify or reproduce particular letters,
THEN... model again how to identify the letters and give students additional writing practice.

Indoors

We fly through the rain.
Quick, indoors!
Remove our boots.
Unzip the wet parkas.
Change into pajamas.
How exciting!

Lesson 4 **Learn the Letters in the Alphabet 2**

Oo	Pp
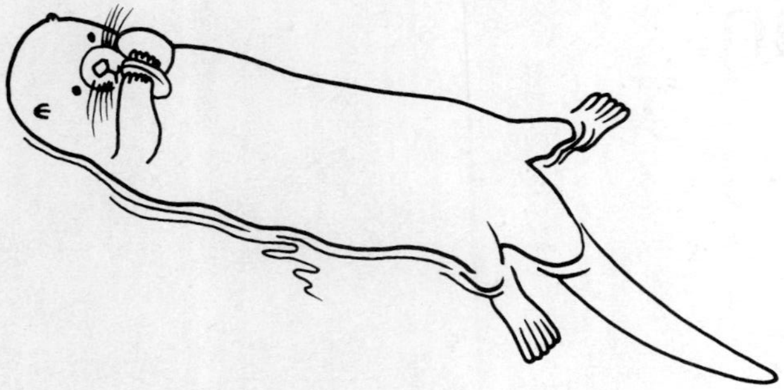	
otter	pie

Open the present now, Pat.

Lesson 4 Learn the Letters in the Alphabet 2

Yy	Zz

yo-yo	zebra

Did you see the zebra at the zoo yet?

Lesson 4

Learn the Letters in the Alphabet 2

ASSESSMENT
LESSONS 3–4

Print Concepts

ASSESS MASTERY Use this Checkpoint to assess students' mastery of upper- and lowercase letters of the alphabet.

ADMINISTER THE TEST Administer the Checkpoint orally to each student. For each student, make two copies of the next page. Give each student a copy and use the other copy for marking the student's responses.

MODEL: Point to *g*. What letter is this? That's right; this is *g*. Now you name as many of these letters as you can. Start here (point to *E*) and go across the page. When you finish one line, go to the next line, and read across the page. If you come to a letter you don't know, I'll name it for you.

SCORING

SKILL/LESSON	SCORE
1. Learn the Letters of the Alphabet 1 and 2 (Lessons 3–4)	____ / 51

An overall score of 80% correct is typically considered mastery. Use your judgment and your individual students' needs as well to determine skill mastery.

IF... students score below the benchmark,
THEN... review the missed letters, going back to the lessons to reteach and scaffold as needed.

ASSESSMENT
LESSONS 3–4

Print Concepts

g	E	v	a	J	o	q	L	R	b	h
s	I	G	c	K	p	t	d	V	S
e	n	f	H	r	m	T	g	Q	M	z
u	A	I	Y	j	F	P	B	k	Z	x
N	O	y	W	U	D	w	C	X

Lesson 5 Identify Rhyming Words and Alliteration

INTRODUCE Explain that when the ending parts of words sound alike, the words rhyme. When the beginning parts of words in a group sound alike, it is called alliteration. Tell students that they will listen to some words and decide which ones rhyme and which ones are alliteration.

MODEL Reinforce the concept of rhyme. Words that rhyme sound the same, such as *bike* and *like*. Other words that sound like those are *Mike* and *trike*. The words rhyme because their ending parts sound the same. Display or write the following lines from Student Page S61.

New Wheels

Mike rides a trike.
What would Mike like?
Mike would like a bike.

TEACH I'm going to say two words. If they rhyme, I will clap my hands. If they do not rhyme, I will not clap my hands. *Rose, pill* (do not clap). *Run, fun* (clap).

Now you try. Read aloud the following single-syllable word pairs: *top, drop; hit, sit; nose, ear; fall, call; nice, neat; date, late; try, fly.*

If students respond incorrectly, say: Listen carefully. Do the ending parts have the same sound? Repeat the pair. Affirm correct responses.

Slowly say: *pat, rip, sat.* Pay attention to how each word ends. *Pat.* The word *pat* ends with /at/. Say it with me: /at/. *Rip.* The word *rip* ends with /ip/. That's not the same as /at/, so those two words do not rhyme. *Sat.* The word *sat* ends with /at/. That's the same ending sound as in *pat. Pat* and *Sat* rhyme.

Introduce the concept of alliteration. Alliteration is the use of the same beginning sound in a group of words. *Big bees buzz.* What sound do you hear that begins each word? That's right: /b/. You just heard alliteration. Listen: *Red rat ran.* What is the same beginning sound? /r/

Use triplets to reinforce alliteration. Say: Listen to three words. Which words begin with the same sound? Slowly say: *dog, pan, dish.* Help students determine that *dog* and *dish* both begin with the letter *d*. Repeat with *key, kite, man.*

OBJECTIVES:

- Determine if spoken pairs of words rhyme.
- Identify which spoken words rhyme.
- Demonstrate phonological awareness by identifying rhyming words.
- Demonstrate phonological awareness by recognizing spoken alliteration or groups of words that begin with the same spoken onset or initial sound.

Lesson 5 Identify Rhyming Words and Alliteration

REMIND STUDENTS THAT …

- words that rhyme have the same ending sound.

PRACTICE 1 Tell students they will practice finding words that rhyme. I'm going to say two words. If they rhyme, clap your hands. If they do not rhyme, do not clap. Let's do one pair of words together. *Fin, pin* (clap).

Now you try. Display and read aloud the single-syllable word pairs from Student Page S62.

got cot (clap)	pit put	cow now (clap)	bed bad

If students respond incorrectly, say: Listen carefully. Do the ending parts have the same sound? Repeat the pair. Affirm correct responses: Yes, those words rhyme.

Read aloud the rhyming pairs from Student Page S62. Have students repeat the words aloud, emphasizing the rhyming sounds.

did, hid	fat, rat	how, wow
mile, pile	roar, soar	

Next, say the following word sets aloud, and have students name the rhyming words.

<u>weak</u>, watch, <u>beak</u>	<u>crab</u>, <u>grab</u>, cup
plan, <u>plane</u>, <u>gain</u>	<u>fin</u>, fat, <u>pin</u>
grin, <u>mug</u>, <u>jug</u>	

☑ **MONITOR PROGRESS** Read the following word pairs aloud to students: *fair, pair; dark, bark; oil, boil; rap, good; send, fan.* After each pair ask: Do these words rhyme? Affirm correct responses.

IF… students cannot identify rhyming words,
THEN… model hearing rhyme by saying two rhyming words, emphasizing the ending in each one.

Lesson 5 Identify Rhyming Words and Alliteration

PRACTICE 2 Ask students to listen to these words: *hot, lot, can.* Say: *hot.* Say the ending /ot/, then have students say it with you. Repeat with *lot*. Then say: *can*. Say its ending: /an/. Have students repeat the ending. Ask: Which words have the same ending? Pause to let students respond. Yes, *hot* and *lot* have the same ending. *Hot* and *lot* rhyme.

Then say each set of words from the first box on Student Page S63 and ask students to name the rhyming words. After doing the oral exercise, you may wish to display Student Page S63 and point out the word endings to reinforce the final sounds and rhymes.

pat pig wig	cat sit mat	joke woke wake

Say: Now we are going to practice finding pairs of words that have the same beginning sound. Read aloud the alliteration groups from the second box on Student Page S63. Have students identify the word pairs that begin with the same sound.

pig post tick	set van sun	corn fed fox

REMIND STUDENTS THAT …

- words that rhyme have the same ending sound.
- words that do not have the same ending sound do not rhyme.
- groups of words can begin with the same sound.

☑ **MONITOR PROGRESS** Say each set of words below and have students name the word pairs that begin with the same sound.

<u>grin</u>, <u>gate</u>, weak
<u>book</u>, watch, <u>box</u>
<u>fin</u>, <u>fat</u>, pine
<u>can</u>, mug, <u>cup</u>

IF… students cannot identify the alliteration pairs in a set,
THEN… say each word in the set and have students repeat the words after you. Ask: Which words begin with the same sound? Repeat the words emphasizing the beginning of each to help students identify the alliterations.

Lesson 5 Identify Rhyming Words and Alliteration

REMIND STUDENTS THAT ...

- words that rhyme have the same ending sound.
- words that do not have the same ending sound do not rhyme.
- rhyming words can have one or more than one syllable.

PRACTICE 3 Tell students that short words can rhyme, and longer words can rhyme as well. Let's start with short words. Here are some short words that rhyme: *lap, tap, map.* All of those words end with the sound /ap/.

Now listen to these longer words: *Pocket, happy, rocket.* The word *pocket* ends with /ok it/. Say it with me: /ok it/. The word *happy* ends with /ap ē/. That is not the same as /ok it/, so those two words do not rhyme. *Pocket, rocket.* The word *rocket* ends with /ok it/; that sounds just like *pocket. Pocket* and *rocket* rhyme.

Here are other longer words: *tower, shower, flicker.* Which two words end with /ow er/? Let's say the words together: *tower, shower.*

Next, display and say each set of words from Student Page S64, and have students name the rhyming words.

pile line fine	rider wider later	pickle label tickle

Say each set of words aloud and have students name the rhyming words.

ring, kick, quick	stumble, bother, crumble
might, fight, spot	cool, pool, rail
sunny, rabbit, funny	phone, yarn, barn

☑ **INDEPENDENT PRACTICE** Say each set of words aloud and have students name the rhyming words.

bread, drip, said	simple, dimple, ticket
drag, snug, plug	sneezy, snazzy, breezy

IF... students cannot identify two-syllable rhyming words in a set,
THEN... say each word in the set and have students repeat the words after you. Guide students to identify the ending sounds in each word. Which endings are the same? Pause for students to respond. The words with the same ending sounds rhyme.

Lesson 5 **Identify Rhyming Words and Alliteration**

New Wheels

Mike rides a trike.
What would Mike like?
Mike would like a bike.

Teacher: This Student Page is intended as an *optional extension* of the lesson. After teaching the phonological awareness lesson orally, you can distribute or display this page to connect the phonological awareness skills (sounds) to phonics skills (sound-spelling).

Lesson 5 Identify Rhyming Words and Alliteration

got cot	pit put	cow now	bed bad

did, hid	fat, rat	how, wow
mile, pile	roar, soar	

Teacher: This Student Page is intended as an *optional extension* of the lesson. After teaching the phonological awareness lesson orally, you can distribute or display this page to connect the phonological awareness skills (sounds) to phonics skills (sound-spelling).

Lesson 5 Identify Rhyming Words and Alliteration

pat pig wig	cat sit mat	joke woke wake

pig post tick	set van sun	corn fed fox

Teacher: This Student Page is intended as an *optional extension* of the lesson. After teaching the phonological awareness lesson orally, you can distribute or display this page to connect the phonological awareness skills (sounds) to phonics skills (sound-spelling).

Lesson 5 Identify Rhyming Words and Alliteration

pile line fine	rider wider later	pickle label tickle

Teacher: This Student Page is intended as an *optional extension* of the lesson. After teaching the phonological awareness lesson orally, you can distribute or display this page to connect the phonological awareness skills (sounds) to phonics skills (sound-spelling).

Lesson 6 Produce Rhyming Words and Alliteration

INTRODUCE Remind students that rhyming words have ending parts that sound the same. Alliteration is when the beginning parts of words in a group sound alike. I'm going to say some words, and then we're going to think of new words that rhyme with the ones I say. We are also going to practice thinking of words that begin with the same sound.

MODEL Display or distribute the passage "My Friend Pat" from Student Page S65. Then, read the passage, emphasizing the ending sounds.

My Friend Pat

My friend Pat
has more than one hat.
One hat has a bat.
One hat has a cat.
One hat has a very fat rat.
That is one ugly hat!

Use the passage as you review the concept of rhyme with students. I want to find a word that rhymes with *cat*. Say *cat* aloud several times, slowly at first, and then at a normal rate. The word *cat* ends with /at/. Say /at/ several times. What other words do I know that end the same way? I know—*bat*. The word *bat* rhymes with *cat:* /k//at/, /b//at/. Repeat with the words *fit* and *hit*.

TEACH Use simple segmenting to reinforce the concept that rhyme involves the ending parts of words. A lot of the words we know have beginning sounds and ending sounds. Listen closely: *Shake. Shake* has the beginning sound /sh/ and the ending sound /āk/. To make a rhyming word, we need another word that ends with /āk/. How about *take? cake? break?* All of those words have the ending sound /āk/. All of the words rhyme with *shake.* Invite students to add other words that rhyme. Examples include *bake, fake, Jake, lake, make,* and *rake*.

Use simple segmenting to reinforce the concept that alliteration involves the beginning parts of words. Now let's think about words that begin with the same sound. Listen: *Four fish feed. Four* has the beginning sound /f/. The words *fish* and *feed* begin with the /f/ sound too. All of the words begin with /f/. Let's try another one. Say: Mice make music. What sound do you hear at the beginning of each word? Help students figure out that *mice, make,* and *music* begin with the /m/ sound. Ask students to think of other word groups that begin with the same sounds.

OBJECTIVES:

- Produce a spoken word to rhyme with another spoken word.
- Demonstrate phonological awareness by identifying and producing rhyming words.
- Demonstrate phonological awareness by recognizing spoken alliteration or groups of words that begin with the same spoken onset or initial sound.

Lesson 6 Produce Rhyming Words and Alliteration

REMIND STUDENTS THAT …

- words that rhyme have the same ending.
- words that do not have the same ending do not rhyme.

PRACTICE 1: Rhyming Words Invite students to help you think of rhyming words. I'll say a word, and we'll all figure out words that rhyme with it. Say *tip*. Have students repeat the word. Say the ending with me: /ip/. What's another word that ends the same way? Pause to let students tell you a word. Yes, (*dip, drip, lip, sip, trip*) rhymes with *tip*.

Follow this procedure to guide practice, using the words from Student Page S66. Accept nonsense words as well as real words that rhyme.

sat (bat, cat, fat, hat, mat, rat, pat)
hug (rug, jug, mug, bug, dug, tug, plug, chug)
fan (man, ran, van, Jan, Dan, can, pan)
bed (fed, led, head, said, red, Ned, Ted)
fox (box, locks, socks, rocks, knocks)

Then give students the following words from Student Page S66 and have them produce rhyming words for each. Accept nonsense words as well as real words that rhyme.

book (cook, look, took, shook, nook, hook, rook)
school (rule, cool, pool, tool, fool)
sit (bit, fit, spit, mitt, hit, pit, quit)
read (bead, feed, lead, need, seed)

☑ **MONITOR PROGRESS** Give students the following words from Student Page S66 and have them produce at least two rhyming words for each.

tap (cap, clap, flap, lap, map, nap, sap, trap)
hop (bop, cop, chop, drop, shop, mop, pop, top)

IF… students say words with similar beginning sounds instead of similar endings,
THEN… say the word again, emphasizing the ending, and model a correct response.

Lesson 6 Produce Rhyming Words and Alliteration

PRACTICE 2: Alliteration Invite students to help you think of alliterations. Listen closely: *lamp.* Have students repeat the word slowly. Say the beginning sound with me: /l/. What's one other word that begins the same way? Pause to let students tell you a word. Yes, (*leaf, lion, lizard, lock, lemon, ladybug, ladder, log*) begins with the same sound as *lamp.* Ask for more words that begin with the same sound until students have produced four or five. Follow this procedure to guide practice, using the following words from Student Page S67. Accept nonsense words as well as real words.

REMIND STUDENTS THAT …

- groups of words can begin with the same sound.

dog (down, dig, deer, doll, daisy, duck)
car (camel, carrot, cup, cat, cone)
sun (spoon, swing, sock, sit, sled)
tent (toe, toad, tooth, table, tiger)

Display and read aloud the following words from Student Page S67, and have students produce alliterations for each. Accept nonsense words as well as real words.

bat (bee, balloon, bag, bus, ball)
goat (grapes, gate, girl, gift, goose)
jet (jeans, jump, juice, jacket, jam)
pen (plane, pencil, plate, pear, pig)

☑ **MONITOR PROGRESS** Read aloud the following words from Student Page S67, and have students produce at least two alliterations.

robot (rainbow, rabbit, rake, rose, ring)
nest (nine, nut, nail, nose, neck)

IF… students cannot produce alliterations,
THEN… say each word slowly. Help students segment the sounds in the word and guide them to identify the beginning sound in the word. Then ask: What other words do you know that have the same beginning sound? Offer one example to help students produce alliterations.

Lesson 6 Produce Rhyming Words and Alliteration

REMIND STUDENTS THAT ...

- words that rhyme have the same ending.
- long words can rhyme.

PRACTICE 3: More Rhyming Words Explain that words of all sizes can rhyme. Some words with just one sound can rhyme. Point to your eye and say: *Eye.* This word has just one sound. What words rhyme with *eye?* Let students respond. Yes, (*buy, fly, why, my, try*) rhymes with *eye.*

What about longer words? If their ending sounds match, they rhyme. Listen: *berry.* The ending sound is /air ē/. What words rhyme with *berry?* Have students respond. Yes, (*fairy, merry, cherry, hairy, scary*) rhymes with *berry.*

What if I want a word that rhymes with *agrees? Agrees* ends with /ēz/. Say /ēz/ several times. What other words end this way? How about *sneeze?* The words *agrees* and *sneeze* both end in /ēz/. They rhyme. So do *bees, knees,* and *chimpanzees!* Follow this procedure to guide practice, using the words below from Student Page S68.

funny (honey, money, sunny, runny, bunny)
better (wetter, sweater, letter, setter)

Next, say each word below from Student Page S68 and have students repeat the word. Ask for a rhyming word: What word rhymes with _______?

many (any, penny, Jenny)
dinner (winner, thinner, spinner, inner)

☑ **INDEPENDENT PRACTICE** Read aloud the following words from Student Page S68, and have students produce at least two rhyming words for each. Accept nonsense words as well as real words that rhyme.

sticker (quicker, thicker, flicker, kicker, sicker)
bend (friend, end, send, spend, lend, depend)

IF... students cannot produce rhyming words with more than one syllable, THEN... model a correct response by saying *mister* and *twister,* emphasizing the ending part in each one. Guide students to suggest other words that end with the /is ter/ sound, such as *sister.* Encourage students to use this process to produce rhyming words.

Lesson 6 **Produce Rhyming Words and Alliteration**

My Friend Pat

My friend Pat
has more than one hat.
One hat has a bat.
One hat has a cat.
One hat has a very fat rat.
That is one ugly hat!

Teacher: This Student Page is intended as an *optional extension* of the lesson. After teaching the phonological awareness lesson orally, you can distribute or display this page to connect the phonological awareness skills (sounds) to phonics skills (sound-spelling).

Lesson 6 Produce Rhyming Words and Alliteration

sat	bed
hug	fox
fan	

book	sit
school	read

tap
hop

Teacher: This Student Page is intended as an *optional extension* of the lesson. After teaching the phonological awareness lesson orally, you can distribute or display this page to connect the phonological awareness skills (sounds) to phonics skills (sound-spelling).

Lesson 6 Produce Rhyming Words and Alliteration

dog car	sun tent

bat goat	jet pen

robot nest

Teacher: This Student Page is intended as an *optional extension* of the lesson. After teaching the phonological awareness lesson orally, you can distribute or display this page to connect the phonological awareness skills (sounds) to phonics skills (sound-spelling).

Lesson 6

Produce Rhyming Words and Alliteration

funny **better**
many **dinner**
sticker **bend**

Teacher: This Student Page is intended as an *optional extension* of the lesson. After teaching the phonological awareness lesson orally, you can distribute or display this page to connect the phonological awareness skills (sounds) to phonics skills (sound-spelling).

Lesson 7 Blend and Count Syllables in Spoken Words

INTRODUCE Remind students that some words are short and some are long. You know that sentences are made of parts called words. Words are made of parts called syllables. Today we will put syllables together to make words.

MODEL Explain that short words have one syllable and longer words have more than one syllable. Listen as I say the syllables that make a word. As you say each syllable, clap your hands: *mu* (clap) *sic* (clap). I will put the syllables together to make the word. I will say them quickly without stopping: *music.*

How many syllables are in the word *music*? Remember, I clapped my hands for the syllables: *mu* (clap) *sic* (clap). *Music* has two syllables. Now let's count on our fingers. Watch: *mu* (raise your thumb) *sic* (raise your index finger on the same hand). Repeat and have students count with you. Follow the same procedure to model blending and then counting the syllables of *rain* and *bow* (*rainbow*) and *af* and *ter* (*after*). After the oral exercise, you may wish to distribute or display Student Page S69.

Explain that changing a syllable makes a new word. Have students repeat the syllables in *after* several times: *af•ter.* Now, change the syllable *af* to *en: en•ter.* What is the new word? (*enter*). Repeat with *later.*

TEACH Wave your hand around the room and say: *classroom.* There are two syllables in *classroom: class* (hold up your thumb) *room* (hold up the index finger). When we put the syllables together, we make a word: *classroom.* Repeat with *playground, classmates,* and *daylight.*

Reinforce hearing and counting syllables. Slowly say *sunset* as you raise two fingers. Listen and count with me: *sun•set.* Then work with students to manipulate the syllables in *sunset* to form new words, such as *sunshine, sunrise,* and *upset.*

OBJECTIVES:

- Identify spoken syllables in words.
- Pronounce and count syllables in spoken words.
- Blend spoken words into compound words.
- Blend syllables to form multisyllabic words.
- Manipulate syllables in spoken words.

Lesson 7 Blend and Count Syllables in Spoken Words

REMIND STUDENTS THAT ...

- words are made of parts called syllables.
- saying a word slowly makes it easy to hear the syllables.
- changing a syllable makes a new word.

PRACTICE 1 Remind students that some words have just one syllable. Other words have two or more syllables.

Let's try some words. First, I will say the syllables. Next, you say the syllables with me. Then, we'll make a word by saying the syllables together.

Say *pic* and *ture*, clapping after you say each syllable. Now say the syllables with me and clap after each one. *Pic* (clap) *ture* (clap). Let's say the syllables without clapping. Speak the syllables distinctly. As you speak, raise your thumb for the first syllable and another finger for the second syllable. Have students repeat what you do. Now, let's say the syllables together in a word: *picture*. Repeat the word: *picture*.

Follow the same procedure with the words *zig•zag* and *cor•ner*.

Say the syllables of each word in the first box on Student Page S70 and have students repeat the syllables with you. Then ask students to say the syllables together as a word. If students falter, model saying the word and have them repeat it with you several times.

air port	run way	rain y

Change a syllable in each word to make a new word with students. Have students repeat the syllables in *airport* several times: *air•port*. Now, change the syllable *air* to *pass*: *pass•port*. What is the new word? (*passport*) Repeat with *subway* and *raincoat*.

MONITOR PROGRESS Say the syllables of each word below and ask students how many syllables they hear. Then have students say the syllables together as a word.

pen cil	bee hive	gar den	cheer ful

IF... students make an error,
THEN... model the correct response by saying the syllables separately, holding up a finger for each syllable and then blending the syllables to say the word.

Lesson 7 Blend and Count Syllables in Spoken Words

PRACTICE 2 Explain that you are going to practice making words that have two or more syllables. We will make words with two or more syllables from shorter words. Here are two short words: *cup* (pause) *cake.* Now I will say the words together to make one word: *cupcake.* Do you know what a cupcake is? Allow students to respond.

Let's try some words together. We will take two short words and make them into one word. Distinctly say the words in each of the following word pairs from Student Page S71. Have students repeat each pair and then combine them into a single word.

cat fish	blue bird	sting ray

Say each of the following pairs of words from Student Page S71. Have students repeat each word distinctly. Then have students combine each pair of words into a single word.

bed room	night light	fire fly

Change a syllable in each word to make a new word with students. Have students repeat the syllables in *bedroom* several times: *bed•room.* Now, change the syllable *bed* to *bath: bath•room.* What is the new word? (*bathroom*) Repeat with *nightgown* and *firewood.*

REMIND STUDENTS THAT ...

- words are made of parts called syllables.
- words sound right when you say syllables together without stopping.
- changing a syllable makes a new word.

☑ **MONITOR PROGRESS** Say each of the following sets of words from Student Page S71. Have students repeat each set of words distinctly and then combine them into a single word. Then have them choose a word and replace one of the syllables to make a new word.

gold fish	sun beam	fire place
____ fish	sun ____	fire ____

IF... students make errors in blending or manipulating syllables,
THEN... model the correct response by saying the syllables together and having students repeat after you. Offer replacement syllables such as *cat, burn,* or *wood* and then say the new words with students.

Lesson 7 Blend and Count Syllables in Spoken Words

REMIND STUDENTS THAT ...

- words are made of parts called syllables.
- to make a word, we say syllables together without stopping.
- changing a syllable makes a new word.

PRACTICE 3 Review hearing and counting syllables. Let's count the syllables, or parts, in the word *sidewalk*. Say the word slowly, and count the parts on your fingers: *side* (raise your thumb) *walk* (raise the next finger). There are two syllables in *sidewalk*, *side* and *walk*. When we put the syllables together, we get *sidewalk*.

Now we will put together some other syllables to make words. Here are two syllables: *kit•chen*. Can you tell what word they make? Have students respond. That's right; the word is *kitchen*. Now replace the syllable *chen* with *ten*. What is the new word? (*kitten*)

Display and say the following syllables from Student Page S72. Have students repeat the syllables distinctly, and then have them say the word.

bath robe	bathrobe
morn ing	morning
count er	counter
toast er	toaster
mi cro wave	microwave

Have students listen closely as you say these sets of distinct syllables from Student Page S72. Have them repeat the syllables separately and then blend the syllables into a word. Allow students to begin slowly and make several attempts to say each word. Then encourage them to change a syllable to make a new word.

sham poo	tooth brush	tel e phone
jack et	um brel la	ad ven ture

☑ **INDEPENDENT PRACTICE** Say the following syllables from Student Page S72 and have students repeat after you. After each set, have them say the syllables together as one word. Allow them to begin slowly and speed up to make the word. Then have them choose a word and replace one of the syllables to make a new word.

nap kin	din ner	in doors	a maz ing
____ kin	____ ner	in ____	a ____ ing

IF... students make an error in blending or manipulating syllables,
THEN... say the word, say the syllables separately, and then blend the syllables back into the word. Offer replacement syllables such as *pump*, *win*, *sect*, and *wak* and then say the new words with students.

Lesson 7 Blend and Count Syllables in Spoken Words

mu sic **rain bow** **af ter**

Teacher: This Student Page is intended as an *optional extension* of the lesson. After teaching the phonological awareness lesson orally, you can distribute or display this page to connect the phonological awareness skills (sounds) to phonics skills (sound-spelling).

Lesson 7 Blend and Count Syllables in Spoken Words

air port run way rain y

pen cil bee hive gar den cheer ful

Teacher: This Student Page is intended as an *optional extension* of the lesson. After teaching the phonological awareness lesson orally, you can distribute or display this page to connect the phonological awareness skills (sounds) to phonics skills (sound-spelling).

Lesson 7

Blend and Count Syllables in Spoken Words

cat fish	blue bird	sting ray

bed room	night light	fire fly

gold fish	sun beam	fire place
____ fish	sun ____	fire ____

Teacher: This Student Page is intended as an *optional extension* of the lesson. After teaching the phonological awareness lesson orally, you can distribute or display this page to connect the phonological awareness skills (sounds) to phonics skills (sound-spelling).

Lesson 7 Blend and Count Syllables in Spoken Words

bath robe
morn ing
count er

toast er
mi cro wave

sham poo
jack et

tooth brush
um brel la

tel e phone
ad ven ture

nap kin
____ kin

din ner
____ ner

in doors
in ____

a maz ing
a ____ ing

Teacher: This Student Page is intended as an *optional extension* of the lesson. After teaching the phonological awareness lesson orally, you can distribute or display this page to connect the phonological awareness skills (sounds) to phonics skills (sound-spelling).

Lesson 8 Segment and Count Syllables in Spoken Words

OBJECTIVES:

- Count syllables in spoken words.
- Segment spoken compound words.
- Segment multisyllabic words into syllables.
- Manipulate syllables within multisyllabic words.

INTRODUCE Remind students that some words have more than one part. Listen as I say a word: *dinosaur*. Can you hear the parts in *dinosaur*? Let me say them slowly: *di•no•saur*. There are three parts, or syllables, in *dinosaur*.

MODEL Refer to Student Page S73. I'm going to say a word: *number*. I'll say the word again as I use my fingers to count each syllable I hear. Say *num•ber* again slowly, holding up your thumb for *num* and your index finger for *ber*.

Use your other hand to point to your raised fingers as you repeat the syllables. Say: *one, two* to count your fingers. Count with me: one, two. I hear two syllables. The syllables are *num•ber*.

Remind students that changing a syllable makes a new word. Have students repeat the syllables in *number* several times: *num•ber*. Now, change the syllable *num* to *bar*: *bar•ber*. What is the new word? (*barber*). Repeat with *barley*.

TEACH Follow the modeling procedure to segment the remaining words on Student Page S73. Let's do some other words together. First, we'll say a word: *sleepy*. Say the word with me: *sleepy*. Next, we will say the syllables and count them. *Sleep* (hold up your thumb and have students imitate you) *y* (hold up your index finger and have students imitate you). How many syllables did we count? Use your other hand to point to your raised fingers and count. Have students imitate you. That's right. We counted two syllables. Continue with the words *bedtime* (*bed•time*) and *seven* (*sev•en*).

Work with students to manipulate the syllables to form new words. Listen to the syllables in the word *sleepy* again: *sleep•y*. Now change the syllable *y* to the syllable *less*. What is the new word? Accept student responses. That's right. The new word is *sleepless*. Continue by replacing *bed* in *bedtime* with *day* to make *daytime* and replacing *sev* in *seven* with *giv* to make *given*.

Lesson 8 Segment and Count Syllables in Spoken Words

REMIND STUDENTS THAT ...

- words may have two or more syllables, or parts.
- they know how to count syllables.
- changing a syllable makes a new word.

PRACTICE I Explain that hearing the separate syllables in words is called segmenting. You have counted syllables in words. Some words are just one syllable. An example is *cow*. Some words have more syllables. An example is *cowboy*. How many parts can we hear in *cowboy*? Let's count them.

Raise your thumb as you say: *cow*. Raise your index finger as you say: *boy*. Point to each finger and say: Count with me. One, two. There are two syllables in *cowboy*. Have students segment each of the following words from Student Page S74.

bunny (bun•ny)	piglet (pig•let)
baby (ba•by)	duckling (duck•ling)
puppy (pup•py)	butterfly (but•ter•fly)
kitten (kit•ten)	caterpillar (cat•er•pil•lar)

Say each of the following words from Student Page S74 and have students repeat each one with you. Then have them count the syllables in the words using the process outlined above.

family (fam•i•ly, 3 syllables)
picnic (pic•nic, 2 syllables)
outdoors (out•doors, 2 syllables)
catnap (cat•nap, 2 syllables)

Challenge students to replace a syllable in one of the words to make a new word. If necessary, provide syllables for students to use, such as *eas* (*easily*), *ture* (*picture*), *ward* (*outward*), and *fish* (*catfish*)

☑ **MONITOR PROGRESS** Display and read the following words from Student Page S74. Have students segment the words and count the syllables.

robot (ro•bot, 2 syllables)
helper (help•er, 2 syllables)
wonder (won•der, 2 syllables)
afternoon (af•ter•noon, 3 syllables)

IF... students have difficulty identifying the correct number of syllables, THEN... review how to count the number of syllables on one hand, and provide some familiar multisyllabic words to help students practice.

Lesson 8 Segment and Count Syllables in Spoken Words

PRACTICE 2 Remind students that they know some words that are made of smaller words. Our school has classrooms. The word *classroom* has two syllables. Each syllable is its own word. Can you hear the two syllables? Let me say them: *class* (pause) *room*. Say the syllables with me: *class* (pause) *room*. If we say these words together quickly, it is like saying syllables together quickly. It makes a word: *classroom*.

Let's take apart some words together. These words have two syllables. Each syllable is a short word. The first word is *armchair*. What are the two syllables? Let students respond. That's right. The two syllables are *arm* and *chair*. Say them with me: *arm* (pause) *chair*.

Repeat the process with the words *eyelash*, *handshake*, *wristwatch*, and *footstep*.

Read aloud the following compound words from Student Page S75. After reading each word, ask students to tell you the two syllables, or short words, that make it up. Then change a syllable in each word to make a new word with students. Have students repeat the syllables in *outside* several times: *out•side*. Now, change the syllable *out* to *be*: *be•side*. What is the new word? (*beside*) Repeat with *hairnet, clubhouse, horseshoe* (requires shifting *shoe* from first syllable to second syllable), *baseball,* and *doorknob*.

outside (out•side)	shoelace (shoe•lace)
haircut (hair•cut)	football (foot•ball)
doghouse (dog•house)	doorway (door•way)

REMIND STUDENTS THAT ...

- syllables are the separate word parts they can hear.
- many longer words are made of syllables that are really two short words.
- changing a syllable makes a new word.

MONITOR PROGRESS Read aloud each of the following compound words from Student Page S75. Have students segment each word. Then have them choose a word and replace one of the syllables to make a new word.

ballpark (ball•park)	ball ______
homework (home•work)	______ work
campfire (camp•fire)	camp ______

IF... students have difficulty segmenting or manipulating syllables,
THEN... model segmenting the word and have students repeat the syllables after you. Provide additional practice with familiar compound words. Create a word chain as you change out syllables in familiar words and have students repeat after you. For example, *ballpark, ballgame, ballroom, lunchroom, lunchtime,* and *classtime*.

Lesson 8 Segment and Count Syllables in Spoken Words

REMIND STUDENTS THAT …

- words may have two or more syllables, or parts.
- segmenting words lets them count the syllables.
- changing a syllable makes a new word.

PRACTICE 3 Tell students they will listen to words and decide which syllables they contain. For example, I can say the word *winter*. I am going to say it slowly so you can hear the parts: *win* (pause) *ter*. The word *winter* contains the syllables *win* and *ter*. Say them with me: *win* (pause) *ter*.

Some words have more syllables. Say this word with me: *sharpener*. Have students say the word. Now let's say it very slowly so that we can hear the syllables. Repeat after me: *sharp* (pause) *en* (pause) *er*. There are three syllables: *sharp* (pause) *en* (pause) and *er*. Now replace the syllable *er* with *ing*. *What is the word?* (*sharpening*).

Repeat the process with the following words from Student Page S76. Guide students to change a syllable to make a new word. (*winner, penny, hammer, garbage*)

window (win•dow)	hamster (ham•ster)
thunderstorm (thun•der•storm)	insect (in•sect)
pencil (pen•cil)	mystery (mys•ter•y)
hamburger (ham•bur•ger)	garden (gar•den)

INDEPENDENT PRACTICE Read the following words from Student Page S76 and have students repeat each word with you. Then ask students to say the word slowly so you can hear the syllables, or parts. Then have them choose a word and replace one of the syllables to make a new word.

birthday (birth•day)	_______ day
monkey (mon•key)	_______ key
sleepover (sleep•o•ver)	sleep _______
doctor (doc•tor)	_______ tor
elephant (el•e•phant)	ele _______

IF… students are unable to segment or manipulate syllables,
THEN… model the correct response by saying the word in distinct syllables as you raise a finger to count each one. Have students repeat after you. If needed, help students brainstorm familiar multisyllabic words for additional practice (for example: *Monday, donkey, sleepy, tractor, elementary*). Have students repeat the word *birthday* after you, syllable by syllable. Then replace *birth* with *Mon* and have students continue repeating the word after you, syllable by syllable. Finally, say the syllables without stopping to blend the new word: *Monday*.

Lesson 8 Segment and Count Syllables in Spoken Words

num ber
sleep y
bed time
sev en

Teacher: This Student Page is intended as an *optional extension* of the lesson. After teaching the phonological awareness lesson orally, you can distribute or display this page to connect the phonological awareness skills (sounds) to phonics skills (sound-spelling).

Lesson 8

Segment and Count Syllables in Spoken Words

bunny	**piglet**
baby	**duckling**
puppy	**butterfly**
kitten	**caterpillar**

family	**outdoors**
picnic	**catnap**

robot	**wonder**
helper	**afternoon**

Teacher: This Student Page is intended as an *optional extension* of the lesson. After teaching the phonological awareness lesson orally, you can distribute or display this page to connect the phonological awareness skills (sounds) to phonics skills (sound-spelling).

Lesson 8 Segment and Count Syllables in Spoken Words

outside	shoelace
haircut	football
doghouse	doorway

ballpark	ball ________
homework	________ work
campfire	camp ________

Teacher: This Student Page is intended as an *optional extension* of the lesson. After teaching the phonological awareness lesson orally, you can distribute or display this page to connect the phonological awareness skills (sounds) to phonics skills (sound-spelling).

Lesson 8 Segment and Count Syllables in Spoken Words

window	hamster
thunderstorm	insect
pencil	mystery
hamburger	garden

birthday	________ day
monkey	________ key
sleepover	sleep ________
doctor	________ tor
elephant	ele ________

Teacher: This Student Page is intended as an *optional extension* of the lesson. After teaching the phonological awareness lesson orally, you can distribute or display this page to connect the phonological awareness skills (sounds) to phonics skills (sound-spelling).

ASSESSMENT
LESSONS 5–8

Phonological Awareness

ASSESS MASTERY Use this Checkpoint to assess students' mastery of rhyming words, alliteration, and syllables in spoken words.

ADMINISTER THE TEST Administer the Checkpoint orally to each student. For each item, model the process as described, and then have the student use the process to respond to your prompts. Record responses on the scoring chart on the next page.

1. Identify Rhyming Words and Alliteration (Lesson 5)
MODEL: I am going to read three words. You tell me which two words rhyme. I could say *pan, can,* and *pin. Pan* and *can* are words that rhyme. Then I will read three words and ask you to tell me the words that begin with the same sound.

ASSESS:	lip, dip, cup	try, hot, fly	bubble, litter, sitter
	nut, nail, pail	ball, fall, big	kite, hop, hit

2. Produce Rhyming Words and Alliteration (Lesson 6)
MODEL: I am going to say a word. Then you will say a word that rhymes. It can be a real word or a made-up word. Then I am going to say the word again and ask you to say a word that begins with the same sound.

ASSESS:	sit	dot	pet	bed	can	two

3. Blend and Count Syllables in Spoken Words (Lesson 7)
MODEL: I will say some syllables. Then you blend them together to say the word. For example, the word *picnic* has two syllables, *pic•nic.* To say the word, we blend the syllables together without stopping: *picnic.*

ASSESS:	high•way	nev•er	re•cess	mu•sic

4. Segment and Count Syllables in Spoken Words (Lesson 8)
MODEL: I will say a word. I will ask you to say each syllable of the word and count the syllables on your fingers. For example, the word *feather* has two syllables. I hold up a finger for each syllable: *feath•er.*

ASSESS:	haircut	family	sandwich	quarter

5. Segment and Count Syllables in Spoken Words (Lesson 8)
MODEL: I will say a word. I will ask you to change one syllable of the word to make a new word. For example, the word *summer* has two syllables: *sum-mer.* I can change the syllable *sum* to the syllable *ham* to make the new word *hammer.*

ASSESS:	lunchroom	puppy

ASSESSMENT
LESSONS 5–8

Phonological Awareness

SCORING

SKILL/LESSON	SCORE
1. Identify Rhyming Words and Alliteration (Lesson 5) lip, dip try, fly litter, sitter nut, nail ball, big hop, hit	_____ / 6
2. Produce Rhyming Words and Alliteration (Lesson 6) sit dot pet bed can two Accept real or made-up words that begin with the sounds /s/, /d/, /p/, /b/, /k/, and /t/.	_____ / 12
3. Blend and Count Syllables in Spoken Words (Lesson 7) highway never recess music	_____ / 4
4. Segment and Count Syllables in Spoken Words (Lesson 8) 2 3 2 2	_____ / 4
5. Segment and Count Syllables in Spoken Words (Lesson 8) Accept any words that include the syllable *lunch, room, pup,* or *py* (e.g., *lunchtime, classroom, puppet, happy*)	_____ / 2

An overall score of 80% correct is typically considered mastery. Use your judgment and your individual students' needs as well to determine skill mastery.

IF... students score below the benchmark,
THEN... review those discrete skills, going back to the lessons to reteach and scaffold as needed.

Lesson 9 Blend Onset and Rime

INTRODUCE Say the word *get* using onset and rime: /g/ (pause) /et/. What word did you hear? Did it sound right? Let me say the sounds together: *get.* Did that sound better? Today we will practice hearing the sounds in words. We will also blend sounds to make words.

MODEL Remind students that rhyming words have the same ending sound (rime). Display or share copies of Student Page S79. Read it aloud. Then say: Watch my face as I say some of these words. Point to *let, wet, pet, net,* and *yet* as you say the words: *let, wet, pet, net, yet.* These words have the same ending sound, or rime: /et/. They have different beginning sounds, or onsets. Listen. Repeat each word as onset and rime: /l/ (pause) /et/, and so on. Elongate each onset for emphasis. I can hear the onset and the rime in each word. I blend them together to make a whole word.

Stop!

Do not let
that wet pet
jump out of
the net yet!

TEACH Point to your face and say: This is my face. Listen to the sounds in the word: *face.* What sound do you hear at the beginning of the word? Make the sound for me. After students respond, slowly say the onset and then the rime: /f/ (pause) /ās/. Now I will make the word by putting together the onset and the rime. I will say them together without stopping: *face.* The word is *face.* Say it with me: *face.*

OBJECTIVES:

- Detect the initial sound (onset) in spoken words.
- Identify the initial sound (onset) in spoken words.
- Blend onset and rime to make a whole word.

Lesson 9 Blend Onset and Rime

REMIND STUDENTS THAT …

- words are made of beginning sounds (onsets) and ending sounds (rimes).
- they can blend onsets and rimes to make whole words.

PRACTICE 1 Help students hear and reproduce onsets. Model, using the following routine.

Routine

1. Model.	Say a word, isolating and elongating the onset. Listen: *lap*. /lap/; /l/ is the onset.
2. Practice together.	Say *lap* with me: *lap*. Say the onset in *lap*: /l/. Yes, /l/ is the onset in *lap*.
3. Extend practice.	Now try it on your own. Say *lap* (pause to have students respond). Say the onset in *lap* (have students respond). Yes, /l/ is the onset in *lap*.

Follow the routine using the following words from Student Page S80.

nap	rip
fog	vet
cut	

Continue by blending. Have students say the distinct sounds of each word and then blend the sounds into a whole word: /n/ /ap/, *nap*, and so on.

Finally, use the list of words to check that students hear onsets correctly. Do you hear the sound /n/ at the beginning of the word *nap?* (yes) Do you hear the sound /n/ at the beginning of the word *cap?* (no) Continue with /f/ *fog* and *dog*, /k/ *cut* and *hut*, /r/ *rip* and *dip*, and /v/ *vet* and *met*.

☑ **MONITOR PROGRESS** Have students distinguish sounds with you and then blend them on their own. Repeat after me: /s/ /ix/. Now blend the sounds into a word. Have students blend. Continue with the words *bake* (/b//āk/), *sip* (/s//ĭp/), *mud* (/m//ud/), and *laugh* (/l//af/).

IF… students make an error when blending onset and rime,
THEN… model the correct response by blending the onset and rime slowly and having students echo you. Repeat with additional words until they develop proficiency.

Lesson 9 Blend Onset and Rime

PRACTICE 2 Have students identify initial sounds (onsets) and then blend onset and rime. Listen closely as I say a word. Then tell me what the onset is. Let's do one together. Here is the word: *red.* What is the onset? Pause for students to respond. Yes, the onset is /r/. Now listen to this word: *save.* What is the onset? Pause for students to respond. Yes, the onset is /s/.

Display the following words from Student Page S81 and read each one aloud. Repeat each word several times and ask: What is the onset?

fun	peek	roll
hop	neck	sing
line	help	van
mine	jump	wow

Provide these words: *bang, cap, day, fish, good, joke, map, nap,* and *run*. For each word, ask: What sound do you hear at the beginning of the word *[bang]*? Then have students blend onset and rime for each word. I will say the sounds in a word. You blend the sounds. Say them together, without stopping, to make a word. Ready? Let's start. Here are the sounds: /b//ang/ Students should blend the onset and rime to make the word *bang*. Continue with the remaining eight words.

REMIND STUDENTS THAT ...

- words are made of beginning sounds (onsets) and ending sounds (rimes).
- they can hear onsets and rimes in words.
- they can blend onsets and rimes to make whole words.

☑ **MONITOR PROGRESS** Say each of the following words. Say each word and ask: What sound do you hear at the beginning of the word? After students respond, you may wish to extend the activity by showing Student Page S81 and pointing out the beginning sounds of the words.

cup	zoo	tub
jet	sit	pal
bite	five	roll

IF... students make an error,
THEN... have students watch your mouth as you repeat the word slowly, and then have them imitate the initial sound you made.

Lesson 9 Blend Onset and Rime

REMIND STUDENTS THAT …

- words are made of different sounds.
- blending all of the sounds together makes a whole word.

PRACTICE 3 Listen as I say some different sounds: /f//i//sh/. Do you hear a word when I say the sounds? Let me say them again: /f//i//sh/. Now I will say them again without stopping: *fish*. The word is *fish*. When I blend the sounds quickly, the word is *fish*.

Remember that onsets are beginning sounds and rimes are ending sounds. I will say some onsets and rimes. Point to a light in the room. Listen to the onset and the rime: /l//īt/. Now you make the word by blending the sounds together quickly. Pause for students to blend the word. That's right! The word is *light*.

Continue the activity with the following words from Student Page S82. When possible, point to an object as you say the onset and the rime.

shoe	wall
roof	book
man	shelf
paint	rug

Continue with sets of words that rhyme. I will say the sounds in a word. Listen carefully. When I finish, you say the word. /l//īk/ (like). Continue with *bike, mike, tyke,* and *hike*. Then repeat the process with the following sets of words: *curl, girl, hurl,* and *pearl*; *red, head, said,* and *fed*; *jar, far, car,* and *tar*.

INDEPENDENT PRACTICE Have students watch your face and listen closely as you say the onset-rime combinations below. After you say each set twice, have students blend the sounds into a whole word.

/n//īs/	/r//īs/	/m//īs/
/l//ās/	/f//ās/	/r//ās/
/p//an/	/j//ak/	/s//ip/

IF… students make an error,
THEN… return to the word later during practice. Model the correct response by blending onset and rime, and have students echo you.

Lesson 9 **Blend Onset and Rime**

Stop!

Do not let
that wet pet
jump out of
the net yet!

Teacher: This Student Page is intended as an *optional extension* of the lesson. After teaching the phonological awareness lesson orally, you can distribute or display this page to connect the phonological awareness skills (sounds) to phonics skills (sound-spelling).

Lesson 9 Blend Onset and Rime

nap	rip
fog	vet
cut	

Teacher: This Student Page is intended as an *optional extension* of the lesson. After teaching the phonological awareness lesson orally, you can distribute or display this page to connect the phonological awareness skills (sounds) to phonics skills (sound-spelling).

Lesson 9 Blend Onset and Rime

fun	peek	roll
hop	neck	sing
line	help	van
mine	jump	wow

cup	zoo	tub
jet	sit	pal
bite	five	roll

Teacher: This Student Page is intended as an *optional extension* of the lesson. After teaching the phonological awareness lesson orally, you can distribute or display this page to connect the phonological awareness skills (sounds) to phonics skills (sound-spelling).

Lesson 9 Blend Onset and Rime

shoe	**wall**
roof	**book**
man	**shelf**
paint	**rug**

Teacher: This Student Page is intended as an *optional extension* of the lesson. After teaching the phonological awareness lesson orally, you can distribute or display this page to connect the phonological awareness skills (sounds) to phonics skills (sound-spelling).

Lesson 10 Segment Onset and Rime

INTRODUCE Remind students that they have learned to break words apart into syllables and that they know how to blend onset and rime to make a word. Remember that an onset is the beginning sound in a word, and a rime is the ending sound in a word. Today we will break words into their onsets and rimes. For example, we know the word *sun*. It has the onset /s/. Hold up one finger. It has the rime /un/. Hold up a second finger. The sounds are /s/ and /un/. We heard two parts in the word.

MODEL Hold up a pen and ask: What is this? Yes, this is a pen. Listen to the word: *pen*. I will break the word *pen* into its onset and rime. Model how to say the onset and rime slowly, pausing between the two: /p/ (pause) /en/. The onset is /p/, and the rime is /en/. Repeat this procedure with the words *map* and *zip*.

Present the following words from Student Page S83 and read the lines aloud from left to right.

four	five	six
pig	bed	fix
saw	ham	mix

TEACH Point to each word as you segment it into onset and rime. I will break the word *four* into its onset and rime. Listen: /f//or/. This time, I will tap my hand on the desk as I say the onset again: /f/ (tap). I'll slide my hand as I say the rime again: /or/ (slide). Say the sounds with me: /f//or/.

Repeat the procedure with the remaining words. Tap as you say the onset. Slide your hand as you say the rime. Have students repeat the onset and rime with you.

OBJECTIVE:

- Segment the sounds of spoken words into onset and rime.

Lesson 10 Segment Onset and Rime

REMIND STUDENTS THAT …

- every word has a beginning sound (onset).
- they can break, or segment, a word into its beginning sound (onset) and ending sound (rime).

PRACTICE 1 Present the following words from Student Page S84. Have students listen for the onset as you say the words in each line. For example, point to the first line and say: Listen as I say these words: *mug, mad, mop.* What sound do you hear at the beginning of each word? Pause for responses. Yes, the beginning sound is /m/. Continue with the remaining lines.

mug	mad	mop
cup	cot	call
lip	lose	like
zoom	zap	zing
net	nut	nip
tap	top	tell

Repeat individual words as you point to them. After you say the word, ask: What is the onset? What is the rime? After students respond, say: Yes, the onset is /m/. The rime is /ug/.

Have students listen for the onset as you say these words: *fun, rug, leg, head, foot, room, mail, pail, sad,* and *ten*. For each word, say: Listen as I say the word: *fun.* What is the onset? Repeat the word: *fun.* What is the rime? Pause for responses after each question.

☑ **MONITOR PROGRESS** Present the following words from Student Page S84. Read each word and ask: What is the onset? What is the rime? Pause for responses after each question.

feet	bug	tag	sell
pot	jump	cake	rag

IF… students struggle to separate the sounds,
THEN… model segmenting by tapping your hand as you say the onset and sliding your hand as you say the rime. Have students repeat the sounds and gestures with you.

Lesson 10 Segment Onset and Rime

PRACTICE 2 Tell students that they will listen to the sounds in words. I will say a word. Then you will say it with me, one time normally and one time slowly. When we say the word slowly, we can hear its onset and its rime. Then we will say the onset by itself and the rime by itself.

Here is the word: *pat*. Say it with me normally, then slowly. Say the word *pat* twice with students, first at a normal pace, then slowly. The onset is /p/. Say it with me: /p/. The rime is /at/. Let's say it together: /at/. Repeat the process with the words *top, dig, back,* and *good*.

Say each of the following words from Student Page S85 slowly, drawing out the vowels and emphasizing the final consonant. For each word, ask: What is the onset? Pause for responses. Repeat the word as many times as necessary for students to isolate the onset. Once they have succeeded, repeat the word and ask: What is the rime? Affirm correct responses by saying: Yes, the onset is /k/. The rime is /ap/. Correct errors as needed.

cap	day	fur	get
big	pot	sip	van

REMIND STUDENTS THAT …

- every word has a beginning sound (onset).
- they can break, or segment, a word into its beginning sound (onset) and ending sound (rime).

☑ **MONITOR PROGRESS** Work with words that students have already segmented successfully. Say the word (for example, *top*). Have students repeat the word slowly. Ask: What is the onset? What is the rime? Pause for responses after each question.

IF… students cannot segment onset and rime,
THEN… model segmenting a familiar CVC word correctly, and have students echo you. Provide other CVC words for practice as needed.

Lesson 10 Segment Onset and Rime

REMIND STUDENTS THAT ...

- they can break, or segment, a word into parts with different sounds.

PRACTICE 3 Present the following words from Student Page S86. Prompt students to listen for the onset and rime as you say each word. Model with the word *hen*. Listen as I say the word: *hen*. What is the onset? Pause for responses. Repeat the word *hen* and ask: What is the rime? Pause for responses. I will say the word *hen* one more time. You will say both the onset and the rime. Repeat the word *hen* and have students say /h//en/. Continue the activity for the remaining words.

hen	cow	pig	lamb
kid	goat	goose	dog
pup	ram	bat	peep

Point to any of these objects that are visible in the classroom: *door, desk, shelf, book, pen, board, wall, map, chair, boot,* and *shoe*. Name each object as you point to it, and ask: What is the onset in the word *door*? What is the rime? Pause for responses after each question.

☑ **INDEPENDENT PRACTICE** Say *cup, knife, pot, jam,* and *soup*. Have students identify the onset in each word. Repeat each word and have students segment it into onset and rime.

IF... students cannot isolate the onset or rime in a word,
THEN... say the onset, tap your fingers on the desk, and then say the rime. Repeat the process and have students pantomime you. Use this method with other CVC words to give students additional practice.

Lesson 10 Segment Onset and Rime

four	five	six
pig	bed	fix
saw	ham	mix

Teacher: This Student Page is intended as an *optional extension* of the lesson. After teaching the phonological awareness lesson orally, you can distribute or display this page to connect the phonological awareness skills (sounds) to phonics skills (sound-spelling).

Lesson 10 Segment Onset and Rime

mug	mad	mop
cup	cot	call
lip	lose	like
zoom	zap	zing
net	nut	nip
tap	top	tell

feet	bug	tag	sell
pot	jump	cake	rag

Teacher: This Student Page is intended as an *optional extension* of the lesson. After teaching the phonological awareness lesson orally, you can distribute or display this page to connect the phonological awareness skills (sounds) to phonics skills (sound-spelling).

Lesson 10 Segment Onset and Rime

cap	**day**	**fur**	**get**
big	**pot**	**sip**	**van**

Teacher: This Student Page is intended as an *optional extension* of the lesson. After teaching the phonological awareness lesson orally, you can distribute or display this page to connect the phonological awareness skills (sounds) to phonics skills (sound-spelling).

Lesson 10 Segment Onset and Rime

hen	cow	pig	lamb
kid	goat	goose	dog
pup	ram	bat	peep

Teacher: This Student Page is intended as an *optional extension* of the lesson. After teaching the phonological awareness lesson orally, you can distribute or display this page to connect the phonological awareness skills (sounds) to phonics skills (sound-spelling).

ASSESSMENT
LESSONS 9–10

Phonological Awareness

ASSESS MASTERY Use this Checkpoint to assess students' mastery of blending and segmenting onsets and rimes of single-syllable words.

ADMINISTER THE TEST Administer the Checkpoint orally to each student. For each item, model the process as described, and then have the student use the process to respond to your prompts. Record responses on the scoring chart on the next page.

1. Blend Onset and Rime (Lesson 9)
MODEL: Every word has an onset, or initial sound. I will say the onset and the rime, or ending, in a word. Then you will say the two parts together without stopping to say the word. For example, I could say /m//ud/. Then you blend the sounds together to say *mud.*

ASSESS:	/s//ink/	/f//ās/	/p//ark/	/w//et/

2. Segment Onset and Rime (Lesson 10)
MODEL: I will say a word. You will listen and then tell me the onset, or initial sound, and the rest of the word, or rime. For example, I could say *coat.* Then you would say /k/ and /ōt/, /k//ōt/.

ASSESS:	toy	big	pup	shoe	laugh

ASSESSMENT
LESSONS 9–10

Phonological Awareness

SCORING

SKILL/LESSON	SCORE
1. Blend Onset and Rime (Lesson 9) sink face park wet	_____ / 4
2. Segment Onset and Rime (Lesson 10) /t//oi/ /b//ig/ /p//up/ /sh//o͞o/ /l//af/	_____ / 5

An overall score of 80% correct is typically considered mastery. Use your judgment and your individual students' needs as well to determine skill mastery.

IF… students score below the benchmark,
THEN… review those discrete skills, going back to the lessons to reteach and scaffold as needed.

Lesson 11 Identify Same and Different Initial Sounds

INTRODUCE Explain that students will learn how to determine whether words begin with the same sounds.

MODEL Display or share copies of the passage "Katy and Ted" from Student Page S89, and read it aloud.

Katy and Ted

Katy had a pet rock.
She named the rock Ted.
Katy made a grass bed for Ted.
She put the bed in a red pan.
She set the bed in the sun.
Ted did not mind.
He liked the warm sun.

same beginning sound (/p/)

different beginning sound (/b/ and /s/)

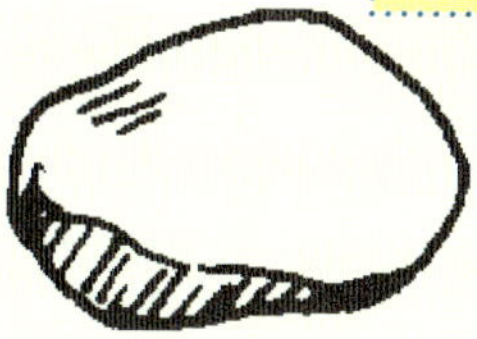

TEACH Listen to these words: *pet, pan.* As I say them again, I'm going to listen carefully to their beginning sounds. Emphasize the beginning sounds as you blend the words. Repeat the words again, drawing out the beginning sounds. Make sure to pronounce the short consonant /p/ (not /puh/). I hear /p/ at the beginning of *pet.* Repeat the word *pet* with me. Listen to make sure students pronounce the word correctly. Do you hear /p/ at the beginning of the word *pan?* Pause for students to respond. Yes, both words have the same beginning sound (/p/).

Repeat the model activity with the words *sun* and *bed* from the passage. Point out that the words have different sounds. I hear /s/ at the beginning of *sun,* but I hear /b/ at the beginning of *bed.*

OBJECTIVES:

- Identify and pronounce the initial sound in CVC words.
- Compare and distinguish among initial sounds.
- Produce words with the same initial sounds.

Lesson 11 Identify Same and Different Initial Sounds

REMIND STUDENTS THAT ...

- they can identify and pronounce continuous initial sounds in words.
- they can compare and distinguish among continuous initial sounds.

PRACTICE 1 Use the following routine to make sure students can identify and pronounce initial sounds.

Routine

1. Model. Say the word. Listen to the word: *sat.* /s//at/. Isolate and elongate the initial sound as you pronounce it. I hear /s/ first: /s//at/.

2. Practice together. Say it with me: *sat.* /s//at/. What is the first sound? Yes, /s/ is the first sound.

3. Extend practice. Have students identify and pronounce the initial sound with other CVC words. First practice with words with continuous initial consonant sounds that are easiest to identify (*l, r, s, m*).

Next, model how to identify same and different initial sounds. Say the words *mat* and *mine* with me: *mat, mine.* What is the first sound you hear in *mat?* (/m/) What is the first sound you hear in *mine?* (/m/) Do the words have the same or different beginning sounds? (same)

Have students follow the same procedure using the word pairs below, which also appear on Student Page S90.

bat, fin (different)	not, nap (same)
fat, fog (same)	net, cut (different)
van, vet (same)	fit, wet (different)

☑ **MONITOR PROGRESS** Have students listen to the following sets of words from Student Page S90. For each set, ask: What is the first sound you hear in the first word? Do you hear the same sound in the second word?

met, mop	rat, bad	sit, so

IF... students make an error,
THEN... have them watch your mouth as you repeat the word pair for clues to whether the beginning sounds are the same.

Lesson 11 Identify Same and Different Initial Sounds

PRACTICE 2 Use the following routine to help students identify and pronounce the initial sound in a word.

Routine

1. Model. Say the word. Listen to the word: *let.* /l//et/. Isolate and elongate the initial sound as you pronounce it. *I hear /l/ first: /l//et/.*

2. Practice together. Say it with me: *let.* /l//et/. What is the first sound? Yes, /l/ is the first sound.

3. Extend practice. Have students identify and pronounce the initial sound with other CVC words. If students can identify continuous initial consonant sounds *l, r, s,* and *m,* have them practice with the short initial consonant sounds *b, d,* and *t.*

Next, have students play a game to practice identifying same and different initial sounds. Model how to play the game. Listen as I say two words: *top, toe.* Raise your hand if these words begin with the same sound. Raise your hand. Repeat the process with the words *cot* and *map.* Do not raise your hand. These words begin with different sounds, so we don't raise our hands.

Continue the game with the following word pairs, which also appear on Student Page S91.

take, tip (hands)	win, vote (no hands)
mop, man (hands)	cat, dog (no hands)
cup, pup (no hands)	gas, go (hands)

REMIND STUDENTS THAT ...

- they can identify and pronounce the initial sound in words.
- they can compare and distinguish among initial sounds.

☑ **MONITOR PROGRESS** Have students listen to the following set of words from Student Page S91. Then ask: What sound do you hear at the beginning of each word? Which words have the same beginning sound? Have students pronounce the words again, if needed.

led	lip	sip	lap

IF... students have difficulty identifying words that have the same initial sound, THEN... have them say each word slowly, paying close attention to the positioning of their lips and tongue as they initiate the word. Have them note which words involve the same positioning of the lips and tongue.

Lesson 11 Identify Same and Different Initial Sounds

REMIND STUDENTS THAT ...

- they can identify and pronounce the initial sound in words.
- they can compare and distinguish among initial sounds.
- they can produce words with the same initial sounds.

PRACTICE 3 Use the following routine to help students identify and pronounce the initial sound in a word.

Routine

1. Model. Say the word. Listen to the word: *put.* Isolate the initial sound as you pronounce it. I hear /p/ first: /p//ut/.

2. Practice together. Say it with me: *put.* /p//ut/. What is the first sound? Yes, /p/ is the first sound.

3. Extend practice. Have students identify and pronounce the initial sound with other CVC words. Have them practice with the short initial consonant sounds *h, p,* and *w.*

Next, have students play a game to name words that begin with the same sound. I will start the game by naming something I could shop for. I went shopping, and I bought a *rug.* Later, I went shopping and bought a *ring.* What else could we shop for that begins with the /r/ sound? Pause for responses. We could buy a *rope* and a *rake.*

Continue the game using the following words from Student Page S92.

cake /k/ (cap, key, kite)	hat /h/ (hose, hen, ham)
van /v/ (vase, vine, vat)	pan /p/ (pin, pot, pie)
bed /b/ (bat, boat, bass)	tub /t/ (tea, toy, top)

☑ **INDEPENDENT PRACTICE** Ask: What is the first sound you hear in the word *hip*? What other words begin with the /h/ sound?

IF... students have difficulty identifying the initial /h/ sound,
THEN... model the correct pronunciation of the /h/ sound and words beginning with /h/ as students pay close attention to the positioning of your mouth. Then have them pantomime your actions until they can correctly identify the sound.

Lesson 11 **Identify Same and Different Initial Sounds**

Katy and Ted

Katy had a pet rock.
She named the rock Ted.
Katy made a grass bed for Ted.
She put the bed in a red pan.
She set the bed in the sun.
Ted did not mind.
He liked the warm sun.

Teacher: This Student Page is intended as an *optional extension* of the lesson. After teaching the phonological awareness lesson orally, you can distribute or display this page to connect the phonological awareness skills (sounds) to phonics skills (sound-spelling).

Lesson 11 Identify Same and Different Initial Sounds

bat, fin
fat, fog
van, vet

not, nap
net, cut
fit, wet

met, mop **rat, bad** **sit, so**

Teacher: This Student Page is intended as an *optional extension* of the lesson. After teaching the phonological awareness lesson orally, you can distribute or display this page to connect the phonological awareness skills (sounds) to phonics skills (sound-spelling).

Lesson 11 Identify Same and Different Initial Sounds

take, tip	win, vote
mop, man	cat, dog
cup, pup	gas, go

led	lip	sip	lap

Teacher: This Student Page is intended as an *optional extension* of the lesson. After teaching the phonological awareness lesson orally, you can distribute or display this page to connect the phonological awareness skills (sounds) to phonics skills (sound-spelling).

Lesson 11 Identify Same and Different Initial Sounds

cake	**hat**
van	**pan**
bed	**tub**

Teacher: This Student Page is intended as an *optional extension* of the lesson. After teaching the phonological awareness lesson orally, you can distribute or display this page to connect the phonological awareness skills (sounds) to phonics skills (sound-spelling).

Lesson 12 Identify Same and Different Final Sounds

INTRODUCE Remind students that they can segment words into beginning sounds and ending sounds. Today we will listen for the last sound in a word. The last sound in a word is called the final sound. We will say two words. Then we will tell if the two words have the same final sound or different final sounds.

MODEL Display or share copies of the passage "Dan and Roy" from Student Page S93, and read it aloud.

Dan and Roy

Dan has a do**g**.
His dog is named Roy.
Roy is a bi**g** dog.
Dan takes Roy for a walk every day.
Dan and Roy have fu**n** on their walks.
Dan loves his pe**t** dog.

dog big
same final sound (/g/)

fun pet
different final sounds (/n/ and /t/)

TEACH After you read the passage aloud, demonstrate how to identify final sounds. Listen to these words: *dog, big*. As I say the words again, I will listen to their final sounds. Emphasize the final sounds as you blend the words. Now, I ask myself if both words end with the same sound or different sounds. Repeat the words, drawing out the final sounds. Say the words *dog* and *big* with me. Listen to make sure that students pronounce the words correctly. The words *dog* and *big* both have the final /g/ sound. Repeat the process for the words *fun* and *pet*. The words *fun* and *pet* have different final sounds. The word *fun* ends with the /n/ sound. The word *pet* ends with the /t/ sound.

OBJECTIVES:

- Identify and pronounce the final sound in CVC words.
- Compare and distinguish among final sounds.
- Produce words with the same final sound.

Lesson 12 Identify Same and Different Final Sounds

REMIND STUDENTS THAT…

- they can identify final sounds in words.
- they can pronounce final sounds in words.
- they can compare among final sounds.

PRACTICE 1 Make sure students can identify and pronounce final sounds in CVC words. Use the following routine.

Routine

1. Model. Say the word: *tin.* /t//i//n/. Isolate and elongate the final sound as you pronounce it for students. I hear /n/ last. /n/ is the final sound in the word *tin.* /t//i//n/.

2. Practice together. Let's say the word together: *tin.* /t//i//n/. What is the final sound in the word? Pause for responses. Yes! The final sound in the word *tin* is /n/.

3. Extend practice. Repeat the routine with other CVC words with continuous final consonant sounds, such as *f, m, n,* and *s.*

For each of the following word pairs from Student Page S94, say the first word and have students repeat it: *gum* What is the final sound you hear in the word? (/m/) Then say the second word and have students repeat it: *fin.* What is the final sound you hear in the second word? (/n/) Do these words have the same final sounds or different final sounds? (different)

gum, fin (different)	beef, seem (different)
moon, ham (different)	van, pin (same)
pass, yes (same)	hiss, mess (same)

MONITOR PROGRESS Say the following word pairs from Student Page S94.

hem, ram	his, pan	hen, win

What is the final sound you hear in the first word? Do you hear the same sound in the second word?

IF… students are unable to distinguish the final sound,
THEN… guide students in segmenting the words into initial, medial, and final sounds (for example, /h//e//m/). Ask them to repeat the final sound they hear. Have students perform these actions for both words and then compare the final sounds.

Lesson 12 Identify Same and Different Final Sounds

PRACTICE 2 Before students compare sounds, make sure they can identify and pronounce final sounds in CVC words. Use the following routine.

Routine

1. Model.	Say the word: *miss.* /m//i//s/. Isolate and elongate the final sound as you pronounce it for students. I hear /s/ last. /s/ is the final sound in the word *miss.* /m//i//s/.
2. Practice together.	Say it with me: *miss.* /m//i//s/. What is the final sound in the word? Pause for responses. Yes! The final sound in the word *miss* is /s/.
3. Extend practice.	Repeat the routine with other CVC words with stop final consonant sounds, such as *d, g, p,* and *t.*

Help students practice identifying same and different final sounds. I will say two words. If the words have the same final sound, we'll clap our hands. If the words have different final sounds, we won't clap our hands. Listen: *bag, pig.* Clap and make sure students do so. Then say *tip* and *dog.* Do not clap. The words *tip* and *dog* end with two different sounds, so we don't clap our hands.

Continue the activity with the following word pairs from Student Page S95.

nut, bet (clap)	log, cap (no clap)
hug, tag (clap)	top, rip (clap)
beg, lap (no clap)	met, ran (no clap)

REMIND STUDENTS THAT ...

- they can identify the final sounds in words.
- they can pronounce the final sounds in words.
- they can compare and distinguish among final sounds.

☑ **MONITOR PROGRESS** Say the following words from Student Page S95.

get	bat	rug	hit

Have students repeat each word. Do you hear the /t/ sound at the end of *get, bat, rug,* or *hit*? What other final sounds do you hear?

IF... students misidentify the final sound,
THEN... have them segment the words into initial, medial, and final sounds and say each sound, focusing on the final sound they hear.

Lesson 12 Identify Same and Different Final Sounds

REMIND STUDENTS THAT …

- they can identify and pronounce the final sounds in words.
- they can compare and distinguish among final sounds.
- they can produce words with the same final sound.

PRACTICE 3 Ensure that students can identify and pronounce final sounds in CVC words before comparing the final sounds of words. Use the following routine if needed.

Routine

1. Model.	Say the word: *tub.* /t//u//b/. Isolate and pronounce the final sound for students. /b/ is the final sound in the word *tub.*
2. Practice together.	Say it with me: *tub.* /t//u//b/. What is the final sound? Pause for responses. Right! The final sound in the word *tub* is /b/.
3. Extend practice.	Repeat the routine with other CVC words with continuous and stop final consonant sounds.

Tell students that they will name words that end with the same sound. Listen to each word I say. Then say a new word that ends with the same final sound. Present the following words from Student Page S96. Say the word *jam* and have students repeat it. What other word has the same final sound as *jam*? (*ham, room,* and so on) Continue for the remaining words. If needed, help students produce appropriate words.

jam	bun	less	bib	red
bug	leg	hop	mat	pot

☑ **INDEPENDENT PRACTICE** Have students name one familiar word for each of the final /n/, /m/, /g/, and /t/ sounds. Then have students produce a new word with the same final sound.

IF… students have difficulty identifying words that have the final /n/, /m/, /g/, and /t/ sounds,
THEN… say a word as a model. Have students repeat the word and emphasize the final sound. Guide them in brainstorming new words with the same final sound.

Lesson 12 **Identify Same and Different Final Sounds**

Dan and Roy

Dan has a dog.
His dog is named Roy.
Roy is a big dog.
Dan takes Roy for a walk every day.
Dan and Roy have fun on their walks.
Dan loves his pet dog.

Teacher: This Student Page is intended as an *optional extension* of the lesson. After teaching the phonological awareness lesson orally, you can distribute or display this page to connect the phonological awareness skills (sounds) to phonics skills (sound-spelling).

Lesson 12 Identify Same and Different Final Sounds

gum, fin
moon, ham
pass, yes

beef, seem
van, pin
hiss, mess

hem, ram

his, pan

hen, win

Teacher: This Student Page is intended as an *optional extension* of the lesson. After teaching the phonological awareness lesson orally, you can distribute or display this page to connect the phonological awareness skills (sounds) to phonics skills (sound-spelling).

Lesson 12 Identify Same and Different Final Sounds

nut, bet	log, cap
hug, tag	top, rip
beg, lap	met, ran

get	bat	rug	hit

Teacher: This Student Page is intended as an *optional extension* of the lesson. After teaching the phonological awareness lesson orally, you can distribute or display this page to connect the phonological awareness skills (sounds) to phonics skills (sound-spelling).

Lesson 12 Identify Same and Different Final Sounds

jam	bun	less	bib	red
bug	leg	hop	mat	pot

Teacher: This Student Page is intended as an *optional extension* of the lesson. After teaching the phonological awareness lesson orally, you can distribute or display this page to connect the phonological awareness skills (sounds) to phonics skills (sound-spelling).

Lesson 13 Identify Same and Different Medial Sounds

INTRODUCE Remind students that they have listened to the beginning and ending sounds in words. Today we will listen for sounds in the middle of words. We will say two words. Then we will say if the two words have the same middle sound or different middle sounds.

MODEL Display or share copies of the passage "A Fun Day for Jan" from Student Page S97, and read it aloud.

A Fun Day for Jan

Jan had a fun day.
She gave her mom a hug.
Then she got her bat.
She played baseball with her friends.
Then the fog came.
Jan went home.
She had a fig for a snack.

fun hug
same medial sound
(/u/)

got fig
different medial
sounds (/o/ and /i/)

TEACH After you read the passage aloud, show students how to identify medial sounds. Listen to these words: *fun, hug.* I will say the words again and listen to the middle sound in each one. Emphasize the medial sounds as you blend the words. Now I ask myself if both words have the same sound or different sounds in the middle. Repeat the words, drawing out the medial sounds. Let's say the words *fun* and *hug* together. Make sure that students pronounce the words correctly. The words *fun* and *hug* both have the /u/ sound in the middle.

Repeat the process for the words *got* and *fig*. The words *got* and *fig* have different middle sounds. The word *got* has the /o/ sound in the middle. The word *fig* has the /i/ sound in the middle.

OBJECTIVES:

- Identify and pronounce the medial sound in CVC words.
- Compare and distinguish among medial sounds.
- Produce words with the same medial sound.

Lesson 13 Identify Same and Different Medial Sounds

REMIND STUDENTS THAT ...

- they can identify the medial sounds in words.
- they can pronounce medial sounds in words.
- they can compare among medial sounds.

PRACTICE 1 Before students compare sounds in CVC words, use the following routine to ensure students can identify and pronounce medial sounds.

Routine

1. Model. Say the word: *fan*. /f//a//n/. Isolate and elongate the medial sound as you pronounce it for students. I hear /a/ in the middle. /a/ is the middle sound in the word *fan*. /f//a//n/.

2. Practice together. Let's say the word together: *fan*. /f//a//n/. What is the middle sound? Pause for responses. Yes! The middle sound in *fan* is /a/.

3. Extend practice. Repeat the routine with other familiar CVC words.

Help students compare medial sounds in CVC words. Listen to these words: *cap, bat*. Say them with me: *cap, bat*. Do these words have the same middle sounds or different middle sounds? (same) Repeat the process with the words *bit* and *pot*.

For each of the following word pairs from Student Page S98, say the first word and have students repeat it. What is the middle sound in the word? Then say the second word and have students repeat it. Do you hear the same middle sound? Correct errors.

gum, bug (same)	wag, pan (same)
get, den (same)	rat, cup (different)
bed, had (different)	dog, leg (different)

☑ **MONITOR PROGRESS** Say the following word pairs from Student Page S98.

hog, big	pen, hem	mug, let	sit, pig

What is the middle sound you hear in the first word? Do you hear the same sound in the second word?

IF... students are unable to distinguish the medial sound,
THEN... guide students in segmenting the words into initial, medial, and final sounds (for example, /h//aw//g/). Ask them to repeat the medial sound they hear. Have students perform these actions for both words and then compare the medial sounds.

Lesson 13 Identify Same and Different Medial Sounds

PRACTICE 2 Use the following routine to help students practice identifying and pronouncing medial sounds in CVC words.

Routine

1. Model. Say the word: *seed.* /s//ē//d/. Isolate and elongate the medial sound as you pronounce it for students. I hear /ē/ in the middle. /ē/ is the middle sound in the word *seed.* /s//ē//d/.

2. Practice together. Say it with me: *seed.* /s//ē//d/. What is the middle sound? Pause for responses. Yes! The middle sound in *seed* is /ē/.

3. Extend practice. Repeat the routine with other familiar and newly learned CVC words.

Practice comparing medial sounds in CVC words. I will say two words. If the words have the same middle sound, raise your hand. If the words have different middle sounds, don't raise your hand. Listen: *peel, meet.* Raise your hand. Repeat the process with the words *bun* and *dig*. Do not raise your hand.

Continue the activity with the following word pairs from Student Page S99. After students indicate whether the medial sounds are the same or different, have them identify the medial sound in each word.

kit, fin (hands)	cat, map (hands)
pit, fed (no hands)	bin, run (no hands)
sad, hut (no hands)	tin, his (hands)

REMIND STUDENTS THAT ...

- they can identify the medial sounds in words.
- they can pronounce the medial sounds in words.
- they can compare and distinguish among medial sounds.

MONITOR PROGRESS Say the following words from Student Page S99.

bag	set	fit	web	hip	nap

Have students repeat each word after you. What sound do you hear in the middle of *bag*? Repeat the process for the remaining words. Then have students identify words with the same medial sound (bag, nap; set, web; fit, hip).

IF... students misidentify the medial sound,
THEN... have them segment the words into initial, medial, and final sounds and say each sound, focusing on the medial sound they hear.

Lesson 13 Identify Same and Different Medial Sounds

REMIND STUDENTS THAT …

- they can identify and pronounce the medial sounds in words.
- they can compare and distinguish among medial sounds.
- they can produce words with the same medial sound.

PRACTICE 3 Use the following routine if needed to ensure that students can identify and pronounce medial sounds in CVC words.

Routine

1. Model. Say the word: *dot*. /dot/. Isolate and pronounce the medial sound for students. /o/ is the middle sound in the word *dot*.

2. Practice together. Say it with me: *dot*. /dot/. What is the middle sound? Pause for responses. Right! The middle sound in *dot* is /o/.

3. Extend practice. Repeat the routine with other familiar and newly learned CVC words.

Tell students that they will play a game. Pam, Ben, Kim, and Ron like words that have the same middle sound as the one in each of their names. Have students say the four names aloud and identify the medial sound in each name. I will say some words. Listen to each word. Then tell me who will like the word. You may wish to display the following words from Student Page S100 to help students connect medial sounds to spellings.

fit	hen	tag	hop
got	lap	dig	pet

Say the word *fit* and have students repeat it. Who likes the word *fit*—Pam, Ben, Kim, or Ron? Have students respond by saying *Kim likes the word* fit. Continue for the remaining words.

☑ **INDEPENDENT PRACTICE** Have students name one CVC word for each of these medial sounds: /a/, /e/, /i/, /o/, /u/. Then have students produce a new word with the same medial sound.

IF… students have difficulty identifying words,
THEN… say a correct word as a model. Have students repeat the word and emphasize the medial sound. Help them brainstorm a new word with the same medial sound.

Lesson 13 **Identify Same and Different Medial Sounds**

A Fun Day for Jan

Jan had a fun day.
She gave her mom a hug.
Then she got her bat.
She played baseball with her friends.
Then the fog came.
Jan went home.
She had a fig for a snack.

Teacher: This Student Page is intended as an *optional extension* of the lesson. After teaching the phonological awareness lesson orally, you can distribute or display this page to connect the phonological awareness skills (sounds) to phonics skills (sound-spelling).

Lesson 13 Identify Same and Different Medial Sounds

gum, bug
get, den
bed, had

wag, pan
rat, cup
dog, leg

hog, big   pen, hem   mug, let   sit, pig

Teacher: This Student Page is intended as an *optional extension* of the lesson. After teaching the phonological awareness lesson orally, you can distribute or display this page to connect the phonological awareness skills (sounds) to phonics skills (sound-spelling).

Lesson 13 Identify Same and Different Medial Sounds

kit, fin	cat, map
pit, fed	bin, run
sad, hut	tin, his

bag set fit web hip nap

Teacher: This Student Page is intended as an *optional extension* of the lesson. After teaching the phonological awareness lesson orally, you can distribute or display this page to connect the phonological awareness skills (sounds) to phonics skills (sound-spelling).

Lesson 13 Identify Same and Different Medial Sounds

fit	hen	tag	hop
got	lap	dig	pet

Teacher: This Student Page is intended as an *optional extension* of the lesson. After teaching the phonological awareness lesson orally, you can distribute or display this page to connect the phonological awareness skills (sounds) to phonics skills (sound-spelling).

Lesson 14 Isolate Initial, Final, and Medial Sounds

OBJECTIVES:

- Recognize and isolate initial, final, and medial sounds in CVC words.
- Blend individual sounds in spoken words to make words.

INTRODUCE Remind students that they have identified and pronounced the beginning, ending, and middle sounds in many words. Today we will listen closely to words and then say just their beginning sounds. Then we will listen closely and say just their final sounds. Next, we will listen closely and say just their middle sounds. Finally, we will say all the sounds together to make words.

MODEL Display or share copies of the passage "Tom Likes to Run" from Student Page S101. Read it aloud, emphasizing the word *run*.

Tom Likes to Run

Tom likes to run.
He runs everywhere he goes.
He runs to school.
He runs home from school, too!
His feet and legs help him to run.
Tom can run very fast!

run
initial sound (/r/)
final sound (/n/)
medial sound (/u/)

TEACH After you read the passage aloud, demonstrate isolating initial, final, and medial sounds in a word and then blending the sounds to say the word. Listen as I say a word: *run*. Say the word slowly. I ask myself what the beginning sound in *run* is. Let's say the word together: *run*. The word *run* begins with /r/. Repeat this process for the final sound /n/ and medial sound /u/. Then have the class say the word.

Repeat the process with other CVC words in the passage, such as *Tom, him,* and *can*. Help students identify the initial, final, and medial sounds in each word.

Lesson 14 Isolate Initial, Final, and Medial Sounds

REMIND STUDENTS THAT …

- every word has a beginning sound and a final sound.
- they can identify and pronounce beginning and final sounds in words.

PRACTICE 1 Help students practice isolating initial and final sounds in CVC words with continuous initial or final consonant sounds, such as *f, m, n,* and *s.* Listen closely as I say a word: *man.* Say the word with me: *man.* Listen to the first sound: /m/. Say the first sound with me: /m/. Repeat this process for the final sound /n/.

Have students practice using the words below. Say the word *fed* and have students repeat it. What is the first sound you hear in the word *fed?* /f/. Repeat the procedure for *mop, nap,* and *sit.* Then use the same process to have students determine the final sounds in the words *miss, van, hum,* and *beef.*

After the oral exercise, you may wish to distribute or display Student Page S102 to help students connect initial and final sounds to specific letters.

Beginning Sound	Final Sound
fed (/f/)	miss (/s/)
mop (/m/)	van (/n/)
nap (/n/)	hum (/m/)
sit (/s/)	beef (/f/)

MONITOR PROGRESS Say each of the following words from Student Page S102.

fan	mad	not	set
yes	pin	him	nod

What is the first sound you hear in the word [*fan, mad, not, set*]? What is the last sound you hear in the word [*yes, pin, him, nod*]?

IF… students make errors pronouncing initial and final sounds,
THEN… model the correct pronunciation and have students echo you. If necessary, provide other familiar CVC words to help students practice pronouncing initial and final sounds correctly.

Lesson 14 Isolate Initial, Final, and Medial Sounds

PRACTICE 2 Help students practice isolating initial and final sounds in CVC words with stop initial or final consonant sounds, such as *b, d, g, k, p,* and *t.* Listen closely as I say a word: *pit.* Let's say the word together: *pit.* Listen to the first sound: /p/. Say the first sound with me: /p/. Repeat this process for the final sound /t/.

Tell students they will identify beginning and ending sounds in words. Say the word *bat* and have students repeat it. What is the first sound you hear in the word *bat?* Repeat the procedure for *dip, get, kit, pan,* and *tap.* Then use the same process for the final sounds in the words *rib, bed, pig, seek, hip,* and *sat.*

After the oral exercise, you may wish to distribute or display Student Page S103 to reinforce the connection between initial and final sounds and their corresponding letters.

Beginning Sound

bat (/b/)	kit (/k/)
dip (/d/)	pan (/p/)
get (/g/)	tap (/t/)

Final Sound

rib (/b/)	bin (/n/)
bed (/d/)	hip (/p/)
pig (/g/)	sat (/t/)

REMIND STUDENTS THAT ...

- every word has a beginning sound and a final sound.
- they can identify and pronounce beginning and final sounds in words.

MONITOR PROGRESS Say each of the following words from Student Page S103.

tin	pot	cap	got	hid	map
bib	sad	hug	big	hop	set

What is the first sound you hear in the word [*tin, pot, jam, got, hid, map*]? What is the final sound you hear in the word [*bib, sad, hug, big, hop, set*]?

IF... students have difficulty identifying initial or final sounds,
THEN... have students say the word slowly; segment it into initial, medial, and final sounds; and then listen carefully as they repeat the initial and final sounds.

Lesson 14 Isolate Initial, Final, and Medial Sounds

REMIND STUDENTS THAT …

- words have beginning sounds, final sounds, and middle sounds.
- they can identify and pronounce beginning, final, and middle sounds in words.
- they can blend beginning, middle, and final sounds to make words.

PRACTICE 3 First, review with students how to isolate initial and final sounds. Say the word *mat* and have students repeat it. Listen to the first sound: /m/. Say it with me: /m/. Now listen to the final sound: /t/. Say it with me: /t/. Remind students that words also have medial sounds. Repeat the word *mat*, emphasizing the medial sound /a/. Let's say the middle sound together: /a/. Now let's say the three sounds together to make the word: *mat*. Repeat this process with other CVC words, such as *hut* and *ram*.

Tell students that they will listen to words. Say the word *lap* and have students repeat it. What is the beginning sound in the word *lap*? What is the middle sound in the word *lap*? What is the final sound in the word *lap*? Now say the sounds together to make the word: *lap*. Repeat the process for the remaining words. You may wish to display the following words from Student Page S104 to help students connect initial, final, and medial sounds to spellings.

lap	peg	rip	sob	mud
can	not	lip	dot	rug

INDEPENDENT PRACTICE Say these words aloud: *rat, led, tin, nod, sum, fib, bag,* and *fit*. Have students identify the initial, medial, and final sound in each word. Then have them blend the sounds to say the word.

IF… students have difficulty blending initial, medial, and final sounds into a word,
THEN… ask them to isolate the initial, medial, and final sound in the word and then practice saying the sounds several times, accelerating the pace until they have blended the sounds successfully.

Lesson 14 **Isolate Initial, Final, and Medial Sounds**

Tom Likes to Run

Tom likes to run.
He runs everywhere he goes.
He runs to school.
He runs home from school, too!
His feet and legs help him to run.
Tom can run very fast!

Teacher: This Student Page is intended as an *optional extension* of the lesson. After teaching the phonological awareness lesson orally, you can distribute or display this page to connect the phonological awareness skills (sounds) to phonics skills (sound-spelling).

Lesson 14 Isolate Initial, Final, and Medial Sounds

Beginning Sound	Final Sound
fed	miss
mop	van
nap	hum
sit	beef

fan	mad	not	set
yes	pin	him	nod

Teacher: This Student Page is intended as an *optional extension* of the lesson. After teaching the phonological awareness lesson orally, you can distribute or display this page to connect the phonological awareness skills (sounds) to phonics skills (sound-spelling).

Lesson 15 Add Initial Phonemes

OBJECTIVES:

- Reinforce the concept of beginning sounds.
- Add single initial phonemes to make new words.

INTRODUCE Remind students that they have identified and pronounced the beginning, final, and middle sounds in words, and that they have blended these sounds to say words. Today we will say a word. We will listen to its sounds, especially at the beginning. Then we will add a sound at the beginning and say a new word.

MODEL Display or share copies of the passage "So Many Hats" from Student Page S107, and read it aloud.

So Many Hats

I went to the store to buy a hat.
There were so many hats at the store!
There was a hat with flowers on it.
There was a short hat and a tall hat, too.
I did not know what hat to buy.
I put on lots of hats at the store.
I bought the one with flowers on it.
I like my new hat!

/h/ + *at* = *hat*
/s/ + *at* = *sat*

/h/ + *it* = *hit*
/s/ + *it* = *sit*

TEACH After you read the passage aloud, point out the word *at* in the second sentence. Listen as I say this word: *at.* Now I will add /h/ to the beginning of *at* to make a new word: *hat.* Say the new word with me: *hat.* Now I will add a /s/ to the beginning of *at* to make a different word: *sat.* Say it with me: *sat.* Repeat the process by adding first a /h/ and then a /s/ to the word *it* in the third sentence.

Lesson 15 Add Initial Phonemes

REMIND STUDENTS THAT …

- words are made of sounds in the beginning, middle, and end.
- adding a sound to the beginning of a word can make a new word.

PRACTICE 1 Show students how to construct new words by adding the continuous consonant sounds *f, m, n,* and *s* to the beginning of existing words. Listen closely as I say a word: *an*. Say the word with me: *an*. Listen to the first sound: /a/. Say it with me: /a/. Listen to the last sound: /n/. Let's say the last sound together: /n/. Now let's add the /f/ sound to the beginning of the word *an*. First, say the sound with me: /f/. Now let's say all the sounds together to make a new word: *fan*. Repeat this process by adding the initial sound /m/ to the word *an*.

	e	a	t

Present the Elkonin boxes on Student Page S108 or have students use letter cards or tiles to make the word *eat*. Say the word aloud and have students repeat it. Have students add the /f/, /m/, /n/, and /s/ sound to the beginning of the word *eat* and say the new words *feat, meat, neat,* and *seat*.

☑ **MONITOR PROGRESS** Say the following five words from Student Page S108.

at	eel	end	it	old

What new word do you get when you add /f/ to the beginning of the words *at* and *eel*? What new word do you get when you add /s/ to the beginning of the words *end, it,* and *old*?

IF… students have trouble identifying the new word created by adding an initial phoneme,
THEN… model the correct response by saying the original word, saying the added initial phoneme, and then blending the sounds into the new word. Have students repeat these steps with one of the other four words.

Lesson 15 Add Initial Phonemes

PRACTICE 2 Show students how to construct new words by adding stop consonant sounds, such as *b, d, g, k, p,* and *t,* to the beginning of existing words. Listen as I say a word: *and.* Say it with me: *and.* Let's add the /b/ sound to the beginning of the word *and.* First, say the sound with me: /b/. Now let's say all the sounds together to make a new word: */band/.* Repeat this process by adding the initial sound /k/ to the word *it.*

	a	r	t

Display the Elkonin boxes on Student Page S109 or have students use letter cards or tiles to make the word *art.* Say the word aloud and have students repeat it. Have students add the /d/, /p/, and /t/ sound to the beginning of the word *art* and say the new words *dart, part,* and *tart.*

REMIND STUDENTS THAT . . .

- words are made of sounds in the beginning, middle, and end.
- adding a sound to the beginning of a word can make a new word.

☑ **MONITOR PROGRESS** Say the following seven words from Student Page S109.

am	ate	ill
an	end	
in	up	

What new words do you make when you add /d/ to the beginning of the words *am* and *ate*? What new words do you make when you add /b/ to the beginning of the words *an* and *end*? What new words do you make when you add /p/ to the beginning of the words *in, up,* and *ill*?

IF… students have difficulty saying the new word after adding the initial phoneme,

THEN… say the initial phoneme, the original word, and the new word and have students repeat after you. Have students follow these steps with one of the other six words.

Lesson 15 Add Initial Phonemes

REMIND STUDENTS THAT …

- words are made of sounds in the beginning, middle, and end.
- adding a sound to the beginning of a word can make a new word.
- there may be more than one sound at the beginning of a word.

PRACTICE 3 Remind students that they have added sounds to the beginnings of words to make new words. Listen to this word: *an*. Say it with me: *an*. Let's add the /t/ sound to the beginning of the word *an*. First, say the sound with me: /t/. Now let's say all the sounds together to make a new word: */tan/*. Repeat this process by adding the /t/ sound to the beginning of the word *wig*. There are now two sounds at the beginning of the word *twig*: /t/ and /w/.

Tell students that they will listen to words. Say the following words aloud, displaying Student Page S110 if desired.

pot	way	lip
rip	ray	rap

Say *pot* aloud and have students echo you. Let's add the /s/ sound to the beginning of the word. What new word do we make? (spot) What are the two sounds at the beginning of the new word? (/s/ and /p/) Have students add the /s/ sound to the beginning of *way* and *lip* to make the new words *sway* and *slip*. Repeat this process by having students add the /t/ sound to the beginning of *rip*, *ray*, and *rap*.

☑ **INDEPENDENT PRACTICE** Say the words *in*, *it*, *or*, *eat*, *lot*, and *nap* aloud. Have students add the /f/ sound to the first three words and the /s/ sound to the last three words. Have them say each new word aloud and identify the sound or sounds at the beginning of each word.

IF… students have difficulty distinguishing the two sounds at the beginning of *slot* and *snap*,
THEN… have them say the /s/ sound and the original word separately, focusing on the initial sound in the original word. Then have them blend the sounds to say the new word, emphasizing the two new sounds at the beginning of the word.

Lesson 15 **Add Initial Phonemes**

So Many Hats

I went to the store to buy a hat.
There were so many hats at the store!
There was a hat with flowers on it.
There was a short hat and a tall hat, too.
I did not know what hat to buy.
I put on lots of hats at the store.
I bought the one with flowers on it.
I like my new hat!

Teacher: This Student Page is intended as an *optional extension* of the lesson. After teaching the phonological awareness lesson orally, you can distribute or display this page to connect the phonological awareness skills (sounds) to phonics skills (sound-spelling).

Lesson 15 Add Initial Phonemes

	e	a	t

at eel end it old

Teacher: This Student Page is intended as an *optional extension* of the lesson. After teaching the phonological awareness lesson orally, you can distribute or display this page to connect the phonological awareness skills (sounds) to phonics skills (sound-spelling).

Lesson 15 Add Initial Phonemes

	a	r	t

am	ate	ill
an	end	
in	up	

Teacher: This Student Page is intended as an *optional extension* of the lesson. After teaching the phonological awareness lesson orally, you can distribute or display this page to connect the phonological awareness skills (sounds) to phonics skills (sound-spelling).

Lesson 15 Add Initial Phonemes

pot	way	lip
rip	ray	rap

Teacher: This Student Page is intended as an *optional extension* of the lesson. After teaching the phonological awareness lesson orally, you can distribute or display this page to connect the phonological awareness skills (sounds) to phonics skills (sound-spelling).

Lesson 16 Add Final Phonemes

INTRODUCE Remind students that they have been saying words and making new words. We know how to say a word and add a sound at the beginning of the word to make a new word. Think of the word *am*. When we add the /h/ sound to the beginning of the word *am*, we make the word *ham*. Today we will say a word. Then we will add a sound at the end of the word and say the new word.

MODEL Display or share copies of "A Trip to the Zoo" from Student Page S111, and read it aloud.

A Trip to the Zoo

My family and I went to the zoo. *zoo + /m/ = zoom*
We saw so many animals there!
We saw a tall animal with a long neck.
We saw lions and monkeys, too.
The monkeys at the zoo did funny things.
They jumped on things and hung from bars.
I saw a big bee in the garden.
We had a fun time at the zoo!

bee + /f/ = beef

TEACH After you read the passage aloud, point out the word *zoo* in the first sentence. Listen as I say this word: *zoo*. Now I will add /m/ to the end of *zoo* to make a new word: *zoom*. Say the new word with me: *zoom*. Repeat this process by adding /f/ to the word *bee* in the seventh sentence.

OBJECTIVES:

- Review naming final phonemes.
- Add final phonemes to make new words.
- Make blends by adding final phonemes.

Lesson 16 Add Final Phonemes

REMIND STUDENTS THAT ...

- every word has a final sound.
- adding a sound to the end of a word can make a new word.

PRACTICE 1 Demonstrate how to make a new word by adding a sound to the end of an existing word. Listen as I say a word: see. Say the word with me: *see*. Listen to the first sound: /s/. Say it with me: /s/. Listen to the last sound: /ē/. Let's say the last sound together: /ē/. Now let's add the /m/ sound to the end of see. First, say the sound with me: /m/. Now let's say all the sounds together to make a new word: *seem*.

f	e	e	

Display the Elkonin boxes on Student Page S112 or have students use letter cards or tiles to make the word *fee*. Say the word aloud and have students repeat it. Have students add the /d/, /l/, and /t/ sound to the end of the word *fee* and say the new words *feed*, *feel*, and *feet*.

☑ **MONITOR PROGRESS** Say each of the following words from Student Page S112.

moo	see	tea	too

What new word do you make when you add /n/ to the end of *moo*?
What new word do you make when you add /d/ to the end of *see*?
What new word do you make when you add /m/ to the end of *tea*?
What new word do you make when you add /l/ to the end of *too*?

IF... students have trouble identifying the new word created by adding a final phoneme,
THEN... model the correct response by saying the original word, saying the added final phoneme, and then blending the sounds into the new word. Have students repeat the process with one of the other words.

Lesson 16 Add Final Phonemes

PRACTICE 2 Have students say the word *ten* and identify the final /n/ sound. Let's add /t/ to the end of *ten*. First, say the sound with me: /t/. Now let's say the sounds together to make a new word: *tent*. Point out that there are two sounds at the end of *tent*: /n/ and /t/. Repeat this process by adding the final sound /d/ to *ten*. Have students identify the final sounds /n/ and /d/ in the new word *tend*.

a	n	

Display the Elkonin boxes on Student Page S113 or have students use letter cards or tiles to make the word *an*. Have students say the word aloud. Then have them add /d/ and /t/ to the end of *an* and say the new words *and* and *ant*. What are the two sounds at the end of [*and, ant*]?

REMIND STUDENTS THAT …

- adding a sound to the end of a word can make a new word.
- there may be more than one sound at the end of a word.

☑ MONITOR PROGRESS Say each of the following words from Student Page S113.

dam	hum	
far	fir	for
ban	pin	tan

What new words do you make when you add /p/ to the end of *dam* and *hum*? What new words do you make when you add /m/ to the end of *far, fir,* and *for*? What new words do you make when you add /k/ to the end of *ban, pin,* and *tan*? Have students identify the two sounds at the end of each new word.

IF… students have difficulty identifying the two sounds at the end of the new word,
THEN… say the new word slowly, emphasizing the two distinct final sounds, and have students repeat after you. Have students follow these steps with one of the other words you presented.

Lesson 16 Add Final Phonemes

REMIND STUDENTS THAT ...

- adding a sound to the end of a word can make a new word.
- there may be more than one sound at the end of a word.

PRACTICE 3 Have students say *bar* and identify the final sound in the word. Let's add /k/ to the end of *bar* to make a new word. When we add /k/ to the end of *bar*, we make the word *bark*. Let's say the words together: *bar, bark*. Have students identify the two distinct sounds at the end of the word. Then repeat the process by adding /d/ to the end of *ten* and *men*.

Read the following words from Student Page S114 aloud, displaying them if desired.

car	for	pan	ran	tar

Repeat each word aloud with students. Now add the /t/ sound to the end of each word. What new words do we make? What are the two sounds at the end of each new word?

☑ **INDEPENDENT PRACTICE** Say these words aloud: *sun, bun, mass*, and *stun*. Have students add /k/ to the end of each word, say each new word aloud, and identify the two sounds at the end of each word.

IF... students have difficulty identifying the two sounds at the end of the new word,
THEN... have them say the original word, emphasizing the final sound, and then say the added final phoneme separately. Then have them combine the two parts into the new word, emphasizing the two distinct final sounds as they say the new word aloud.

Lesson 16 **Add Final Phonemes**

A Trip to the Zoo

My family and I went to the zoo.
We saw so many animals there!
We saw a tall animal with a long neck.
We saw lions and monkeys, too.
The monkeys at the zoo did funny things.
They jumped on things and hung from bars.
I saw a big bee in the garden.
We had a fun time at the zoo!

Teacher: This Student Page is intended as an *optional extension* of the lesson. After teaching the phonological awareness lesson orally, you can distribute or display this page to connect the phonological awareness skills (sounds) to phonics skills (sound-spelling).

Lesson 16 Add Final Phonemes

f	e	e	

moo see tea too

Teacher: This Student Page is intended as an *optional extension* of the lesson. After teaching the phonological awareness lesson orally, you can distribute or display this page to connect the phonological awareness skills (sounds) to phonics skills (sound-spelling).

Lesson 16 Add Final Phonemes

a	n	

dam	hum	for
far	fir	tan
ban	pin	

Teacher: This Student Page is intended as an *optional extension* of the lesson. After teaching the phonological awareness lesson orally, you can distribute or display this page to connect the phonological awareness skills (sounds) to phonics skills (sound-spelling).

Lesson 16 Add Final Phonemes

car	**for**	**pan**	**ran**	**tar**

Teacher: This Student Page is intended as an *optional extension* of the lesson. After teaching the phonological awareness lesson orally, you can distribute or display this page to connect the phonological awareness skills (sounds) to phonics skills (sound-spelling).

Lesson 17 Delete or Change Initial Phonemes

INTRODUCE Remind students that words have beginning, middle, and ending sounds. We know how to add a beginning sound to a word and say the new word. We can add /s/ to the beginning of *end* and say the new word: *send*. We can also take away or change the beginning sound in a word to make a new word. Today we will say a word. Then we will take away or change the beginning sound and say the new word.

OBJECTIVES:

- Reinforce the concepts of beginning sounds.
- Delete or change initial phonemes to make new words.

MODEL Display or share copies of the passage "A Day at the Beach" from Student Page S115, and read it aloud.

A Day at the Beach

sat – /s/ = at
sat /s/ to /h/ = hat

Nan went to the beach today.
She sat in the sun and played in the sand.
She went for a swim in the sea.
Her mom and dad helped her fly a kite.
It was such a nice day at the beach!
Nan wants to go back very soon.

sand – /s/ = and
sand /s/ to /b/ = band

TEACH After you read the passage aloud, point out the word *sat* in line 2. Listen as I say this word: *sat*. I will take away the /s/ to make another new word: *at*. Say it with me: *at*. Now I will change the /s/ to /h/ to make a new word: *hat*. Let's say the new word together: *hat*. Repeat the process with the word *sand* by first deleting the /s/ and then changing the /s/ to a /b/.

Lesson 17 Delete or Change Initial Phonemes

REMIND STUDENTS THAT ...

- words have beginning sounds.
- deleting a word's beginning sound makes a new word.

PRACTICE 1 Help students focus on isolating and deleting initial sounds. Listen as I say a word. Then we'll say the word together. We will name the beginning sound. After that, we'll take away the beginning sound and say the new word.

Listen as I say the word: *fin*. Say the word with me: *fin*. Repeat the word, blending each sound slowly. The beginning sound in the word *fin* is /f/. Now let's take away the beginning /f/ sound and say the new word: *in*. Repeat this procedure for the word *man*.

Follow the above procedure with the words below, which appear on Student Page S116. Listen to each word I say. First, say the word. Then tell me the first sound in the word. Next, take away the first sound in the word and say the new word.

can (an)	win (in)	lend (end)	cart (art)

MONITOR PROGRESS Say the following words from Student Page S116.

wall	meat	hill	sink
mask	self	hand	wax

Have students say the word *wall* and identify the beginning sound.

What new word do you make when you take away the beginning sound in *wall*? (all) Repeat this procedure for the remaining words.

IF... students have difficulty identifying the new word created after deleting the initial phoneme,
THEN... model the correct response with one of the words in the activity, and have students repeat after you. Return to the same word later in the practice and invite students to delete the initial phoneme and say the new word.

Lesson 17 Delete or Change Initial Phonemes

PRACTICE 2 Review with students initial, medial, and final sounds. Let's practice making a new word by taking away the beginning sound of the old word. Listen as I say a word: *ham*. Say it with me: *ham*. Repeat the word, blending each sound slowly. Now let's take away the /h/ sound from the beginning of *ham*. Say the new word: *am*.

Help students recall that some words have more than one beginning sound. Listen to this word: *stop*. What are the two sounds at the beginning of *stop*? (/s/ and /t/) Now let's take away the /s/ sound from the beginning of *stop*. Say the new word: *top*.

Say the following words, displaying Student Page S117 if desired. Listen to each word I say. Repeat each word after me. Tell me the first sound or sounds you hear in the word. Then take away the very first sound in the word and say the new word. Guide and assist students as needed.

bin (in)   kit (it)   spot (pot)   tray (ray)   year (ear)

REMIND STUDENTS THAT ...

- words are made up of sounds.
- there may be more than one sound at the beginning of a word.
- deleting a word's beginning sound makes a new word.

MONITOR PROGRESS Say the following words from Student Page S117.

jam	stub	ran	grow	pup
part	sway	flip	task	glow

Have students say each word and identify its beginning sound(s). Then have them omit the very first sound they hear and say the new word.

IF... students have difficulty determining which sound they should omit in a word with two distinct initial sounds,
THEN... model how to omit the very first initial sound in one of the words they are having trouble with. Revisit the same word later in the practice and have students try deleting the initial phoneme and saying the new word on their own.

Lesson 17 Delete or Change Initial Phonemes

REMIND STUDENTS THAT ...

- words have one or more beginning sounds.
- changing a word's beginning sound makes a new word.

PRACTICE 3 Isolate an initial sound. The word *dip* has three sounds: /d//i//p/. The beginning sound is /d/. If I change the /d/ to a /t/, I make a new word: *tip*. Isolate the two initial sounds in *drip*. If I change the /d/ to a /t/, I make a new word: *trip*.

Listen as I say a word: *fan*. Say it with me: *fan*. The beginning sound in *fan* is /f/. Let's change the /f/ to /t/: /t//a//n/. The new word is *tan*. Let's say it together: *tan*. Present the word *slow*, identifying the two beginning sounds. Replace /s/ with /g/ to produce the word *glow*.

Say the following words from Student Page S118.

had /h/ to /p/ (pad)
sun /s/ to /r/ (run)
jump /j/ to /b/ (bump)
slip /s/ to /f/ (flip)

Say the word *had*. Have students repeat it and identify the initial /h/ sound. Change the /h/ sound to a /p/ sound. What new word do you get? Repeat the procedure for the remaining words. Make sure students identify the two distinct initial sounds in *slip*.

☑ **INDEPENDENT PRACTICE** Say *keep, grip, tar,* and *glow*. Have students identify the beginning sound(s) in each word. Ask them to replace the beginning sound in *keep* and *grip* with /d/ and the beginning sound in *tar* and *glow* with /f/. Have them say the new words.

IF... students have difficulty replacing initial phonemes to create new words, THEN... model the correct response by saying the original word, naming the sound to be replaced as well the new initial sound, and then saying the new word. Have them use this procedure with one or more of the other featured words.

Lesson 18 Delete or Change Final Phonemes

INTRODUCE Remind students that they have practiced hearing the final sound in a word. When we say *bat*, the final sound is /t/. We say words slowly to hear the sounds.

MODEL Let's say the word *cup* together and listen for its sounds. Say it with me: *cup*. It has the sounds /k//u//p/.

Here is another word: *seed*. It has the sounds /s//ē//d/. If I take away the last sound, I make a new word: *see*. If I add the sound /n/ to the end, I have a new word, *seen*.

Read the first column of words from Student Page S119 aloud. Repeat the words *beef* and *bee* and ask: What sound did I take away? Pause for responses. Yes, I took the /f/ sound away and made the word *bee*. Repeat *beef* and *beet* and ask: What sound did I change? Pause. Yes, I changed /f/ to /t/ at the end and made the word *beet*.

beef	seam	feel
bee	sea	fee
beet	seat	feed

TEACH Repeat the process with the other two columns of words. Then help students delete phonemes on their own, using the words below. I will say a word. You take away the last sound and say the new word. For example, I will say *feet*. You take away the last sound and say *fee*.

boot (boo) seem (see) weed (wee) ink (in)

OBJECTIVES:

- Identify individual sounds in spoken words.
- Produce a spoken word when the final phoneme is removed.
- Recognize a spoken word when the final phoneme is replaced.

Lesson 18 Delete or Change Final Phonemes

REMIND STUDENTS THAT ...

- they can hear the sounds that make up a word.
- they can take away sounds to make new words.

PRACTICE 1 Review isolating final sounds. We know how to hear the sounds in short words. Here is a word: *tap*. If I say it very slowly, you can hear all the sounds: /t//a//p/. Tell me the sounds that you heard. Pause for responses. That's right. *Tap* has three sounds: /t/ (pause) /a/ (pause) /p/. Now listen as I say another word: *sit*. What are the sounds in *sit*? Pause for responses. The sounds in sit are /s//i//t/.

Listen as I say another word: *mine*. Now let's say the sounds slowly together: /m//ī//n/. The last sound is /n/. If we take it away, what word do we have? *My*. Say it with me: *my*.

Present the following words from Student Page S120. I will say a word. We will say the word together, slowly, so we can hear the sounds. Then we will take away the last sound and say the new word. After practicing each deletion orally, you may wish to write the original words on the board and erase the final letter to emphasize deleting it.

seed see	zoom zoo	team tea
moon moo	week wee	fort for

☑ **MONITOR PROGRESS** Ask students to repeat the words *tool, heap,* and *light* with you, and to then remove the final sound of each. Have students say the new words on their own.

IF... students have difficulty saying a new word,
THEN... model orally segmenting the sounds in the original word, and then say the new word. Have students repeat the new word after you. Provide other suitable words for additional practice as needed.

Lesson 18 Delete or Change Final Phonemes

PRACTICE 2 Have students review adding final phonemes. I will say a word, and then you add a sound to the end and make a new word. For example, if I say *sea*, you can add /l/ to make the new word *seal*. Say the following words, and have students add final phonemes to make new words, such as the ones suggested in parentheses.

for (form, fort, fork)	moo (moon, mood, move, moose)
go (goat, goal, ghost)	say (sail, safe, same, sake, save)

Tell students that instead of adding a final sound, now they will change a final sound to make a new word. Earlier, we made the word *seal*. If we change the /l/ at the end of *seal* to /t/, what word will we have? (seat) What if we change the /t/ at the end of *seat* to /m/? (seam)

Use the routine below to have students change the final phonemes of the following words from Student Page S121.

Routine

1. Say a word.	Here is the beginning word: *mat*.
2. Give the new sound.	Change the /t/ at the end of *mat* to /d/.
3. Elicit the new word.	What will the new word be? (mad)

mat /d/ (mad)	hit /m/ (him)
web /t/ (wet)	jam /b/ (jab)
run /g/ (rug)	bag /d/ (bad)
hot /p/ (hop)	dim /p/ (dip)

REMIND STUDENTS THAT ...

- they can take away or add final sounds to make new words.

☑ **MONITOR PROGRESS** Have students change the following final phonemes as indicated to make new words: *tan* /p/, *kit* /n/, *pat* /n/, and *ham* /d/.

IF... students have trouble saying the new word,
THEN... say the beginning part of the original word and have students repeat it. Then add the new final sound, say the new word, and have students repeat it. If necessary, provide other familiar CVC words for additional practice.

Lesson 18 Delete or Change Final Phonemes

REMIND STUDENTS THAT ...

- they can change final sounds to make new words.

PRACTICE 3 Demonstrate changing a final phoneme. Listen as I say a word: *hat.* The sounds in the word are /h//a//t/. The last sound is /t/: *hat.* If I change the final sound from /t/ to /z/, I can make a new word, /h//a//z/, *has.* I made the word *has.*

We can change the ending again, from /z/ to /m/. That makes another new word, /h//a//m/, *ham.*

Say each of the following words from Student Page S122. For each word, have students change the final phoneme to make at least two new words. Provide guidance and assistance as needed.

cat cab, can, cap	bag bad, ban, bat
hub hug, hum, hut	cod cob, cop, cot
dig did, dim, dip	pan pad, pal, pat

If students falter, suggest that they try different final sounds to see if one makes a real word. For example, students could say *cab, caf, caj, cak,* and so on.

☑ **INDEPENDENT PRACTICE** Have students change the final phonemes of the following words to make at least two new words: *bed, big, map, him,* and *sat.*

IF... students have trouble identifying appropriate final phonemes to use to create new words,
THEN... say the original word, repeating it without the final sound, and then encourage students to try various letters to see which ones can replace the existing final phoneme to create a new word.

Lesson 18 Delete or Change Final Phonemes

beef	seam	feel
bee	sea	fee
beet	seat	feed

Teacher: This Student Page is intended as an *optional extension* of the lesson. After teaching the phonological awareness lesson orally, you can distribute or display this page to connect the phonological awareness skills (sounds) to phonics skills (sound-spelling).

Lesson 18 Delete or Change Final Phonemes

seed	**zoom**	**team**
see	**zoo**	**tea**
moon	**week**	**fort**
moo	**wee**	**for**

Teacher: This Student Page is intended as an *optional extension* of the lesson. After teaching the phonological awareness lesson orally, you can distribute or display this page to connect the phonological awareness skills (sounds) to phonics skills (sound-spelling).

Lesson 18 Delete or Change Final Phonemes

mat	**hit**
web	**jam**
run	**bag**
hot	**dim**

Teacher: This Student Page is intended as an *optional extension* of the lesson. After teaching the phonological awareness lesson orally, you can distribute or display this page to connect the phonological awareness skills (sounds) to phonics skills (sound-spelling).

Lesson 18 Delete or Change Final Phonemes

cat	bag
hub	cod
dig	pan

Teacher: This Student Page is intended as an *optional extension* of the lesson. After teaching the phonological awareness lesson orally, you can distribute or display this page to connect the phonological awareness skills (sounds) to phonics skills (sound-spelling).

Lesson 19 Change Medial Phonemes

INTRODUCE You know that words are made of sounds. Different sounds make different words. You can change the sounds in a word and make a new word. For example, think about the word *tug*. Say it with me: *tug*. If you change the beginning sound in *tug* to /m/, you make a new word, *mug*.

MODEL Display or share copies of Student Page S123, which features the chart below. These are pictures of words that have the same beginning sounds, /b/, and the same final sounds, /g/. Their middle sounds are different. Listen as I say the words: *bag, beg, big, bog, bug*.

We can say the word *bag* and listen to the sounds. The middle sound is /a/. We can change the middle sound to /e/. The new word is *beg*.

bag	beg	big	bog	bug
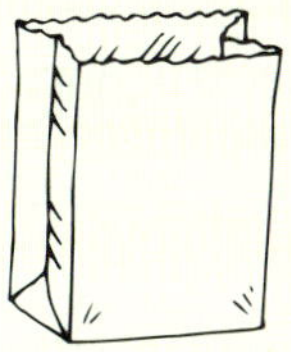				

TEACH Use the chart to demonstrate changing medial phonemes. I will say each word slowly. After I say a word, we will say the word together *very* slowly. Listen for the sound in the middle.

The first word is *bag*. Draw out the vowel as you say the word. Say it slowly with me: *bag*. What is its middle sound? Pause. Yes, the middle sound is /a/. Repeat with the other four words. After each, say: The middle sound changed from [previous middle sound] to [present middle sound].

OBJECTIVES:

- Recognize a spoken word when a phoneme is replaced with a different phoneme.

Lesson 19 Change Medial Phonemes

REMIND STUDENTS THAT ...

- words are made of different sounds they can hear.
- by saying a word slowly, they can hear the middle sound.

PRACTICE 1 Use the routine to have students isolate and then change medial short vowels. First, model listening for a middle phoneme. I am going to say a word very slowly so I can hear its middle sound. Listen with me: *red*. I will say the sounds in the word: /r/ (pause) /e/ (pause) /d/. The middle sound is /e/.

Routine

1. Segment the word.	Listen as I say the word very slowly: *tag*. The sounds are /t//a//g/.
2. Isolate the middle sound.	The middle sound I hear is /a/.
3. Name a new sound.	Let's change the middle sound to /u/. Say it with me: /u/.
4. Say the new sounds together.	Let's say the sounds of the new word: /t//u//g/.
5. Blend the sounds.	Now say the sounds together without stopping: *tug*.

Continue the activity using the following words and phonemes from Student Page S124.

pod, /a/, pad	pig, /e/, peg	fan, /i/, fin
hop, /i/, hip	lip, /a/, lap	pen, /a/, pan
rag, /u/, rug	at, /i/, sit	dug, /o/, dog

MONITOR PROGRESS Guide students to isolate the middle sound in the following words. Then tell them to change the middle sound, as shown, and say the new word.

hit, /u/, (hut) bud, /e/, (bed) sad, /e/, (said)

IF... students have trouble distinguishing the middle sound,
THEN... slowly sound out the word together several times until students can identify it successfully.

Lesson 19 Change Medial Phonemes

PRACTICE 2 Demonstrate changing one medial short vowel to another medial short vowel. Listen as I say a word: /h//o//t/, *hot.* Wave your hand as if fanning your face and repeat the word, drawing out the vowel. The sound in the middle of *hot* is /o/. If I change the middle sound from /o/ to /i/, I can make a new word, /h//i//t/, *hit.* Bump your fists together and repeat the word, drawing out the vowel.

Let's try another: *leg.* Say it with me slowly: /l//e//g/. What is the middle sound? Pause for responses. The sound in the middle of leg is /e/. Now let's change that middle sound to /a/: /l//a//g/, *lag.* The new word is *lag.* Say it with me: *lag.* Repeat the procedure with the following words from Student Page S125. When possible, use gestures to reinforce the differences between words.

hum, /i/, him	pan, /i/, pin
pat, /e/, pet	wig, /a/, wag
cup, /a/, cap	bat, /i/, bit

REMIND STUDENTS THAT ...

- by saying a word slowly, they can hear the middle sound.
- they can change the middle sound in a word to make a new word.

☑ **MONITOR PROGRESS** Have students try changing some medial sounds on their own. I will say a word and we'll say it together. You say the middle sound. I will tell you a new middle sound to use. Then you say the new word. Ready? The word is *net.* Say it with me: *net.* What is the middle sound? (/e/) Now change the middle sound to /u/. What is the new word? (nut) Repeat with the following words:

cut, /a/, (cat) mop, /a/, (map) fix, /o/, (fox)

IF... students have trouble remembering the beginning and ending sounds of a word,
THEN... prompt them by voicing the beginning sound, asking for the new middle sound, and voicing the ending sound. Then have students echo you as you blend the sounds into the new word.

Lesson 19 Change Medial Phonemes

REMIND STUDENTS THAT ...

- changing the middle sound in a word makes a new word.

PRACTICE 3 Demonstrate how to say the middle sound in a word, change the middle sound, and say a new word. I am going to say a word, and I want to know its middle sound. The word is *rap*. I will say it slowly: /r//a//p/. The middle sound is /a/.

Now I want to change the middle sound to /i/. The beginning sound is /r/, the new middle sound is /i/, and the ending sound is /p/. That's /r//i//p/. The new word is *rip*.

Now you try. I will say a word. You tell me the middle sound. Then I will say a new middle sound, and you say the new word. Here is the word: *zip*. What is the middle sound? Pause for responses. Right, the middle sound is /i/. Change the middle sound to /a/. What is the new word? Pause for responses. Yes, the new word is *zap*.

Continue by substituting vowels in the middle of the word frames below, which also appear on Student Page S126.

p__t	h__m	h__t	c__t

INDEPENDENT PRACTICE Have students try substituting short vowels as middle phonemes in the spoken words below. Encourage them to experiment in order to find new real words.

him (ham, hum)	tip (top, tap)	net (not, nut)
flip (flap, flop)	bet (bat, bit, but)	map (mat, man)
pop (pep, pup)	get (got, gut)	bed (bad, bid, bud)

IF... students make an error,
THEN... model the correct response by saying the original word, the new medial sound, and the new word. Revisit the word later in the practice.

Lesson 19 Change Medial Phonemes

bag	beg	big	bog	bug

Teacher: This Student Page is intended as an *optional extension* of the lesson. After teaching the phonological awareness lesson orally, you can distribute or display this page to connect the phonological awareness skills (sounds) to phonics skills (sound-spelling).

Lesson 19 Change Medial Phonemes

pod, /a/	pig, /e/	fan, /i/
hop, /i/	lip, /a/	pen, /a/
rag, /u/	sat, /i/	dug, /o/

Teacher: This Student Page is intended as an *optional extension* of the lesson. After teaching the phonological awareness lesson orally, you can distribute or display this page to connect the phonological awareness skills (sounds) to phonics skills (sound-spelling).

Lesson 19 Change Medial Phonemes

hum, /i/	**pan, /i/**
pat, /e/	**wig, /a/**
cup, /a/	**bat, /i/**

Teacher: This Student Page is intended as an *optional extension* of the lesson. After teaching the phonological awareness lesson orally, you can distribute or display this page to connect the phonological awareness skills (sounds) to phonics skills (sound-spelling).

Lesson 19 Change Medial Phonemes

p___t   h___m   h___t   c___t

Teacher: This Student Page is intended as an *optional extension* of the lesson. After teaching the phonological awareness lesson orally, you can distribute or display this page to connect the phonological awareness skills (sounds) to phonics skills (sound-spelling).

Lesson 20 Blend and Segment Two to Three Phonemes into Words

INTRODUCE Remind students that by listening closely, they can hear the separate sounds in words. We learned that words are made of sounds. Some very short words have just two sounds. Many words have more than two sounds. We will put sounds together to make words. Then we will separate words into sounds.

MODEL I am going to say the sounds that make up a word: /m/ (pause) /ē/. Now I will blend the sounds together to make the word. To do this, I will say the sounds quickly without stopping: *me*. Then, model segmenting the *me* back into its sounds, /m//ē/.

Repeat the process to model blending /y/ and /o͞o/ into *you*, /w/ and /ē/ into *we*, and /m/ and /ā/ into *may*, and then segmenting the words back into sounds. Then display the passage from Student Page S127.

OBJECTIVES:

- Blend two phonemes into spoken words.
- Blend three phonemes into spoken words.
- Segment words into two phonemes.
- Segment words into three phonemes.

Say Hi!

Do you know who Sue is?
Sue is new.
She is why I say hi.
We all say hi to Sue.

TEACH Have students blend two phonemes into words. I am going to say two or three sounds. You will make a word from the sounds. For example, I will say /ĭ/ (pause) /t/. The sounds are /ĭ//t/. You will make a word by saying the sound quickly without stopping: *it*. Have students make words from the following sounds:

/n//ō/	/s//ā/	/aw//l/	/wh//ī/	/sh//ē/
/h//ă//t/	/w//ĭ//n/	/b//ō//t/	/s//ĕ//d/	/t//ā//k/

Explain: You can segment a word into two or three sounds by saying the word slowly and stopping after each new sound. For example, I will say *Sue*. I then say it slower, stopping after each sound: /s/ (pause) /o͞o/. Have students practice segmenting the following words:

we	do	you	new	who
bag	knot	map	him	meet

Lesson 20 Blend and Segment Two to Three Phonemes into Words

REMIND STUDENTS THAT ...

- words are made of sounds.
- some words have just two sounds.
- saying sounds together without stopping makes a word.
- saying a word slowly with stops can reveal the sounds.

PRACTICE 1 Some short words, such as *me, my,* and *you*, have just two sounds. Can you hear them? The word *me* has the sounds /m/ and /ē/. What are the sounds in *my*? Pause for responses as students segment sounds. Yes, the sounds are /m//ī/; *my*. The sounds in *you* are /y//ōō/; *you*. Use the routine to have students blend two sounds into words.

Routine

1. Model. I can blend two sounds to make a word. For example, the sounds /b//ē/ can make a word. When I say them quickly without stopping, they make *be*.

2. Voice two sounds. Listen to these two sounds: /t//ī/. Listen again: /t//ī/.

3. Have students blend. Say the sounds quickly to make the word. (tie)

Have students blend the following sounds:

/ĭ//z/ /d//ā/ /s//ē/ /g//ō/ /ă//t/

Say the word *eat*. Guide students to segment the word into sounds by saying the word slower and slower with them and then have them pause between the sounds /ē/ and /t/. Continue practicing segmenting sounds with the words in the sentences from Student Page S128.

They say to eat an egg.
We may do it.

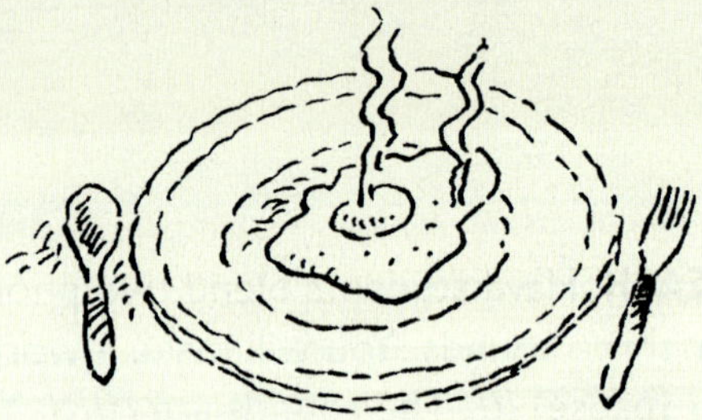

MONITOR PROGRESS Give students the following sounds and words and ask them to blend the sounds into a word or segment the word into sounds.

/ă//m/ /ā//k/ /b//ī/ row on my

IF... students have trouble blending or segmenting the sounds,
THEN... tell them the word and sounds and have them repeat it after you. Then have them try to blend or segment the sounds again.

Lesson 20 Blend and Segment Two to Three Phonemes into Words

PRACTICE 2 Let's try blending some sounds into words. We will say the sounds, and then we will make the word by blending the sounds together. Here are the sounds: /ā/ (pause) /m/. Say the sounds with me: /ā/ (pause) /m/. Now let's say the sounds quickly without stopping: *aim*. The word is *aim*. Repeat the process with the following words.

/th//ā/ /m//ā/ /ĭ//t/ /ă//t/ /m//ē/

Now, let's make some words out of three sounds. We will do it the same way. I will say the sounds. Then we will say the sounds together. After that, we will blend the sounds together into a word. The first sounds we will say are /b//aw//l/. Say them with me: /b//aw//l/. Now we will say them quickly without stopping: *ball*. The word is *ball*. Repeat the process with the following words.

/k//ĭ//k/ /g//ā//m/ /w//ĭ//n/ /b//ă//k/ /t//ē//m/

Display Student Page S129 and read it aloud. Next, we will say a word and listen for the sounds that make the word. Say the word *they* with me: *they*. Repeat it slowly: /th//ā/. Now pause between sounds: /th/ (pause) /ā/. The sounds in the word are /th/ and /ā/. Read other words from the passage on S129 with two phonemes and have students segment the words into sounds.

You can separate some words into three sounds. Listen as I say *will*: *will*. Now listen as I say it slower: /w//ĭ//l/; /w/ (pause) /ĭ/ (pause) /l/. The sounds are /w/ and /ĭ/ and /l/. Have students segment the other words from the passage with three phonemes, *kick* and *back*.

They may aim it at me.
I will kick it back.

REMIND STUDENTS THAT ...

- some words have just two or three sounds.
- blending sounds together makes a word.
- saying a word slowly with stops can reveal the sounds.

☑ **MONITOR PROGRESS** Give students the following sounds and words, and have them blend the sounds into words or segment the word into sounds.

/r//ŭ//n/ /s//ŏ//k/ /d//ā//t/ /s//ŭ//n/ /l//ĕ//g/

bite neat toad kneel goal

IF... students have trouble blending or segmenting three phonemes,
THEN... have them blend or segment the first two phonemes and then add the third.

Lesson 20 Blend and Segment Two to Three Phonemes into Words

REMIND STUDENTS THAT ...

- blending sounds together makes a word.
- they can blend two sounds together to make a word.
- some short words have three sounds.
- saying a word slowly with stops can reveal the sounds.

PRACTICE 3 Review the blending process. We will blend sounds into words. I will say some sounds. Then we will say the sounds together. After that, we will make the word by blending the sounds without stopping. Here are three sounds: /r/ (pause) /u/ (pause) /n/. Say the sounds with me: /r/ (pause) /u/ (pause) /n/. Now let's blend the sounds together without stopping: *run*. The word is *run*. Repeat the process with the following sounds.

/m//ŏ//m/	/s//ĕ//d/	/h//ă//t/	/k//ō//t/
/b//ă//t/	/b//aw//l/	/s//ĭ//t/	/s//ē//t/
/r//ā//s/	/s//ŏ//k/	/p//l//ā/	/n//o͞o//n/
/s//ŭ//n/	/r//ā//n/	/w//ĭ//sh/	/t//ŏ//p/

Display Student Page S130 to have students segment the words into their individual sounds. We will segment words into sounds. I will say the words. Then we will say the words slowly until we hear each sound in the word. Listen to the word *mom*. *Mom*. Say it slowly with me: /m//ŏ//m/. Now, we'll pause between sounds: /m/ (pause) /ŏ/ (pause) /m/. The sounds are /m//ŏ//m/. Repeat with the other words on S130.

mom	said	hat	coat
bat	ball	sit	seat
race	sock	play	noon
sun	rain	wish	top

☑ INDEPENDENT PRACTICE Mix practicing with two sounds and three sounds. Have students blend the following sounds into words and segment the following words into sounds.

/b//ē/	/s//ā//f/	/wh//ĕ//n/	/y//o͞o/
/t//ī/	/b//ō/	/b//ō//l/	/ē//t//s/
met	low	cup	lace
shoe	that	pin	my

IF... students make an error,
THEN... model the correct response by repeating the sounds and then blending them into a word or repeating the word and then segmenting it into sounds.

Lesson 20 **Blend and Segment Two to Three Phonemes into Words**

Say Hi!

Do you know who Sue is?
Sue is new.
She is why I say hi.
We all say hi to Sue.

Teacher: This Student Page is intended as an *optional extension* of the lesson. After teaching the phonological awareness lesson orally, you can distribute or display this page to connect the phonological awareness skills (sounds) to phonics skills (sound-spelling).

Lesson 20 Blend and Segment Two to Three Phonemes into Words

They say to eat an egg.
We may do it.

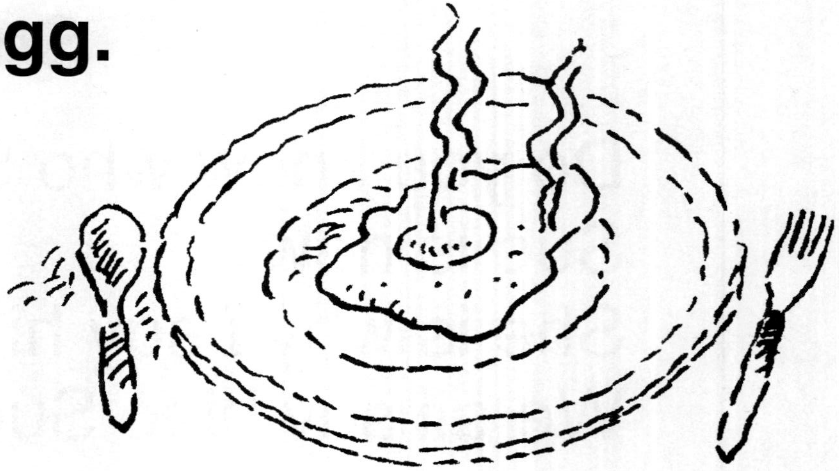

Teacher: This Student Page is intended as an *optional extension* of the lesson. After teaching the phonological awareness lesson orally, you can distribute or display this page to connect the phonological awareness skills (sounds) to phonics skills (sound-spelling).

Lesson 20 Blend and Segment Two to Three Phonemes into Words

They may aim it at me.
I will kick it back.

Teacher: This Student Page is intended as an *optional extension* of the lesson. After teaching the phonological awareness lesson orally, you can distribute or display this page to connect the phonological awareness skills (sounds) to phonics skills (sound-spelling).

Lesson 20 Blend and Segment Two to Three Phonemes into Words

mom	said	hat	coat
bat	ball	sit	seat
race	sock	play	noon
sun	rain	wish	top

Teacher: This Student Page is intended as an *optional extension* of the lesson. After teaching the phonological awareness lesson orally, you can distribute or display this page to connect the phonological awareness skills (sounds) to phonics skills (sound-spelling).

ASSESSMENT
LESSONS 15–20

Phonological Awareness

ASSESS MASTERY Use this Checkpoint to assess students' mastery of phonemes.

ADMINISTER THE TEST Administer the Checkpoint orally to each student. Model the process as described and then have the student use the process to respond. Record responses using the scoring chart on the next page.

1. Add Initial Phonemes (Lesson 15)
MODEL: I will ask you to add a new sound at the beginning of some words. For example, I could add /s/ to the beginning of the word *at*: *sat*. I want you to add /p/ to the beginning of these words.

ASSESS:	it	an	at	in	eel

2. Add Final Phonemes (Lesson 16)
MODEL: I will ask you to add a new sound at the end of some words. For example, I could add /t/ to the end of the word *go*: *goat*. I want you to add /m/ to the end of these words.

ASSESS:	bee	say	tie	far	hoe

3. Delete or Change Initial Phonemes (Lesson 17)
MODEL: I am going to have you take away a beginning sound to make a new word. For example, take /f/ away from *fit* to make *it*. Then you will add a new beginning sound to make another word. Add /b/ to *it* to make *bit*.

ASSESS:	cat, /p/	bone, /f/	game, /s/	ball, /w/

4. Delete or Change Final Phonemes (Lesson 18)
MODEL: I want you to take away an ending sound to make a new word. For example, take /p/ away from *heap* to make *he*. Then I will have you add a new ending sound. Add /l/ to *he* to make the word *heel*.

ASSESS:	bike, /t/	rope, /d/	mail, /n/	tool, /b/

5. Change Medial Phonemes (Lesson 19)
MODEL: I will say a word, such as *tag*. Then I will say a new middle sound, such as /u/. You will use the new middle sound to make a new word. In the example, the new word is *tug*.

ASSESS:	pen, /a/	dog, /i/	not, /e/	fizz, /u/

6. Blend and Segment Two to Three Phonemes into Words (Lesson 20)
MODEL: I will say some sounds. You will blend the sounds together into a word. If I say /b//u//g/, you will say *bug*. Then I will say a word. You will say each sound in the word. If I say *tap*, you will say /t//a//p/.

ASSESS:	/s//ō/	/w//aw//k/	/n//ē/	mice	bell

ASSESSMENT
LESSONS 15–20

Phonological Awareness

SCORING

SKILL/LESSON	SCORE
1. Add Initial Phonemes (Lesson 15) pit pan pat pin peel	_____ / 5
2. Add Final Phonemes (Lesson 16) beam same time farm home	_____ / 5
3. Delete or Change Initial Phonemes (Lesson 17) cat, at, pat bone, own, phone game, aim, same ball, all, wall	_____ / 4
4. Delete or Change Final Phonemes (Lesson 18) bike, by, bite rope, row, rode mail, may, main tool, too, tube	_____ / 4
5. Change Medial Phonemes (Lesson 19) pen, pan dog, dig not, net fizz, fuzz	_____ / 4
6. Blend and Segment Two to Three Phonemes into Words (Lesson 20) so; walk; knee; /m//ī//s/; /b//e//l/	_____ / 5

An overall score of 80% correct is typically considered mastery. Use your judgment and your individual students' needs as well to determine skill mastery.

IF... students score below the benchmark,
THEN... review those discrete skills, going back to the lessons to reteach and scaffold as needed.

Lesson 21 Connect Sound and Letter: Consonants 1

INTRODUCE Write the letters *Mm*, say the name *(m)*, and have students repeat after you. Explain that *m* is a consonant and spells the sound /m/. Point to something that begins with *m*, such as a map. What sound do you hear at the beginning of *map?* Write the word *map*. In this lesson, we'll learn how letters and sounds connect.

MODEL Display or share copies of the following passage, "Mac and Sam," from Student Page S133, and read it aloud. The words in this story have the letters and sounds *l* /l/, *r* /r/, *s* /s/, *m* /m/, *t* /t/, and *p* /p/.

Mac and Sam

I have a tiny pup.
His name is Mac.
Mac likes to run for his ball.
I have a tiny cat.
Her name is Sam.
Sam likes to sit on my lap!

TEACH Use examples of words to help students recognize letter-sound correspondences. Say: The first word in the title is *Mac*. It begins with the letter *M*. The other name in the title is *Sam*. It begins with the letter *S*. The letter *M* stands for the sound /m/ and the letter *S* stands for the sound /s/. Point out letter-sound correspondences in the story for *l* /l/, *r* /r/, *t* /t/, and *p* /p/.

OBJECTIVES:

- Recognize letters *l, r, s, m, t, p* and sounds *l* /l/, *r* /r/, *s* /s/, *m* /m/, *t* /t/, and *p* /p/.
- Connect letters and sounds *l* /l/, *r* /r/, *s* /s/, *m* /m/, *t* /t/, and *p* /p/.
- Identify *l* /l/, *r* /r/, *s* /s/, *m* /m/, *t* /t/, *and p* /p/ in words.

Lesson 21 Connect Sound and Letter: Consonants l

REMIND STUDENTS THAT …

- they can recognize the letters *l* and *r* and the sounds /l/ and /r/.
- they can connect the letters and sounds *l* /l/ and *r* /r/.
- they can identify *l* /l/ and *r* /r/ in words.

PRACTICE 1 Follow the routine below to teach one-to-one letter-sound correspondences for *l* /l/ and *r* /r/.

Routine

1. Teach the letters and sounds. Write capital and lowercase *Ll*. This is the letter *l*. It stands for the sound /l/. Write capital and lowercase *Rr*. This is the letter *r*. It stands for the sound /r/.

2. Model letter-sound correspondence. Write the word *log* and circle the *l*. The word *log* begins with the letter *l* and the sound /l/. Write the word *red* and circle the *r*. The word *red* begins with the letter *r* and the sound /r/.

3. Practice letter-sound correspondence. Write *lot, lid,* and *lap*. Have students circle the letter *l* in each word. What sound does *l* make in each word? Write *rid, run,* and *rag*. Have students follow the same process for letter *r*.

Ll	Rr
 leg	 rabbit
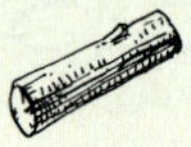 log	 ring

Distribute Student Page S134. Have students cut out the picture cards. Pairs put letter cards *Ll* and *Rr* face up and mix the picture cards face down. They select picture cards, say the word for the picture, say the first sound of each word, and match the card to *Ll* or *Rr*.

☑ **MONITOR PROGRESS** Display the following sentence from Student Page S134. Have students identify each example of *l* /l/ and *r* /r/.

Lions like to roar, and robins like to sing.

IF… students cannot connect the letters and sounds in the words,
THEN… review key steps in the routine, and provide additional words beginning with *l* /l/ and *r* /r/ for practice.

Lesson 21 Connect Sound and Letter: Consonants 1

PRACTICE 2 Follow the routine below to teach one-to-one letter-sound correspondences for *s* /s/ and *m* /m/.

Routine

1. Teach the letters and sounds. Write capital and lowercase *Ss*. This is the letter *s*. It stands for the sound /s/. Write capital and lowercase *Mm*. This is the letter *m*. It stands for the sound /m/.

2. Model letter-sound correspondence. Write the word *sun* and circle the *s*. The word *sun* begins with the letter *s* and the sound /s/. Write the word *men* and circle the *m*. The word *men* begins with the letter *m* and the sound /m/.

3. Practice letter-sound correspondence. Write the words *sip, sit,* and *sat*. Have students circle the letter *s* in each word. What sound is connected with the letter *s* in each word? Write the words *map, mop,* and *mat*. Have students follow the same process for letter *m*.

REMIND STUDENTS THAT ...

- they can recognize the letters *s* and *m* and the sounds /s/ and /m/.
- they can connect the letters and sounds *s* /s/ and *m* /m/.
- they can identify *s* /s/ and *m* /m/ in words.

Ss	Mm
 six	 man
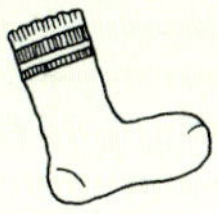 sock	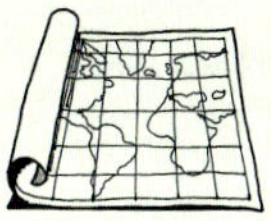 map

Distribute Student Page S135. Have students cut out the picture cards. Pairs put letter cards *Ss* and *Mm* face up and mix the picture cards face down. They select picture cards, say the word for the picture, say the first sound of each word, and match the card to *Ss* or *Mm*.

MONITOR PROGRESS Display the following sentence from Student Page S135. Have students identify each example of s /s/ and m /m/.

Sis can mix the salad, and Mike can make jam.

IF... students cannot identify the letter-sound correspondences,
THEN... review key steps in the routine, and have students practice with other *s* /s/ and *m* /m/ words.

Lesson 21 Connect Sound and Letter: Consonants 1

REMIND STUDENTS THAT …

- they can recognize the letters *t* and *p* and the sounds /t/ and /p/.
- they can connect the letters and sounds *t* /t/ and *p* /p/.
- they can identify *t* /t/ and *p* /p/ in words.

PRACTICE 3 Tell students you will focus on the letters and sounds *t* /t/ and *p* /p/. Follow this routine.

Routine

1. Teach the letters and sounds.	Write capital and lowercase *Tt*. This is the letter *t*. It stands for the sound /t/. Write capital and lowercase *Pp*. This is the letter *p*. Its sound is /p/.
2. Model letter-sound correspondence.	Write the word *ten* and circle the *t*. The word *ten* begins with the letter *t* and the sound /t/. Write the word *pin* and circle the *p*. The word *pin* begins with the letter *p* and the sound /p/.
3. Practice letter-sound correspondence.	Write the words *tan, tip,* and *tub*. Have students circle the letter *t* in each word. What sound is connected with the letter *t* in each word? Write the words *pot, pat,* and *pet*. Have students circle the letter *p* in each word. What sound is connected with the letter *p* in each word?

Tt	Pp
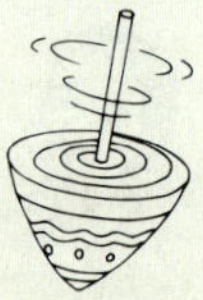 top	 pan
 tiger	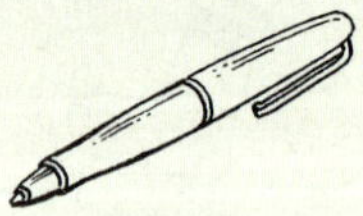 pen

Distribute Student Page S136. Have students cut out the picture cards. Pairs put letter cards *Tt* and *Pp* face up and mix the picture cards face down. They select picture cards, say the word for the picture, say the first sound of each word, and match the card to *Tt* or *Pp*.

☑ **INDEPENDENT PRACTICE** Display the following sentence from Student Page S136. Have individuals identify each example of *t* /t/ and *p* /p/, one at a time.

Ten pet pigs play tag.

IF… students cannot identify the one-to-one letter-sound correspondences, THEN… review key steps in the routine, and have students practice with additional words that contain *t* /t/ and *p* /p/.

Lesson 21 Connect Sound and Letter: Consonants I

Mac and Sam

I have a tiny pup.
His name is Mac.
Mac likes to run for his ball.
I have a tiny cat.
Her name is Sam.
Sam likes to sit on my lap!

Lesson 21 Connect Sound and Letter: Consonants l

Ll	Rr
 leg	 rabbit
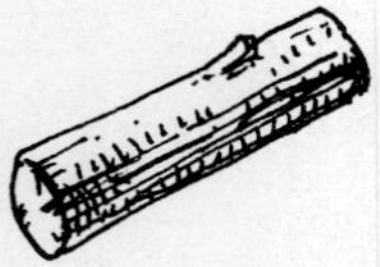 log	 ring

Lions like to roar, and robins like to sing.

Lesson 21 Connect Sound and Letter: Consonants 1

Ss	Mm
 six	 man
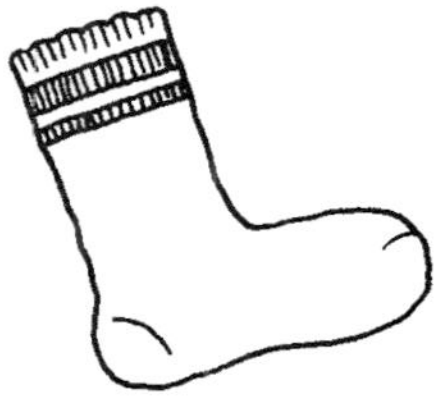 sock	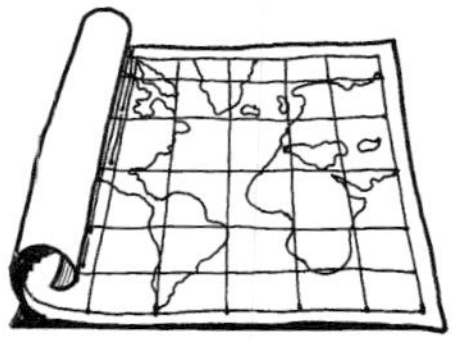 map

Sis can mix the salad, and Mike can make jam.

Lesson 21 Connect Sound and Letter: Consonants I

Tt	Pp
 top	 pan
 tiger	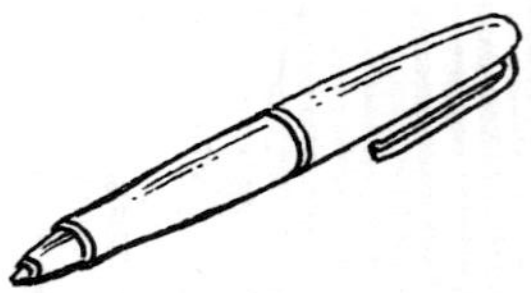 pen

Ten pet pigs play tag.

Lesson 22 Connect Sound and Letter: Consonants 2

INTRODUCE Write the letters *Nn*, say the name *n*, and have students repeat after you. Explain that *n* is a consonant and spells the sound /n/. Point to a student whose name begins with *N*, such as *Nat*. What sound do you hear at the beginning of *Nat?* Write the name *Nat*. In this lesson, we'll connect sounds and consonant letters.

MODEL Display or share copies of the passage "Who Fits in the Car?" from Student Page S137, and read it aloud. Say: The words in this story have the letters and sounds *n* /n/, *b* /b/, *c* /k/, *f* /f/, *d* /d/, and *g* /g/.

Who Fits in the Car?

The dog got in the car.
The duck got in the car.
The goat got in the car.
The fox with the big bag
did not fit in the car!

TEACH Use examples to help students recognize letter-sound correspondences. Say: We read the word *dog*. The first letter in *dog* is *d*. The letter *d* stands for the sound /d/. Point to other words in the story that begin with *d* /d/. Help students identify the words *duck* and *did* as words beginning with *d* /d/. Circle each *d*. Continue the process for *n* /n/, *b* /b/, *c* /k/, *f* /f/, and *g* /g/, circling each letter as you identify it.

OBJECTIVES:

- Recognize letters *n, b, c, f, d, g* and sounds /n/, /b/, /k/, /f/, /d/, /g/.
- Connect letters and sounds *n* /n/, *b* /b/, *c* /k/, *f* /f/, *d* /d/, and *g* /g/.
- Identify *n* /n/, *b* /b/, *c* /k/, *f* /f/, *d* /d/, and *g* /g/in words.

Lesson 22 Connect Sound and Letter: Consonants 2

REMIND STUDENTS THAT ...

- they can recognize the letters *n* and *b* and the sounds /n/ and /b/.
- they can connect the letters and sounds *n* /n/ and *b* /b/.
- they can identify *n* /n/ and *b* /b/ in words.

PRACTICE 1 Follow this routine to teach one-to-one letter-sound correspondences for *n* /n/ and *b* /b/.

Routine

1. Teach the letters and sounds. Write capital and lowercase *Nn*. This is the letter *n*. It stands for the sound /n/. Write capital and lowercase *Bb*. This is the letter *b*. It stands for the sound /b/.

2. Model letter-sound correspondence. Write the word *nap* and circle the *n*. The word *nap* begins with the letter *n* and the sound /n/. Repeat the word *nap* after me. Write the word *bat* and circle the *b*. The word *bat* begins with the letter *b* and the sound /b/. Say the word *bat*.

3. Practice letter-sound correspondence. Write the words *not, nip,* and *net*. Have students circle the letter *n* in each word. What sound is connected with the letter *n* in each word? Write the words *bad, big,* and *bit*. Have students circle the letter *b* in each word. What sound is connected with the letter *b* in each word?

4. Extend practice. Extend practice by having students find examples of the letters *Nn* and *Bb* in words in the titles of classroom books. Have them read the words and identify the sound.

Distribute Student Page S138. Have students cut apart the word cards. Have pairs place the cards face down and take turns picking a card. They identify the first letter of the word, say the sound of the first letter, read the word, and use the word in a sentence.

net	bat	ball
nut	bed	not
bud	nod	nip

MONITOR PROGRESS Display the following sentence from Student Page S138. Have students identify all instances of *n* /n/ and *b* /b/. Then check that students can print each letter.

Ben has the bat, but Ned does not have a ball.

IF... students confuse the letters,
THEN... read the sentence aloud, emphasizing each *b* /b/ and *n* /n/ word. Ask students to identify the first letter. Offer corrective feedback and repeat with other words as needed.

Lesson 22 Connect Sound and Letter: Consonants 2

PRACTICE 2 Follow this routine to teach one-to-one letter-sound correspondences for *c* /k/ and *f* /f/.

Routine

1. Teach the letters and sounds. Write capital and lowercase *Cc*. This is the letter *c*. It stands for the sound /k/. Write capital and lowercase *Ff*. This is the letter *f*. It stands for the sound /f/.

2. Model letter-sound correspondence. Write the word *cat* and circle the *c*. The word *cat* begins with the letter *c* and the sound /k/. Repeat the word *cat* after me. Write the word *fan* and circle the *f*. The word *fan* begins with the letter *f* and the sound /f/. Say the word *fan*.

3. Practice letter-sound correspondence. Write the words *cap*, *car*, and *cab*. Have students circle the letter *c* in each word. What sound is connected with the letter *c* in each word? Write the words *fit*, *fun*, and *fin*. Have students circle the letter *f* in each word. What sound is connected with the letter *f* in each word?

4. Extend practice. Extend practice by having students say the names of objects they see in the room that begin with *c* /k/ and *f* /f/.

Distribute Student Page S139. Have students cut apart the word cards. Have pairs place the cards face down and take turns picking a card. They identify the first letter of the word, say the sound of the first letter, read the word, and use the word in a sentence.

can	fun	fib
cub	cut	fan
fin	fox	cat

MONITOR PROGRESS Display the following sentence from Student Page S139. Have students identify all instances of each of the letters taught. Then check that students can print each letter.

Can you find the cat and fix her food?

IF... students struggle to identify c /k/ and f /f/,
THEN... give students additional words for practice writing these letters. Review the steps of the routine as needed.

REMIND STUDENTS THAT ...

- they can recognize the letters *c* and *f* and the sounds /k/ and /f/.
- they can connect the letters and sounds *c* /k/ and *f* /f/.
- they can identify *c* /k/ and *f* /f/ in words.

Lesson 22 Connect Sound and Letter: Consonants 2

REMIND STUDENTS THAT ...

- they can recognize the letters *d* and *g* and the sounds /d/ and /g/.
- they can connect the letters and sounds *d* /d/ and *g* /g/.
- they can identify *d* /d/ and *g* /g/ in words.

PRACTICE 3 Follow this routine to teach one-to-one letter-sound correspondences for *d* /d/ and *g* /g/.

Routine

1. Teach the letters and sounds. Write capital and lowercase *Dd*. This is the letter *d*. It stands for the sound /d/. Write capital and lowercase *Gg*. This is the letter *g*. It stands for the sound /g/.

2. Model letter-sound correspondence. Write the word *dip* and circle the *d*. The word *dip* begins with the letter *d* and the sound /d/. Write the word *gab* and circle the *g*. The word *gab* begins with the letter *g* and the sound /g/.

3. Practice letter-sound correspondence. Write the words *did, dot,* and *dog*. Have students circle the letter *d* in each word. What sound is connected with the letter *d* in each word? Write the words *got, get,* and *gas*. Have students circle the letter *g* in each word. What sound is connected with the letter *g* in each word?

4. Extend practice. Have students write the letters *Dd* and *Gg* on sticky notes. Ask them to find an object in the classroom that begins with *d*/d/ and put the *Dd* sticky note on it. Have them repeat the process with the *Gg* sticky note.

Distribute Student Page S140. Have students cut apart the word cards. Have pairs place the cards face down and take turns picking a card. They identify the first letter of the word, say the sound of the first letter, read the word, and use the word in a sentence.

dad	good	dot
dim	gag	gap
Don	gave	duck

INDEPENDENT PRACTICE Display the following sentence from Student Page S140. Have individuals identify all instances of *d* /d/ and *g* /g/.

Gram gave Dot a doll for a gift.

IF... students struggle to identify the words with *d* /d/ and *g* /g/,
THEN... give students additional words beginning with *d* /d/ and *g* /g/ to practice writing the letters. Review the steps of the routine as needed.

Lesson 22 Connect Sound and Letter: Consonants 2

Who Fits in the Car?

The dog got in the car.
The duck got in the car.
The goat got in the car.
The fox with the big bag
did not fit in the car!

Lesson 22 Connect Sound and Letter: Consonants 2

net	bat	ball
nut	bed	not
bud	nod	nip

Ben has the bat, but Ned does not have a ball.

Lesson 22 Connect Sound and Letter: Consonants 2

can	fun	fib
cub	cut	fan
fin	fox	cat

Can you find the cat and fix her food?

Lesson 22 Connect Sound and Letter: Consonants 2

dad	good	dot
dim	gag	gap
Don	gave	duck

Gram gave Dot a doll for a gift.

Lesson 23 Connect Sound and Letter: Consonants 3

INTRODUCE Write the letters *Hh* and say the name *(h)*. Explain that *h* is a consonant and spells the sound /h/. Ask students to hold up a hand. The word *hand* begins with the letter *h* and the sound /h/. Write or display the word *hand*. In this lesson, we'll learn to connect more sounds and consonant letters.

MODEL Display or share copies of the passage "Can You Do It?" from Student Page S141, and read it aloud. The words in this passage have the letters and sounds *h* /h/, *v* /v/, *k* /k/, *j* /j/, *z* /z/, *w* /w/, *y* /y/, *q* /kw/ and *x* /ks/.

Can You Do It?

Can you hug a hippo?
Can you kiss a zebra?
Can you jog with an ox to the vet?
Yes, I can!
I am the queen!

TEACH Use examples to help students recognize letter-sound correspondences. We read the word *hug*. The first letter in *hug* is *h*. The letter *h* stands for the sound /h/. Do the words *hug* and *hippo* begin with the same sound or different sounds? Circle each *h*. Continue the process until you have identified the relevant letter and sound in each of the following words: *you, kiss, zebra, jog, with, ox, vet, Yes,* and *queen*. Explain to students that the letter *x* and sound /ks/ usually come at the end of the word.

OBJECTIVES:

- Recognize letters *h, v, k, j, z, w, y, q, x* and sounds /h/, /v/, /k/, /j/, /z/, /w/, /y/, /kw/, /ks/.
- Connect letters and sounds *h* /h/, *v* /v/, *k* /k/, *j* /j/, *z* /z/, *w* /w/, *y* /y/, *q* /kw/, and *x* /ks/.
- Identify *h* /h/, *v* /v/, *k* /k/, *j* /j/, *z* /z/, *w* /w/, *y* /y/, *q* /kw/, and *x* /ks/ in words.

Lesson 23 Connect Sound and Letter: Consonants 3

REMIND STUDENTS THAT ...

- they can recognize the letters *h*, *v*, and *k* and the sounds /h/, /v/, and /k/.
- they can connect the letters and sounds *h* /h/, *v* /v/, and *k* /k/.
- they can identify *h* /h/, *v* /v/, and *k* /k/ in words.

PRACTICE I Follow this routine to teach one-to-one letter-sound correspondences for *h* /h/, *v* /v/, and *k* /k/.

Routine

1. Teach the letters and sounds. Write capital and lowercase *Hh*. This is the letter *h*. It stands for the sound /h/. Repeat for *Vv* and *Kk*.

2. Model letter-sound correspondence. Write the word *hid* and circle the *h*. The word *hid* begins with the letter *h* and the sound /h/. Say the word *hid* after me. Repeat the process with the words *van* and *kit*.

3. Practice letter-sound correspondence. Write the words *hip*, *hat*, and *him*. Have students circle the letter *h* in each word. What sound is connected with the letter *h* in each word? Write the words *vent*, *vest*, *kid*, and *Kim*. Have students circle the letters *v*, *k*, and *K* and identify the sounds /v/ and /k/.

4. Extend practice. Have students write the letters *h*, *v*, and *k* and one example of a word that begins with each letter. They can use words from the lists in steps 2 and 3.

Distribute Student Page S142. Have students cut apart the word cards. Pairs place the cards face down and take turns selecting a card. They identify the first letter of the word, say the sound of the first letter, read the word, and then use it in a sentence.

hop	kid	vet
vent	kit	her
ham	hum	hid
hat	kind	van

MONITOR PROGRESS Display the following sentence from Student Page S142. Have students identify all instances of *h* /h/, *v* /v/, and *k* /k/. Then check that students can print each letter.

Kit has a helmet, and Kim has a vest.

IF... students struggle with the words,
THEN... help them find additional words with those letters in signs or posters in the room. Review steps from the routine as needed.

Lesson 23 Connect Sound and Letter: Consonants 3

PRACTICE 2 Follow this routine to teach one-to-one letter-sound correspondences for *j* /j/, *z* /z/, and *w* /w/.

Routine

1. Teach the letters and sounds. Write capital and lowercase *Jj*. This is the letter *j*. It stands for the sound /j/. Repeat for *Zz* and *Ww*.

2. Model letter-sound correspondence. Write the word *jam* and circle the *j*. The word *jam* begins with the letter *j* and the sound /j/. Say the word *jam* after me. Repeat the process with the words *zip* and *win*.

3. Practice letter-sound correspondence. Write the words *jet, jog,* and *job*. Have students circle the letter *j* in each word. What sound is connected with the letter *j* in each word? Write the words *zap, zoo, was,* and *web*. Have students circle the letters z and *w* and identify the sounds /z/ and /w/.

4. Extend practice. Have students write *j, z,* and *w* and say a word that begins with each letter. Ask them to use the word in a sentence.

Distribute Student Page S143. Have students cut apart the word cards. Pairs place the cards face down and take turns selecting a card. They identify the first letter of the word, say the sound of the first letter, read the word, and then use it in a sentence.

Zak	jot	jet
wed	will	zap
wig	jar	Jon
zest	were	went

REMIND STUDENTS THAT …

- they can recognize the letters *j, z,* and *w* and the sounds /j/, /z/, and /w/.
- they can connect the letters and sounds *j* /j/, z /z/, and *w* /w/.
- they can identify *j* /j/, z /z/, and *w* /w/ in words.

☑ **MONITOR PROGRESS** Display the following sentence from Student Page S143. Have students identify all instances of *j* /j/, z /z/, and *w* /w/. Then check that students can print each letter.

We just went to the zoo to see the baby zebra.

IF… students struggle with the words,
THEN… help them hunt for additional words with these letters in classroom books. Review steps from the routine as needed.

Lesson 23 Connect Sound and Letter: Consonants 3

REMIND STUDENTS THAT ...

- they can recognize the letters *y*, *q*, and *x* and the sounds /y/, /kw/, and /ks/.
- they can connect the letters and sounds *y* /y/, *q* /kw/, and *x* /ks/.
- they can identify *y* /y/, *q* /kw/, and *x* /ks/ in words.

PRACTICE 3 Follow this routine to teach one-to-one letter-sound correspondences for *y* /y/, *q* /kw/, and *x* /ks/.

Routine

1. Teach the letters and sounds. Write capital and lowercase *Yy*. This is the letter *y*. It stands for the sound /y/. Repeat for *Qq* and *Xx*.

2. Model letter-sound correspondence. Write the word *yet* and circle the *y*. The word *yet* begins with the letter *y* and the sound /y/. Say the word *yet* after me. Repeat the process with the words *quiz* and *fix*.

3. Practice letter-sound correspondence. Write the words *yum, yap,* and *yes*. Have students circle the letter *y* in each word. What sound is connected with the letter *y* in each word? Write the words *quit, queen, ax,* and *ox*. Have students circle the letters *q* and *x* in each word. What sounds are connected with the letters *q* and *x*?

4. Extend practice. Have students write *y, q,* and *x* and say a word that begins with each letter. Have them write a word for each letter using the lists in steps 2 and 3.

Distribute Student Page S144. Have students cut apart the word cards. Pairs place the cards face down and take turns selecting a card, reading the word, and using it in a sentence. Point out that *x* /ks/ is at the end of a word in this lesson.

quit	wax	fox
yes	Max	you
yank	fix	yellow
quick	mix	quiet

☑ **INDEPENDENT PRACTICE** Display the following sentence from Student Page S144. Have students identify all instances of *y* /y/, *q* /kw/, and *x* /ks/. Then check that students can print each letter.

The fox gave the queen a yard of yellow yarn.

IF... students struggle with the words,
THEN... guide them as they look for additional words with these letters in classroom books. Review steps from the routine as needed.

Can You Do It?

Can you hug a hippo?
Can you kiss a zebra?
Can you jog with an ox to the vet?
Yes, I can!
I am the queen!

Lesson 23 Connect Sound and Letter: Consonants 3

hop	kid	vet
vent	kit	her
ham	hum	hid
hat	kind	van

Kit has a helmet, and Kim has a vest.

Lesson 23 Connect Sound and Letter: Consonants 3

Zak	jot	jet
wed	will	zap
wig	jar	Jon
zest	were	went

We just went to the zoo to see the baby zebra.

Lesson 23 Connect Sound and Letter: Consonants 3

quit	wax	fox
yes	Max	you
yank	fix	yellow
quick	mix	quiet

The fox gave the queen a yard of yellow yarn.

Lesson 24 Spelling: Soft Consonant Sounds

INTRODUCE Explain that some sounds can be spelled in more than one way. This lesson focuses on new spellings for the sounds /s/, /j/, and /z/.

MODEL Display or share copies of the following passage, "At the Circus," from Student Page S145, and read it aloud. The words in this passage have some sounds we know but with different spellings for the sounds.

At the Circus

He has a big, red nose.
He wears a hat with a rose.
You see him in the center of a big ring.
When he walks on tall poles, he is a giant.
Can you say who he is?

TEACH Connect to previously learned sound-spellings. Write *see* and *say*. What do you know about reading these words? Elicit from students that both begin with /s/ spelled *s*. Repeat /s/ with me: /s/. Today you will learn how to spell and read words with /s/ spelled *c*. Write the word *center*. This is the word *center*. What is the first letter? How do you say the sound? Help students recognize that the first letter is *c* but the sound is /s/. You will also learn how to read words with /j/ spelled *g* as in *giant* and /z/ spelled *s* as in *nose*, *rose*, *poles*, and *is*.

OBJECTIVES:

- Recognize multiple sounds of consonants.
- Connect letters and sounds *c* /s/, *g* /j/, *s* /z/.
- Identify *c* /s/, *g* /j/, *s* /z/ in words.

Lesson 24 Spelling: Soft Consonant Sounds

REMIND STUDENTS THAT ...

- they can recognize multiple sounds of consonants.
- they can connect letters and sounds s /s/ and c /s/.
- they can identify s /s/ and c /s/ in words.

PRACTICE 1 Use this routine to help students connect /s/ with *c*.

Routine

1. Connect sound to spelling. Remind students that some sounds can be spelled in more than one way. The letter *c* can stand for /s/.

2. Model. Write and say *cell.* What is the first sound in this word? Students should respond with /s/. In this word, the sound /s/ is spelled with *c*. The *c* is followed by *e*. Point to *c* and have students say /s/. Now let's read this word together: /s//e//l/.

3. Guide practice. Have students identify the first letter in *cent, celery,* and *circus.* What sound do you hear for the letter *c* in *cent* and *celery?* What sound do you hear for the first letter *c* in *circus?* Point to the second *c* in *circus.* What sound do you hear for this letter *c* in *circus?*

4. Extend practice. Write and say *cider, candle, certain, circle, cubby,* and *cereal.* Have students say each word and identify the sound of each *c* as /s/ or /k/.

Have students cut apart the word cards from Student Page S146 and sort them into two piles: one with words with the sound /s/ spelled *c*, the other with words with the sound /k/ spelled *c*.

cent	cup	cell	circle
cat	cabin	cement	city

☑ **MONITOR PROGRESS** Display the following word pairs from Student Page S146 and read them aloud. Have students read the words and then ask individuals to identify the word in the pair with the sound /s/ spelled *c*.

cat, city	cupcake, cement	center, color

IF... students struggle to identify the word with the sound /s/ spelled *c*,
THEN... provide additional word pairs for practice and review the routine.

Lesson 24 Spelling: Soft Consonant Sounds

PRACTICE 2 Use this routine to help students connect /j/ with *g*.

Routine

1. Connect sound to spelling. Remind students that some sounds can be spelled in more than one way. The letter *g* can stand for /j/.

2. Model. Write and say *jet* and *June*. What are the first sound and letter in these words? (/j/ and *j*). Write and say *gem*. In this word, the sound /j/ is spelled with *g*. Point to *g* and have students say /j/. Blend the word with students.

3. Guide practice. Write and say *germ* and *giant*. Have students say the words and identify the first letter in each one. What sound do you hear for the letter *g* in each word?

4. Extend practice. Write and say *giraffe, garden, gas, ginger, gerbil,* and *gorilla*. Have students say each word and identify the sound of each *g* as /g/ or /j/.

Have students cut apart the word cards from Student Page S147 and sort them into two piles: one with words with the sound /j/ spelled *g*, the other with words with the sound /g/ spelled *g*.

gem	grass	gerbil	giraffe
gum	glad	gentle	germ

REMIND STUDENTS THAT …

- they can recognize multiple sounds of consonants.
- they can connect letters and sounds *g* /g/ and *g* /j/.
- they can identify *g* /g/ and *g* /j/ in words.

MONITOR PROGRESS Display the following word pairs from Student Page S147 and read them aloud. Have students read the words and then ask individuals to identify the word in the pair with the sound /j/ spelled *g*.

gentle, gallon   gap, gym   Gene, girl

IF… students struggle to identify the word with the sound /j/ spelled *g*,
THEN… provide additional word pairs for practice and review the routine.

Lesson 24 Spelling: Soft Consonant Sounds

REMIND STUDENTS THAT ...

- they can recognize multiple sounds of consonants.
- they can connect letters and sounds s /s/ and s /z/.
- they can identify s /s/ and s /z/ in words.

PRACTICE 3 Use this routine to help students connect /z/ with s.

Routine

1. Connect sound to spelling. Remind students that some sounds can be spelled in more than one way. The letter s can stand for /z/.

2. Model. Write and say *his*. Let's read this word together: /h//i//z/. Where do you hear the sound /z/ in *his*? Students should say they hear /z/ at the end. The sound /z/ is sometimes spelled with s. When s has the sound /z/, it is often at the end of the word.

3. Guide practice. Write and say *has, is,* and *dogs*. Have students repeat the words and identify the sound at the end of each one.

4. Extend practice. Write and say *these, dress,* and *bells*. Have students identify the sound of each s as /s/ or /z/.

Have students cut apart the word cards from Student Page S148 and sort them into two piles: words with the sound /s/ spelled s and words with the sound /z/ spelled s.

is	less	frogs
grows	this	us

INDEPENDENT PRACTICE Display the following word pairs from Student Page S148 and read them aloud. Have students read the words and then ask individuals to identify the word in the pair with the sound /z/ spelled s.

plays, books	bus, as	miss, rose

IF... students cannot identify words with /s/ and /z/ spelled s,
THEN... provide additional examples for practice and review the routine.

Lesson 24 **Spelling: Soft Consonant Sounds**

At the Circus

He has a big, red nose.
He wears a hat with a rose.
You see him in the center of a big ring.
When he walks on tall poles, he is a giant.
Can you say who he is?

Lesson 24 Spelling: Soft Consonant Sounds

cent	cup	cell	circle
cat	cabin	cement	city

cat, city cupcake, cement center, color

Lesson 24

Spelling: Soft Consonant Sounds

gem	grass	gerbil	giraffe
gum	glad	gentle	germ

gentle, gallon	gap, gym	Gene, girl

Lesson 24 Spelling: Soft Consonant Sounds

is	less	frogs
grows	this	us

plays, books	bus, as	miss, rose

ASSESSMENT LESSONS 21–24 Phonics, Morphology, and Spelling

ASSESS MASTERY Use this Checkpoint to assess students' mastery of one-to-one letter-sound correspondences for consonants.

ADMINISTER THE TEST Administer the Checkpoint orally to each student. Give each student a copy of the next page. Have students listen as you read each sentence aloud, and then have them circle each letter you name. Then have students say the sound each letter represents. For example, if students circle *r* and *l* in *real,* they should then say /r/ and /l/.

Print the next page for students.

1. Connect Sound and Letter: Consonants 1 (Lesson 21)
Circle each of these letters in the sentence: *l, r, s, m, t, p.*

2. Connect Sound and Letter: Consonants 2 (Lesson 22)
Circle each of these letters in the sentence: *n, b, c, f, d, g.*

3. Connect Sound and Letter: Consonants 3 (Lesson 23)
Circle each of these letters in the sentence: *h, v, k, j, z, w, y, q, x.*

4. Spelling: Soft Consonant Sounds (Lesson 24)
Circle each of these letters in the sentence: *c* that sounds like /s/, *g* that sounds like /j/, *s* that sounds like /z/.

SCORING

SKILL/LESSON	SCORE
1. Connect Sound and Letter: Consonants 1 (Lesson 21) Tim tasted a ripe lemon slice.	_____ / 11
2. Connect Sound and Letter: Consonants 2 (Lesson 22) A bug crawled out from the bin.	_____ / 7
3. Connect Sound and Letter: Consonants 3 (Lesson 23) Max likes the zoo with yellow wasps just hovering above a quilt.	_____ / 12
4. Spelling: Soft Consonant Sounds (Lesson 24) The giraffe put ice cubes in those glasses.	_____ / 5

An overall score of 80% correct is typically considered mastery. Use your judgment and your individual students' needs as well to determine skill mastery.

IF… students score below the benchmark,
THEN… review those discrete letters and sounds, going back to the lessons to reteach and scaffold as needed.

ASSESSMENT
LESSONS 21–24

Phonics, Morphology, and Spelling

1. **Tim tasted a ripe lemon slice.**
2. **A bug crawled out from the bin.**
3. **Max likes the zoo with yellow wasps just hovering above a quilt.**
4. **The giraffe put ice cubes in those glasses.**

Lesson 25 Short *a*

INTRODUCE Remind students that words are made up of consonant and vowel sounds. You learned that /ă/ is spelled with the letter *a*, and you learned how to blend letters to read words with this sound. Today we will learn another way to read words with the short *a* sound.

MODEL Display or share copies of the following passage, "Pat and Sam," from Student Page S151, and read it aloud.

Pat and Sam

Pat's pal is Sam.
He is in her class.
Pat and Sam have lunch.
Sam eats jam.
Pat eats ham.

ends with *-al*

ends with *-am*

ends with *-at*

TEACH Point to the word *pal* in the first line. The word *pal* has a consonant, then a vowel, and then another consonant. Each letter has its own sound. Point to the word *Pat* in the third sentence. Changing a letter in a word makes a new word. When the *l* in *pal* is changed to a *t*, the word *pal* becomes *Pat*.

Point out the words with the short *a* sound. Explain that students can read more words when they learn how to recognize letter combinations that include a short *a*. *Jam* and *ham* both have a short *a* sound and end with *-am*. Now that I know *-am* has a short *a* sound, I can use this letter combination to make new words. When I change, add, or delete a letter, I make a new word. Reinforce this idea by pointing out other words in the model that have the short *a* sound, such as *pal*, *Pat*, and *Sam*.

Now point to the *-at* letter combination at the end of *Pat*. Now that I know what the letters *at* sound like, when I hear a word that ends with those sounds, I can spell the word. The word *hat* ends with the sounds /ă/ and /t/. I can write the letter combination *-at*. The word starts with the sound /h/. I know the letter *h* makes the /h/ sound. I can add the letter *h* to the beginning of *-at* to make *hat*. Work through other examples, such as *cat*, *at*, and *sat* by changing, adding, and deleting letters.

OBJECTIVES:

- Read words with the short *a* sound.
- Form words using the short *a* sound.
- Change, add, and delete sounds to make new words.
- Spell VC, CVC, and CCVC words.

Lesson 25 Short *a*

REMIND STUDENTS THAT ...

- they can recognize the short *a* sound.
- they can read words with the short *a* sound.
- they can make new words using *-at* and *-am* by changing, adding, and deleting letters.
- they can spell words using familiar letter combinations.

PRACTICE I Remind students that one way to read words is to break them into word parts and read the parts one after the other. Use the following routine to guide students as they identify words with the short *a* sound.

Routine

1. Connect. Write and say *mat.* This is a word you know. Let's read it together. Knowing how to read *-at* can help you read many words with this word part.

2. Model and give examples. Read *mat* aloud again: *mat.* Have students say *-at* with you several times. *Mat* is one of many words with the word part *-at.* Help students think of other words that use *-at,* such as *cat, rat,* and *flat.*

3. Model blending. Write *at* and slowly blend it several times with students. Then write *m* at the beginning. Cover the word part *-at* and point to *m.* Say *m* aloud: /m/. Then cover *m* and read the word part *-at* aloud: *at.* Now look at the word part that comes before the vowel. The two parts are *m* and *-at.* Let's read together: *m, at, mat.* Delete *m* and add *c,* and blend the word with students. Repeat with *rat* and *flat,* changing and adding letters as you go. Point out that *flat* has a consonant, consonant, vowel, consonant pattern.

4. Model spelling. Say *bat* slowly several times. I hear the letter combination *-at* at the end of the word. Write *at.* Model sounding out the beginning sound and write *b.* Have students blend the word with you.

Repeat this routine with the word part *-am.*

	at		am

Display the Elkonin boxes from Student Page S152 and have students use them to spell and blend words. If needed, offer letters such as *b, h,* and *p.*

☑ **MONITOR PROGRESS** Display the following sentence from Student Page S152. Have students identify and blend the short *a* words with the *-at* and *-am* letter combinations.

Pam has a red hat.

IF... students incorrectly blend words with the short *a* sound,
THEN... offer corrective feedback by showing the words one letter at a time and blending them with students.

Lesson 25 Short *a*

PRACTICE 2 Use the following routine to guide students as they identify words with the short *a* sound. Point out that students will focus on words that have the *-ad* or *-ag* word part.

Routine

1. Connect.	Write and say *sad*. This is a word you know. Let's read it together. Knowing how to read *-ad* can help you read many words with this word part.
2. Model and give examples.	Read *sad* aloud again: *sad*. Have students say *-ad* with you several times. *Sad* is one of many words with the word part *-ad*. Help students think of other words that use *-ad*, such as *bad, mad,* and *glad*.
3. Model blending.	Write *ad* and slowly blend it several times with students. Then write *s* at the beginning. Cover the word part *-ad* and point to *s*. Say *s* aloud: /s/. Then cover *s* and read the word part *-ad* aloud: *ad*. Now look at the word part that comes before the vowel. The two parts are *s* and *-ad*. Let's read together: *s, ad, sad*. Delete *s* and add *b*, and blend the word with students. Repeat with *mad* and *glad*, changing and adding letters as you go. Point out that *glad* has a consonant, consonant, vowel, consonant pattern.
4. Model spelling.	Say *dad* slowly several times. I hear the letter combination *-ad* at the end of the word. Write *ad*. Model sounding out the beginning sound and write *d*. Have students blend the word with you.

Repeat this routine with the word part *-ag*.

	ad		ag

Display the Elkonin boxes from Student Page S153 and have students use them to spell and blend words. If needed, offer letters such as *h, p,* and *t*. Then have students use one or two of the words in their own oral sentences.

REMIND STUDENTS THAT . . .

- they can recognize the short *a* sound.
- they can read words with the short *a* sound.
- they can make new words using *-ad* and *-ag* by changing, adding, and deleting letters.
- they can spell words using familiar letter combinations.

MONITOR PROGRESS Display the following sentence from Student Page S153. Have students identify and blend the words with the short *a* sound.

The bat had a tag.

IF... students incorrectly blend words with the short *a* sound,
THEN... offer corrective feedback by showing the words one letter at a time and blending them with students.

Lesson 25 Short *a*

REMIND STUDENTS THAT …

- they can recognize the short *a* sound.
- they can read words with the short *a* sound.
- they can make new words using *-ab*, *-an*, and *-ap* by changing, adding, and deleting letters.
- they can spell words using familiar letter combinations.

PRACTICE 3 Use the following routine to guide students as they identify words with the short *a* sound and word parts *-ab*, *-an*, or *-ap*.

Routine

1. Connect. Write and say *cab.* This is a word you know. Let's read it together. Knowing how to read *-ab* can help you read many words with this word part.

2. Model and give examples. Read *cab* aloud again: *cab.* Have students say *-ab* with you several times. *Cab* is one of many words with the word part *-ab.* Help students think of other words that use *-ab*, such as *lab, tab,* and *grab*.

3. Model blending. Write *ab* and slowly blend it several times with students. Then write *c* at the beginning. Cover the word part *-ab* and point to *c*. Say *c* aloud: /k/. Then cover *c* and read the word part *-ab* aloud: *ab.* Now look at the word part that comes before the vowel. The two parts are *c* and *-ab.* Let's read together: *c, ab, cab.* Delete *c* and add *l*, and blend the word with students. Repeat with *tab* and *grab*, changing and adding letters as you go. Point out that *grab* has a consonant, consonant, vowel, consonant pattern.

4. Model spelling. Say *jab* slowly several times. I hear the letter combination *-ab* at the end of the word. Write *ab*. Model sounding out the beginning sounds and write *j*. Have students blend the word with you.

Repeat this routine with the word parts *-an* and *-ap*.

	ab		an
	ap		

Display the Elkonin boxes from Student Page S154 and have students use them to spell and blend words. If needed, offer letters such as *c, m, n,* and *t*. Then have students use at least two of the words in their own oral sentences.

☑ **INDEPENDENT PRACTICE** Display the following sentence from Student Page S154. Have students blend the words with the short *a* sound.

The cat sat on the man's cap.

IF… students incorrectly blend words with the short *a* sound,
THEN… offer corrective feedback by showing the words one letter at a time and blending them with students.

Lesson 25 **Short *a***

Pat and Sam

ends with *-al*

Pat's pal is Sam.
He is in her class.
Pat and Sam have lunch.
Sam eats jam.
Pat eats ham.

ends with *-am*

ends with *-at*

Lesson 25 **Short *a***

	at		am

Pam has a red hat.

Lesson 25 **Short *a***

	ad		ag

The bat had a tag.

Lesson 25 **Short *a***

	ab		an
	ap		

The cat sat on the man's cap.

Lesson 26 Short *i*

OBJECTIVES:

- Read words with the short *i* sound.
- Form words using the short *i* sound.
- Change, add, and delete sounds to make new words.
- Spell VC, CVC, and CCVC words.

INTRODUCE Emphasize that words are made up of consonant and vowel sounds. You learned that /ĭ/ is spelled with the letter *i*, and you learned how to blend letters to read words with this sound. Today we will learn another way to read words with the short *i* sound.

MODEL Display or share copies of the following passage, "Sid Did," from Student Page S155, and read it aloud.

Sid Did

Did Sid see a pig?
Sid did.
Did Sid see a big cat?
Sid did.
Did Sid see a kid?
Sid did.

ends with *-id*

ends with *-ig*

TEACH Point to *Did* in the first line. The word *did* has a consonant, then a vowel, and then another consonant. Each letter has its own sound. Point to the word *Sid*. Changing a letter in a word makes a new word. When the first *d* in *did* is changed to an *s*, the word *did* becomes *Sid*.

Point out the words with the short *i* sound. Explain that students can read more words when they learn how to recognize letter combinations that include a short *i*. *Sid* and *did* both have a short *i* sound and end with *-id*. Now that I know that *-id* has a short *i* sound, I can use this letter combination to make new words. When I change, add, or delete a letter, I make a new word. Reinforce this idea by pointing out other words in the model that have the short *i* sound, such as *big* and *kid*.

Now point to the *-ig* letter combination at the end of *pig* in the first sentence. Say: Now that I know what the letters *-ig* sound like, when I hear a word that ends with those sounds, I can spell the word. The word *dig* ends with the sounds /ĭ/ and /g/. I can write the letter combination *-ig*. The word starts with the sound /d/. I know the letter *d* makes the /d/ sound. I can add the letter *d* to the beginning of *-ig*. Work through other examples, such as *fig*, *wig*, and *zig* by changing, adding, and deleting letters.

Lesson 26 Short *i*

REMIND STUDENTS THAT ...

- they can recognize the short *i* sound.
- they can read words with the short *i* sound.
- they can make new words using *-ig* and *-it* by changing, adding, and deleting letters.
- they can spell words using familiar letter combinations.

PRACTICE 1 Remind students that one way to read words is to break them into word parts and read the parts one after the other. Use the following routine to guide students as they identify words with the short *i* sound.

Routine

1. Connect. Write and say *sit*. This is a word you know. Let's read it together. Knowing how to read *-it* can help you read many words with this word part.

2. Model and give examples. Read *sit* aloud again: *sit*. Have students say *-it* with you several times. *Sit* is one of many words with the word part *-it*. Help students think of other words that use *-it*, such as *bit*, *kit*, and *fit*.

3. Model blending. Write *it* and slowly blend it several times with students. Then write *s* at the beginning. Cover the word part *-it* and point to *s*. Say *s* aloud: /s/. Then cover *s* and read the word part *-it* aloud: *it*. Now look at the word part that comes before the vowel. The two parts are *s* and *-it*. Let's read together: *s*, *it*, *sit*. Delete *s* and add *b*, and blend the word with students. Repeat with *kit*, *it*, and *fit*, changing, deleting, and adding letters as you go.

4. Model spelling. Say *pit* slowly several times. I hear the letter combination *-it* at the end of the word. Write *it*. Model sounding out the beginning sound and write *p*. Have students blend the word with you.

Repeat this routine with the word part *-ig*.

	it		ig

Display the Elkonin boxes from Student Page S156 and have students use them to spell and blend words. If needed, offer letters such as *b* and *p*.

✓ MONITOR PROGRESS Have students read the following words from Student Page S156. Then have them make two new words: one with *-it* and one with *-ig*.

bit	lit	hit	___
rig	gig	dig	___

IF... students misread or misspell a word,
THEN... guide them to identify the letters and sounds in the word. Then have them blend or spell the word with you and independently.

Lesson 26 Short *i*

PRACTICE 2 Use the following routine to guide students as they identify words with the short *i* sound. Point out that students will focus on words that have the *-in* or *-ip* word part.

Routine

1. Connect. Write and say *pin*. This is a word you know. Let's read it together. Knowing how to read *-in* can help you read many words with this word part.

2. Model and give examples. Read *pin* aloud again: *pin*. Have students say *-in* with you several times. *Pin* is one of many words with the word part *-in*. Help students think of other words that use *-in*, such as *tin*, *fin*, and *win*.

3. Model blending. Write *in* and slowly blend it several times with students. Then write *p* at the beginning. Cover the word part *-in* and point to *p*. Say *p* aloud: /p/. Then cover *p* and read the word part *-in* aloud: *in*. Now look at the word part that comes before the vowel. The two parts are *p* and *-in*. Let's read it together: *p*, *in*, *pin*. Delete *p* and add *t*, and blend the word with students. Repeat with *fin*, *in*, and *win*, changing, deleting, and adding letters as you go.

4. Model spelling. Say *tin* slowly several times. I hear the letter combination *-in* at the end of the word. Write *in*. Model sounding out the beginning sound and write *t*. Have students blend the word with you.

Repeat this routine with the word part *-ip*.

	in		ip

Display the Elkonin boxes from Student Page S157 and have students use them to spell and blend words. If needed, offer letters such as *z*, *l*, and *t*. Then have students use one or two of the words in their own oral sentences.

REMIND STUDENTS THAT ...

- they can recognize the short *i* sound.
- they can read words with the short *i* sound.
- they can make new words using *-in* and *-ip* by changing, adding, and deleting letters.
- they can spell words using familiar letter combinations.

☑ **MONITOR PROGRESS** Have students read the following words from Student Page S157. Then have them make two new words: one with *-in* and one with *-ip*.

bin	tin	win	___
lip	rip	dip	___

IF… students misread or misspell a word,
THEN…guide them as they sound out the word. Then have them blend or spell the word with you and independently.

Lesson 26 Short *i*

REMIND STUDENTS THAT ...

- they can recognize the short *i* sound.
- they can read words with the short *i* sound.
- they can make new words using *-ib*, *-im*, and *-is* by changing, adding, and deleting letters.
- they can spell words using familiar letter combinations.

PRACTICE 3 Use the following routine to guide students as they identify words with the short *i* sound and word parts *-ib*, *-im*, or *-is*.

Routine

1. Connect. Write and say *him*. This is a word you know. Let's read it together. Knowing how to read *-im* can help you read many words with this word part.

2. Model and give examples. Read *him* aloud again: *him*. Have students say *-im* with you several times. *Him* is one of many words with the word part *-im*. Help students think of other words that use *-im*, such as *dim*, *Jim*, and *rim*.

3. Model blending. Write *im* and slowly blend it several times with students. Then write *h* at the beginning. Cover the word part *-im* and point to *h*. Say *h* aloud: /h/. Then cover *h* and read the word part *-im* aloud: *im*. Now look at the word part that comes before the vowel. The two parts are *h* and *-im*. Let's read together: *h*, *im*, *him*. Delete *h* and add *d*, and blend the word with students. Repeat with *Jim*, *rim*, and *trim*, changing and adding letters as you go. Point out that *trim* has a consonant, consonant, vowel, consonant pattern.

4. Model spelling. Say *slim* slowly several times. I hear the letter combination *-im* at the end of *slim*. Write *im*. Model sounding out the beginning sounds and write *sl*. Have students blend the word with you.

Repeat this routine with the word parts *-ib* and *-is*.

	ib		im
	is		

Display the Elkonin boxes from Student Page S158 and have students use them to spell and blend words. If needed, offer letters such as *b*, *h*, and *t*. Then have students use at least two of the words in their own oral sentences.

☑ **INDEPENDENT PRACTICE** Display the following sentences from Student Page S158. Have students blend the words with the short *i* sound.

> Jim and Kim have a bin.
> It is big.

IF... students incorrectly blend words with the short *i* sound,
THEN... offer corrective feedback by showing the words one letter at a time and blending them with students.

Lesson 26 **Short *i***

Sid Did

Did Sid see a pig?
Sid did.
Did Sid see a big cat?
Sid did.
Did Sid see a kid?
Sid did.

ends with *-id*

ends with *-ig*

Lesson 26 **Short *i***

	it		ig

bit	lit	hit	____
rig	gig	dig	____

Lesson 26 **Short *i***

	in		ip

bin	tin	win	______
lip	rip	dip	______

Lesson 26 **Short *i***

	ib		im
	is		

Jim and Kim have a bin.

It is big.

ASSESSMENT
LESSONS 25–26

Phonics, Morphology, and Spelling

ASSESS MASTERY Use this Checkpoint to assess students' mastery of the short *a* sound and the short *i* sound.

ADMINISTER THE TEST Administer the Checkpoint orally to each student. For each item, model the process as described, and then have the student use the process to respond to your prompts. Record responses on the scoring chart on the next page.

1. Short *a* (Lesson 25)
MODEL: I will display two words that have the short *a* sound. You will read them to me and tell me what short *a* word part is in both words. For example, I see the words *bad* and *mad*. When I read them, I can hear that the short *a* word part is *-ad*.

ASSESS:	jam, ham	cat, rat	bag, tag

2. Short *a* (Lesson 25)
MODEL: I will display two words that have the short *a* sound and you will make a word that has the same short *a* word part. For example, I read the words *pat* and *hat*. I can see that the short *a* word part is *-at*. I can use this word part to make the word *mat*.

ASSESS:	ban, pan, ___	tab, lab, ___	map, cap, ___

3. Short *i* (Lesson 26)
MODEL: I will display two words that have the short *i* sound. You will read them to me and tell me what short *i* word part is in both words. For example, I see the words *pig* and *big*. When I read them, I can hear that the short *i* word part is *-ig*.

ASSESS:	tin, pin	sit, kit	bib, rib

4. Short *i* (Lesson 26)
MODEL: I will display two words that have the short *i* sound and you will make a word that has the same short *i* word part. For example, I read the words *his* and *tis*. I can see that the short *i* word part is *-is*. I can use this word part to make the word *sis*.

ASSESS:	rip, nip, ___	Tim, rim, ___	did, hid, ___

ASSESSMENT
LESSONS 25–26

Phonics, Morphology, and Spelling

SCORING

SKILL/LESSON	SCORE
1. Short *a* (Lesson 25) jam, ham (*-am*) cat, rat (*-at*) bag, tag (*-ag*)	_____ / 3
2. Short *a* (Lesson 25) ban, pan, (Sample Answer: man) tab, lab, (Sample Answer: cab) map, cap, (Sample Answer: tap)	_____ / 3
3. Short *i* (Lesson 26) tin, pin (*-in*) sit, kit (*-it*) bib, rib (*-ib*)	_____ / 3
4. Short *i* (Lesson 26) rip, nip, (Sample Answer: lip) Tim, rim, (Sample Answer: him) did, hid, (Sample Answer: kid)	_____ / 3

An overall score of 80% correct is typically considered mastery. Use your judgment and your individual students' needs as well to determine skill mastery.

IF… students score below the benchmark,
THEN… review those discrete skills, going back to the lessons to reteach the scaffold as needed.

Lesson 27 Short o

INTRODUCE Remind students that words are made up of consonant and vowel sounds. You learned that /ŏ/ is spelled with the letter *o*, and you learned how to blend letters to read words with this sound. Today we will learn another way to read words with the short *o* sound.

MODEL Display or share copies of the following passage, "Hot Pot," from Student Page S161, and read it aloud.

Point to the word *pot* in the first line. The word *pot* has a consonant, then a vowel, and then another consonant. Each letter has its own sound. Point to the word *hot*. Changing a letter in a word makes a new word. When the *p* in *pot* is changed to an *h*, the word *pot* becomes *hot*.

Hot Pot

ends with *-ot*

The pot is hot.
The lid is on the pot.
Cod is in the pot.
Pop got the cod.

ends with *-op*

TEACH Point out the words with the short *o* sound. Explain that students can read more words when they learn how to recognize letter combinations that include a short *o*. *Pot* and *hot* both have a short *o* sound and end with *-ot*. I can use the *-ot* letter combination to make new words that have the short *o* sound. When I change, add, or delete a letter, I make a new word. Reinforce this idea by pointing out other words in the model that have the short *o* sound, such as *Pop*.

Now point to the *-od* letter combination at the end of *Cod* in the third sentence. Now that I know what the letters *-od* sound like, when I hear a word that ends with those sounds, I can spell the word. The word *Cod* ends with the sounds /ŏ/ and /d/. I can write the letter combination *-od*. The word starts with the sound /k/. I know the letter *c* makes the /k/ sound. I can add the letter *c* to the beginning of *-od*. Work through spelling other examples, such as *pod*, *nod*, and *rod* by changing, adding, and deleting letters.

OBJECTIVES:

- Read words with the short *o* sound.
- Form words using the short *o* sound.
- Change, add, and delete sounds to make new words.
- Spell VC, CVC, and CCVC words.

Lesson 27 Short *o*

REMIND STUDENTS THAT ...

- they can recognize the short *o* sound.
- they can read words with the short *o* sound.
- they can make new words using *-op* and *-ot* by changing, adding, and deleting letters.
- they can spell words using familiar letter combinations.

PRACTICE 1 Remind students that they can read words by breaking them into word parts and reading the parts one after the other. Use the following routine to guide students as they identify words with the short *o* sound.

Routine

1. Connect. Write and say *pop*. This is a word you know. Let's read it together. Knowing how to read *-op* can help you read many words with this word part.

2. Model and give examples. Read *pop* aloud again: *pop*. Have students say *-op* with you several times. *Pop* is one of many words with the word part *-op*. Help students think of other words that use *-op*, such as *hop*, *mop*, and *top*.

3. Model blending. Write *op* and slowly blend it several times with students. Then write *p* at the beginning. Cover the word part *-op* and point to *p*. Say the sound aloud: /*p*/. Then cover *p* and read the word part *-op* aloud: *op*. The two parts are *p* and *-op*. Read the parts one after the other. Let's read together: *p*, *op*, *pop*. Delete *p* and add *h*, and blend the word with students. Repeat with *mop* and *top*, changing and adding letters as you go.

4. Model spelling. Say *mop* slowly several times. I hear the letter combination *-op* at the end of the word. Write *op*. Sound out the initial /m/ for students. Write *m*. Have students blend the word with you.

Repeat this routine with the word part *-ot*.

	op		ot

Display the Elkonin boxes from Student Page S162 and have students use them to spell and blend words. If needed, offer letters such as *c*, *g*, and *t*.

✔ **MONITOR PROGRESS** Display the following sentence from Student Page S162. Have students identify the words with the short *o* sound.

Dot and Pop got a top.

IF... students misidentify words with the short *o* sound,
THEN... offer corrective feedback by pointing out the four words with the short *o* sound.

Lesson 27 Short *o*

PRACTICE 2 Use the following routine to guide students as they identify words with the short *o* sound. Point out the *-ob* or *-om* word part.

Routine

1. Connect. Write and say *job*. This is a word you know. Let's read it together. Knowing how to read *-ob* can help you read many words with this word part.

2. Model and give examples. Read *job* aloud again: *job*. Have students say *-ob* with you several times. *Job* is one of many words with the word part *-ob*. Help students think of other words that use *-ob*, such as *mob, sob,* and *rob*.

3. Model blending. Write *ob* and slowly blend it several times with students. Then write *j* at the beginning. Cover the word part *-ob* and point to *j*. Say j aloud: */j/*. Then cover *j* and read the word part *-ob* aloud: *ob*. The two parts are *j* and *-ob*. Read the parts one after the other. Let's read together: *j, ob, job*. Delete *j* and add *m*, and blend the word with students. Repeat with *sob* and *rob*, changing and adding letters as you go.

4. Model spelling. Say *lob* slowly several times. I hear the letter combination *-ob* at the end of the word. Write *ob*. Sound out the initial /l/ for students. Write *l*. Have students blend the word with you.

Repeat this routine with the word part *-om*.

	ob		om

Display the Elkonin boxes from Student Page S163 and have students use them to spell and blend words. If needed, offer letters such as *c* and *m*. Then have students use one or two of the words in their own oral sentences.

REMIND STUDENTS THAT . . .

- they can recognize the short *o* sound.
- they can read words with the short *o* sound.
- they can make new words using *-ob* and *-om* by changing, adding, and deleting letters.
- they can spell words using familiar letter combinations.

☑ **MONITOR PROGRESS** Display the following sentence from Student Page S163. Have students identify the words with the short *o* sound.

Mom and Tom got jobs.

IF... students misidentify words with the short *o* sound,
THEN... offer corrective feedback by pointing out the four words with the short *o* sound.

Lesson 27 Short *o*

REMIND STUDENTS THAT ...

- they can recognize the short *o* sound.
- they can read words with the short *o* sound.
- they can make new words using *-od*, *-og*, and *-on* by changing, adding, and deleting letters.
- they can spell words using familiar letter combinations.

PRACTICE 3 Use the following routine to guide students as they identify words with the short *o* sound. Point out the *-od*, *-og*, or *-on* word part.

Routine

1. Connect. Write and say *fog*. This is a word you know. Let's read it together. Knowing how to read *-og* can help you read many words with this word part.

2. Model and give examples. Read *fog* aloud again: *fog*. Have students say *-og* with you several times. Help students think of other words that use *-og*, such as *bog*, *dog*, and *log*.

3. Model blending. Write *og* and slowly blend it several times with students. Then write *f* at the beginning. Cover the word part *-og* and point to *f*. Say *f* aloud: /f/. Then cover *f* and read the word part *-og* aloud: *og*. The two parts are *f* and *-og*. Let's read together: *f*, *og*, *fog*. Delete *f* and add *b*, and blend the word with students. Repeat with *dog*, *log*, and *frog*, changing, adding, and deleting letters as you go. Point out that *trim* has a consonant, consonant, vowel, consonant pattern.

4. Model spelling. Say *blog* slowly several times. I hear the letter combination *-og* at the end of the word. Write *og*. Sound out the initial /b/ and /l/ for students. Write *bl*. Have students blend the word with you.

Repeat this routine with the word parts *-od* and *-on*.

	od		on
	og		ox

Display the Elkonin boxes from Student Page S164 and have students use them to spell and blend words. If needed, offer letters such as *c*, *h*, and *j*. Then have students use at least two of the words in their own oral sentences.

☑ **INDEPENDENT PRACTICE** Display the following sentences from Student Page S164. Have students identify and blend the words with the short *o* sound.

Fog is on the bog. The bog has a log.

IF... students incorrectly blend words with the short *o* sound,
THEN... offer corrective feedback by showing the words one letter at a time and blending them with students.

Lesson 27 **Short *o***

Hot Pot

ends with *-ot*

The pot is hot.
The lid is on the pot.
Cod is in the pot.
Pop got the cod.

ends with *-op*

Lesson 27 Short o

	op		ot

Dot and Pop got a top.

Lesson 27 **Short *o***

	ob		om

Mom and Tom got jobs.

Lesson 27 **Short *o***

	od		on
	og		ox

Fog is on the bog.

The bog has a log.

Lesson 28 Short e

OBJECTIVES:

- Read words with the short e sound.
- Form words using the short e sound.
- Change, add, and delete sounds to make new words.
- Spell VC, CVC, and CCVC words.

INTRODUCE Emphasize that words are made up of consonant and vowel sounds. You learned that /ĕ/ is spelled with the letter e, and you learned how to blend letters to read words with this sound. Today we will learn another way to read words with the short e sound.

MODEL Display or share copies of the following passage, "Ben's Pet," from Student Page S165, and read it aloud.

Point to the word *red* in the last line. The word *red* has a consonant, then a vowel, and then another consonant. Each letter has its own sound. Point to the word *bed*. Changing a letter in a word makes a new word. When the *r* in *red* is changed to a *b*, the word *red* becomes *bed*.

Ben's Pet

ends with *-et*

Ben gets a pet.
He gets a dog.
He gets the dog a red bed.

ends with *-ed*

TEACH Point out the words with the short e sound. Explain that students can read more words when they learn how to recognize letter combinations that include a short e. *Red* and *bed* both have a short e sound and end with *-ed*. Now that I know *-ed* has a short e sound, I can use this letter combination to make new words. When I change, add, or delete a letter, I make a new word. Reinforce this idea by pointing out other words in the model that have the short e sound, such as *Ben* and *pet*.

Now point to the *-et* letter combination at the end of *pet* in the first sentence. Now that I know what the letters *-et* sound like, when I hear a word that ends with those sounds, I can spell the word. The word *pet* ends with the sounds /ĕ/ and /t/. I can write the letter combination *-et*. The word starts with the sound /p/. I know the letter *p* makes the /p/ sound. I can add the letter *p* to the beginning of *-et*. Work through spelling other examples, such as *let*, *met*, and *bet* by changing, adding, and deleting letters.

Lesson 28 Short e

REMIND STUDENTS THAT ...

- they can recognize the short e sound.
- they can read words with the short e sound.
- they can make new words using *-eg* and *-et* by changing, adding, and deleting letters.
- they can spell words using familiar letter combinations.

PRACTICE I Remind students that one way to read words is to break them into word parts and read the parts one after the other. Use the following routine to guide students as they identify words with the short e sound.

Routine

1. Connect. Write and say *vet*. This is a word you know. Let's read it together. Knowing how to read *-et* can help you read many words with this word part.

2. Model and give examples. Read *vet* aloud again: *vet*. Have students say *-et* with you several times. *Vet* is one of many words with the word part *-et*. Help students think of other words that use *-et*, such as *bet*, *let*, and *wet*.

3. Model blending. Write *et* and slowly blend it several times with students. Then write *v* at the beginning. Cover the word part *-et* and point to *v*. Say *v* aloud: /v/. Then cover *v* and read the word part *-et* aloud: *et*. The two parts are *v* and *-et*. Read the parts one after the other. Let's read together: *v*, *et*, *vet*. Delete *v* and add *b*, and blend the word with students. Repeat with *let* and *wet*, changing and adding letters as you go.

4. Model spelling. Say *get* slowly several times. I hear the letter combination *-et* at the end of the word. Write *et*. Sound out the initial /g/ for students. Write *g*. Have students blend the word with you.

Repeat this routine with the word part *-eg*.

	eg		et

Display the Elkonin boxes from Student Page S166 and have students use them to spell and blend words. If needed, offer letters such as *b* and *p*.

✔ **MONITOR PROGRESS** Have students read the following words from Student Page S166. Then have them spell and blend two new words: one with *-eg* and one with *-et*.

peg	beg	___
let	net	___

IF... students misread or misspell a word,
THEN... guide them to identify the letters and sounds in the word. Then have them spell and blend the word with you and independently.

Lesson 28 Short e

PRACTICE 2 Use the following routine to guide students as they identify words with the short e sound. Point out the *-ed* or *-em* word part.

Routine

1. Connect. Write and say *fed*. This is a word you know. Let's read it together. Knowing how to read *-ed* can help you read many words with this word part.

2. Model and give examples. Read *fed* aloud again: *fed*. Have students say *-ed* with you several times. *Fed* is one of many words with the word part *-ed*. Help students think of other words that use *-ed,* such as *bed, red,* and *wed*.

3. Model blending. Write *ed* and slowly blend it several times with students. Then write *f* at the beginning. Cover the word part *-ed* and point to *f*. Say *f* aloud: */f/*. Then cover *f* and read the word part *-ed* aloud: *ed*. The two parts are *f* and *-ed*. Read the parts one after the other. Let's read together: *f, ed, fed*. Delete *f* and add *b*, and blend the word with students. Repeat with *red* and *wed*, changing and adding letters as you go.

4. Model spelling. Say *sled* slowly several times. I hear the letter combination *-ed* at the end of the word. Write *ed*. Sound out the initial /s/ and /l/ for students. Write *sl*. Have students blend the word with you.

Repeat this routine with the word part *-em*.

	ed		em

Display the Elkonin boxes from Student Page S167 and have students use them to spell and blend words. If needed, offer letters such as *g, h* and *l*. Then have students use one or two of the words in their own oral sentences.

REMIND STUDENTS THAT ...

- they can recognize the short e sound.
- they can read words with the short e sound.
- they can make new words using *-ed* and *-em* by changing, adding, and deleting letters.
- they can spell words using familiar letter combinations.

✓ **MONITOR PROGRESS** Have students read the following words from Student Page S167. Then have them use one or two of the words in their own oral sentences.

fed	led	red
hem	gem	

IF... students misread a word,
THEN... guide them as they sound out the word. Then have them blend the word with you and independently.

Lesson 28 Short e

REMIND STUDENTS THAT …

- they can recognize the short e sound.
- they can read words with the short e sound.
- they can make new words using *-eb, -el,* and *-en* by changing, adding, and deleting letters.
- they can spell words using familiar letter combinations.

PRACTICE 3 Use the following routine to guide students as they identify words with the short e sound. Point out the *-eb, -el,* or *-en* word part.

Routine

1. Connect. Write and say *ten*. This is a word you know. Let's read it together. Knowing how to read *-en* can help you read many words with this word part.

2. Model and give examples. Read *ten* aloud again: *ten*. Have students say *-en* with you several times. *Ten* is one of many words with the word part *-en*. Help students think of other words that use *-en*, such as *hen, Ken,* and *pen*.

3. Model blending. Write *en* and slowly blend it several times with students. Then write *t* at the beginning. Cover the word part *-en* and point to *t*. Say *t* aloud: /t/. Then cover *t* and read the word part *-en* aloud: *en*. The two parts are *t* and *-en*. Let's read together: *t, en, ten.* Delete *t* and add *h*, and blend the word with students. Repeat with *Ken*, *pen*, and *glen*, changing, adding, and deleting letters as you go. Point out that *glen* has a consonant, consonant, vowel, consonant pattern.

4. Model spelling. Say *den* slowly several times. I hear the letter combination *-en* at the end of the word. Write *en*. Sound out the initial /d/ for students. Write *d*. Have students blend the word with you.

Repeat this routine with the word parts *-eb* and *-el*.

	eb		en
	el		

Display the Elkonin boxes from Student Page S168 and have students use them to spell and blend words. If needed, offer letters such as *d, g, m,* and *w*. Then have students use at least two of the words in their own oral sentences.

☑ **INDEPENDENT PRACTICE** Display the following sentence from Student Page S168. Have students identify and blend the words with the short e sound.

Mel the hen sits in a pen.

IF… students incorrectly blend words with the short e sound,
THEN… offer corrective feedback by showing the words one letter at a time and blending them with students.

Lesson 28 **Short e**

Ben's Pet

ends with -*et*

Ben gets a pet.
He gets a dog.
He gets the dog a red bed.

ends with -*ed*

Lesson 28 **Short e**

	eg		et

peg	beg	______
let	net	______

Lesson 28 **Short e**

	ed		em

fed	led	red
hem	gem	

Lesson 28 **Short e**

	eb		en
	el		

Mel the hen sits in a pen.

Lesson 29 Short *u*

INTRODUCE Remind students that words are made up of consonant and vowel sounds. You learned that /ŭ/ is spelled with the letter *u*, and you learned how to blend letters to read words with this sound. Today we will learn another way to read words with the short *u* sound.

MODEL Display or share copies of the following passage, "Gus Has Fun," from Student Page S169, and read it aloud.

Gus Has Fun

Gus is out of the hut.
Gus is on a fun walk.
Gus can hum as he walks.
But Gus will not run.
It is too hot in the sun!

ends with *-un*

TEACH Point to *fun* in the second line. The word *fun* has a consonant, then a vowel, and then another consonant. Each letter has its own sound. Point to the word *run*. Changing a letter in a word makes a new word. When the *f* in *fun* is changed to an r, the word *fun* becomes *run*. Repeat with the word *sun*. *Fun, run,* and *sun* all have a short u sound and end with *-un*.

Explain that students can read more words when they learn how to recognize letter combinations that include a short *u*. Point to the word *hut* in the first line Say: When I hear a word that ends with the *-ut* sounds, I can spell the word. The word *hut* ends with the sounds /ŭ/ and /t/. I can write the letter combination *-ut*. The word starts with the sound /h/. I know the letter *h* makes the /h/ sound. I can add the letter *h* to the beginning of *-ut*. Work through other examples, such as *but, cut,* and *nut* by changing, adding, and deleting letters. Point to the word *Gus* in the first line. Note that the name *Gus* is the word *us* with a *G* at the beginning.

OBJECTIVES:

- Read words with the short *u* sound.
- Form words using the short *u* sound.
- Change, add, and delete sounds to make new words.
- Spell VC, CVC, and CCVC words.
- Understand that different short *u* CVC words are easily formed just by changing the consonants.

Lesson 29 Short *u*

REMIND STUDENTS THAT ...

- they can recognize the short *u* sound.
- they can read and spell words with the short *u* sound.
- they can make new short *u* words by changing, adding, and deleting consonants.
- they can spell words using familiar letter combinations.

PRACTICE 1 Remind students that one way to read words is to break them into word parts and read the parts one after the other. Use the following routine to guide students as they identify words with the short *u* sound.

Routine

1. Connect. Write and say *bug*. This is a word you know. Let's read it together. Knowing how to read -*ug* can help you read many words with this word part.

2. Model and give examples. Read *bug* aloud again: *bug*. Have students say -*ug* with you several times. *Bug* is one of many words with the word part -*ug*. Help students think of other words that use -*ug*, such as *dug* and *tug*.

3. Model blending. Write *ug* and slowly blend it several times with students. Then write *b* at the beginning. Cover the word part -*ug* and point to *b*. Say *b* aloud: /b/. Then cover *b* and read the word part -*ug* aloud: *ug*. The two parts are *b* and -*ug*. Let's read together: *b*, *ug*, *bug*. Delete *b* and add *d*, and blend the word with students. Repeat with *tug*.

4. Model spelling. Say *rug* slowly several times. I hear the letter combination -*ug* at the end of the word. Write it. Model sounding out the beginning sound and write *r*. Have students blend the word with you.

Repeat this routine with the word part -*ub*.

	ub		ug

Display the Elkonin boxes from Student Page S170 and have students use them to spell and blend words. If needed, offer letters such as *c* and *t*.

MONITOR PROGRESS Have students read the following words from Student Page S170. Then have them make two new words with -*ub* and -*ug*.

hub	sub	rub	___
mug	lug	jug	___

IF... students misread a word,
THEN... guide them to identify the letters and sounds in the word. Then have them blend the word with you and independently.

Lesson 29 Short *u*

PRACTICE 2 Use the following routine to guide students as they identify words with the short *u* sound. Point out that students will focus on words that have the *-ud* or *-ut* word part.

Routine

1. Connect. Write and say *nut*. This is a word you know. Let's read it together. Knowing how to read *-ut* can help you read many words with this word part.

2. Model and give examples. Read *nut* aloud again: *nut*. Have students say *-ut* with you several times. *Nut* is one of many words with the word part *-ut*. Help students think of other words that use *-ut*, such as *but* and *cut*.

3. Model blending. Write *ut* and slowly blend it several times with students. Then write *n* at the beginning. Cover the word part *-ut* and point to *n*. Say *n* aloud: /n/. Then cover *n* and read the word part *-ut* aloud: *ut*. The two parts are *n* and *-ut*. Let's read together: *n*, *ut*, *nut*. Delete *n* and add *b*, and blend the word with students. Repeat with *cut*.

4. Model spelling. Say *shut* slowly several times. I hear the letter combination *-ut* at the end of the word. Write *ut*. Model sounding out the beginning sound and write *sh*. Point out that *shut* has a CCVC pattern. Have students blend the word with you.

Repeat this routine with the word part *-ud*.

	ud		ut

Display the Elkonin boxes from Student Page S171 and have students use them to spell and blend words. Then have students use one or two of the words in their own oral sentences.

REMIND STUDENTS THAT ...

- they can recognize the short *u* sound.
- they can read and spell words with the short *u* sound.
- they can make new short *u* words by changing, adding, and deleting consonants.
- they can spell words using familiar letter combinations.

☑ **MONITOR PROGRESS** Have students read the following words from Student Page S171. Then have them make two new words with *-ud* and *-ut*.

mud	___	
cut	gut	___

IF... students misread a word,
THEN... guide them as they sound out the word. Then have them blend the word with you and independently.

Lesson 29 Short *u*

REMIND STUDENTS THAT …

- they can recognize the short *u* sound.
- they can read and spell words with the short *u* sound.
- they can make new short *u* words by changing, adding, and deleting consonants.
- they can spell words using familiar letter combinations.

PRACTICE 3 Use the following routine to guide students as they identify words with the short *u* sound. Point out that students will focus on words that have the *-um* or *-un* word part.

Routine

1. Connect. Write and say *run*. This is a word you know. Let's read it together. Knowing how to read *-un* can help you read many words with this word part.

2. Model and give examples. Read *run* aloud again: *run*. Have students say *-un* with you several times. *Run* is one of many words with the word part *-un*. Help students think of other words that use *-un*, such as *pun* and *sun*.

3. Model blending. Write *un* and slowly blend it several times with students. Then write *r* at the beginning. Cover the word part *-un* and point to *r*. Say *r* aloud: /r/. Then cover *r* and read the word part *-un* aloud: *un*. The two parts are *r* and *-un*. Let's read together: *r*, *un*, *run*. Delete *r* and add *p*, and blend the word with students. Repeat with *sun*.

4. Model spelling. Say *spun* slowly several times. I hear the letter combination *-un* at the end of *spun*. Write *un*. Model sounding out the beginning sounds and write *sp*. Point out that *spun* has a CCVC pattern. Have students blend the word with you.

Repeat this routine with the word part *-um*.

	um		un

Display the Elkonin boxes from Student Page S172 and have students use them to spell and blend words. Then have students use at least two of the words in their own oral sentences.

☑ **INDEPENDENT PRACTICE** Display the following sentence from Student Page S172. Have students identify the words with the short *u* sound.

Dogs run in the mud for fun.

IF… students misidentify words with the short *u* sound,
THEN… offer corrective feedback by pointing out the three words with the short *u* sound.

Lesson 29 **Short *u***

Gus Has Fun

Gus is out of the hut.
Gus is on a fun walk.
Gus can hum as he walks.
But Gus will not run.
It is too hot in the sun!

Lesson 29 **Short *u***

	ub		ug

hub	sub	rub	______
mug	lug	jug	______

Lesson 29 Short *u*

	ud		ut

mud	______	
cut	gut	______

Lesson 29 **Short *u***

	um		un

Dogs run in the mud for fun.

ASSESSMENT
LESSONS 27–29

Phonics, Morphology, and Spelling

ASSESS MASTERY Use this Checkpoint to assess students' mastery of the short *o* sound, the short e sound, and the short *u* sound.

ADMINISTER THE TEST Administer the Checkpoint orally to each student. For each item, model the process as described, and then have the student use the process to respond to your prompts. Record responses on the scoring chart on the next page.

ACTIVITY A

MODEL: I will say two words and you will tell me what short vowel word part is in both words. For example, I might say *got* and *not*. I can hear that the short *o* word part is *-ot*.

1. Short *o* (Lesson 27)

ASSESS:	pop, top	job, Bob	pod, cod

2. Short e (Lesson 28)

ASSESS:	pet, wet	gel, Mel	hem, gem

3. Short *u* (Lesson 29)

ASSESS:	mud, bud	gum, hum	hub, sub

ACTIVITY B

MODEL: I will say two words and you will make a word that has the same short vowel word part. For example, I might say *bop* and *cop*. The short *o* word part is *-op*. I can use this word part to make the word *mop*.

4. Short *o* (Lesson 27)

ASSESS:	fog, hog, ___	rod, sod, ___	hot, lot, ___

5. Short e (Lesson 28)

ASSESS:	red, bed, ___	leg, peg, ___	Ken, pen, ___

6. Short *u* (Lesson 29)

ASSESS:	jug, mug, ___	cut, rut, ___	bun, sun, ___

ASSESSMENT
LESSONS 27–29

Phonics, Morphology, and Spelling

SCORING

SKILL/LESSON	SCORE
1. Short *o* (Lesson 27) pop, top (*-op*) job, Bob (*-ob*) pod, cod (*-od*)	____ / 3
2. Short *e* (Lesson 28) pet, wet (*-et*) gel, Mel (*-el*) hem, gem (*-em*)	____ / 3
3. Short *u* (Lesson 29) mud, bud (*-ud*) gum, hum (*-um*) hub, sub (*-ub*)	____ / 3
4. Short *o* (Lesson 27) fog, hog, (Sample Answer: log) rod, sod, (Sample Answer: cod) hot, lot, (Sample Answer: pot)	____ / 3
5. Short *e* (Lesson 28) red, bed, (Sample Answer: fed) leg, peg, (Sample Answer: beg) Ken, pen, (Sample Answer: hen)	____ / 3
6. Short *u* (Lesson 29) jug, mug, (Sample Answer: bug) cut, rut, (Sample Answer: but) bun, sun, (Sample Answer: fun)	____ / 3

An overall score of 80% correct is typically considered mastery. Use your judgment and your individual students' needs as well to determine skill mastery.

IF… students score below the benchmark,
THEN… review those discrete skills, going back to the lessons to reteach the scaffold as needed.

Lesson 30 Long *a*, *i*, and *o*

INTRODUCE Connect today's lesson to short vowel sound-spellings by writing *cap* and *at* for students. You can read words like these. They both have short *a*, pronounced /a/, spelled *a*. Repeat the short *a* sound with me: /a/. Explain that students will learn how to spell and read words with long *a*, pronounced /ā/ as in *cape*. Use the same routine to review the short vowel sounds for *i* and *o*. Point out that students will also learn about long *i* and long *o* in this lesson.

MODEL Display or share copies of "Bike Ride" from Student Page S175, and read it aloud.

long *a* spelled *a_e*

Bike Ride

Jane and Sid ride bikes side by side.
Jane and Sid ride a mile at a time.
Jane and Sid race home.

long *a* spelled *a_e*

TEACH Explain that students can read more words when they learn how long vowel sounds are spelled. Remind students that long vowels say their name.

Write *a*_e and say its sound: /ā/. Point out *Jane* and *race*. *Jane* and *race* both have a long *a* sound spelled *a*_e. The letter e is silent but gives the vowel *a* its long sound. The blank shows where a consonant will go. Write *J* in front of the pattern and blend the sounds /j//ā/. Have students blend with you as you run your hand under the letters. Write *n* in the blank and have students say its sound with you. Then blend the whole word, pointing to *a* and e as you say /ā/. This is how I blend this word: /j//ā//n/, *Jane*. Say the word with me. Then review the silent e rule with students. Remember that the e at the end is silent but makes the vowel say its name. Cover the e and ask what the new word is. (*Jan*) This is another example of how adding a letter forms a new word. The e at the end turns *Jan* into *Jane*.

Follow this procedure to model words with the long *i* sound and long *o* sound, such as *side* and *home*. Point out how *Sid* becomes *side* when the letter e is added to the end.

OBJECTIVES:

- Understand that long vowels are pronounced like the letter names.
- Learn the silent e rule.
- Learn the long vowel spelling patterns *ay*, *i*, *y*, and *o*.
- Apply knowledge of letter-sound correspondence to read and spell long *a*, *i*, and *o* words.
- See that words can share the same letter patterns.
- Understand that different words are easily formed by adding, deleting, or changing letters.

Lesson 30 Long *a*, *i*, and *o*

REMIND STUDENTS THAT . . .

- they can recognize words with long vowel sounds.
- they can recognize vowel patterns and learn to read and spell many words.
- they can make new long *a* words by adding, deleting, or changing letters.

WORD LIST

late	date
take	make
face	pace
made	wade
lay	ray

PRACTICE I: Long *a* (Spelled *a_e* and *ay*) Use the routine below to help students connect /ā/ with *a_e* and to blend words with two long *a* spelling patterns.

Routine

1. Connect sound and spelling. Write *a_e*. The long *a* sound, /ā/, can be spelled *a_e*. Point to *a_e*. Have students say /ā/ several times as you point to *a_e*.

2. Model blending. Write *a_e* and say its sound: /ā/. Write *c* in front of the pattern and blend the sounds: /k//ā/. Have students blend with you as you run your hand under the letters. Write *m* in the blank and have students say its sound with you: /m/. Then blend the whole word, pointing to *a* and *e* as you say /ā/. This is how I blend this word: /k//ā//m/, *came*. Have students practice saying the word without pausing between sounds. Say the sounds quickly to say the word. What's the word? Yes, it's *came*.

Repeat this routine to model *male* and *sale*. Point out how changing just the first letter makes a new word, so once students learn spelling patterns such as *-ale* they can read and spell many new words. Have them write *pale* and *tale* as examples. Then, complete the procedure to model *day* and *may*. Begin each word by writing the vowel spelling *ay* as a unit. Use the Word List in the sidebar for additional practice with both spellings.

Next, you may wish to distribute or display Student Page S176. Have students write the letter *e* in the boxes to make a new word. Then have them read each pair of words.

tap	→	tape
cap	→	cape
at	→	ate
mad	→	made

☑ **MONITOR PROGRESS** Use the Word List from Student Page S176 to check that students can read more words with /ā/.

cake	game	safe	race
say	hay	pay	way

IF... students have difficulty reading a word,
THEN... model blending as you run your hand under the letters. Then have students blend the word with you.

Lesson 30 Long *a*, *i*, and *o*

PRACTICE 2: Long *i* (Spelled *i*, *i_e*, and *y*) Write or display the word *hi*. Point out its spelling. I can blend this word: /h//ī/. Then continue to teach long *i* spelling patterns using the following routine.

Routine

1. Connect sound and spelling. Write *i_e*. The long *i* sound, /ī/, can be spelled *i_e*. Point to *i_e*. Have students say /ī/ several times as you point to *i_e*.

2. Model blending. Write *r* in front of the pattern and blend the sounds: /r//ī/. Have students blend with you as you run your hand under the letters. Write *c* in the blank and have students say its sound with you: /s/. Then blend the whole word, pointing to *i* and e as you say /ī/. This is how I blend this word: /r//ī//s/, *rice*. Have students practice saying the word without pausing between sounds. Say the sounds quickly to say the word. What's the word? Yes, it's *rice*. Cover the *r* and point out that the new word is *ice*. Then ask what word is formed when the *r* is changed to *n*. (*nice*)

Repeat the routine to model how to read words with long *i* spelled *y*, such as *my*. Then, use the Word List in the sidebar for additional practice with the long *i* vowel spellings.

Next, distribute or display Student Page S177. Have students write the letter *e* in the boxes to make a new word. Then have them read each pair of words.

pin → pine
fin → fine
rid → ride
dim → dime

REMIND STUDENTS THAT ...

- they can recognize words with long vowel sounds.
- they can apply long vowel patterns that they learn to read and spell many words.
- they can make new long *i* words by adding, deleting, or changing letters.

WORD LIST:

I	side
hike	like
lime	time
my	by

☑ **MONITOR PROGRESS** Use the Word List from Student Page S177 to check that students can read more words with /ī/.

bike	dive	side	life
my	by		

IF... students have difficulty reading a word,
THEN... model blending as you run your hand under the letters. Then have students blend the word with you.

Lesson 30 Long *a*, *i*, and *o*

REMIND STUDENTS THAT …

- they can recognize words with long vowel sounds.
- they can apply long vowel patterns that they learn to read and spell many words.
- they can make new long *o* words by adding, deleting, or changing letters.

WORD LIST

no	so
cone	bone
hope	rope

PRACTICE 3: Long *o* (Spelled *o* and *o_e*) Use the routine to teach the long *o* sound and how to read words spelled *o* and *o_e*.

Routine

1. Connect sound and spelling Write or display the word *go*. Point out its spelling. I can blend this word: /g//ō/.

2. Model blending Next, write or display *o_e* and have students say its sound: /ō/. Write *h* in front of the pattern and blend the sounds /h//ō/. Write *m* in the blank and say its sound. Then blend the whole word, pointing to *o* and *e* as you say /ō/. This is how I blend this word: /h//ō//m/, *home.* Let's say it together several times. Remind students that now they can read and spell other words such as *dome* and *Rome*.

Use other words from the Word List for additional practice with long *o* vowel spellings. Follow the routine above to model for students how to read these words.

After the routine, distribute or display Student Page S178. Have students write the letter *e* in the boxes to make new words. Then have them read each pair of words.

not → note
cod → code
mop → mope
rob → robe

INDEPENDENT PRACTICE Use the Word List from Student Page S178 to check that students can read more words with /ō/.

rope	vote	nose	joke
go	no		

IF… students have difficulty reading the words,
THEN… model breaking each word into sounds. Help students say each sound and write its spelling.

Bike Ride

Jane and Sid ride bikes side by side.
Jane and Sid ride a mile at a time.
Jane and Sid race home.

Lesson 30 **Long *a*, *i*, and *o***

tap	→	tap	
cap	→	cap	
at	→	at	
mad	→	mad	

cake	game	safe	race
say	hay	pay	way

Lesson 30 Long *a*, *i*, and *o*

pin	→	pin	
fin	→	fin	
rid	→	rid	
dim	→	dim	

bike	dive	side	life
my	by		

Lesson 30 Long *a*, *i*, and *o*

not	→	not	
cod	→	cod	
mop	→	mop	
rob	→	rob	

rope	vote	nose	joke
go	no		

Lesson 31 Long e and *u*

INTRODUCE Remind students that vowel sounds can be short or long. You have learned how to read words with long *a* spelled *a*_e and *ay*; long *i* spelled *i*, *i*_e, and *y*; and long *o* spelled *o* and *o*_e. Today we will learn to read words with the long e and *u* sounds.

MODEL Display or share copies of the following passage, "My Rat Zeke" from Student Page S179, and read it aloud.

My Rat Zeke

long e spelled e_e

Zeke is my rat.
He is very nice.
I made him a maze in a tube.
He likes his maze.

long e spelled *y*

long *u* spelled *u*_e

TEACH Explain that students can read more words when they learn how long vowel sounds are spelled.

Write e_e and say its sound: /ē/. Point out *Zeke*. *Zeke* has a long e sound spelled e_e. The letter e at the end of the word gives the vowel e its long sound, and the blank shows where a consonant will go. Write *Z* and blend the sounds /z//ē/. Have students blend with you as you run your hand under the letters. Write *k* in the blank and have students say its sound with you: /k/. Then blend the whole word, pointing to e and e as you say /ē/. This is how I blend this word: /Z//ē//k/, *Zeke*. Have students practice saying the word without pausing between sounds. Repeat the process with *he* (/ē/ spelled e) and *very* (/ē/ spelled *y*). When I change, add, or delete a letter, I make a new word. Then, follow this routine to model words with the long *u* sound, such as *tube*.

OBJECTIVES:

- Teach the concept of long vowel sounds.
- Introduce long e spelled e and *y*.
- Introduce long e spelled e_e.
- Introduce long *u* spelled *u*_e.
- Change, add, and delete sounds to make new words.

Lesson 31 Long e and *u*

REMIND STUDENTS THAT …

- they can recognize words with long vowel sounds.
- they can recognize words with the long e sound spelled e and *y*.
- they can read words with the long e sound.
- they can make new words by changing, adding, and deleting letters.

WORD LIST

be	we
ruby	baby

PRACTICE I: Long e (Spelled e and y) Use the routine below to help students connect /ē/ with e and *y* and to blend words with these two long e spellings.

Write e. Have students say /ē/ several times with you. Write *m*. Then blend the whole word: /m//ē/, *me*. When a word or a syllable ends with one vowel, the vowel sound is usually long.

Explain to students that vowel sounds can be spelled in different ways. Today we're going to learn that the sound /ē/ can be spelled with a *y* at the end of a word.

Write *y*. Explain that the long e sound can be spelled *y*. Write *copy*. When the letter *y* comes at the end of a word with more than one syllable, it usually stands for /ē/. Have students say *copy*. Use this procedure to help students read the words from the Word List in the sidebar.

Then distribute or display Student Page S180 to reinforce the long e sound. Have students read each pair of words and identify the word that has the long e sound. Guide students to note that adding or deleting a letter makes a new word.

met, me (me)	be, bet (be)
lady, lad (lady)	wet, we (we)

MONITOR PROGRESS Use the Word List from Student Page S180 to check that students can read more words with /ē/.

he	very	body	we

IF… students cannot read a word,
THEN… have them use sound-by-sound blending. For example, if students cannot read *body*, write out *body* and move your hand in a continuous motion from letter to letter /b//o//d//ē/.

Lesson 31 Long e and *u*

PRACTICE 2: Long e (Spelled e_e) Use the routine below to help students connect /ē/ with e_e and to blend words with this long e spelling pattern.

Routine

1. Connect sound to spelling. Write e_e and have students say /ē/ as you point to the letters. The letter e at the end of the word gives the first e its long sound, and the blank shows where a consonant will go.

2. Model blending. Say the word *gene*, then write e_e and say its sound: /ē/. Write *g* and blend the sounds: /j//ē/. Have students blend with you as you point to the letters. Write *n* in the blank and have students say its sound with you: /n/. Then blend the whole word, pointing to the first and second e as you say /ē/. This is how I blend this word: /j//ē//n/, *gene*. Have students practice saying the word without pausing between sounds.

Follow this procedure to model the long e, /ē/, spelled e_e as in *eve*. Then distribute or display Student Page S181 to reinforce the long e sound spelled e_e. Have students read each word aloud. Point out the letters that are added or changed to make a new word.

eve	Pete	Zeke

REMIND STUDENTS THAT ...

- they can recognize words with long vowel sounds.
- they can recognize words with the long e sound spelled *e_e*.
- they can read words with the long e sound.
- they can make new words by changing, adding, and deleting letters.

☑ **MONITOR PROGRESS** Use the Word List from Student Page S181 to check that students can read more words with /ē/, spelled e_e.

Steve	here	gene

IF... students have difficulty reading a word,
THEN... help them identify the consonant and vowel sounds in each word. Guide students to blend the sounds together to read the word.

Lesson 31 Long e and *u*

REMIND STUDENTS THAT ...

- they can recognize words with long vowel sounds.
- they can recognize words with the long *u* sound spelled *u_e*.
- they can read words with the long *u* sound.
- they can make new words by changing, adding, and deleting letters.

WORD LIST

tube
use
fume
rule

PRACTICE 3: Long *u* (Spelled *u_e*) Write the first two words from the Word List in the sidebar and say each aloud several times. What vowel sounds do you hear when I say the words *tube* and *use*? Point out that sometimes the sound for long *u* is /ū/, as in *tube*, and sometimes it is /yū/, as in *use*. When you see the spelling *u_e* in a word, try the long *u* sound, /ū/. Say /ū/ aloud with students as you point to *u_e*. Then point to the initial consonant, in *tube*, say its sound, and blend the first two sounds: /t//ū/. Point to the next consonant and say its sound: /b/. Now blend the word with me: /t//ū//b/. Repeat the procedure with *use*.

Use other words from the Word List for additional practice. Follow the procedure above to model for students how to read these words.

Then distribute or display Student Page S182 to reinforce the long *u* sound. Have students add the letter e in the boxes to make new words. Then have them read each pair of words.

cub → cube	hug → huge
tub → tube	cut → cute

INDEPENDENT PRACTICE Distribute Student Page S182. Have students read the Word List independently to check that they can read words with /ū/ and /ē/. Then have them identify the spelling of the long vowel sound in each word.

duke (u_e)	be (e)	baby (y)
eve (e_e)	June (u_e)	

IF... students cannot read a word,
THEN... have them use sound-by-sound blending. For example, if students cannot read *duke*, write out *duke* and move your hand in a continuous motion from letter to letter: /d//ū//k/.

Lesson 31 **Long *e* and *u***

My Rat Zeke

Zeke is my rat.
He is very nice.
I made him a maze in a tube.
He likes his maze.

Lesson 31 Long e and *u*

met, me	be, bet
lady, lad	wet, we

he	very	body	we

Lesson 31 Long e and *u*

eve	Pete	Zeke
Steve	here	gene

Lesson 31 **Long e and *u***

cub → cub		hug → hug	
tub → tub		cut → cut	

duke	be	baby
eve	June	

ASSESSMENT
LESSONS 30–31

Phonics, Morphology, and Spelling

ASSESS MASTERY Assess students' mastery of the long vowel sounds.

ADMINISTER THE TEST Administer the Checkpoint orally to each student. Give each student a copy of the next page. Instruct students as follows.

MODEL: I will display words that have a long vowel sound. You will tell me what long vowel spelling is in each word. For example, *day*: long *a* spelled *ay*.

1. Long *a* (Lesson 30)

ASSESS:	make	say	face	way

2. Long *i* (Lesson 30)

ASSESS:	mile	hi	dive	by

3. Long *o* (Lesson 30)

ASSESS:	go	Rome	hope	no

4. Long *e* (Lesson 31)

ASSESS:	we	eve	baby	Pete

5. Long *u* (Lesson 31)

ASSESS:	cute	huge	cube	tube

SCORING

SKILL/LESSON	SCORE
1. Long *a* (Lesson 30) make (*a*_e), say (*ay*), face (*a*_e), way (*ay*)	_____ / 4
2. Long *i* (Lesson 30) mile (*i*_e), hi (*i*), dive (*i*_e), by (*y*)	_____ / 4
3. Long *o* (Lesson 30) go (*o*), Rome (*o*_e), hope (*o*_e), no (*o*)	_____ / 4
4. Long *e* (Lesson 31) we (*e*), eve (*e*_e), baby (*y*), Pete (*e*_e)	_____ / 4
5. Long *u* (Lesson 31) cute (*u*_e), huge (*u*_e), cube (*u*_e), tube (*u*_e)	_____ / 4

An overall score of 80% correct is typically considered mastery. Use your judgment and your individual students' needs as well to determine skill mastery.

IF... students score below the benchmark,
THEN... review those discrete skills, reteaching as needed.

ASSESSMENT
LESSONS 30–31

Phonics, Morphology, and Spelling

make	say	face	way
mile	hi	dive	by
go	Rome	hope	no
we	eve	baby	Pete
cute	huge	cube	tube

Lesson 32 Consonant Blends

INTRODUCE Emphasize that students can segment and blend sounds to read words. Explain that they will read and spell words with consonant blends. Say: Consonant blends are two consonants that are read together. The sounds blend into each other. Words with consonant blends at the beginning are spelled with two consonants, then the vowel, and then a consonant. Words with consonant blends at the end are spelled with one consonant, then the vowel, and then two more consonants.

OBJECTIVES:

- Read and spell CCVC words with initial consonant blends.
- Read and spell CVCC words with final consonant blends.

MODEL Display or distribute the passage "The Sled" from Student Page S185 and read it aloud.

starts with *sl-*

The Sled

ends with *-nd*

I held my sled in my hand.
I went up the hill.

ends with *-nt*

I set my sled on the top of the hill.
I sat on it.
I went fast! I did not stop!

starts with *st-*

ends with *-st*

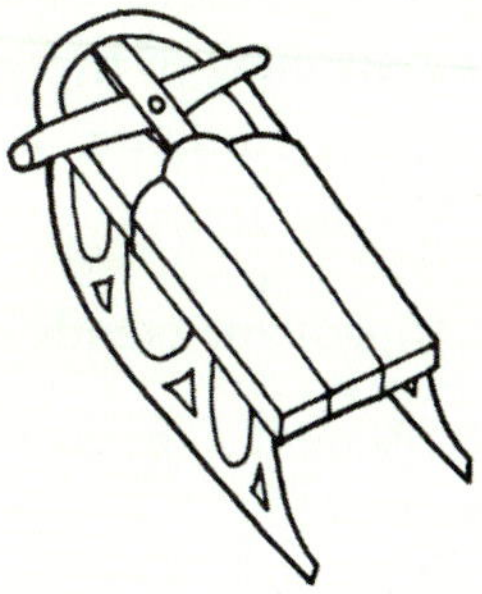

TEACH Point out the words with initial and final consonant blends. Explain that students will learn to read more words when they learn to recognize consonant blends. Say: The word *sled* begins with the letters s and *l*. This is a consonant blend. We blend the letter sounds together as we read. The sounds /s/ and /l/ are read /sl/. Once we blend the consonants, we can read the rest of the word: /sl/ /ĕ/ /d/. Repeat with the final consonant blend in the word *hand*.

Explain that some consonant blends appear only at the beginning of words and others may appear only at the end of words. Then say: Some consonant blends with s can be found at the beginning and end of words. Point out the words *fast* and *stop* in the passage. Blend the words with students.

Now point to the -*st* letter combination at the end of *fast* in the last line. Now that I know what the consonant blend -*st* sounds like, when I hear a word with those sounds, I can spell the word. The word *test* ends with the sounds /st/. I can write the letter combination *st*. The word starts with the sounds /t/ and /ĕ/. I know the letters *t* and *e* make those sounds. I can write *te* at the beginning of the word.

Lesson 32 Consonant Blends

REMIND STUDENTS THAT ...

- they can read words that begin with consonant blends.
- they can spell words that begin with consonant blends.

PRACTICE 1: Initial Consonant Blends Say: One way to read words is to break them into word parts and read each part. Use the following routine to guide students as they read and spell words with initial consonant blends.

Routine

1. Connect. Write and say *plan*. Let's read it together. Knowing how to read consonant blends with *l* at the beginning of words can help you read many words with this blend.

2. Model and give example. Read *plan* aloud again: *plan*. Have students say *pl-* with you several times. *Plan* is one of many words with a consonant blend with *l* at the beginning. Help students think of other words that use a consonant blend with *l* at the beginning of the word, such as *plot, slip,* and *flag*.

3. Model blending. Write *pl-* and slowly blend it several times with students. Then write *an* at the end. Cover the word part *-an* and point to the consonant blend *pl*. Say *pl* aloud: /pl/. Then cover *pl* and point to the word part *-an*. Say *-an* aloud: /ăn/. The two parts are *pl* and *-an*. Let's read together: *pl, an, plan*. Delete *an* and add *ot*, and blend the word with students. Repeat with *slot* and *slip*.

4. Model spelling. Say *flag* slowly several times. I hear the consonant blend *fl* at the beginning of the word. Write *fl*. Sound out the /ă/ and /g/ for students. Write *ag*. Have students blend the word with you.

Repeat this routine with initial consonant blends with *r*.

Display the Elkonin boxes from Student Page S186 and have students use them to spell and blend words. If needed, offer letters such as *a, b, d, e, g, o,* and *t*.

bl		cr	
fl		dr	

MONITOR PROGRESS Have students read the words on Student Page S186. Then have them spell two new words: one with an initial consonant blend with *l* and one with *r*.

glad	flap	________
slid	trip	________

IF... students misread or misspell a word,
THEN... guide them to identify the letters and sounds in the word. Then have them blend or spell the word with you and independently.

Lesson 32 Consonant Blends

PRACTICE 2: Final Consonant Blends Use the following routine to guide students as they read and spell words with final consonant blends.

Routine

1. Connect. Write and say *melt*. Let's read it together: *melt*. Knowing how to read consonant blends with *l* at the end of words can help you read many words with this blend.

2. Model and give example. Read *melt* aloud again: *melt*. Have students say *-lt* with you several times. *Melt* is one of many words with a consonant blend with *l* at the end. Help students think of other words that use a consonant blend with *l* at the end of the word, such as *held* and *bulb*.

3. Model blending. Write *-lt* and slowly blend it several times with students. Then write *me* at the beginning. Cover the consonant blend *-lt* and point to the word part *me-*. Say *me-* aloud: /mĕ/. Then cover *me-* and point to the consonant blend *-lt*. Say *-lt* aloud: /lt/. The two parts are *me-* and *-lt*. Let's read together: *me*, *lt*, *melt*. Delete *m* and add *b* and blend the word with students. Repeat with *weld* and *hilt*.

4. Model spelling. Say *held* slowly several times. I hear the consonant blend *-ld* at the end of the word. Write *-ld*. Sound out the /h/ and /ĕ/ for students. Write *he*. Have students blend the word with you.

Repeat this routine with final consonant blends with *n*.

Display the Elkonin boxes from Student Page S187 and have students use them to spell and blend words. If needed, offer letters such as *e*, *i*, *l*, and *w*.

	ld		nd
	lt		nt

REMIND STUDENTS THAT ...

- they can read words that end with consonant blends.
- they can spell words that end with consonant blends.

☑ **MONITOR PROGRESS** Have students read the following words from Student Page S187. Then have them spell two new words: one with a final consonant blend with *l* and one with *n*.

pelt	hand	________
tilt	mint	________

IF... students misread or misspell a word,
THEN... guide them to identify the letters and sounds in the word. Then have them blend or spell the word with you and independently.

Lesson 32 Consonant Blends

REMIND STUDENTS THAT ...

- they can read words that start and end with consonant blends *st* and *sk*.
- they can spell words that start and end with consonant blends *st* and *sk*.

PRACTICE 3: Initial and Final Consonant Blends Remind students that words can begin or end with consonant blends. Use the following routine to guide students as they read and spell words with initial and final consonant blends.

Routine

1. Connect. Write and say *past*. Let's read it together. Knowing how to read consonant blends with *st* can help you read many words with this blend.

2. Model and give example. Read *past* aloud again: *past*. Have students say *-st* with you several times. *Past* is one of many words with a consonant blend with *st*. This consonant blend can start or end a word. Help students think of other words that use the consonant blend *st* at the beginning or end of the word, such as *list*, *step*, and *stag*.

3. Model blending. Write *-st* and slowly blend it several times with students. Then write *pa* at the beginning. Cover the consonant blend *-st* and point to the word part *pa-*. Say *pa-* aloud: /pă/. Then cover *pa-* and point to the consonant blend *-st*. Say *-st* aloud: /st/. The two parts are *pa-* and *-st*. Let's read together: *pa*, *st*, *past*. Delete *p* and add *l* and blend the word with students. Repeat with *stop* and *stun*.

4. Model spelling. Say *best* slowly several times. I hear the consonant blend *st* at the end of the word. Write *-st*. Sound out the /b/ and /ĕ/ for students. Write *be*. Have students blend the word with you.

Repeat this routine with initial and final consonant blends with *sk*.

st			st
sk			sk

Display the Elkonin boxes from Student Page S188 and have students use them to spell and blend words. If needed, offer letters such as *a*, *e*, *i*, *l*, *p*, and *t*.

☑ **INDEPENDENT PRACTICE** Have students read the following words from Student Page S188. Then have them spell two new words: one with the consonant blend *st* and one with the consonant blend *sk*.

pest	Stan	________
ask	skim	________

IF... students misread or misspell a word,
THEN... guide them to identify the letters and sounds in the word. Then have them blend or spell the word with you and independently.

Lesson 32 **Consonant Blends**

starts with *-sl*

The Sled

I held my sled in my hand.

ends with *-nd*

I went up the hill.

ends with *-nt*

I set my sled on the top of the hill.

I sat on it.

I went fast! I did not stop!

ends with *-st*

starts with *st-*

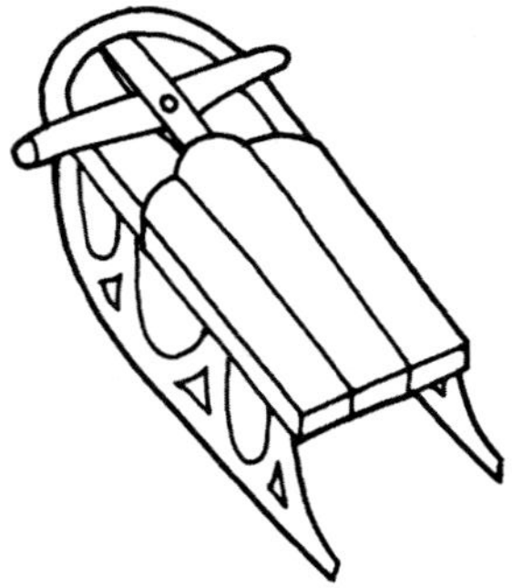

Lesson 32 Consonant Blends

bl		cr	
fl		dr	

glad	flap	______
slid	trip	______

Lesson 32 Consonant Blends

	ld		nd
	lt		nt

pelt	hand	______
tilt	mint	______

Lesson 32 Consonant Blends

st			st
sk			sk

pest	Stan	________
ask	skim	________

ASSESSMENT
LESSON 32

Phonics, Morphology, and Spelling

ASSESS MASTERY Use this Checkpoint to assess students' mastery of consonant blends.

ADMINISTER THE TEST Display or print the following page for students. Then administer the Checkpoint to each student. Read the directions aloud, then have students respond. Record responses on the scoring chart below.

DIRECTIONS: I will read and show you groups of words. Tell me the consonant blend you hear in the first word. Then tell me the other word in the group that has the same consonant blend.

1. Consonant Blends (Lesson 32)

ASSESS:	**flag**	sled	flat	plan

2. Consonant Blends (Lesson 32)

ASSESS:	**trap**	trip	crack	drag

3. Consonant Blends (Lesson 32)

ASSESS:	**hand**	belt	went	mend

4. Consonant Blends (Lesson 32)

ASSESS:	**must**	step	task	skim

SCORING

SKILL/LESSON	**SCORE**
1. Consonant Blends (Lesson 32) consonant blend *fl*; *flat*	_____ / 2
2. Consonant Blends (Lesson 32) consonant blend *tr*; *trip*	_____ / 2
3. Consonant Blends (Lesson 32) consonant blend *nd*; *mend*	_____ / 2
4. Consonant Blends (Lesson 32) consonant blend *st*; *step*	_____ / 2

An overall score of 80% correct is typically considered mastery. Use your judgment and your individual students' needs as well to determine skill mastery.

IF... you determine that students have not demonstrated sufficient mastery of one or more skills,
THEN... review the skill(s), going back to the lessons to reteach and scaffold as needed.

ASSESSMENT
LESSON 32

Phonics, Morphology, and Spelling

1.	**flag**	**sled**	**flat**	**plan**

2.	**trap**	**trip**	**crack**	**drag**

3.	**hand**	**belt**	**went**	**mend**

4.	**must**	**step**	**task**	**skim**

Lesson 33 High-Frequency Words 1

INTRODUCE Remind students that we form words by putting letters together. We learn to read some words by saying the sounds that the letters make. Other words we have to learn just by remembering the letters. These are words that we see a lot. Let's look at some of these words.

MODEL Display or share copies of the following passage, "Jon and Max," from Student Page S191 and read it aloud.

Jon and Max

I am Jon.

I have a little cat.

His name is Max.

Max likes to sleep in the tub!

Words to learn and remember

TEACH Point out the first set of high-frequency words from the first word list on Student Page S192. Remind students that the words they are learning by sight are common words found in many texts. The words we are learning now are words we'll see a lot when reading new texts. Reinforce this idea by showing that almost half of the words in the model are high-frequency words.

Next, follow the routine on T192 to introduce high-frequency words. Teach the meaning, pronunciation, and spelling of these words. Help students apply this knowledge to independently recognize and read the words in new contexts.

OBJECTIVES:

- Recognize common high-frequency words by sight.
- Correctly pronounce and fluently read common high-frequency words in text.

Lesson 33 High-Frequency Words I

REMIND STUDENTS THAT ...

- they can recognize the words *a, am, have, I, is, little, the,* and *to* by sight.
- they can identify and read these high-frequency words in texts.

PRACTICE 1 Display the words *a, am, have, I, is, little, the,* and *to* from Student Page S192. Follow the routine to teach each word. You may wish to create separate word cards for student practice.

a	am	have	I
is	little	the	to

Routine

1. Introduce the word. Display the word card for *am*. This word is *am*.

2. Say and spell it. *Am* has two letters. Touch each letter as you spell the word. It is spelled *a-m, am*. Have students say the word with you and without you. Ask: How do you spell *am*? Right, *a-m*. If students are still having trouble, then spell the word again.

3. Use the word. I use the word in sentences to help me understand it: *I am a student. I* am *happy. I* am *ready for school.*

4. Read the word. Display a sentence that includes the word, such as *I* am *happy*. Ask: Where is the word *am*? Circle it. Say the word and then read the complete sentence, emphasizing the word *am*.

Follow the routine for each word on the list.

☑ **MONITOR PROGRESS** Display high-frequency word cards in random order and have students read each of them. Then have students use one or two of the words in their own oral sentences. Display the following sentences from Student Page S192 and ask each student to identify the high-frequency words you say aloud.

> I am Kim.
> I have to go.
> I am a little late.

IF... students have trouble using the word in a sentence,
THEN... identify the word and model how to use it. For example, say: *The word is* to. *I go to the store.* Have students repeat the sentence and then say their own sentence.

Lesson 33 High-Frequency Words I

PRACTICE 2 Display the words *for, he, like, me, my, she, we,* and *with* from Student Page S193. Follow the routine to teach each word. You may wish to create separate word cards for student practice.

for	he	like	me
my	she	we	with

Routine

1. Introduce the word. Display the *for* word card. This word is *for.*

2. Say and spell it. *For* has three letters. Touch each letter as you spell the word. It is spelled *f-o-r, for.* Have students say the word with you and then without you. Ask: How do you spell *for*? Right, *f-o-r.*

3. Use the word. I use the word in sentences to help me understand it: *I look* for *my coat. I have a toy* for *you. Are you ready* for *lunch?*

4. Read the word. Display a sentence that includes the word, such as *I will go* for *a walk.* Ask: Where is the word *for*? Circle it. Say the word and then read the complete sentence, emphasizing the word *for.*

Follow the routine for each word on the list.

REMIND STUDENTS THAT ...

- they can recognize the high-frequency words *for, he, like, me, my, she, we,* and *with* by sight.
- they can identify and read these high-frequency words in texts.

☑ **MONITOR PROGRESS** Choose a word from the list and have students use it in a sentence. Display a sentence that includes the word and have students identify the word in context. For each word on the list, display the word card and have students say the word. Then display the following sentences from Student Page S193 for students to read aloud with you.

We like my dog, Bud.
He likes to run with me.
He can run a lot!

IF… students cannot read a particular word,
THEN… model how to say and spell any problematic high-frequency words, such as *like* or *with*, and use sound-by-sound blending for decodable words. Then have students read the sentence aloud independently.

Lesson 33 High-Frequency Words I

REMIND STUDENTS THAT ...

- they can recognize the high-frequency words *are, do, look, of, see, that, they,* and *you* by sight.
- they can identify and read these high-frequency words in texts.

PRACTICE 3 Display the words *are, do, look, of,* see, *that, they,* and *you* from Student Page S194. Follow the routine to teach each word. You may wish to create separate word cards for student practice.

are	do	look	of
see	that	they	you

Routine

1. Introduce the word. Display the *are* word card. This word is *are.*

2. Say and spell it. *Are* has three letters. Touch each letter as you spell the word. It is spelled *a-r-e, are.* Have students say the word with you and then without you. Ask: How do you spell *are?* Right, *a-r-e.*

3. Use the word. I use the word in sentences to help me understand it: *We are home. Are you coming? They are my shoes.*

4. Read the word. Display a sentence that includes the word, such as *You* are so *kind.* Ask: Where is the word *are?* Circle it. Say the word and then read the complete sentence, emphasizing the word *are.*

Follow the routine for any words on the list.

✓ MONITOR PROGRESS Display sentences including the high-frequency words and have students identify the words in context. For each word on the list, hold up a word card and have students say the word and then use it in a sentence. Then display the following sentences from Student Page S194 for students to read aloud with you.

Do you see the little bugs?
I like to look for bugs.
They are fun!

IF... students have trouble using the words in sentences,
THEN... identify the word and model how to use it. For example, say: *The word is that. I want to play with that red ball.* Have students repeat the sentence and then say their own sentence.

Lesson 33 High-Frequency Words I

PRACTICE 4 Display the words *one, two, three, four, five, from, go,* and *here* from Student Page S195. Follow the routine to teach each word. You may wish to create separate word cards for student practice.

one	two	three	four
five	from	go	here

Routine

1. Introduce the word. Display the word card for *one*. This word is *one*.

2. Say and spell it. *One* has three letters. Touch each letter as you spell the word. It is spelled *o-n-e, one*. Have students say the word with you and then without you. Ask: How do you spell *one*? Right, *o-n-e*.

3. Use the word. I use the word in sentences to help me understand it: *I have* one *book.* One *day I want to go to Africa.*

4. Read the word. Display a sentence that includes the word, such as *I have* one *little fish*. Ask: Where is the word *one*? Circle it. Say the word and then read the complete sentence, emphasizing the word *one*.

Follow the routine for each word on the list. Point out the difference between the homophones *for/four* and *to/two*.

REMIND STUDENTS THAT …

- they can recognize the high-frequency words *one, two, three, four, five, from, go,* and *here* by sight.
- they can identify and read these high-frequency words in texts.

MONITOR PROGRESS Choose the word cards *four* and *two* from the list and have students use them in oral sentences. Display sentences including the words *for, four, to,* and *two*, and ask students to identify the words in context. Then display the following sentences from Student Page S195 and ask students to read them aloud.

> Here we go!
> Here are three balls for you and two for me.
> I have to look for that one.

IF… students mix up *for/four* or *to/two*,
THEN… model how to say and spell the words, pointing out differences in spelling and meaning. Then have students create sentences using the words correctly.

Lesson 33 High-Frequency Words I

REMIND STUDENTS THAT ...

- they can recognize the high-frequency words *yellow, blue, green, come, said, was, what,* and *when* by sight.
- they can identify and read these high-frequency words in texts.

PRACTICE 5 Display the words *yellow, blue, green, come, said, was, what,* and *when* from Student Page S196. Follow the routine to teach each word. You may wish to create separate word cards for student practice.

yellow	blue	green	come
said	was	what	when

Routine

1. Introduce the word. Display the word card for *blue*. This word is *blue*.

2. Say and spell it. *Blue* has four letters. Touch each letter as you spell the word. It is spelled *b-l-u-e, blue.* Have students say the word with you and then without you.

3. Use the word. I use the word in sentences to help me understand it: *I have a* blue *hat. The sky is* blue.

4. Read the word. Display a sentence that includes the word, such as *She has a* blue *dress.* Ask: Where is the word *blue*? Circle it. Say the word and then read the complete sentence, emphasizing the word *blue*.

Follow the routine for other words on the list.

☑ **INDEPENDENT PRACTICE** Choose two words from the list and have students use them in oral sentences. Display a sentence including the words and have students identify both words in context. For each word on the list, hold up a word card and have students say the word and use it in a sentence. Then display the following sentences from Student Page S196 and have individual students read them aloud.

> Do you see what I see?
> Dad said that we have five hats.
> Two are blue. Three are green.
> What hat was yellow?

IF... students have trouble identifying the words,
THEN... review any problematic high-frequency words, reteaching as necessary.

Lesson 33 High-Frequency Words I

Jon and Max

I am Jon.
I have a little cat.
His name is Max.
Max likes to sleep in the tub!

Lesson 33 High-Frequency Words I

a	am	have	I
is	little	the	to

I am Kim.
I have to go.
I am a little late.

Lesson 33 High-Frequency Words 1

for	he	like	me
my	she	we	with

We like my dog, Bud.
He likes to run with me.
He can run a lot!

Lesson 33 High-Frequency Words 1

are	do	look	of
see	that	they	you

Do you see the little bugs?
I like to look for bugs.
They are fun!

Lesson 33 High-Frequency Words I

one	two	three	four
five	from	go	here

Here we go!
Here are three balls for you and two
for me.
I have to look for that one.

Lesson 33 High-Frequency Words 1

yellow	blue	green	come
said	was	what	when

Do you see what I see?
Dad said that we have five hats.
Two are blue.
Three are green.
What hat was yellow?

Lesson 34 High-Frequency Words 2

INTRODUCE Remind students that we form words by putting letters together. We learn to read some words by saying the sounds that the letters make. Other words we have to learn just by remembering the letters. These are words that we see a lot. We've learned some of these words. Let's look at more of them today.

MODEL Display or distribute "Kitten at Play," from Student Page S197, and read it aloud.

Kitten at Play

I need to get my pen.

Did it fall on the rug?

Is it in the den?

It must be here, but where?

Look at Mugs play with it!

TEACH Point out the first set of high-frequency words from the word list on Student Page S198. Remind students that the words they are learning by sight are common words found in many texts. The words we are learning now are words we'll see a lot when reading new texts. Reinforce this idea by pointing out how many of the words in the model are high-frequency words.

Next, follow the routine on T198 to introduce high-frequency words. Teach the meaning, pronunciation, and spelling of these words, and help students apply this knowledge to independently recognize and read the words in new contexts.

OBJECTIVES:

- Recognize common high-frequency words by sight.
- Correctly pronounce and fluently read common high-frequency words in text.

Lesson 34 High-Frequency Words 2

REMIND STUDENTS THAT ...

- they can recognize the words *and, but, get, did, be, in, on,* and *at* by sight.
- they can identify and read these high-frequency words in texts.

PRACTICE 1 Display the words *and, at, be, but, did, get, in, and on* for students using Student Page S198. You may wish to create separate word cards for student practice.

and	at	be	but
did	get	in	on

Follow the routine below to teach each word.

Routine

1. Introduce the word.	Display the word card for *and.*
2. Say and spell it.	*And* has three letters. Touch each letter as you spell the word. Have students say the word with you and without you. Ask: How do you spell *and?* Right, *a-n-d.* If students are still having trouble, then spell the word again.
3. Use the word.	I use the word in sentences to help me understand it: *Pal* and *Spot are my pets. Meg* and *I run together.*
4. Read the word.	Display a sentence that includes the word, such as *Pal* and *Spot are my pets.* Ask: Where is the word *and?* Circle it. Say the word and then read the complete sentence, emphasizing the word *and.*

Repeat the routine using the other words in the list.

☑ **MONITOR PROGRESS** Display the following sentences from Student Page S198 and ask individuals to identify the high-frequency words you say aloud.

He did get the ham and eggs.
The buns are in the pan.
Can you be here at six?

IF... students have trouble identifying a high-frequency word,
THEN... identify the word and model how to use it. For example, say: *The word is did. I did clean my desk.*

Lesson 34 High-Frequency Words 2

PRACTICE 2 Display the words *help, her, him, make, people, play, them,* and *water* for students using Student Page S199. You may wish to create separate word cards for student practice.

help	her	him	make
people	play	them	water

Follow the routine below to teach each word.

Routine

1. Introduce the word.	Display the word card for *help.*
2. Say and spell it.	*Help* has four letters. Touch each letter as you spell the word. Have students say the word with you and without you. Ask: How do you spell *help?* Yes, *h-e-l-p.*
3. Use the word.	I use the word in sentences to help me understand it: *You* help *at home. I* help *students learn.*
4. Read the word.	Display a sentence that includes the word, such as *You* help *at home.* Ask: Where is the word *help?* Circle it. Say the word and then read the complete sentence, emphasizing the word *help.*

Repeat the routine using the other words in the list.

REMIND STUDENTS THAT ...

- they can recognize the words *help, her, him, make, people, play, them,* and *water* by sight.
- they can identify and read these high-frequency words in texts.

MONITOR PROGRESS For each word on the list, display the word card and have students say the word. Choose several of the words and have students use them in sentences. Then display the following sentences from Student Page S199 for students to read aloud with you.

The people can play in the water.
I will make up games for them.
He can help me.

IF... students cannot read one of the words,
THEN... model how to say and spell it. Have the student read the sentence aloud independently.

Lesson 34 High-Frequency Words 2

REMIND STUDENTS THAT …

- they can recognize the words *been, can, jump, many, ride, run, some,* and *take* by sight.
- they can identify and read these high-frequency words in texts.

PRACTICE 3 Display the words *been, can, jump, many, ride, run, some,* and *take* for students using Student Page S200. You may wish to create separate word cards for student practice.

been	can	jump	many
ride	run	some	take

Follow the routine below to teach each word.

Routine

1. Introduce the word. Display the word card for *been.*

2. Say and spell it. Been has four letters. Touch each letter as you spell the word. Have students say the word with you and without you. Ask: How do you spell *been*? Yes, *b-e-e-n.*

3. Use the word. I use the word in sentences to help me understand it: *I have* been *to a zoo. Have you* been *sick?*

4. Read the word. Display a sentence that includes the word, such as *Dad has* been *to see Gram.* Ask: Where is the word *been*? Circle it. Say the word and then read the complete sentence, emphasizing the word *been.*

Repeat the routine using the other words in the list.

☑ **MONITOR PROGRESS** Display the following sentences from Student Page S200 and have students read them aloud with you. Ask them to identify the high-frequency words.

> Jan can run and jump into the water.
> She can take a ride on a boat.
> She has many ways to have fun.

IF… students have trouble identifying the high-frequency words,
THEN… identify the word and model using it. For example, say and write: *The word is* some. *I want* some *pens!*

Lesson 34 High-Frequency Words 2

PRACTICE 4 Display the words *came, down, out, sit, this, these, up,* and *use* for students using Student Page S201. You may wish to create separate word cards for student practice.

came	down	out	sit
this	these	up	use

Follow the routine below to teach each word.

Routine

1. Introduce the word.	Display the word card for *came*.
2. Say and spell it.	*Came* has four letters. Touch each letter as you spell the word. Have students say the word with you and without you. Ask: How do you spell *came*? Yes, *c-a-m-e*. If students are still having trouble, then spell the word again.
3. Use the word.	I use the word in sentences to help me understand it: *Nan came to see us. She came at five.*
4. Read the word.	Display a sentence that includes the word, such as *She* came *to play a game with us.* Ask: Where is the word *came*? Circle it. Say the word and then read the complete sentence, emphasizing the word *came*.

Repeat the routine using the other words in the list.

REMIND STUDENTS THAT . . .

- they can recognize the words *came, down, out, sit, this, these, up,* and *use* by sight.
- they can identify and read these high-frequency words in texts.

☑ **MONITOR PROGRESS** Display the following sentences from Student Page S201 and ask students to identify high-frequency words in context. Then ask students to read the sentences aloud.

> This old car did not make it up the hill.
> It slid back down.
> These people need a ride.

IF... students have trouble identifying the high-frequency words in sentences,
THEN... identify the words and model using them.

Lesson 34 High-Frequency Words 2

REMIND STUDENTS THAT …

- they can recognize the words *black, brown, does, picture, red, show, were,* and *white* by sight.
- they can identify and read these high-frequency words in texts.

PRACTICE 5 Display the words *black, brown, does, picture, red, show, were,* and *white* for students using Student Page S202. You may wish to create separate word cards for student practice.

black	brown	does	picture
red	show	were	white

Follow the routine below to teach each word.

Routine

1. Introduce the word. Display the word card for *black.*

2. Say and spell it. Black has five letters. Touch each letter as you spell the word. Have students say the word with you and without you. Ask: How do you spell *black?* Right, *b-l-a-c-k.* If students are still having trouble, then spell the word again.

3. Use the word. I use the word in sentences to help me understand it: *Jack has* black *hair. I need a* black *marker.*

4. Read the word. Display a sentence that includes the word, such as *Ned has a* black *cat.* Ask: Where is the word *black?* Circle it. Say the word and then read the complete sentence, emphasizing the word *black.*

Repeat the routine using the other words in the list.

☑ **INDEPENDENT PRACTICE** Display the following sentences from Student Page S202. Then have students identify the high-frequency words and use them in an oral sentence.

T.S. has a black cap.
My cap is brown.
Were their caps red or yellow?

IF… students have trouble using the high-frequency words in oral sentences,
THEN… identify the words and model using them. For example, say: *The word* is white. *I need a piece of* white *paper.*

Kitten at Play

I need to get my pen.
Did it fall on the rug?
Is it in the den?
It must be here, but where?
Look at Mugs play with it!

Lesson 34 High-Frequency Words 2

and	at	be	but
did	get	in	on

He did get the ham and eggs.
The buns are in the pan.
Can you be here at six?

Lesson 34 High-Frequency Words 2

help	her	him	make
people	play	them	water

The people can play in the water.
I will make up games for them.
He can help me.

Lesson 34 High-Frequency Words 2

been	can	jump	many
ride	run	some	take

Jan can run and jump into the water.
She can take a ride on a boat.
She has many ways to have fun.

Lesson 34 High-Frequency Words 2

came	down	out	sit
this	these	up	use

This old car did not make it up the hill.
It slid back down.
These people need a ride.

Lesson 34 High-Frequency Words 2

black	brown	does	picture
red	show	were	white

T.S. has a black cap.
My cap is brown.
Were their caps red or yellow?

Lesson 35 High-Frequency Words 3

INTRODUCE Remind students that we form words by putting letters together. We learn to read some words by saying the sounds that the letters make. We have been learning about other words by remembering the letters. We call these sight words. Let's learn more of these words.

MODEL Display or share copies of the passage "What Is It?" from Student Page S203, and read it aloud.

OBJECTIVES:

- Recognize common high-frequency words by sight.
- Correctly pronounce and fluently read common high-frequency words in text.

What Is It?

Soon it will be time to eat.
First you mix, and then you bake.
After it bakes, let it cool.
Before you cut it, find the butter.
Now give me a slice.

TEACH Point out the first set of high-frequency words from the word list on Student Page S204. Remind students that the words they are learning by sight are common words found in many texts. The words we are learning now are words we'll see a lot when we read. Reinforce this idea by pointing out how many of the words in the model are high-frequency words.

Next, follow the routine on T204 to introduce high-frequency words. Teach the meaning, pronunciation, and spelling of these words, and help students apply this knowledge to independently recognize and read the words in new contexts.

Lesson 35 High-Frequency Words 3

REMIND STUDENTS THAT ...

- they can recognize the words *after, before, first, now, soon, then, time,* and *when* by sight.

PRACTICE 1 Display the words *after, before, first, now, soon, then, time,* and *when* for students using Student Page S204. You may wish to create separate word cards for student practice.

after	before	first	now
soon	then	time	when

Follow the routine below to teach each word.

Routine

1. Introduce the word. Display the word card for *after.*

2. Say and spell it. *After* has five letters. Touch each letter as you spell the word. Have students say the word with you and without you. Ask: How do you spell *after?* Right, *a-f-t-e-r.* If students are still having trouble, then spell the word again.

3. Use the word. I use the word in sentences to help me understand it: After *dinner, we will read a book. Tuesday comes* after *Monday.*

4. Read the word. Display a sentence that includes the word, such as *We will swim* after *school.* Ask: Where is the word *after?* Circle it. Say the word and then read the complete sentence, emphasizing the word *after.*

Repeat the routine for each word on the list.

☑ **MONITOR PROGRESS** Display the following sentences from Student Page S204 and read them aloud. Ask each student to identify the high-frequency words.

Soon it will be time to race.
First, get in a line.
Then, listen to me.
You can go when I say, "Now!"

IF... students have difficulty identifying high-frequency words,
THEN... say the word and model how to use it. For example, say: The word is *first. First, you pick a color.*

Lesson 35 High-Frequency Words 3

PRACTICE 2 Display the words *away, different, home, live, move, new, place,* and *same* using Student Page S205. You may wish to create separate word cards for student practice.

away	different	home	live
move	new	place	same

Follow the routine below to teach each word.

Routine

1. Introduce the word. Display the word card for *away.*

2. Say and spell it. Away has four letters. Touch each letter as you spell the word. Have students say the word with you and without you. Ask: How do you spell *away?* Right, *a-w-a-y.* If students are still having trouble, then spell the word again.

3. Use the word. I use the word in sentences to help me understand it: *Please go away now. Gran is away on a trip.*

4. Read the word. Display a sentence that includes the word, such as *Stay* away *from the stove.* Ask: Where is the word *away?* Circle it. Say the word and then read the complete sentence, emphasizing the word *away.*

Repeat the routine for each word on the list.

REMIND STUDENTS THAT ...

- they can recognize the words *away, different, home, live, move, new, place,* and *same* by sight.
- they can identify and read these high-frequency words in texts.

MONITOR PROGRESS Display the following sentences from Student Page S205 and read them aloud. Ask each student to identify the high-frequency words.

I will move to a different home.
It is away from here.
Do you live in the same place?

IF... students respond incorrectly,
THEN... offer corrective feedback for the high-frequency words they cannot identify.

Lesson 35 High-Frequency Words 3

REMIND STUDENTS THAT ...

- they can recognize the words *answer, ask, know, learn, read, study, work,* and *write* by sight.
- they can identify and read these high-frequency words in texts.

PRACTICE 3 Display the words *answer, ask, know, learn, read, study, work,* and *write* for students using Student Page S206. You may wish to create separate word cards for student practice.

answer	ask	know	learn
read	study	work	write

Follow the routine below to teach each word.

Routine

1. Introduce the word. Display the word card for *answer.*

2. Say and spell it. Answer has six letters. Touch each letter as you spell the word. Have students say the word with you and without you. Ask: How do you spell *answer?* Right, *a-n-s-w-e-r.* If students are still having trouble, then spell the word again.

3. Use the word. I use the word in sentences to help me understand it: *Who can* answer *the question? Your* answer *is correct.*

4. Read the word. Display a sentence that includes the word, such as *She will* answer *the bell.* Ask: Where is the word *answer?* Circle it. Say the word and then read the complete sentence, emphasizing the word *answer.*

Repeat the routine for each word on the list.

☑ **MONITOR PROGRESS** Display the following sentences from Student Page S206 for students to read aloud with you. Then have students identify the high-frequency words used.

> You can study and learn.
> Ask me what you do not know.
> Read the book, and write your answer.

IF... students cannot identify the high-frequency words or read the sentences, THEN... point out the high-frequency words and help student pronounce the words they cannot identify.

Lesson 35 High-Frequency Words 3

PRACTICE 4 Display the words *eat, family, father, give, good, mother, our,* and *which* for students using Student Page S207. You may wish to create separate word cards for student practice.

eat	family	father	give
good	mother	our	which

Follow the routine below to teach each word.

Routine

1. Introduce the word.	Display the word card for *eat*.
2. Say and spell it.	*Eat* has three letters. Touch each letter as you spell the word. Have students say the word with you and without you. Ask: How do you spell *eat*? Right, *e-a-t*. If students are still having trouble, then spell the word again.
3. Use the word.	I use the word in sentences to help me understand it: *It is time to* eat. *What will your family* eat *for dinner?*
4. Read the word.	Display a sentence that includes the word, such as Eat *your corn now!* Ask: Where is the word *eat*? Circle it. Say the word and then read the complete sentence, emphasizing the word *eat*.

Repeat the routine for each word on the list.

REMIND STUDENTS THAT …

- they can recognize the words *eat, family, father, give, good, mother, our,* and *which* by sight.
- they can identify and read these high-frequency words in texts.

MONITOR PROGRESS Display the following sentences from Student Page S207 and ask students to identify the words in context.

> Our family is on a trip.
> We get to eat out.
> Father wants to show us a good time.

IF… students cannot identify the high-frequency words in the sentences,
THEN… say the word and model how to use it. For example, say: The word is *eat*. I eat *lunch*.

Lesson 35 High-Frequency Words 3

REMIND STUDENTS THAT ...

- they can recognize the words *animal, because, change, land, need, over, try,* and *under* by sight.
- they can identify and read these high-frequency words in texts.

PRACTICE 5 Display the words *animal, because, change, land, need, over, try,* and *under* for students using Student Page S208. You may wish to create separate word cards for student practice.

animal	because	change	land
need	over	try	under

Follow the routine below to teach each word.

Routine

1. Introduce the word. Display the word card for *animal.*

2. Say and spell it. *Animal* has six letters. Touch each letter as you spell the word. Have students say the word with you and without you. Ask: How do you spell *animal?* Right, *a-n-i-m-a-l.* If students are still having trouble, then spell the word again.

3. Use the word. I use the word in sentences to help me understand it: *An elephant is an* animal. *It's fun to have a pet* animal.

4. Read the word. Display a sentence that includes the word, such as *A pig is an* animal. Ask: Where is the word *animal?* Circle it. Say the word and then read the complete sentence, emphasizing the word *animal.*

Repeat the routine for each word on the list.

☑ **INDEPENDENT PRACTICE** For each word on the list, hold up a word card and have students say the word and use it in a sentence. Then display the following sentences from Student Page S208 and have individual students read them aloud.

This animal lives on land.
That animal lives under water.
Animals eat because they need food.
It helps them grow and change.

IF... students have trouble identifying the words,
THEN... review any problematic high-frequency words and model how to use them.

Lesson 35 **High-Frequency Words 3**

What Is It?

Soon it will be time to eat.
First you mix, and then you bake.
After it bakes, let it cool.
Before you cut it, find the butter.
Now give me a slice.

Lesson 35 High-Frequency Words 3

after	before	first	now
soon	then	time	when

Soon it will be time to race.
First, get in a line.
Then, listen to me.
You can go when I say, “Now!”

Lesson 35 High-Frequency Words 3

away	different	home	live
move	new	place	same

I will move to a different home.
It is away from here.
Do you live in the same place?

Lesson 35 High-Frequency Words 3

answer	ask	know	learn
read	study	work	write

You can study and learn.
Ask me what you do not know.
Read the book, and write your answer.

Lesson 35 High-Frequency Words 3

eat	family	father	give
good	mother	our	which

Our family is on a trip.
We get to eat out.
Father wants to show us a good time.

Lesson 35 **High-Frequency Words 3**

animal	because	change	land
need	over	try	under

This animal lives on land.
That animal lives under water.
Animals eat because they need food.
It helps them grow and change.

ASSESSMENT
LESSONS 33–35

Phonics, Morphology, and Spelling

ASSESS MASTERY Use this Checkpoint to assess students' mastery of high-frequency words.

ADMINISTER THE TEST Administer the Checkpoint to each student. Give each student a copy of the next page. Have students follow along as you read each sentence aloud, and then have them identify each high-frequency word. Then have students use one or more of the words in a new oral sentence. Check their answers using the scoring chart.

1. High-Frequency Words 1 (Lesson 33)

ASSESS: There are two blue hats.

2. High-Frequency Words 2 (Lesson 34)

ASSESS: I saw this picture.

3. High-Frequency Words 3 (Lesson 35)

ASSESS: After today, we will live in a different place.

SCORING

SKILL/LESSON	SCORE
1. High-Frequency Words 1 (Lesson 33) There are two blue hats. (Answers will vary.)	_____ / 4
2. High-Frequency Words 2 (Lesson 34) I saw this picture. (Answers will vary.)	_____ / 4
3. High-Frequency Words 3 (Lesson 35) After today, we will live in a different place. (Answers will vary.)	_____ / 8

An overall score of 80% correct is typically considered mastery. Use your judgment and your individual students' needs as well to determine skill mastery.

IF… students score below the benchmark,
THEN… review those discrete skills, going back to reteach as needed.

ASSESSMENT
LESSONS 33–35

Phonics, Morphology, and Spelling

1. There are two blue hats.
2. I saw this picture.
3. After today, we will live in a different place.

Lesson 36 Define Unfamiliar Words

DIRECTIONS Follow along as your teacher reads aloud the title and article, "Underwater Fliers." Look at the picture.

Underwater Fliers

Adélie (uh DAY lee) penguins live in Antarctica, an area covered in ice. The water around Antarctica is ice cold. Adélie penguins spend hours or days flying through the icy water. They do this to get food for their babies, called chicks. Adélie parents come up to breathe every minute or so.

Adélie penguins eat small animals called krill. Krill look like tiny shrimp. Billions of tons of krill live in Antarctic waters. Every kind of penguin in Antarctica needs krill to survive.

Lesson 36 Define Unfamiliar Words

Underwater Fliers, *continued*

To find food, Adélie parents dive in the icy water. They tuck their heads to stay streamlined. They hold their feet by their tails to steer. To fly underwater, they use their wings, just like birds in the air do. Water is much heavier than air. Flying underwater is much harder than flying in air. Penguins have very strong chest and wing muscles. You could say they use their wings like flippers. When penguins fly, they swim.

Adélie penguins return to shore to feed their chicks. Where the land is rocky or icy, the penguins jump straight out of the water. They can sometimes jump more than 9 feet (3 meters) into the air! Their hungry chicks are happy to see them.

Lesson 36 Define Unfamiliar Words

INTRODUCE Explain that people are always learning new words. Say: Sometimes a new word makes sense right away, but often readers have to stop and find out what the new word means.

MODEL Distribute or display Student Page S213 and read it aloud.

Underwater Fliers

Adélie (uh DAY lee) penguins live in Antarctica, an area covered in ice. The water around Antarctica is ice cold. Adélie penguins spend hours or days flying through the icy water. They do this to get food for their babies, called chicks. Adélie parents come up to breathe every minute or so.

TEACH Read the first sentence aloud. Say: Antarctica is where the penguins live, so it must be a place. How could I find out more about it? Reference materials, such as picture dictionaries and online dictionaries, can be good ways to learn more.

Say: A picture dictionary is arranged alphabetically and tells you what a word means. It shows a picture to help you understand the definition of a word. Show students a picture dictionary and choose several words to look up together.

Tell students: You can also look up a word using a digital resource such as an online dictionary. This type of dictionary helps you find the meaning of a word quickly. You might also see a picture of the word. You might be able to hear how the word is pronounced. Show students how to look up several words using an online source.

Read the first sentence and point to *covered*. Say: I know that a *cover* can be a lid or something that goes on top of something else. I think *covered* means "on top of something." If the area is *covered* in ice, that means ice is on top of it. That makes sense. Later, I can check a dictionary or ask questions to make sure I know the correct meaning of *covered*.

Read the last sentence and point to *breathe*. Say: I know that breath comes out of my mouth. To *breathe* means to make air go in and out of my mouth. Tell students when they see an unfamiliar word, they can use what they know to guess what it means.

OBJECTIVES:

- Ask about unfamiliar words.
- Tell about unfamiliar words.
- Use picture dictionaries or online dictionaries to define unfamiliar words.
- Use context clues from illustrations or text to help determine the meaning of unfamiliar words.

BUILD VOCABULARY

Use Prefixes

Point out *return* in the last paragraph.

Say: *Return* begins with the prefix *re-*. This word part has the meaning "again."

Read aloud the sentence with *return*. "Adélie penguins return to shore to feed their chicks." The penguins *turn again*, or come back to, the shore.

Have students identify other *re-* words and explain how the prefix helps determine the meaning of those words.

Lesson 36 Define Unfamiliar Words

REMIND STUDENTS THAT...

- people are always learning new words.
- there are many ways to find out the meaning of a new word.
- picture dictionaries or online dictionaries can help them find the meaning of words.
- words around the word you don't know can give clues about its meaning.

PRACTICE 1: Ask About Unfamiliar Words Remind students that a question often begins with the word *who, what, when, where, why,* or *how.* Say: When you hear an unfamiliar word, you can ask questions to learn what it means. Some questions are: *What do I already know about this word? What other word does this word sound like?* What words around the word give clues about its meaning? *Where can I find out more about this word? Who can I ask about this word?*

Distribute or display Student Page S214 and read the paragraph aloud.

> Adélie penguins eat small animals called krill. Krill look like tiny shrimp. Billions of tons of krill live in Antarctic waters. Every kind of penguin in Antarctica needs krill to survive.

Say: You can ask questions to learn what the word *krill* means. I will help you get started. What is the paragraph mostly about? (what the penguins eat) What other questions could we ask? Pause for responses. Some questions could be *Does* krill *refer to what a penguin eats?* or *What is krill like?*

MONITOR PROGRESS Display or distribute Student Page S214. Read the following sentences aloud several times.

> Water is much heavier than air. Flying underwater is much harder than flying in air. Penguins have very strong chest and wing muscles.

Have students articulate questions they could ask to learn the meaning of the word *muscles.*

IF... students struggle to pose questions about the word *muscles,*
THEN... point out that the sentences compare and contrast moving in air and in water. Help students see that muscles help penguins swim in water.

Lesson 36 Define Unfamiliar Words

PRACTICE 2: Talk About Unfamiliar Words Say: When you have guessed or learned the meaning of an unfamiliar word, you can talk about it with others.

Display or distribute Student Page S215. Read it aloud.

> Adélie penguins eat small animals called krill. Krill look like tiny shrimp. Billions of tons of krill live in Antarctic waters. Every kind of penguin in Antarctica needs krill to survive.

Ask students to tell you what the word *survive* means by using details in the text. Ask: What do penguins do with krill? (eat them) How important are krill to penguins? (Krill are important. All penguins in Antarctica need them.) So if penguins need krill to survive, what do you think *survive* means? ("to live" or "to stay alive")

REMIND STUDENTS THAT…

- unfamiliar words may sound like words they already know.
- they can ask questions to learn about unfamiliar words.
- words around the word you don't know can give clues about its meaning.

☑ **MONITOR PROGRESS** Display the same paragraph from Student Page S215 and read it aloud again. Ask: What do you think the word *billions* means? How do details about penguins and krill help you understand *billions*?

IF… students cannot infer that *billions* is a very high number,
THEN… refer back to the passage and point out that every kind of penguin eats krill. Krill are very small. For penguins to survive, they must eat a large amount of krill.

Lesson 36 Define Unfamiliar Words

REMIND STUDENTS THAT…

- they can ask questions to learn about unfamiliar words.
- there are many ways to find out the meaning of a new word.
- picture dictionaries or online dictionaries can help them find the meaning of words.
- words around the word you don't know can give clues about its meaning.

PRACTICE 3: Use Strategies to Identify Unfamiliar Words Remind students they can use references, ask questions, look for smaller words, and try substituting a definition to explore the meaning of an unfamiliar word. Display or distribute Student Page S216 and read the first excerpt aloud.

> To find food, Adélie parents dive in the icy water. They tuck their heads to stay streamlined. They hold their feet by their tails to steer.

Ask students to picture a penguin in their minds. Reread the sentences, and then ask: What does the word *streamlined* mean? Guide students to use the context and prior knowledge of the words *stream* and *line* to guess a meaning of *streamlined*. Demonstrate *streamlined* by tucking your head and making your body as tight as possible, like a diver, to give students a visual. Also show students how to confirm the definition in a dictionary.

☑ **INDEPENDENT PRACTICE** Display or distribute Student Page S216 and read the second excerpt aloud.

> Penguins have very strong chest and wing muscles. You could say they use their wings like flippers. When penguins fly, they swim.

Ask students to use strategies to determine a meaning of the word *flippers*.

IF… students struggle to suggest a meaning for the word *flippers*,
THEN… demonstrate a flying motion with your arms, ask how a swimmer might use the motion, then return to the sentences and help students infer that flippers push on or through water.

Lesson 36 **Define Unfamiliar Words**

Underwater Fliers

Adélie (uh DAY lee) penguins live in Antarctica, an area covered in ice. The water around Antarctica is ice cold. Adélie penguins spend hours or days flying through the icy water. They do this to get food for their babies, called chicks. Adélie parents come up to breathe every minute or so.

Lesson 36 Define Unfamiliar Words

Adélie penguins eat small animals called krill. Krill look like tiny shrimp. Billions of tons of krill live in Antarctic waters. Every kind of penguin in Antarctica needs krill to survive.

Water is much heavier than air. Flying underwater is much harder than flying in air. Penguins have very strong chest and wing muscles.

Lesson 36 **Define Unfamiliar Words**

Adélie penguins eat small animals called krill. Krill look like tiny shrimp. Billions of tons of krill live in Antarctic waters. Every kind of penguin in Antarctica needs krill to survive.

Lesson 36 **Define Unfamiliar Words**

To find food, Adélie parents dive in the icy water. They tuck their heads to stay streamlined. They hold their feet by their tails to steer.

Penguins have very strong chest and wing muscles. You could say they use their wings like flippers. When penguins fly, they swim.

Lesson 37 Sort Words into Categories

INTRODUCE Say: You know that people can be related yet different. The same is true for words. Some words fit into the same groups. Some are opposites. That means that they are the complete other thing. They are as different from each other as they can possibly be. Some words are similar yet also different in ways you can recognize.

OBJECTIVES:
- Recognize related words.
- Recognize antonyms.
- Understand shades of meaning among verbs.

MODEL Display or distribute Student Page S217.

Colors: red, orange, yellow, green, blue
Opposites: cold/hot, strong/weak, win/lose, arrive/leave

Similar yet different: walk, stomp, march, hike, stride

TEACH Read aloud the first category, *Colors*. Say: You can put some words together in groups. For example, these words all stand for colors.

Say: Other words are opposites. Point to the illustrations. For example, *cold* and *hot* are opposites. Read aloud the second category, *Opposites*.

Next, say: Some words describe similar actions that are a bit different. Read aloud the third category, *Similar yet different*. For example, *walk* and *hike* are two words about using one's legs, but walking and hiking are different in some ways.

Explain that students can sort words into groups. Say: If I say *cereal, salad, jacket,* and *socks,* you would put *cereal* and *salad* in a group called "food." You would put *jacket* and *socks* in a group called "clothes." You can recognize opposites. If I say *asleep, juggling,* and *awake,* you would probably say that *awake* and *asleep* are opposites. You can also describe the differences between similar words. If I say *sleep, snooze,* and *nap,* you can tell me how the words are alike and different.

Lesson 37 Sort Words into Categories

REMIND STUDENTS THAT...

- they can recognize related words.
- they can sort words into groups.

PRACTICE 1: Sort Words into Categories Say: You can put words with related meanings into groups. This is called sorting. Groups can be anything—words about temperatures, foods, ways to travel from place to place, shapes, colors, times, feelings, and more. What are some groups you can think of? After students respond, choose one of the groups they suggested and ask: What are some words you can put into this group?

Then display or distribute Student Page S218. Point to and read the three headings. Ask students to suggest words, such as those that appear below, to go under each heading.

Pets	Games	Family
dog	tag	uncle
fish	hide and seek	aunt
lizard	video games	grandparent
hamster	board games	sister

MONITOR PROGRESS Display or distribute Student Page S218. Read aloud the following words. Have students tell you the group to which each word belongs: *pets, family,* or *games.*

gerbil	cousin	grandmother
pets	family	family
soccer	mother	turtle
games	family	pets
cat	baseball	brother
pets	games	family

IF... students struggle to place related words into categories,
THEN... discuss the meaning of each category with students, read aloud a word that goes in each, and have students try sorting again.

Lesson 37 Sort Words into Categories

PRACTICE 2: Identify Opposites Review the concept of verbs. Verbs are action words. They tell about what happens. Some actions are opposites of each other. That is, they are as different from each other as they can possibly be. For example, *fall asleep* and *wake up* are opposites. Then briefly introduce the concept of adjectives, or words that describe. Words can describe things that are the same and things that are opposites. For example, you can describe a person as *sleepy* or *wide awake*. Those are opposites.

Then display or distribute Student Page S219.

neat	messy	tiny	huge
true	false	rise	fall
close	open	lose	find

Read aloud the six words and define unfamiliar words as needed. Then reread the word *neat* and ask: What word has the opposite meaning from *neat?* Elicit that *messy* would be a word with the opposite meaning, and write *messy* beside *neat*. You may want to point out that some words have more than one opposite if the opposites are very close in meaning. For example, *sloppy* is also the opposite of *neat*. Continue with the other words, guiding students to offer the word that completes each pair of opposites.

Extend the activity by listing pairs of words, such as *hot/cold, clean/neat, night/day,* and *small/tiny*. Define unfamiliar words. Then have students tell you which pairs are opposites.

REMIND STUDENTS THAT...

- they can recognize related words.
- they can sort words into groups.

☑ **MONITOR PROGRESS** Display or distribute Student Page S219. Read aloud the following sets of words, and then have students identify the opposites in each set.

safe, loose, unsafe	safe, unsafe
top, outside, bottom	top, bottom
take, give, miss	take, give

IF... students cannot identify the opposites,
THEN... work through the meanings of one set of words and help students rule out the unrelated word; repeat as necessary.

Lesson 37 Sort Words into Categories

REMIND STUDENTS THAT...

- they can recognize related words.
- they can sort words into groups.
- some words have opposite meanings.

PRACTICE 3: Identify Shades of Meaning in Verbs Write *Hello* on the board and read the word aloud. Have students say the word with you in a whisper, then in a normal speaking voice, and then in a shout. Say: We just whispered, talked, and shouted. These words all refer to ways of speaking, but the meanings of the words are different. You can act out the different meanings.

Display or distribute Student Page S220.

touch	press	push
stare	look	peek
hold	hug	squeeze

Explain that you will read words about things a person can do. Read aloud each set of three words in a row and have students act out each word in the set. Help students with meanings as necessary. After each set, say: Now you know the differences among these words. They are close in meaning but not the same.

☑ **INDEPENDENT PRACTICE** Display or distribute Student Page S220. Read aloud each set of three words in a row, and then have students act out the words in each set.

cry	whimper	sob
giggle	chuckle	laugh

IF... students cannot identify shades of meaning in the verbs,
THEN... act out one set of words with students, and then have them act out the other set.

Lesson 37 Sort Words into Categories

Colors: red, orange, yellow, green, blue

Opposites: cold/hot, strong/weak, win/lose, arrive/leave

Similar yet different: walk, stomp, march, hike, stride

Lesson 37 Sort Words into Categories

Pets	Games	Family

gerbil	cousin	grandmother
soccer	mother	turtle
cat	baseball	brother

Lesson 37 Sort Words into Categories

neat ____________

true ____________

close ____________

tiny ____________

rise ____________

lose ____________

safe, loose, unsafe

top, outside, bottom

take, give, miss

Lesson 37 Sort Words into Categories

touch	press	push
stare	look	peek
hold	hug	squeeze

cry	whimper	sob
giggle	chuckle	laugh

ASSESSMENT
LESSONS 36–37

Vocabulary

ASSESS MASTERY Use this Checkpoint to assess students' mastery of the Level A vocabulary skills listed here.

ADMINISTER THE TEST Administer the Checkpoint orally to each student. Distribute copies of the following page. Read aloud the passage as students follow along. Then read aloud questions 1–5 below and have students respond. Check their answers using the scoring chart.

1. Which words give the best clue to the meaning of *regularly*: "every week," "Water gets dirty," or "things living in it"?
2. The word *steady* can have these meanings: "staying the same," "calm," or "regular." Which meaning makes the most sense in the passage?
3. What words in the passage are about moving in water?
4. Which word is the opposite of *dirty*: "big," "clean," or "healthy"?
5. What is the difference between *fresh* and *clean* water?

SCORING

SKILL/LESSON	ANSWER	SCORE
1. Define Unfamiliar Words (Lesson 36)	"every week"	_____ / 1
2. Define Unfamiliar Words (Lesson 36)	"staying the same"	_____ / 1
3. Sort Words into Categories (Lesson 37)	"float" and "swim"	_____ / 2
4. Sort Words into Categories (Lesson 37)	"clean"	_____ / 1
5. Sort Words into Categories (Lesson 37)	Fresh water is all new water. Clean water is water without dirt in it.	_____ / 2

An overall score of 80% is typically considered mastery. Use your judgment and your individual students' needs as well to determine skill mastery.

IF... you determine that students have not demonstrated sufficient mastery of one or more skills,
THEN... review needed skills, going back to the lessons to reteach and scaffold as needed.

ASSESSMENT
LESSONS 36–37

Vocabulary

Your New Pet Fish

by Delia Clark

Congratulations! You have brought home your new pets. These healthy fish will be easy to take care of if you do just three things.

1. Keep the temperature steady. Leave your fish in their bags. Float the bags in your fish tank for half an hour. This makes the temperature in the bags the same as it is in the tank. Then, open the bags and let your fish swim out!
2. Do not feed the fish too much! Follow the instructions you got at the pet store.
3. Change some of their water every week. Water gets dirty with things living in it. Your fish need fresh water regularly.

If you really like taking care of your fish, think about moving them to a big tank. Then you can control the water temperature and make sure their water is clean all the time.

PART 2

READING, WRITING, AND LANGUAGE

Lesson 38 Genre: Traditional Tales

DIRECTIONS Follow along as your teacher reads each story. Look at the pictures.

The Fox and the Grapes

One summer day, Fox went to a farm. He saw grapes hanging high over his head.

I'll eat those grapes, thought Fox.

Fox jumped to get the grapes, but he missed. He jumped again and again, but he could not reach the grapes.

Fox walked away. He said, "I'm sure those grapes are sour."

It is easy to hate what you cannot have.

The Princess and the Pea

Once upon a time, a prince wanted to marry a *real* princess. He met princesses, but were they real?

One rainy night, a princess came to the castle. She was wet and muddy, but she said she was a real princess. To test her, the Queen put a pea on the bed. She piled on twenty mattresses and twenty feather beds.

"Sleep here," said the Queen.

Lesson 38 Genre: Traditional Tales

The Princess and the Pea, *continued*

In the morning, the princess said, "I couldn't sleep. That bed had a hard spot."

Only a real princess could have such delicate skin. The prince had found his wife.

Stone Soup

Long ago, a hungry traveler came to a village. He asked, "May I have a meal?" The villagers said no.

The traveler said, "Then I will make stone soup to share." He filled a pot with water. He dropped in a stone.

"This stone soup will be good," said the traveler. "But it would be better with a potato." A villager put a potato in the pot.

The traveller said the soup would be better with a cabbage , an onion, a carrot. Villagers added each food to the pot.

The stone soup was finished. The whole village shared it.

Lesson 38 Genre: Traditional Tales

INTRODUCE Discuss traditional tales. Say: Folktales, fables, and fairy tales are stories that have been told for many years. These kinds of stories are called traditional tales. Point out the special features of traditional tales. Say: Fables are short stories that usually have animal characters who act like people. Fairy tales are often about queens or kings or magical creatures, such as elves or giants. There are magical events in fairy tales. Folktales have imaginary characters and events, but may tell about real-life problems. In fact, in many traditional tales there is a problem to be solved. These stories may teach a lesson or send a message.

MODEL Display and read aloud the fable "The Fox and the Grapes" on Student Page S225.

character

The Fox and the Grapes

setting

One summer day, Fox went to a farm. He saw grapes hanging high over his head.

I'll eat those grapes, thought Fox.

Fox jumped to get the grapes, but he missed. He jumped again and again, but he could not reach the grapes.

Fox walked away. He said, "I'm sure those grapes are sour."

It is easy to hate what you cannot have.

TEACH Say: "The Fox and the Grapes" is a fable. There is just one animal character in this fable. Who is it? (Fox)

Point out details that reveal the setting. Say: The setting is when and where a story takes place. Guide students to identify the setting. (one summer day at a farm)

Next, point out the first event in the fable. Say: Fox thinks about eating the grapes he sees at a farm. This is one event, or thing that happens, in the fable.

Then, discuss the problem and solution. Ask: What is Fox's problem? (Fox wants to eat the grapes, but he can't reach them.) Point out that Fox doesn't solve his problem by getting the grapes, but by claiming they are sour and walking away.

Say: This fable teaches a lesson. The lesson is written at the end: "It is easy to hate what you cannot have." In a fable, the lesson is usually stated at the end, but in other kinds of stories you may have to figure out the lesson for yourself.

OBJECTIVES:

- Understand that traditional tales include fables, fairy tales, and folktales.
- Identify characters, settings, and events in traditional tales.
- Identify problem and solution in traditional tales.
- Determine the morals and lessons of traditional tales.

Lesson 38 Genre: Traditional Tales

REMIND STUDENTS THAT...

- traditional tales have characters, settings, and events.
- the characters are the people or animals in a story.
- the setting is where and when the story takes place.
- events are things that happen in the story.

PRACTICE 1: Identify Characters, Setting, and Main Events Say: Traditional tales have characters, settings, and events. Review that the characters are the people and animals in a story, and the setting is where and when the story takes place. Point out that stories are made up of events, or things that happen. Display or distribute Student Page S226. Read the text aloud.

The Princess and the Pea

Once upon a time, a prince wanted to marry a *real* princess. He met princesses, but were they real?

One rainy night, a princess came to the castle. She was wet and muddy, but she said she was a real princess. To test her, the Queen put a pea on the bed. She piled on twenty mattresses and twenty feather beds.

Say: "The Princess and the Pea" is a fairy tale. Fairy tales often begin with the words "Once upon a time." That lets you know that the story takes place a long time ago. Where does this fairy tale take place? (in a castle)

Ask: Who are the characters in this fairy tale? (the prince, the princess, the Queen) Point out that the Queen is the prince's mother.

Ask: What happens in this part of the story? (The princess comes to the castle on a rainy night. The Queen puts a pea under twenty mattresses and twenty feather beds to test the princess.)

☑ **MONITOR PROGRESS** Read aloud the first paragraph from the folktale "Stone Soup" on Teacher Page T224. Have students name the setting and the characters and describe the main event in this part of the story. (long ago in a village; the traveler, the villagers; The traveler asks for a meal, but the villagers say no.)

IF... students have difficulty identifying story elements,
THEN... set a focus before rereading the paragraph. Listen for the time and place as I reread this part of the story. Listen for the people. Listen for what the traveler and the villagers do. You can reread the text multiple times to focus on each element individually.

Lesson 38 Genre: Traditional Tales

PRACTICE 2: Identify Problem and Solution Say: Traditional tales often have a problem that a character needs or wants to fix. How the problem gets fixed is called the solution.

Read aloud the first paragraph of "Stone Soup" on Teacher Page T224. Ask: What problem does the traveler have? (The traveler is hungry and asks the villagers to share a meal, but they say no.)

Display or distribute Student Page S227.

Stone Soup

"This stone soup will be good," said the traveler. "But it would be better with a potato." A villager put a potato in the pot.

The traveller said the soup would be better with a cabbage, an onion, a carrot. Villagers added each food to the pot.

The stone soup was finished. The whole village shared it.

Ask: What does the traveler do to solve his problem? (The traveler makes stone soup. He convinces the villagers to help him make the soup by adding their food to the pot, and then they all share the soup.)

☑ **MONITOR PROGRESS** Read aloud "The Princess and the Pea" on Teacher Pages T223–T224. Pause after the first paragraph and ask students to tell about the prince's problem. (He wants to marry a real princess, but he cannot be sure of finding one.) Then read the rest of the passage and ask students to tell how the problem is solved. (The Queen sets up a test. She knows that only a real princess can feel a pea hidden under twenty mattresses and twenty feather beds, and this princess does.)

IF... students cannot identify the problem and solution,
THEN... review the meaning of each element before asking: What trouble does the prince have? What does the Queen do to find out if the princess is a real princess?

REMIND STUDENTS THAT...

- traditional tales often have a problem and a solution.
- characters may need help from one another to solve a problem.

Lesson 38 Genre: Traditional Tales

REMIND STUDENTS THAT...

- traditional tales often have a lesson to teach.
- sometimes lessons are stated and sometimes lessons or messages must be figured out.
- they can use text evidence to understand the lesson of a traditional tale.

PRACTICE 3: Determine Story Lessons Say: In traditional tales, storytellers often teach a lesson or send a message. Sometimes, as in fables, the lesson is included at the end of the story. Other times, you must figure out the lesson or message for yourself.

Display or distribute Student Page S228. Read the text aloud.

> **The Princess and the Pea**
>
> In the morning, the princess said, "I couldn't sleep. That bed had a hard spot."
>
> Only a real princess could have such delicate skin. The prince had found his wife.

Say: The writer does not state the lesson in this fairy tale. You must figure it out by using text evidence. Guide students to use text evidence that will help them think about the lesson. Ask: What does the princess look like when she arrives at the castle? (She is wet and muddy.) She does not look like a real princess, so the Queen is not sure she is one. What do the Queen and the prince learn about the princess after they test her with the pea in the bed? (She is a real princess.) Ask students to think about the lesson to be learned from this fairy tale. If students need help, offer possible ideas for discussion, such as *appearances can fool you* or *first meetings do not always give the right idea.*

☑ **INDEPENDENT PRACTICE** Read aloud "Stone Soup" on Teacher Page T224 as students follow along. Ask individual students to tell about the lesson the folktale teaches.

IF... students need support determining the story lesson,
THEN... have them think about the actions of the traveler and the villagers. Ask: How do the traveler and the villagers work together? What happens at the end of the story? Elicit that the theme could be *When people work together, everyone is helped.*

Lesson 38 **Genre: Traditional Tales**

The Fox and the Grapes

One summer day, Fox went to a farm. He saw grapes hanging high over his head.

I'll eat those grapes, thought Fox.

Fox jumped to get the grapes, but he missed. He jumped again and again, but he could not reach the grapes.

Fox walked away. He said, "I'm sure those grapes are sour."

It is easy to hate what you cannot have.

character

setting

Lesson 38 **Genre: Traditional Tales**

The Princess and the Pea

Once upon a time, a prince wanted to marry a *real* princess. He met princesses, but were they real?

One rainy night, a princess came to the castle. She was wet and muddy, but she said she was a real princess. To test her, the Queen put a pea on the bed. She piled on twenty mattresses and twenty feather beds.

Lesson 38 **Genre: Traditional Tales**

Stone Soup

"This stone soup will be good," said the traveler. "But it would be better with a potato." A villager put a potato in the pot.

The traveller said the soup would be better with a cabbage, an onion, a carrot. Villagers added each food to the pot.

The stone soup was finished. The whole village shared it.

The Princess and the Pea

In the morning, the princess said, “I couldn’t sleep. That bed had a hard spot.”

Only a real princess could have such delicate skin. The prince had found his wife.

Lesson 39 **Genre: Fiction**

DIRECTIONS Follow along as your teacher reads "A Good Catch" and "At the Game." Look at the pictures.

A Good Catch

Early one morning, Chad and Mom stepped from the dock onto the fishing boat. "Welcome aboard," said Captain Joe.

Captain Joe piloted the boat over to a bay. "Lots of fish here," he said. "There should be a good catch." Just then the wind almost blew Chad's hat off.

"Hold on!" smiled Captain Joe. "Don't be like me. I lost my favorite hat yesterday. The wind tossed it right into the bay."

By midmorning, Mom had caught three fish. Chad just came up empty. Then it was time to return to shore.

Reluctantly, Chad reeled in. He felt something a little heavy. "I got one!" he cried.

But no, he hadn't. It was a hat, a bright blue hat.

Captain Joe laughed and held the hat up. "Good catch! That's the hat I lost yesterday!"

Lesson 39 **Genre: Fiction**

At the Game

On Sunday, Aunt Karla took me to the baseball park. We got to the stadium just in time. It was my first baseball game ever.

"Our seats are over here, Wendy," said Aunt Karla. She was grinning. "There is *nothing* more exciting than being at the ballpark."

We had great seats! We were so close we were almost *in* the game. "This is fantastic," I told Aunt Karla. I wondered how I could thank her.

I put my baseball glove on. Aunt Karla had told me to watch for foul balls. Suddenly, I heard a crack. A ball was high up and coming our way. I jumped. I caught the ball! Everyone cheered.

Then it came to me. I handed the baseball to Aunt Karla and hugged her. "This is for you—to thank you for today."

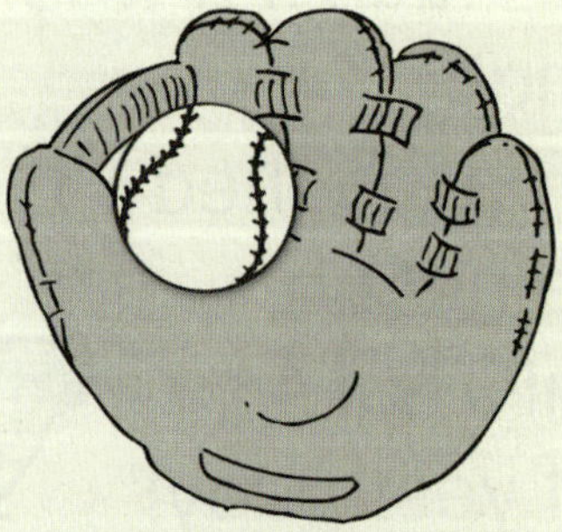

Lesson 39 Genre: Fiction

INTRODUCE Tell students that they will hear and read many kinds of texts. Say: One kind of text you will hear and read is fiction.

MODEL Display and read aloud each excerpt on Student Page S231.

A Good Catch

Early one morning, Chad and Mom stepped from the dock onto the fishing boat. "Welcome aboard," said Captain Joe.

At the Game

On Sunday, Aunt Karla took me to the baseball park. We got to the stadium just in time. It was my first baseball game ever.

"Our seats are over here, Wendy, said Aunt Karla.

TEACH Say: Each excerpt is the beginning of a fiction story. Fiction is a story made up by an author. In some stories the characters are like real people, and the events could happen in real life. Other stories might have characters and events that aren't at all like real life. Point out the character names in each excerpt. Say: The characters are Chad, Mom, and Captain Joe. In the second story, Aunt Karla and Wendy are the characters.

Point out details that reveal setting. Say: The setting is where and when a story takes place. The first story takes place in the morning on a fishing boat. The second story takes place on a Sunday at a baseball park or stadium.

Next, point out the first event in each excerpt (boarding the boat; arriving at the stadium). Say: This is one event, or thing that happens, in the story. Could this event happen in real life? (yes)

In fiction, a character usually has a challenge or problem that needs to be solved. Can you think of a fiction story we have read in which the character had a problem and then solved it?

OBJECTIVES:

- Recognize the characteristics of fiction.
- Understand that fiction has characters, settings, and events.
- Understand that fiction usually has a problem and resolution.
- Listen to and experience first- and third-person texts.

Lesson 39 Genre: Fiction

REMIND STUDENTS THAT...

- some fiction has characters and settings that could be real.
- characters are the people and animals in a story.
- the setting is where and when a story takes place.

PRACTICE 1: Identify Characters and Setting Remind students that characters are the people or animals in a story. In some stories, the characters are like people in real life. Have students name a fiction story they have read. Ask: Who are the characters? Are the characters like people in real life? Where does the story take place? Could that be a real place?

Read aloud the first three paragraphs of "At the Game" on Teacher Page T230. Ask: Who are the characters in this story? Are they like real people? (Aunt Karla, Wendy; yes) Encourage students to describe the characters and tell what they do that show they are like real people. Ask: When does the story take place? (on Sunday) Where does it take place? (at a baseball park)

Display or distribute Student Page S232. Read the text aloud.

A Good Catch

Captain Joe piloted the boat over to a bay. "Lots of fish here," he said. "There should be a good catch." Just then the wind almost blew Chad's hat off.

"Hold on!" smiled Captain Joe. "Don't be like me. I lost my favorite hat yesterday. The wind tossed it right into the bay."

Ask: Who are the characters in this part of the story? (Captain Joe, Chad) How do you know these characters could be real? (They do things people could do in real life.) How would you describe Captain Joe? (a good sailor, kind) Ask students to describe the setting. Where does this part of the story take place? (on the boat, in a bay)

✔ **MONITOR PROGRESS** Read aloud the first paragraph from "A Good Catch" on Teacher Page T229. Ask *who, what, where,* and *when* questions to help students describe the characters and setting. Who was on the dock? (Chad and Mom) Who welcomed the fishers on board? (Captain Joe) When were Chad and Mom on the dock? (early morning) Where did Chad and Mom go? (on the fishing boat)

IF... students are not able to name the characters and identify the setting, THEN... set a focus before rereading the first paragraph. Listen for the people (time, place) as I reread the first paragraph. You can reread the text multiple times to focus on each element individually.

Lesson 39 Genre: Fiction

PRACTICE 2: Identify Main Events Explain that an event is something that happens. In fiction, the events could happen in real life. What is the main thing that happened at the beginning of "A Good Catch?" (Chad and Mom got on the fishing boat.) Ask students to discuss whether this event could happen in real life.

Display or distribute Student Page S233 and read it aloud.

A Good Catch

By midmorning, Mom had caught three fish. Chad just came up empty. Then it was time to return to shore.

Reluctantly, Chad reeled in. He felt something a little heavy. "I got one!" he cried.

Ask: What happens in this part of the story? (Mom catches three fish, but Chad catches none. Captain Joe is ready to return to shore.) After students respond, ask them if the events could really happen and why they think so.

REMIND STUDENTS THAT...

- stories have events, or things that happen.
- fiction has events that could happen in real life.

☑ **MONITOR PROGRESS** Read aloud the last two paragraphs of "A Good Catch" on Teacher Page T229. What main events happen at the end of the story? (Chad catches a blue hat. Captain Joe laughs and says it's the one he lost yesterday.)

IF... students have difficulty distinguishing main events from details,
THEN... read each paragraph, pausing after each to ask questions that focus attention on the main events. Ask: What happens when Chad reels in his fishing line? (Chad thinks he has caught a fish, but he hasn't.) What does Captain Joe do? (Captain Joe laughs and takes the hat because it's the one he lost yesterday.)

Lesson 39 Genre: Fiction

REMIND STUDENTS THAT...

- in fiction there is usually a problem and a solution.
- they can identify the problem and solution in a story.

PRACTICE 3: Identify Problem and Solution Remind students that in fiction a character usually has a problem, or something the character needs or wants to fix. The way the character fixes the problem is called the solution.

Display or distribute Student Page S234. Read aloud the excerpt from "At the Game."

At the Game

We had great seats! We were so close we were almost *in* the game. "This is fantastic," I told Aunt Karla. I wondered how I could thank her.

I put my baseball glove on. Aunt Karla had told me to watch for foul balls. Suddenly, I heard a crack. A ball was high up and coming our way. I jumped. I caught the ball! Everyone cheered.

Then it came to me. I handed the baseball to Aunt Karla and hugged her. "This is for you—to thank you for today."

Ask students to identify the problem and solution in the text. What does Wendy want to do for Aunt Karla? (She wants to thank her but wonders how to do it.) How does Wendy solve the problem? (She gives Aunt Karla the baseball she has caught.)

☑ **INDEPENDENT PRACTICE** Read aloud "A Good Catch" on Teacher Page T229 as students follow along. Have students work independently to identify Captain Joe's problem and the solution.

IF... students struggle to identify the problem and solution,
THEN... refer them to specific paragraphs in the story. Reread the fourth paragraph and have students name the problem. Reread the last two paragraphs and have them name the solution.

Lesson 39 **Genre: Fiction**

A Good Catch

Early one morning, Chad and Mom stepped from the dock onto the fishing boat. “Welcome aboard,” said Captain Joe.

At the Game

On Sunday, Aunt Karla took me to the baseball park. We got to the stadium just in time. It was my first baseball game ever.

“Our seats are over here, Wendy, said Aunt Karla.

Lesson 39 **Genre: Fiction**

A Good Catch

Captain Joe piloted the boat over to a bay. “Lots of fish here,” he said. “There should be a good catch.” Just then the wind almost blew Chad’s hat off.

“Hold on!” smiled Captain Joe. “Don’t be like me. I lost my favorite hat yesterday. The wind tossed it right into the bay.”

Lesson 39 Genre: Fiction

A Good Catch

By midmorning, Mom had caught three fish. Chad just came up empty. Then it was time to return to shore.

Reluctantly, Chad reeled in. He felt something a little heavy. “I got one!” he cried.

Lesson 39 **Genre: Fiction**

At the Game

We had great seats! We were so close we were almost *in* the game. “This is fantastic,” I told Aunt Karla. I wondered how I could thank her.

I put my baseball glove on. Aunt Karla had told me to watch for foul balls. Suddenly, I heard a crack. A ball was high up and coming our way. I jumped. I caught the ball! Everyone cheered.

Then it came to me. I handed the baseball to Aunt Karla and hugged her. “This is for you—to thank you for today.”

Lesson 40 **Genre: Poetry and Drama**

DIRECTIONS Follow along as your teacher reads the play and the poems aloud. How are this play and the poems different from stories you have read or heard?

Time with Miss Prime

Characters: Teacher, Sam, Pat, Jake
Setting: A classroom on the first day of school
(*Teacher and students sit in a circle.*)
TEACHER. Let's say our names and something we like. You go first, Sam.
SAM. I am Sam, and I like jam.
PAT. (*raises her hand*) I am Pat, and I like my cat.
JAKE. (*grinning*) I like cats too! I am Jake, and I like to swim in a lake.
SAM. I like cats too! (*turning to Jake*) And I visited a lake!
TEACHER. I am Miss Prime, and I like to rhyme! Let's eat jam and a yam. Then let's pat a cat. Then let's pretend to take a break in a lake!
(*Students all cheer.*)

Lesson 40 **Genre: Poetry and Drama**

Wishing

The boy wishes for a drum set.
He wished and wished all day.
His mother said, "You get one
As soon as you can pay."

One day he took a bus ride
And gave his seat away
To one sad man on crutches
Who thanked him in this way:

"I used to be a drummer,
But now I cannot play.
If you would take my drum set,
I'd thank you every day."

Blow, Wind, Blow

Blow, wind, blow.
And go, mill, go.
That the miller may grind his corn
That the baker may take it
And into bread make it
And bring us a loaf in the morn.

Lesson 40 Genre: Poetry and Drama

INTRODUCE Tell students that drama and poetry are alike in some ways and different in other ways. Explain that both drama and poetry are different from stories students have read.

Say: Drama tells a story using characters, setting, and action. It is meant to be acted out on a stage by actors. Drama includes dialogue, or lines for actors to speak, and stage directions that tell actors what to do. A work of drama is called a play.

Say: Poetry tells about ideas or feelings. It is organized into groups of lines called stanzas. Sometimes the lines end in words that rhyme. Poets often use words that help you create pictures in your mind. A piece of poetry is called a poem.

MODEL Display or distribute Student Page S237. Read the excerpts aloud. Use the labels to identify the characters, setting, stage directions, and dialogue in the play. Then, identify the stanza and a line in the poem.

characters | setting

Time with Miss Prime

Characters: Teacher, Sam, Pat, Jake
Setting: A classroom on the first day of school
(*Teacher and students sit in a circle.*)
TEACHER. Let's say our names and something we like. You go first, Sam.

dialogue

stanza | line

Wishing

The boy wishes for a drum set.
He wished and wished all day.
His mother said, "You get one
As soon as you can pay."

TEACH Point to each callout in the drama and explain it. Make sure that students understand which words are spoken (by actors) and which are not. In addition, point to the italic stage directions and explain that they tell actors what to do.

Point out the stanza from the poem "Wishing." Say: There are four lines in this stanza. Let's count them: 1, 2, 3, 4. Remind students that a poem tells about ideas or feelings. Say: This poem tells about what a boy wishes for.

Ask students to share other poems or plays they may have read and share how they knew it was poetry or drama.

OBJECTIVES:

- Recognize the characters and main events in a drama.
- Recognize the structure of poetry, including lines and stanzas.
- Recognize rhyme and rhythm in poetry.

Lesson 40 Genre: Poetry and Drama

REMIND STUDENTS THAT…

- drama has characters and events.
- drama includes dialogue between characters, which is used to move the story along.

PRACTICE 1: Structure of Drama Remind students that drama, like stories, has characters and events. It has action that is introduced at the beginning and that concludes at the end of the play.

Display or distribute Student Page S238.

> **Time with Miss Prime**
>
> **Characters:** Teacher, Sam, Pat, Jake
> **Setting:** A classroom on the first day of school
> (*Teacher and students sit in a circle.*)
> **TEACHER.** Let's say our names and something we like. You go first, Sam.
> **SAM.** I am Sam, and I like jam.
> **PAT.** (*raises her hand*) I am Pat, and I like my cat.

Point to the characters and read them aloud. Ask: Who are the characters? (Teacher, Sam, Pat, Jake) Explain that the action of the play takes place in a classroom. Ask: What do these first stage directions tell us that the characters are doing? (sitting in a circle)

Model reading the three pieces of dialogue, using different voices for each. Use a narrator-like voice to read the stage directions. Remind students that characters speak only the dialogue, not the character's name or stage directions. Then choose four students to read the excerpt, each taking on a role. Ask: What action takes place at the beginning? (The students are introducing themselves.)

Display or distribute the whole play on Teacher Page T235. Have groups of five students read the rest of the play together, filling the roles of Teacher, Sam, Pat, Jake, and a stage direction reader. When they are done, ask: How does this drama end? (The students cheer after Miss Prime uses all of their rhymes.)

✔ **MONITOR PROGRESS** Display Student Page S238 and point to the last line. Have students identify the character, the stage directions, and the dialogue spoken by the character.

IF… students have trouble differentiating dialogue from stage directions,
THEN… model reading aloud several lines, pointing out the dialogue and stage directions. Guide students to see that the stage directions are in italics, or written in a different print, and that it probably sounds funny when they are said aloud.

Lesson 40 Genre: Poetry and Drama

PRACTICE 2: Rhyme and Rhythm Tell students that poems and songs are alike in some ways. They use rhythm to bring attention to words and ideas. Say the following lines, placing heavy emphasis on the bold words. **Hump**ty Dumpty **sat** on a wall. **Hump**ty Dumpty **had** a great fall. Read the lines again. Tap or clap each stressed beat. Explain: The words or word portions *Hump-, sat, Hump-,* and *had* have a strong beat. Other words have a weak beat. Repeating weak and strong beats in a pattern creates a rhythm.

Display or distribute the second stanza from "Wishing" on Student Page S239.

Wishing

One day he took a bus ride
And gave his seat away
To one sad man on crutches
Who thanked him in this way:

Read aloud the stanza. Ask: Which two lines end with words that rhyme? (the second and fourth lines) Ask: And what are the words that rhyme? Pause for responses. Then say: Yes, *away* and *way* rhyme. They both end with the *ay* sound.

Reread the stanza aloud again, emphasizing slightly the strong beats in the rhythm. Ask: What words get emphasis, or a strong beat, in the first two lines? (*day, bus, gave*, the final syllable of *away*). Continue through the stanza and give students increasing responsibility for reading and identifying the words that get the strong beat. If needed, tap or clap the beats as you or a student says each line. Guide students to recognize that strong beats emphasize important things the poet wants readers to know or to think about.

REMIND STUDENTS THAT...

- rhyme is two or more words with the same ending sound.
- the lines of a poem have rhythm made up of weak and strong beats.

☑ **MONITOR PROGRESS** Read aloud the last stanza of "Wishing" on Teacher Page T236. Have students identify the rhyming words in the stanza. Then have them identify the words or word parts that get the strong beat in the first two lines.

IF... students have difficulty identifying rhyme and rhythm,
THEN... read aloud the stanza again. Suggest pairs of words to lead students to the rhyming words. And if necessary, clap or tap as you read aloud to help students hear the strong and weak beats.

Lesson 40 Genre: Poetry and Drama

REMIND STUDENTS THAT...

- poets use words to tell about ideas and feelings.
- sensory words tell about our five senses.
- feeling words tell about our emotions and how things make us feel.

PRACTICE 3: Rhyme and Rhythm in a Nursery Rhyme Tell students that a nursery rhyme is a traditional song or poem for children. Explain: Many nursery rhymes have been around for a long time. In most cases, we do not know who wrote them. Like other poems, nursery rhymes have rhyme and rhythm. Take a moment to have students name any nursery rhymes with which they are familiar.

Say: We already read one poem and looked at its rhyming words and its rhythm. Let's take a close look and find the rhyme and the rhythm in this nursery rhyme. Have students name the five senses. (sight, sound, smell, touch, taste)

Display "Blow, Wind, Blow" on Student Page S240. Read the poem aloud. As needed, explain that a miller is someone who grinds up corn into a flour-like substance called cornmeal so that it can be used for baking.

Blow, Wind, Blow

Blow, wind, blow.
And go, mill, go.
That the miller may grind his corn
That the baker may take it
And into bread make it
And bring us a loaf in the morn.

Now have students read the stanza along with you. Then ask: Who hears words that rhyme in the first two lines? What are they? Allow students to note that there are rhyming words throughout both lines, not just at the line endings.

Reread the stanza with students and clap or tap the strong beats. Then ask students to read a line and clap or tap the beat without your help. Help students with the fact that lines 3 and 6 have a different rhythm than do lines 1, 2, 4, and 5.

✓ **INDEPENDENT PRACTICE** Display or distribute "Blow, Wind, Blow" on Student Page S240. Ask students to identify another pair of lines that end with rhyme. (lines 4 and 5 and lines 3 and 6) Then have partners read aloud together and clap or tap on the words that get a strong beat.

IF... students have difficulty identifying rhyming words or rhythm,
THEN... reread the first two lines aloud and ask prompting questions to lead students to the rhyme and rhythm. Repeat with the fourth and fifth lines for additional practice.

Time with Miss Prime

Characters: Teacher, Sam, Pat, Jake
Setting: A classroom on the first day of school
(*Teacher and students sit in a circle.*)
TEACHER. Let's say our names and something we like. You go first, Sam.

Wishing

The boy wishes for a drum set.
He wished and wished all day.
His mother said, "You get one
As soon as you can pay."

Time with Miss Prime

Characters: Teacher, Sam, Pat, Jake
Setting: A classroom on the first day of school
(*Teacher and students sit in a circle.*)
TEACHER. Let's say our names and something we like. You go first, Sam.
SAM. I am Sam, and I like jam.
PAT. (*raises her hand*) I am Pat, and I like my cat.

Lesson 41 Character, Plot, and Setting

DIRECTIONS Follow along as your teacher reads aloud the title and the story "What Is Wrong?" Look at the picture.

What Is Wrong?

It was lunchtime on a beautiful spring day. Gary took his dog, Roxy, to the dog park. He knew how much Roxy loved to run outside.

The park had everything Roxy liked. It had shady trees, squirrels, and big open spaces to play.

Gary opened the park gate. He took off Roxy's leash. Roxy ran off like a rocket.

Moments later Roxy limped back to Gary. She held up one front paw. She could not put the paw on the ground. Gary was worried.

"What is wrong, Roxy?" Gary asked. Of course, Roxy couldn't answer. Gary decided to take her to the vet.

Gary called the vet's office to say they were on the way. Then he jumped in his car with Roxy.

What Is Wrong?, *continued*

In ten minutes they hurried into the vet's office. The office was very busy, but Dr. Velez soon came out to see them. She smiled and said, "Let's make you better, Roxy!"

In the examining room, she bent down and gently lifted Roxy's hurt paw.

"Is it serious?" asked Gary.

Dr. Velez replied, "Not at all." She picked up some tweezers and pulled something out of Roxy's paw. She held it up. "It is a little thorn. It was poking into Roxy's paw. That's why she didn't want to put her foot down. She will be fine now."

"What a relief!" said Gary. "Now we can go back to the park." Roxy wagged her tail. She was ready to go.

Lesson 41 Character, Plot, and Setting

INTRODUCE Name the elements of a story. Say: A story has characters, a setting, and events. There is usually a problem and a solution in a story, too.

MODEL Display and read aloud Student Page S245.

What Is Wrong?

It was lunchtime on a beautiful spring day. Gary took his dog, Roxy, to the dog park. He knew how much Roxy loved to run outside.

TEACH Say: Characters are the people or animals in a story. Call attention to the character names in the text. Ask: Who is Gary? Who is Roxy? (Gary is a person, and Roxy is his dog.)

Point out the setting. Say: The setting is where and when a story takes place. Ask: Where are the characters? (at the dog park) When does the story happen? (at lunchtime on a spring day)

Next, point out the first event in the excerpt. Say: Gary and Roxy went to the dog park. This is one event, or thing that happens, in the story.

In a story, a character often has a problem and needs to find a solution. Can you think of a story we have read in which the character has a problem and then solves it? Ask students to describe the problem and solution.

OBJECTIVES:

- Identify and describe the main characters in a story.
- Describe plot elements, including the main events and problem and resolution.
- Describe the setting of a story.

Lesson 41 Character, Plot, and Setting

REMIND STUDENTS THAT...

- characters are the people and animals in a story.
- the setting is the place and time in which a story takes place.

PRACTICE 1: Identify Characters and Setting Say: You can learn more about characters by paying attention to what they do and say. You can learn more about the setting of a story by looking for details.

Display or distribute Student Page S246. Read the excerpt aloud.

> It was lunchtime on a beautiful spring day. Gary took his dog, Roxy, to the dog park. He knew how much Roxy loved to run outside.
>
> The park had everything Roxy liked. It had shady trees, squirrels, and big open spaces to play.

Say: Gary is one character in the story. What is he like? Encourage students to find a detail that tells something about this character. (He is kind to his dog.) The setting is lunchtime at the dog park. Tell what the dog park is like. (It has shady trees and open spaces.)

☑ **MONITOR PROGRESS** Reread the first two paragraphs on Teacher Page T244. Ask students to name the new character and the new setting in this part of the story. Ask: What is Dr. Velez like? (She is friendly and kind.) What is the vet's office like? (It is very busy.)

IF... students are not able to identify and describe the character and the setting,
THEN... reread the first paragraph on Teacher Page T244 and have students visualize the vet's office before describing it. Have students think about what Dr. Velez says and does as you reread the first and second paragraphs. Then have students tell what she is like.

Lesson 41 Character, Plot, and Setting

PRACTICE 2: Identify Main Events Say: In a story, the events are things that happen to characters and what the characters do. Understanding the events helps you understand the story. Review the main events at the beginning of the story. Gary and Roxy go to the dog park. Roxy hurts her paw.

Display or distribute Student Page S247. Read the excerpt aloud.

> Gary called the vet's office to say they were on the way. Then he jumped in his car with Roxy.
>
> In ten minutes, they hurried into the vet's office. The office was very busy, but Dr. Velez soon came out to see them. She smiled and said, "Let's make you better, Roxy!"

Guide students to identify the main events in this part of the story. Ask: What does Gary do at the dog park? (He calls the vet and gets in his car with Roxy.) What happens at the vet's office? (Dr. Velez comes out to see Gary and Roxy and says she will help Roxy feel better.)

MONITOR PROGRESS Read aloud the last paragraph on Teacher Page T244. Ask: What happens at the end of the story?

IF... students need support naming a main event,
THEN... reread the last paragraph again and ask: What happens to Roxy? (Her paw is fine after the thorn is removed.) What does Gary say he and Roxy will do? (go back to the dog park)

REMIND STUDENTS THAT...

- stories have events, or things that happen.
- identifying main events can help readers understand and remember a story.

Lesson 41 Character, Plot, and Setting

REMIND STUDENTS THAT...

- stories often have a problem and a solution.
- they can identify the problem and solution in a story.

PRACTICE 3: Identify Problem and Solution Say: In a story, a character often has a problem, something the character needs or wants to fix. The way the character fixes the problem is called the solution.

Display or distribute Student Page S248. Read aloud the first excerpt.

> Gary opened the park gate. He took off Roxy's leash. Roxy ran off like a rocket.
>
> Moments later Roxy limped back to Gary. She held up one front paw. She could not put the paw on the ground. Gary was worried.

Ask: What problem does Roxy have? (She has hurt her paw and cannot stand on it.)

Display the second excerpt on Student Page S248 and read it aloud.

> Dr. Velez replied, "Not at all." She picked up some tweezers and pulled something out of Roxy's paw. She held it up. "It is a little thorn. It was poking into Roxy's paw. That's why she didn't want to put her foot down. She will be fine now."

Ask: What is the solution to the problem? (Dr. Velez removes a thorn from Roxy's paw.)

✔ **INDEPENDENT PRACTICE** Have students draw or write to fill out a problem-and-solution chart for "What Is Wrong?"

IF... students have difficulty identifying the problem and solution, THEN... ask specific questions to focus their thinking. What is wrong with Roxy? (She has a sore paw.) How does Dr. Velez help Roxy? (She pulls a thorn from Roxy's paw.)

Lesson 41 **Character, Plot, and Setting**

What Is Wrong?

It was lunchtime on a beautiful spring day. Gary took his dog, Roxy, to the dog park. He knew how much Roxy loved to run outside.

Lesson 41 Character, Plot, and Setting

It was lunchtime on a beautiful spring day. Gary took his dog, Roxy, to the dog park. He knew how much Roxy loved to run outside.

The park had everything Roxy liked. It had shady trees, squirrels, and big open spaces to play.

Lesson 41 **Character, Plot, and Setting**

Gary called the vet's office to say they were on the way. Then he jumped in his car with Roxy.

In ten minutes they hurried into the vet's office. The office was very busy, but Dr. Velez soon came out to see them. She smiled and said, "Let's make you better, Roxy!"

Lesson 41 **Character, Plot, and Setting**

Gary opened the park gate. He took off Roxy's leash. Roxy ran off like a rocket.

Moments later Roxy limped back to Gary. She held up one front paw. She could not put the paw on the ground. Gary was worried.

Dr. Velez replied, "Not at all." She picked up some tweezers and pulled something out of Roxy's paw. She held it up. "It is a little thorn. It was poking into Roxy's paw. That's why she didn't want to put her foot down. She will be fine now."

Lesson 42

Set a Purpose for Reading and Activate Prior Knowledge

DIRECTIONS Follow along as your teacher reads aloud the passages. Look at the picture.

The Bear in Winter

The bear woke up.
It was dark.
She was cold.
There was snow on her fur!
She curled up tight.
She went back to sleep.

Lions

Lions are big.
They look a lot like big cats.
They have tails and claws.
Lions sleep a lot!

Lesson 42 Set a Purpose for Reading and Activate Prior Knowledge

The Rabbit and the Mouse

A rabbit met a mouse.
The rabbit had long ears.
The mouse had short ears.
The rabbit was big.
The mouse was small.
But they both could run fast!

The Turtle

The turtle swam and swam.
Soon it was tired.
It found a rock in the sun.
It pulled its legs into its shell.
Now it was warm and dry!

Lesson 42 Set a Purpose for Reading and Activate Prior Knowledge

INTRODUCE Tell students that when they read, they can use what they already know to help them understand what the author is saying. Let's say you read a story about a ladybug. What do you know about a ladybug? Pause for students to respond. Yes, it's small and it has wings.

Students can also use what they don't know to set a purpose—or a reason—for reading. What would you like to learn about ladybugs? Pause for students to respond. Say: I want to learn what ladybugs eat and where they live.

MODEL Tell students that they will be reading a passage about a bear in the wintertime. Explain that you know some things about winter. What you know about winters helps you see a picture in your mind. You may also have some questions. Asking questions helps you set a purpose for reading.

Display the following passage, "The Bear in Winter," from Student Page S251, and read it aloud.

The Bear in Winter

The bear woke up.
It was dark.
She was cold.
There was snow on her fur!
She curled up tight.
She went back to sleep.

Tell students that what you know about winter helped you understand the passage. What you want to know helped you set a purpose for reading.

TEACH Remind students that the passage is about a bear. What do you know and what would you like to learn about bears? Ask guiding questions such as: *Are bears big or small? What do bears like to do?*

OBJECTIVES:

- Establish a purpose for reading.
- Activate prior knowledge before reading a text.
- Draw pictures to show prior knowledge.
- Discuss prior knowledge with classmates.
- Monitor comprehension by rereading, using background knowledge, checking for visual cues, and asking questions.

Lesson 42

Set a Purpose for Reading and Activate Prior Knowledge

REMIND STUDENTS THAT ...

- they can picture what they read about in their minds.
- they can use what they know to help them understand a text.
- they can ask questions to set a purpose for reading.

PRACTICE I Tell students that they are going to use what they know and the questions they have about a topic to help them understand a text. We are going to read a text about a lion. What do you know about lions? What do you want to know? Are they big or small? What color can lions be? What do lions do? What do they look like? Help students state a purpose for reading. (I want to learn what lions look like.)

Have students draw pictures to show what they know about lions. Then ask them to tell a partner what the picture shows. See if you and your partner agree about lions. Maybe you can learn something about lions from your partner.

Display the passage from Student Page S252 and read it with students.

Lions

Lions are big.
They look a lot like big cats.
They have tails and claws.
Lions sleep a lot!

Reread the text one line at a time. Ask students to raise their hands if their pictures tell about that line. For instance, students whose pictures show an animal with a tail and claws should raise their hands when you read the third line.

☑ **MONITOR PROGRESS** Have students look at the following sentence from Student Page S252.

I like to look at birds.

Ask students to name some things they know about birds. Then ask them to say what they would like to learn about birds.

IF... students have trouble thinking of facts and questions about birds,
THEN... ask guiding questions, such as *How do birds get from one place to another? How many legs do birds have?*

Lesson 42 Set a Purpose for Reading and Activate Prior Knowledge

PRACTICE 2 Review with students that they can draw a picture to help them show what they know about a topic. Next we will read a passage about two animals. One animal is a rabbit. The other is a mouse. Think about what you know about these animals. Then draw a picture that shows both of them.

When students have completed their drawings, ask them to share their work with a partner. Then invite a volunteer to tell one thing they would like to learn about rabbits. Have other students add ideas of their own as appropriate. Repeat the activity for the mice drawings.

Explain that students can use what they know about rabbits and mice to help them understand the passage from Student Page S253. They can also use what they would like to learn to set a purpose for reading. (I want to find out if a mouse is fast or slow.) Let's read the passage together. Picture in your mind what is happening.

REMIND STUDENTS THAT …

- they can use what they know about a topic to help them understand what they read.
- they can draw pictures to show what they know.
- they can ask questions to set a purpose for reading.

The Rabbit and the Mouse

A rabbit met a mouse.
The rabbit had long ears.
The mouse had short ears.
The rabbit was big.
The mouse was small.
But they both could run fast!

Ask students how the pictures they drew helped them understand the passage better.

☑ **MONITOR PROGRESS** Have students draw a picture to show what they know about cows and horses. Ask them to tell about their pictures and say what they would like to learn about cows and horses.

IF… students cannot tell what they know or ask questions based on the picture, THEN… model by saying something you see, such as: *I can tell that cows have four legs.* Ask questions such as: *How long do cows live? What colors can horses be?*

Lesson 42 Set a Purpose for Reading and Activate Prior Knowledge

REMIND STUDENTS THAT ...

- they can use what they know about a topic to help them understand what they read.
- they can draw pictures to show what they know about a topic.
- they can talk with a partner to share what they know and learn more about a topic.
- they can ask questions about the topic to set a purpose for reading.

PRACTICE 3 Tell students that they will be working in small groups to share what they know and to ask questions about a topic. Review that when students already know something about a topic, it is easier for them to understand a text about it. When they ask questions about a topic, they can set a purpose for reading.

Ask if anyone has ever seen a turtle. Think about what a turtle looks like. How many legs does it have? Think about what a turtle does. How does it move from one place to another? Think about what questions you have about turtles.

Divide the class into groups of four. Ask them to take turns telling their group members some things they know about turtles. We will read a passage about turtles. It's good to know as much about turtles as we can before reading the passage. Have them set a purpose for reading by saying what they want to learn about turtles.

When groups have finished discussion, have them share with the class one or two facts about turtles. Then read the following passage from Student Page S254 with students.

The Turtle

The turtle swam and swam.
Soon it was tired.
It found a rock in the sun.
It pulled its legs into its shell.
Now it was warm and dry!

Ask students how their discussions helped them learn more about turtles. Have students discuss how knowing about turtles can help them read and understand a text about turtles.

☑ **INDEPENDENT PRACTICE** Ask students to choose an animal they like. Have them use words and drawings to tell what they know about that animal. Have them ask questions about what they want to learn and set a purpose for reading a text about the animal.

IF... students have difficulty describing the drawing they made,
THEN... model by pointing to different features in the drawing and asking about those features.

Lesson 43 Make and Confirm Predictions

PRACTICE 2 Tell students that they can make predictions about what will happen in a text. If possible, remind students of a time when someone made a prediction about what would happen in a book, or ask students to tell about a prediction they made. These guesses are called predictions. It can be fun to make predictions about what will happen next in a story! You can use clues in the story and what has already happened to make a good prediction.

Read the text on Student Page S259 with students.

The Big Noise

Jeff was playing at home.
Then he heard a big noise.
The noise was very loud!
Jeff ran to the window.
He looked out.

Point out that the passage is not yet over. Ask students to predict what Jeff will see. Emphasize that what Jeff sees must be able to make a loud noise. Have students draw pictures of their predictions on the board or on chart paper.

☑ **MONITOR PROGRESS** Display Student Page S259. Ask students which of the endings to the passage would make the most sense.

Jeff saw a tiny little bug!
Jeff saw a dog asleep on the deck!
Jeff saw a big loud truck!

IF... students do not answer the question correctly,
THEN... point out the description in the text and ask them to tell which of those objects makes a big noise.

REMIND STUDENTS THAT ...

- a prediction is a good guess about what will happen or what a book might be about.
- they can use what they know about a story or text so far to make predictions.
- they can draw a picture to predict what will happen next.

Lesson 43 Make and Confirm Predictions

REMIND STUDENTS THAT ...

- they can make predictions about what a text will be about.
- they can make predictions orally about what will happen next in a passage.
- they can make predictions using the title and pictures.

PRACTICE 3 Explain that students can use clues in the text when they make predictions about a story. You can use the title. You can use any pictures that are in the text. You can use what happens at the beginning of the text.

Tell students that they will be reading another passage. Display Student Page S260 and cover everything but the title. Then read the title with students. Ask them to use the title to predict what the passage will be about. Record predictions if possible.

Then reveal the first line of the text. Ask students to predict orally what will happen next. Again, record predictions if you can.

Continue as above until one line remains. Reveal the last line of the passage. Ask students if they were surprised by the ending and why.

My Snack

First, I ate an apple.
Then, I ate some crackers.
Next, I ate some cheese.
After that, I ate two carrots.
And after that...

I wasn't hungry any more!

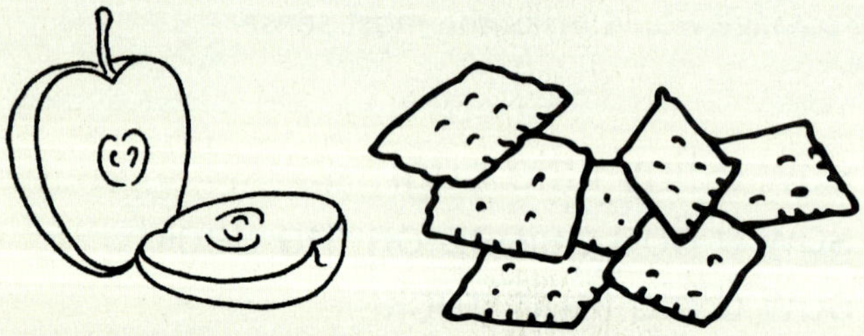

☑ **INDEPENDENT PRACTICE** Ask students what predictions they made that turned out to match the passage. Ask them how they knew to make that prediction.

IF... students have difficulty recalling the predictions they made,
THEN... review the passage with them.

Lesson 43 **Make and Confirm Predictions**

My Pet

My pet is bigger than a mouse.
It's smaller than a dog.
I call my pet Kitty!
What kind of pet do you think I have?

My pet is…a cat!
(Meow!)

Lesson 43 **Make and Confirm Predictions**

How to Make a Sandwich

My Favorite Sport

The Ride

The Girl and the Red Bird

Lesson 43 Make and Confirm Predictions

The Big Noise

Jeff was playing at home.
Then he heard a big noise.
The noise was very loud!
Jeff ran to the window.
He looked out.

Jeff saw a tiny little bug!
Jeff saw a dog asleep on the deck!
Jeff saw a big loud truck!

Lesson 43 **Make and Confirm Predictions**

My Snack

First, I ate an apple.
Then, I ate some crackers.
Next, I ate some cheese.
After that, I ate two carrots.
And after that…

I wasn't hungry any more!

ASSESSMENT
LESSONS 41–43

Reading Literature

ASSESS MASTERY Use this Checkpoint to assess students' mastery of characters, setting, plot, activating prior knowledge, and making predictions.

ADMINISTER THE TEST Administer the Checkpoint orally to each student. Before distributing copies of the following page, ask questions 1–2. Then distribute and read aloud the story on the next page. Read aloud questions 3–5 and have students respond. Check their answers using the scoring chart.

1. I'm going to read you a story with the title, "Lost Cat." What do you think this story will be about?
2. What do you already know about how a cat might get lost?
3. Who are the characters in "Lost Cat"?
4. What is the setting?
5. What is the problem and solution in the story?

SCORING

SKILL/LESSON	ANSWER	SCORE
1. Make and Confirm Predictions (Lesson 43)	Predictions will vary. Accept reasonable predictions. Sample Answer: Someone loses a pet cat.	____ / 1
2. Activate Prior Knowledge (Lesson 42)	Answers will vary. Accept answers that show connection to prior knowledge. Sample Answer: A cat might get out of the house or hide somewhere.	____ / 1
3. Character, Plot, and Setting (Lesson 41)	Characters: Mia and her cat Sam	____ / 2
4. Character, Plot, and Setting (Lesson 41)	Setting: After school at Mia's home	____ / 1
5. Character, Plot, and Setting (Lesson 41)	Problem: Mia can't find Sam. Solution: Mia finds Sam on the top shelf of a closet.	____ / 2

An overall score of 80% correct is typically considered mastery. Use your judgment and your individual students' needs as well to determine skill mastery.

IF... you determine that students have not demonstrated sufficient mastery of one or more skills,
THEN... review the skill(s), going back to the lessons to reteach and scaffold as needed.

ASSESSMENT
LESSONS 41–43

Reading Literature

Lost Cat

Mia's cat Sam always greeted her when she came home from school.

One day Mia came home and Sam was not there.

"Sam, where are you?" Mia called.

Sam did not come.

Mia looked under her bed. Sam was not there.

Mia looked in a box. Sam was not there.

Mia looked in a closet. Sam was not there.

Mia was still looking in the closet when she heard, "Meow!" It came from above her head. She looked on the top shelf. There curled up on some sweaters was Sam!

Lesson 44 Ask and Answer Questions

DIRECTIONS Follow along as your teacher reads aloud the title and the story, "A Chore for Angela." Look at the picture.

A Chore for Angela

"Come here, Angela!" Papa calls.

"Yes, come!" Mama says. They are in the kitchen.

Angela is busy with her stuffed animals. "What is it, Papa and Mama?" she calls. Her parents are quiet. Angela is curious. She goes to the kitchen.

"We are sending a letter to your sister. Would you like to sign it?" asks Papa.

"No," says Angela. Angela is mad at her sister for going away.

"Well then," says Mama, "would you please take the letter to the mailbox? Maybe you could ride your donkey to the mailbox."

Lesson 44 **Ask and Answer Questions**

A Chore for Angela, *continued*

"OK," Angela replies. She hates chores, but she loves her donkey. She likes to climb the stool and put the blanket and saddle on the donkey. Then Angela puts the bridle around the donkey's neck.

"Bye, Papa! Bye, Mama!" calls Angela.

"Wait! Here is the letter," says Papa. He waves for Angela to stop.

Papa and Mama then watch Angela ride her donkey to the end of the driveway. They smile when Angela puts the letter in the mailbox.

Lesson 44 Ask and Answer Questions

INTRODUCE Say: When you hear or read a story, asking and answering questions will make the story easier to understand and remember.

MODEL Display and read aloud Student Page S265. After you read, model asking and answering questions about each set of highlighted words.

details about events

A Chore for Angela

details about Angela

Angela is busy with her stuffed animals. "What is it, Papa and Mama?" she calls. Her parents are quiet. Angela is curious. She goes to the kitchen.

"We are sending a letter to your sister. Would you like to sign it?" asks Papa.

"No," says Angela. Angela is mad at her sister for going away.

multiple-meaning word

TEACH Ask: What is Angela like? Pause for responses. The story says she is *busy* with her stuffed animals. The story says she is curious, too, so she goes to find out what her parents want. The story also says Angela is mad. Why is Angela mad? Read aloud the conversation about the letter. What is the answer to my question? Pause for responses. I read what comes after "Angela is mad." I learn that Angela is mad at her sister for going away.

Point to the word *sign*. Say: Papa asks Angela if she would like to sign the letter. When I hear the word *sign*, I think of writing that gives information, such as on a street sign. I wonder what *sign* means here. Does anyone know? Pause for responses. In this story, the word *sign* means to write your name at the end of a letter so that people know who sent it.

Say: I just asked and answered questions about key details and a word in the story. You can do this too!

OBJECTIVES:

- Ask questions about key details.
- Ask questions about unfamiliar words.
- Provide an oral or pictorial response to a text.
- Answer questions about a text.

BUILD VOCABULARY

Familiar Word Meanings

Point out the word *ride* in paragraph 6.

Say: When I read the word *ride*, I think of something you go on at an amusement park, such as a merry-go-round. But *ride* has another meaning.

Read aloud the sentence that contains *ride*. Mama says that Angela can ride her donkey to the mailbox. In this sentence, *ride* is something you do. It means "to sit and travel on something."

Have students use the same strategy to distinguish the meaning of the verb *calls* in paragraph 1 from that of the plural noun *calls*.

Lesson 44 Ask and Answer Questions

REMIND STUDENTS THAT...

- they can ask and answer questions about a story.
- asking and answering questions about a story makes the story easier to understand and remember.
- they can respond to a text aloud or with pictures.

PRACTICE 1: Ask Questions About Key Details Say: To understand a story, you need to know what happens at the beginning, in the middle, and at the end. Things that happen are called *events*. In this story, Angela's parents ask her to do a chore. Angela doesn't want to do the chore. At the end, she does the chore. To understand and remember the events, ask questions about key details.

Display or distribute Student Page S266. Read it aloud.

> "Come here, Angela!" Papa calls.
>
> "Yes, come!" Mama says. They are in the kitchen.
>
> Angela is busy with her stuffed animals. "What is it, Papa and Mama?" she calls. Her parents are quiet. Angela is curious. She goes to the kitchen.

Ask: What part of the story is this? (the beginning) What details did you hear? Through discussion, guide students to see that the details tell about the characters and the setting. To understand the first event in the story, what other questions could you ask about these details? Help students formulate questions such as *Where are the characters? What makes Angela go to the kitchen?*

Invite students to tell or draw what happens at the beginning of the story.

☑ MONITOR PROGRESS Read aloud paragraphs 4 through 6 on Teacher Page T263. Have students use *who, what, where, when, why,* and *how* to ask questions about key details in this section of the story.

IF... students cannot formulate questions about details,
THEN... model asking a question about the first sentence in paragraph 4, such as *What are Mama and Papa doing?* Then prompt students to use *who, what, where, when, why,* or *how* in a question about each remaining sentence.

Lesson 44 Ask and Answer Questions

PRACTICE 2: Ask Questions About Unfamiliar Words Say: When you hear or read a word you don't know, ask questions about how the word is used in the story. Often the details in the story or a picture on the page will help you answer the questions. This will help you better understand the meaning of the word.

Display or distribute Student Page S267. Read it aloud.

"OK," Angela replies. She hates chores, but she loves her donkey. She likes to climb the stool and put the blanket and saddle on the donkey.

Say: I wonder what a saddle is. What questions could you ask to help me find out? Prompt students to use the story and illustration to generate *who, what, where, when, why,* and *how* questions about the word *saddle.*

REMIND STUDENTS THAT...

- they can ask questions to find out what unfamiliar words mean.
- even familiar words may have different meanings depending on how they are used.
- knowing what words mean can help them understand a text.

MONITOR PROGRESS Read aloud these sentences from the story: *She likes to climb the stool and put the blanket and saddle on the donkey. Then Angela puts the bridle around the donkey's neck.*

Ask students what questions could help them determine what *bridle* means. Remind them that they can use the story and the illustration for help. Model a question based on the illustration, such as *Where is the bridle?* or *Who wears it?*

IF... students struggle to ask questions about a word,
THEN... reread the sentence in which the word occurs, and help students explore context by asking why the author includes the word.

Lesson 44 Ask and Answer Questions

REMIND STUDENTS THAT...

- they can ask questions about key details and unfamiliar words in a story.
- asking about key details will help them understand story events.
- knowing what words mean will help them understand a text.

PRACTICE 3: Answer Questions About a Text Say: The first time you hear a story, ask questions about it. Try to find the answers. When you hear the story again, use the answers to understand it.

Display or distribute Student Page S268. Read it aloud.

> "Well then," says Mama, "would you please take the letter to the mailbox? Maybe you could ride your donkey to the mailbox."
>
> "OK," Angela replies. She hates chores, but she loves her donkey. She likes to climb the stool and put the blanket and saddle on the donkey. Then Angela puts the bridle around the donkey's neck.

Pose some questions and pause for students to answer. Ask: What does Mama ask Angela to do? Even though Angela hates chores, what does she do? Remind students that their answers to the questions help make the story events clear. Help them use text and picture details to find the answers.

☑ **INDEPENDENT PRACTICE** Read aloud the last three paragraphs of the story on Teacher Page T264. Ask individual students these questions: Why does Papa say, "Wait"? (Angela has forgotten the letter.) What does *wait* mean here? (to stay in a place until something happens) What details in the text help you find out? (Papa waves for Angela to stop, or stay in a place.) What makes Papa and Mama smile? (seeing Angela put the letter in the mailbox) How will answering questions about the story help you remember it?

IF... students cannot answer the questions,
THEN... reread the story and help them ask their own questions about key details and unfamiliar words. Generate answers through discussion, and then return to the Independent Practice questions.

A Chore for Angela

Angela is busy with her stuffed animals. “What is it, Papa and Mama?” she calls. Her parents are quiet. Angela is curious. She goes to the kitchen.

“We are sending a letter to your sister. Would you like to sign it?” asks Papa.

“No,” says Angela. Angela is mad at her sister for going away.

Lesson 44 Ask and Answer Questions

"Come here, Angela!" Papa calls.

"Yes, come!" Mama says. They are in the kitchen.

Angela is busy with her stuffed animals. "What is it, Papa and Mama?" she calls. Her parents are quiet. Angela is curious. She goes to the kitchen.

Lesson 44 Ask and Answer Questions

"OK," Angela replies. She hates chores, but she loves her donkey. She likes to climb the stool and put the blanket and saddle on the donkey.

Lesson 44 Ask and Answer Questions

"Well then," says Mama, "would you please take the letter to the mailbox? Maybe you could ride your donkey to the mailbox."

"OK," Angela replies. She hates chores, but she loves her donkey. She likes to climb the stool and put the blanket and saddle on the donkey. Then Angela puts the bridle around the donkey's neck.

Lesson 45 Retell Stories

DIRECTIONS Follow along as your teacher reads aloud the title and the story, "A Steady Pace." Look at the picture.

A Steady Pace

Turtle and Rabbit were best friends, even though they were unalike. Rabbit loved trying new things—new foods, new dances, new vacation spots.

Turtle loved keeping everything the same—same foods, same dances, same vacation spots. Turtle felt happiest with things he knew all about. Turtle knew all about Rabbit.

Lesson 45 **Retell Stories**

A Steady Pace, *continued*

So when Rabbit shouted, "Let's race to the road!" Turtle just said, "Fine, fine." Turtle gasped when Rabbit jumped right over him to get ahead.

But Turtle was unsurprised when Rabbit ran back and said, "Come on! Come on!" Rabbit ran to the road again, and again, and again.

Turtle began to walk toward the road at a steady pace. When Turtle got to the road, Rabbit was way back at home.

Rabbit came hopping up, out of breath. "I won," Turtle said. "As I tell you every time, 'slow and steady wins the race.'"

"I know," smiled Rabbit. "I can count on you to say that."

Lesson 45 Retell Stories

INTRODUCE Remind students that characters are the people and animals in a story. Say: When you read, look for details about each character. Also look for information about where and when the story takes place. Try to remember the main things that happen.

MODEL Display and read aloud Student Page S271.

details about Rabbit and Turtle

A Steady Pace

details about Rabbit

Turtle and Rabbit were best friends, even though they were unalike. Rabbit loved trying new things—new foods, new dances, new vacation spots.

Turtle loved keeping everything the same—same foods, same dances, same vacation spots. Turtle felt happiest with things he knew all about. Turtle knew all about Rabbit.

So when Rabbit shouted, "Let's race to the road!" Turtle just said, "Fine, fine."

details about Turtle

TEACH Ask students to name the characters. Then elicit details about them: What does Rabbit love? What does Turtle love? Affirm correct answers. How are Rabbit and Turtle unalike? Help students incorporate their previous answers into their responses.

Point out that the story is just beginning. Ask: What has happened so far? Affirm the correct response: Yes, Rabbit has challenged Turtle to a race, and Turtle has agreed. Remind students that the place and time of a story make up the setting. Read the passage aloud again, and then ask: Where does Rabbit want to race? What does that tell you about the setting? Guide students to state that the story takes place near a road.

OBJECTIVES:

- Identify characters and settings.
- Identify major events and other key details.
- Retell a story.

BUILD VOCABULARY

Use Prefixes

Point out the word *unalike* in the first paragraph.

Say: To find out what *unalike* means, I can look for a familiar word part. The word *alike* is part of the word *unalike*. I know that *alike* means "almost the same."

The word part *un-* means "not." So *unalike* means "not almost the same." Rabbit and Turtle are not almost the same. They are very different.

Have students use a similar strategy to determine the meaning of *unsurprised* in the third paragraph.

Lesson 45 Retell Stories

REMIND STUDENTS THAT...

- characters are the people and animals in a story.
- the setting is the place and time in which the story takes place.

PRACTICE 1: Identify Characters and Settings Point out that most stories are about characters. Have students identify a character from a familiar story to show they understand what a character is.

Read aloud the first two paragraphs of "A Steady Pace" on Teacher Page T269. Ask: Who are the characters in this story? Tell what you know about each character. Encourage students to include as many details about the characters as they can.

Display or distribute Student Page S272. Read it aloud.

> So when Rabbit shouted, "Let's race to the road!" Turtle just said, "Fine, fine." Turtle gasped when Rabbit jumped right over him to get ahead.
>
> But Turtle was unsurprised when Rabbit ran back and said, "Come on! Come on!" Rabbit ran to the road again, and again, and again.

Ask: Where do you think Turtle and Rabbit are when the race begins? Where does Rabbit go? How far away is that? Invite students to use details from the text to picture and describe the scene.

☑ **MONITOR PROGRESS** Read aloud the first sentence of the story on Teacher Page T269: *Turtle and Rabbit were best friends, even though they were unalike.* Have students tell you how they know that Turtle and Rabbit are unalike. Encourage them to use any information they remember from the whole story.

IF... students cannot explain why the characters are unalike,
THEN... reread the sentences about what each character loved, and help students describe how "new" and "the same" are unalike, or different.

Lesson 45 Retell Stories

PRACTICE 2: Identify Major Events and Other Key Details Say: An event is something that happens. In "A Steady Pace," two friends have a race. What are the main things that happened in the story?

Display or distribute Student Page S273 and read it aloud.

So when Rabbit shouted, "Let's race to the road!" Turtle just said, "Fine, fine." Turtle gasped when Rabbit jumped right over him to get ahead.

But Turtle was unsurprised when Rabbit ran back and said, "Come on! Come on!" Rabbit ran to the road again, and again, and again.

Explain that *gasped* means Turtle nearly choked or lost his breath. Demonstrate a gasp for students. Point out that people (or animals) gasp when they are scared or surprised. Ask: What did Rabbit do that made Turtle gasp? Continue with other questions about the events and details in the paragraph. What did Rabbit do next? How is Rabbit racing?

REMIND STUDENTS THAT...

- stories are about things that happen to characters and how characters behave.
- a story has a beginning, a middle, and an end.

MONITOR PROGRESS Read aloud the first two paragraphs on Teacher Page T270. Ask: Why is Rabbit at home when Turtle reaches the road?

IF... students cannot explain that Rabbit is running back and forth,
THEN... refer students to the following details in the first paragraph on Teacher Page T270: "Rabbit ran back" and "ran to the road again, and again, and again." Have students visualize Rabbit running back and forth, and then pose the question again.

Lesson 45 Retell Stories

REMIND STUDENTS THAT…

- they can identify the characters in a story.
- they can describe where and when a story takes place.
- they can remember the main things that happen in a story.

PRACTICE 3: Retell a Story Ask: What happened at the beginning and in the middle of "A Steady Pace"? After students respond, display or distribute Student Page S274 and read it aloud.

> Turtle began to walk toward the road at a steady pace. When Turtle got to the road, Rabbit was way back at home.
>
> Rabbit came hopping up, out of breath. "I won," Turtle said. "As I tell you every time, 'slow and steady wins the race.'"
>
> "I know," smiled Rabbit. "I can count on you to say that."

Ask: What happens at the very end of the story? After students respond, ask: Is this the way the friends always race? (yes) Have students explain how they know. (Turtle says he tells Rabbit the same thing "every time," and Rabbit says she "can count on" Turtle to say the same thing. This shows that Rabbit and Turtle race this way often.)

INDEPENDENT PRACTICE On the board, write the headings *Beginning, Middle, End.* Have individual students retell various parts of "A Steady Pace," indicating whether the event they are recounting occurs in the beginning, middle, or end of the story. Provide corrective feedback as needed, and place a checkmark next to the appropriate segment of the story.

IF… students struggle to retell events in sequence,
THEN… work with them to create a numbered list of events in chronological order.

A Steady Pace

Turtle and Rabbit were best friends, even though they were unalike. Rabbit loved trying new things—new foods, new dances, new vacation spots.

Turtle loved keeping everything the same—same foods, same dances, same vacation spots. Turtle felt happiest with things he knew all about. Turtle knew all about Rabbit.

So when Rabbit shouted, "Let's race to the road!" Turtle just said, "Fine, fine."

Lesson 45 **Retell Stories**

So when Rabbit shouted, “Let’s race to the road!” Turtle just said, “Fine, fine.” Turtle gasped when Rabbit jumped right over him to get ahead.

But Turtle was unsurprised when Rabbit ran back and said, “Come on! Come on!” Rabbit ran to the road again, and again, and again.

So when Rabbit shouted, “Let’s race to the road!” Turtle just said, “Fine, fine.” Turtle gasped when Rabbit jumped right over him to get ahead.

But Turtle was unsurprised when Rabbit ran back and said, “Come on! Come on!” Rabbit ran to the road again, and again, and again.

Lesson 45 **Retell Stories**

Turtle began to walk toward the road at a steady pace. When Turtle got to the road, Rabbit was way back at home.

Rabbit came hopping up, out of breath. “I won,” Turtle said. “As I tell you every time, ‘slow and steady wins the race.’”

“I know,” smiled Rabbit. “I can count on you to say that.”

Lesson 46 Genre: Nonfiction Texts

INTRODUCE Remind students that they read lots of fiction. Fiction texts are made-up stories. They are written to entertain you. But now we are going to focus on nonfiction. Nonfiction texts are true. They are written to give you information about real life. Confirm that students understand the difference between fiction and nonfiction by asking: Which type of texts tells about real life—fiction or nonfiction? (nonfiction)

Authors write nonfiction texts for different reasons. They might write a text to explain how to do or make something. They might write a text to try to persuade, or convince, you to do something or believe something.

MODEL Display or distribute Student Page S279. Have students follow along as you read aloud the first excerpt.

A Good Home for a Cat

A cat is a nice pet. There are three things to do to make a good home for a cat.

Why Cats Are the Best Pets

I think cats are the best pets. Let me tell you why.

TEACH After reading the first excerpt, ask: Does this text tell a story or give information? Yes. It gives information. It explains how to do something. What do you think the text will explain? Reread the last sentence of the excerpt. Yes, the text will give three steps to make a good home for a cat.

Read aloud the second excerpt on Student Page S279. Ask: Does this text tell a story or give information? Yes. It gives information. It gives information about cats being the best pets. This kind of text is called persuasive text. Point out and read the title of the excerpt. The title lets us know that the author believes cats are the best pets. He wants us to believe that cats are the best, too.

We will look at more characteristics of nonfiction texts that are written to inform or persuade, so you will know what to look for as you read them.

OBJECTIVES:

- Recognize the characteristics of informational text, including procedural and persuasive texts.
- Identify the central idea of informational text.
- Identify the usefulness of presenting steps in sequential order.
- Understand the difference between first-person and third-person texts.

Lesson 46 Genre: Nonfiction Texts

REMIND STUDENTS THAT…

- nonfiction texts give information about real life and might explain how to do something.
- as they learn about different types of nonfiction texts, they can learn what things to look for to help them know what type of text they are reading.
- text and illustrations work together.

PRACTICE 1: Recognize Characteristics of Informational Text Say: Some nonfiction texts explain how to do or make something. The author organizes the text in a way that helps readers understand the steps. Explain that this type of text may include numbered steps, lists, or pictures.

Review the central idea of "A Good Home for a Cat." Ask: What does the author want you to learn? (the things to do to make a home for a cat) Display or distribute Student Page S280 and read it aloud.

A Good Home for a Cat

Make a cat bed. Get a box of a good size. Cut a hole in one side so the cat can get into and out of the box. Line the box with a soft cloth. A cat that lives indoors needs a litter box too.

Buy or make some fun things for the cat to play with. Find a pine log. The cat will like to scratch it!

Set up a place for the cat to eat and drink. Get the best cat food you can.

The author organized the information in steps. How many steps does the author say to do? (Count them out: three.) I notice the first sentence of each step tells what to do. The other sentences and pictures tell us more. What are the three steps? (Make a cat bed. Get things for the cat to play with. Set up a place for the cat to eat.) Why are there pictures? (They are illustrations that show the steps.) Texts that tell how to do something often have illustrations. The text and pictures work together to give information.

☑ **MONITOR PROGRESS** Reread the steps from the excerpt on Student Page S280 as students follow along and look at the pictures. Ask students to gain information from the text and pictures. Ask a question such as: *What do the words and pictures tell us would be good toys for cats?*

IF… students cannot locate information in text and pictures,
THEN… read aloud, point to, and discuss both the text and the illustrations. Ask: What does Step 2 say about cat toys? What does the picture show about what cats play with?

Lesson 46 Genre: Nonfiction Texts

PRACTICE 2: Recognize the Characteristics of Persuasive Text Say: Some nonfiction text tries to persuade readers to believe something or to do something. In a persuasive text, the author states his or her belief and tells why.

Review the central idea of "Why Cats Are the Best Pets." Ask: What does the author want you to believe? (that cats are the best pets) Display or distribute Student Page S281 and read it aloud.

Why Cats Are the Best Pets

First, cats like to snuggle. My cat is so soft!

Cats are also fun to play with. It is funny just to see them play too.

Cats do not eat too much. So it does not cost a lot to have a cat.

Please think about getting a cat. Many cats need a safe place to live.

In each of the paragraphs, the author gives a reason why he thinks cats are the best. What is the first reason? (Cats are nice to hold.) What is another reason? (Cats are fun. Cats do not cost much to feed.) The last reason is that many cats need a safe place to live. How does this make you feel? Pause for answers. Point out that the author wants readers to feel good about helping cats.

Point out the picture. Say: This picture is also used to make readers feel good about helping cats. The boy and the cat both look happy. The picture shows how great it is to have a cat as a pet.

REMIND STUDENTS THAT...

- nonfiction texts give information about real life and might explain how to do something or try to persuade you to think or do something.
- as they learn about different types of nonfiction texts, they can learn what things to look for to help them know what type of text they are reading.
- text and illustrations work together.

MONITOR PROGRESS Reread the excerpt on Student Page S281. Ask students to name one reason the author gives for believing that cats are the best pets.

IF... students cannot identify a reason,
THEN... read the paragraphs, one at a time, and ask: What does the author say he likes about cats?

Lesson 46 Genre: Nonfiction Texts

REMIND STUDENTS THAT...

- nonfiction texts give information about real life and might explain how to do something or try to persuade you to think or do something.
- as they learn about different types of nonfiction texts, they can learn what things to look for to help them know what type of text they are reading.

PRACTICE 3: Recognize First- and Third-Person Texts Display or distribute Student Page S282. Read aloud the two excerpts. Emphasize the underlined words in the second excerpt as you read.

A Good Home for a Cat

A cat is a nice pet. There are three things to do to make a good home for a cat.

It is easy to make a good home for a cat. A cat with a good home will be a happy cat!

Why Cats Are the Best Pets

<u>I</u> think cats are the best pets. Let <u>me</u> tell you why.

Now you see why cats are such good pets. If you want a pet, <u>I</u> say get a cat like <u>mine</u>!

Remind students that in the first passage, the author is telling how to do something. When authors write this type of nonfiction text, they give facts about the topic. They do not tell about themselves or use the word "I." Say: The author of the first text does not talk about herself. She just gives facts about cats. This author is writing to give information.

Reread the second passage and point out the underlined words. Say: The author of the second text does talk about himself. He uses words such as *I*, *my*, and *mine*. He tells his own thoughts and feelings about cats. He uses his own voice to try to convince us that he is right.

☑ **INDEPENDENT PRACTICE** Ask students why the author uses the words *I*, *my*, and *mine* in "Why Cats Are the Best Pets."

IF... students are not able to answer the question,
THEN... remind them that this text is persuasive. It is written to tell what the author believes and to try to convince readers to feel the same. Explain: The author uses *I* and *me* to say what he believes and to try to persuade readers.

Lesson 46 **Genre: Nonfiction Texts**

A Good Home for a Cat

A cat is a nice pet. There are three things to do to make a good home for a cat.

Why Cats Are the Best Pets

I think cats are the best pets. Let me tell you why.

A Good Home for a Cat

Make a cat bed. Get a box of a good size. Cut a hole in one side so the cat can get into and out of the box. Line the box with a soft cloth. A cat that lives indoors needs a litter box too.

Buy or make some fun things for the cat to play with. Find a pine log. The cat will like to scratch it!

Set up a place for the cat to eat and drink. Get the best cat food you can.

Why Cats Are the Best Pets

First, cats like to snuggle. My cat is so soft!

Cats are also fun to play with. It is funny just to see them play too.

Cats do not eat too much. So it does not cost a lot to have a cat.

Please think about getting a cat. Many cats need a safe place to live.

Lesson 46 **Genre: Nonfiction Texts**

A Good Home for a Cat

A cat is a nice pet. There are three things to do to make a good home for a cat.

It is easy to make a good home for a cat. A cat with a good home will be a happy cat!

Why Cats Are the Best Pets

I think cats are the best pets. Let me tell you why.

Now you see why cats are such good pets. If you want a pet, I say get a cat like mine!

Lesson 47 **Identify Main Topic and Key Details**

DIRECTIONS Follow along as your teacher reads aloud the title and the article, "Sandcastles." Look at the picture.

Sandcastles

At the beach or in a sandbox, building castles is fun! All you need is sand and water. Having additional tools can make your work more interesting. Here are some ideas:

bucket with a bottom
bucket without a bottom
cups of different sizes
shovel
spatula
spoon
knife
imagination

Lesson 47 Identify Main Topic and Key Details

Sandcastles, *continued*

Begin with sand and water. Do tests to find out how much water you need. Too much water will make the sand wet. Too little water will keep the sand from sticking together.

Mix sand and water in the bucket with a bottom. Make a ball of the sand and water in your hand. Does your ball of sand stay in shape when you set it on the ground? Then you have the right amount! You are ready to begin.

Start by making your biggest shapes. Use your hands to pile the sand, or use the bucket without the bottom. Fill the bucket with wet sand, turn the bucket over, tap the sides, and push gently on the sand while you lift the bucket off. There is your first tower!

After that, make more towers with the bucket, or use cups of different sizes. Use a shovel to dig. Use a spatula to smooth corners or rough spots. A spoon and a knife can help you make more shapes and carve details.

Before you stop, make sure to use your imagination. Make a sandcastle like nobody else's. That's the most fun of all!

Lesson 47 Identify Main Topic and Key Details

INTRODUCE Remind students that a *topic* is what a passage is mostly about. Say: An article, like the one about making sandcastles, has a topic. No matter how many details there are, there is only one main topic. Often, the title of an article gives a clue about the topic. Inside the article, you will read key details about the topic. Key details are the most important details. They help you understand the topic. Other details may be interesting but are less important.

MODEL Display Student Page S285 and read the two excerpts aloud.

Sandcastles

At the beach or in a sandbox, building castles is fun! All you need is sand and water. Having additional tools can make your work more interesting.

. . .

Before you stop, make sure to use your imagination. Make a sandcastle like nobody else's. That's the most fun of all!

TEACH Say: The title of this article is a compound word. That is one word made up of two smaller ones. Say *sandcastles*. What two words do you hear in *sandcastles*? Point to the highlighted words *sand, castle,* and *sandcastle* in the excerpts. This article is not about sand. It is not about castles. The title and the part both use the word *sandcastles*. The article is about sandcastles.

Say: Articles have key details about the main topic. Point to the second sentence and read it aloud: *All you need is sand and water.* A key detail about sandcastles is that to make them, you need two things. What are those things? (sand, water) To retell the main topic and these key details, you would say that the article is about sandcastles, which are castles made out of sand and water.

Explain: The article says building sandcastles is fun. This is another detail. It is interesting, but it is not important to understanding how to build sandcastles. This is not a key detail.

OBJECTIVES:

- Ask and answer questions about a main topic.
- Ask and answer questions about key details.
- Provide an oral or pictorial response to a text.
- Retell a main topic and key details.
- Know the difference between important and less important details.

BUILD VOCABULARY

Familiar Word Meanings

Point out *sand* in paragraph 1

Say: When I read the word *sand*, I think of something you find at the beach that is gritty and can feel scratchy. But *sand* has another meaning. As a verb, *sand* means "to polish" or "to smooth something by using sandpaper."

Read aloud the sentence with *sand*. "All you need is sand and water."

Have students explain how the meaning of the plural noun *tests* in paragraph 2 is different from that of the verb in *The teacher tests his students.*

Lesson 47 Identify Main Topic and Key Details

REMIND STUDENTS THAT...

- a topic is what a text is mostly about.
- the title of an article may have a clue to its topic.

PRACTICE 1: Ask and Answer Questions About a Main Topic Say: You can often learn the main topic of a text from its title. Sometimes, other parts of the text tell you about the main topic.

Reread the story's title and draw attention to the illustration on Teacher Page T283. Say: Just from the picture, what do you think the topic of the text might be? Pause for responses. It might be about a family at the beach. Point to the title. From the title, you know the topic is sandcastles. You can use the picture to ask questions about the topic, such as *How big is a sandcastle?* What other questions can you ask based on the picture?

MONITOR PROGRESS Display Student Page S286. Read it aloud.

> At the beach or in a sandbox, building castles is fun! All you need is sand and water. Having additional tools can make your work more interesting.

Ask: What is this paragraph about? (building sandcastles) Have students tell you a question they could ask about building sandcastles.

IF... students cannot pose a question about building sandcastles,
THEN... let them study the illustration on Teacher Page T283, and prompt them to ask how the family made the structure shown.

Lesson 47 Identify Main Topic and Key Details

PRACTICE 2: Ask and Answer Questions About Key Details Say: Texts have many details. Some are key details. Without them, the text would not make sense. Key details teach about the topic. Other details are interesting, but you could still understand the text without them.

Display or distribute Student Page S287, and read it aloud. Ask students to listen for key details.

> Begin with sand and water. Do tests to find out how much water you need. Too much water will make the sand wet. Too little water will keep the sand from sticking together.
>
> Mix sand and water in the bucket with a bottom. Make a ball of the sand and water in your hand. Does your ball of sand stay in shape when you set it on the ground? Then you have the right amount! You are ready to begin.

Ask: What are these paragraphs about? (using the right mix of sand and water) Which details in this text help you understand why you should test your mix? (the details about what goes wrong if there is too much or too little water) Invite students to tell or draw what happens with too much or too little water.

REMIND STUDENTS THAT...

- a topic is what a text is mostly about.
- they can ask and answer questions about a topic.
- they can respond to a text orally or with pictures.

☑ **MONITOR PROGRESS** Display and read aloud the same excerpt from Student Page S287. Ask: What does the detail about a ball of sand keeping its shape help you understand? (the right mixture of sand and water)

IF... students cannot interpret the detail about a ball of sand keeping its shape, THEN... invite them to act out the two paragraphs, and then pose the question again.

Lesson 47 Identify Main Topic and Key Details

REMIND STUDENTS THAT...

- a topic is what a text is mostly about.
- they can ask and answer questions about a topic.
- key details help readers understand a text.
- they can ask and answer questions about key details.

PRACTICE 3: Retell the Main Topic and Key Details Have students follow along while you read aloud Student Page S288.

> Start by making your biggest shapes. Use your hands to pile the sand, or use the bucket without the bottom. Fill the bucket with wet sand, turn the bucket over, tap the sides, and push gently on the sand while you lift the bucket off. There is your first tower!
>
> After that, make more towers with the bucket, or use cups of different sizes. Use a shovel to dig. Use a spatula to smooth corners or rough spots. A spoon and a knife can help you make more shapes and carve details.

Ask: What is the main topic of these paragraphs? (how to build a sandcastle) What are the key details in these paragraphs that tell about how to build a sandcastle? (Sample response: The first paragraph tells how to make the first tower of the sandcastle with your hands or the bucket without the bottom. The second paragraph tells how to make more towers with the bucket or cups of different sizes. It also tells what to use the shovel, spatula, spoon, and knife for.)

☑ **INDEPENDENT PRACTICE** Reread Teacher Pages T283–T284 aloud as students follow along. Have students work independently to identify the main topic and key details of "Sandcastles." Then call on individual students to retell the main topic and key details of the article in their own words. Provide corrective feedback as needed.

IF... students struggle to retell the main topic and key details,
THEN... create a three-step sequence diagram and use it to help students describe testing the sand-water mix, making the first tower, and adding details to their sandcastles. Ask students to draw each step in the sequence.

Sandcastles

At the beach or in a sandbox, building castles is fun! All you need is sand and water. Having additional tools can make your work more interesting.

Before you stop, make sure to use your imagination. Make a sandcastle like nobody else's. That's the most fun of all!

Lesson 47 **Identify Main Topic and Key Details**

At the beach or in a sandbox, building castles is fun! All you need is sand and water. Having additional tools can make your work more interesting.

Lesson 47 **Identify Main Topic and Key Details**

Begin with sand and water. Do tests to find out how much water you need. Too much water will make the sand wet. Too little water will keep the sand from sticking together.

Mix sand and water in the bucket with a bottom. Make a ball of the sand and water in your hand. Does your ball of sand stay in shape when you set it on the ground? Then you have the right amount! You are ready to begin.

Lesson 47 **Identify Main Topic and Key Details**

Start by making your biggest shapes. Use your hands to pile the sand, or use the bucket without the bottom. Fill the bucket with wet sand, turn the bucket over, tap the sides, and push gently on the sand while you lift the bucket off. There is your first tower!

After that, make more towers with the bucket, or use cups of different sizes. Use a shovel to dig. Use a spatula to smooth corners or rough spots. A spoon and a knife can help you make more shapes and carve details.

Lesson 48 **Reading Strategies**

DIRECTIONS Follow along as your teacher reads aloud the title and the passage "Skating On and Off the Ice." Look at the pictures.

Skating On and Off the Ice

Ice skating has been a popular sport for a long, long time. Scientists discovered ice skates at the bottom of a lake in Switzerland. The skates were more than 3,000 years old!

Today people ice skate indoors, at a skating rink where loud music blasts through the speakers. They also skate outdoors, on a silent frozen pond or lake. Even at an indoor rink, skaters bundle up in thick wool sweaters and warm mittens. The air must be very cold to keep the ice frozen.

Ice skaters need good balance to stay upright on the thin, sharp metal blades of their skates. When skaters use their legs to push hard, they can go very fast. *Whoooooosh!* Skating fast can feel like flying on the ice!

Skating On and Off the Ice, *continued*

Roller skating has been around a long time, but not as long as ice skating. Roller skates were invented more than 250 years ago. Roller skating is like ice skating in some ways. For example, most people aren't good at it at first! But the sports are also different. Roller skates have wheels instead of blades. People may roller skate on an indoor rink, but the rink has wood floors, not ice. Many people roller skate outside too.

Roller skaters usually don't need warm clothing, but they need safety gear. They wear helmets and wrist pads, elbow pads, and kneepads. This equipment protects them if they fall. Just like ice skaters, roller skaters can pump their legs hard and move fast as the wind!

Lesson 48 Reading Strategies

INTRODUCE Tell students that they can use different strategies to understand the information in a text. Say: A strategy is a plan you can use when you hear or read a text.

MODEL Display and read aloud Student Page S291. Then model the reading strategies using details from the text.

Skating On and Off the Ice

text evidence

Ice skating has been a popular sport for a long, long time. Scientists discovered ice skates at the bottom of a lake in Switzerland. The skates were more than 3,000 years old!

Today people ice skate indoors, at a skating rink where loud music blasts through the speakers. They also skate outdoors, on a silent frozen pond or lake. Even at an indoor rink, skaters bundle up in thick wool sweaters and warm mittens. The air must be very cold to keep the ice frozen.

details

TEACH Say: When you read, you can visualize, or make pictures in your mind. An author uses describing words to help you visualize. Point out the descriptive details. What picture do these details help you make in your mind?

Say: When you read, you can also connect ideas in the text to what you know, to other texts you have read, and to the world around you. This text is about skating. What do you know about ice skating? Have you ever gone skating? If so, was your experience like what the author writes about?

Say: You can also use what you know and information in the text to figure out something the author doesn't tell you. Make an inference and cite the text evidence that supports it. It must be winter when people skate outdoors. I infer that because the text says they skate on a "frozen pond or lake."

OBJECTIVES:

- Visualize text to deepen understanding.
- Make connections to personal experiences, ideas in other texts, and the world.
- Make inferences based on evidence to support understanding.

Lesson 48 Reading Strategies

REMIND STUDENTS THAT...

- they can make connections between what they read and their own life.
- they can make connections to ideas in other texts.
- they can make connections to the world around them.

PRACTICE 1: Make Connections Say: You can make connections when you hear or read a text. Making connections will help you understand the text better.

Display or distribute Student Page S292. Read it aloud.

> Today people ice skate indoors, at a skating rink where loud music blasts through the speakers. They also skate outdoors, on a silent frozen pond or lake. Even at an indoor rink, skaters bundle up in thick wool sweaters and warm mittens. The air must be very cold to keep the ice frozen.
>
> Ice skaters need good balance to stay upright on the thin, sharp metal blades of their skates. When skaters use their legs to push hard, they can go very fast. *Whooooooosh!* Skating fast can feel like flying on the ice!

Ask: Have you ever gone ice skating or watched other people doing it? Encourage students to tell how their skating experience is like or unlike what the text describes. Have you heard or read any books about ice skating? Encourage students to connect ideas about ice skating among texts. What did you already know about ice skating?

✓ **MONITOR PROGRESS** Reread aloud the first paragraph on each of Teacher Pages T289 and T290. Ask: What ideas are the same in both paragraphs? What connections can you make between the paragraphs?

IF... students have difficulty making connections between paragraphs,
THEN... ask questions to help them focus on the connections. Ask questions such as these: *Do both paragraphs tell about kinds of skating? How are they alike?*

Lesson 48 Reading Strategies

PRACTICE 2: Visualize Say: You can visualize, or make pictures in your mind, when you hear or read a text. Visualizing will help you understand the text better.

Display or distribute Student Page S293. Read the text aloud.

Ice skaters need good balance to stay upright on the thin, sharp metal blades of their skates. When skaters use their legs to push hard, they can go very fast. *Whooooosh!* Skating fast can feel like flying on the ice!

Say: The author uses details to help readers visualize the information. What words does the author include to help you visualize ice skating? (thin, sharp blades; very fast; *Whoooooosh!* flying on the ice) What picture did you make in your mind?

REMIND STUDENTS THAT...

- authors use describing words to help readers visualize.

MONITOR PROGRESS Reread the second paragraph on Teacher Page T290 aloud. Say: Visualize a roller skater wearing safety gear. What picture did you make in your mind?

IF... students cannot visualize the text,
THEN... name each item of safety gear one at a time and guide students to visualize what it looks like and where a roller skater wears it.

Lesson 48 Reading Strategies

REMIND STUDENTS THAT...

- they can use what they know and text evidence to make inferences

PRACTICE 3: Make Inferences Say: You can make inferences, or figure out things the author doesn't tell you, when you hear or read a text. Making inferences will help you understand the text better.

Display or distribute Student Page S294. Read the excerpt aloud.

> Roller skating has been around a long time, but not as long as ice skating. Roller skates were invented more than 250 years ago. Roller skating is like ice skating in some ways. For example, most people aren't good at it at first! But the sports are also different. Roller skates have wheels instead of blades. People may roller skate on an indoor rink, but the rink has wood floors, not ice. Many people roller skate outside too.

Ask questions to help students make inferences. Guide them to cite text evidence to support each inference. Can people roller skate year-round? What evidence in the text helps you figure that out? (Yes; the text says people roller skate inside and outside.) Does it take practice to get good at roller skating? What evidence in the text helps you figure that out? (Yes; the text says people aren't good at it at first.)

☑ INDEPENDENT PRACTICE Reread aloud the second paragraph on Teacher Page T289 and the first paragraph on Teacher Page T290. Have individual students answer these questions to make inferences about the text: *How does each piece of safety gear help roller skaters? What evidence in the text helps you figure that out? Is roller skating or ice skating more dangerous? What evidence in the text helps you figure that out?*

IF... students have difficulty answering the questions,
THEN... reread the parts of the text that support the inferences: the items of safety gear for roller skaters and the warm clothing for ice skaters.

Lesson 48 **Reading Strategies**

Skating On and Off the Ice

Ice skating has been a popular sport for a long, long time. Scientists discovered ice skates at the bottom of a lake in Switzerland. The skates were more than 3,000 years old!

Today people ice skate indoors, at a skating rink where loud music blasts through the speakers. They also skate outdoors, on a silent frozen pond or lake. Even at an indoor rink, skaters bundle up in thick wool sweaters and warm mittens. The air must be very cold to keep the ice frozen.

text evidence

details

Lesson 48 **Reading Strategies**

Today people ice skate indoors, at a skating rink where loud music blasts through the speakers. They also skate outdoors, on a silent frozen pond or lake. Even at an indoor rink, skaters bundle up in thick wool sweaters and warm mittens. The air must be very cold to keep the ice frozen.

Ice skaters need good balance to stay upright on the thin, sharp metal blades of their skates. When skaters use their legs to push hard, they can go very fast. *Whoooooosh!* Skating fast can feel like flying on the ice!

Lesson 48 **Reading Strategies**

Ice skaters need good balance to stay upright on the thin, sharp metal blades of their skates. When skaters use their legs to push hard, they can go very fast. *Whoooooosh!* Skating fast can feel like flying on the ice!

Lesson 48 **Reading Strategies**

Roller skating has been around a long time, but not as long as ice skating. Roller skates were invented more than 250 years ago. Roller skating is like ice skating in some ways. For example, most people aren't good at it at first! But the sports are also different. Roller skates have wheels instead of blades. People may roller skate on an indoor rink, but the rink has wood floors, not ice. Many people roller skate outside too.

Lesson 49 Examine the Presentation of Information

INTRODUCE Say: Authors write words. When you write a letter or a story or a report, you are its author.

MODEL Display or distribute Student Page S299 and read it aloud.

Sedan or Sports Car? .... title

by Jenna Burns .... author

Today, people have many choices of cars. Cars come in many different types and sizes. People who like the outdoors often drive a kind of car called an SUV. Police have cruisers. Families have vans.

At one time, there were not that many different kinds of cars. Drivers used to have one main choice: sedan or sports car? .... topic

TEACH Point to the byline. Say: The author's name is Jenna Burns. The title gives a clue to her topic. Point to the last line of the excerpt. The author says people had to choose whether to drive a sedan or a sports car. I will look in the text for the points she makes and the reasons she gives for her points.

Read aloud the following sentences from "Sedan or Sports Car?": *Sedans are great for families.* and *Sports cars are great for one or two people, but they are not so great for families.* Say: The author has two key points: sedans are good for families, but sports cars are great for one or two people. What reasons support these points? Pause for student responses. The author writes, "A sedan has a hard top and either two or four doors. A sedan can seat four or more people." That sounds like a good reason for a family to have a sedan. She also writes, "Most sports cars do not have backseats. Their trunks are tiny." That is a reason sports cars would not be good for a family.

OBJECTIVES:

- Identify an author and the author's role.
- Identify the author's key points.
- Identify reasons that support each point.

BUILD VOCABULARY

Word Parts as Clues to Meaning

Point out plural nouns in the first paragraph. *(choices, cars, types, sizes, cruisers, vans)*

Say: When I see a word that ends in *-s* or *-es*, I have a clue that the word might be a plural noun. I know that both those spellings show that a word means "more than one."

Have students look through classroom books to find words that end with *-ing*. Have them use the above strategy to explain how that word part gives a clue to a word's part of speech (usually a verb) and its meaning.

Lesson 49 Examine the Presentation of Information

REMIND STUDENTS THAT…

- all texts have at least one author.
- a text may have an author and an illustrator.

PRACTICE 1: Identify the Author's Role Hold up a dictionary or other nonfiction text. Ask: Did someone write this book? Help students acknowledge that someone wrote it. When you read words on pages, you know that an author wrote them. You may not always know the name of an author. Sometimes, books have more than one author. However, we do always know that an author is the person who presents ideas and information in a text.

Display or distribute Student Page S300. Point to each line as you read the page aloud.

Sedan or Sports Car?
by Jenna Burns

Today, people have many choices of cars.

Point to the byline. Say: This line tells me who the author is. The author of this passage is Jenna Burns. She wrote the article we just read. That article has the title "Sedan or Sports Car?"

MONITOR PROGRESS Have students choose a book from a classroom library or a textbook. Ask students to point to the author's name and explain what the person has done.

IF… students cannot identify the author and define the author's role,
THEN… share several fiction and nonfiction texts in the classroom and discuss who provided the words in each text.

Lesson 49 Examine the Presentation of Information

PRACTICE 2: Identify the Author's Key Points Display or distribute Student Page S301. Read the paragraph aloud. Encourage students to listen for the author's key point.

> A sedan has a hard top and either two or four doors. A sedan can seat four or more people. A sedan can be plain or fancy. Long ago, sedans looked like the one in the picture. People drove these cars for fun. Of course, they also used them to get from one place to another. Sedans are great for families.

Ask: What information does the author include about a sedan? Encourage students to give details that describe a sedan. It has a hard top, it can seat four or more people, and it can be plain or fancy.

Explain that the author uses pieces of information to make a point. Say: The information about the sedan tells me that the author's point in this paragraph is that sedans are great for families.

REMIND STUDENTS THAT...

- an author provides ideas and information in a text.

✔ **MONITOR PROGRESS** Read aloud the following paragraph from Teacher Page T298.

Sports cars are for fun. Some sports cars used to look like the one in the picture. Does it look fun to you? A sports car often has just two seats. The first sports cars had no top at all. They could go out only in good weather.

Ask: In this paragraph, what is the author's key point about sports cars?

IF... students do not recognize the key point that sports cars are for fun,
THEN... tell students to pay special attention to the first sentence and the last sentence, and then reread the paragraph for students.

Lesson 49 Examine the Presentation of Information

REMIND STUDENTS THAT...

- an author provides information and ideas in a text.
- in informational texts, authors make key points.

PRACTICE 3: Identify Reasons that Support the Author's Points Say: If I say, "vanilla is the best flavor of ice cream," do you know why I think that? Pause for responses. No, you probably do not know my reason. You would need to hear my reason. In the same way, an author has to tell you his or her reasons for the key points in a text.

Display or distribute Student Page S302, and read the first paragraph aloud.

> A sedan has a hard top and either two or four doors. A sedan can seat four or more people. A sedan can be plain or fancy. Long ago, sedans looked like the one in the picture. People drove these cars for fun. Of course, they also used them to get from one place to another. Sedans are great for families.

Say: Imagine there are five people in your family. Why would a sedan be good for your family? (A sedan can seat four or more people.) This is one reason that supports the author's point that a sedan would be great for families.

☑ **INDEPENDENT PRACTICE** Distribute Student Page 302. Read the second paragraph aloud as students follow along.

> Sports cars are great for one or two people, but they are not so great for families. Most sports cars do not have backseats. Their trunks are tiny. Sports cars are light and fast.

Have students work independently to identify the author's point and two reasons that support that point. Call on volunteers to share their responses aloud. Provide corrective feedback as needed.

IF... students have difficulty identifying reasons that support the author's point that sports cars are "not so great for families,"
THEN... ask guiding questions, such as Do sports cars have backseats? Do they have big trunks? How would these features affect a family going on a car trip?

Lesson 49 **Examine the Presentation of Information**

Sedan or Sports Car?

by Jenna Burns

Today, people have many choices of cars. Cars come in many different types and sizes. People who like the outdoors often drive a kind of car called an SUV. Police have cruisers. Families have vans.

At one time, there were not that many different kinds of cars. Drivers used to have one main choice: sedan or sports car?

Sedan or Sports Car?

by Jenna Burns

Today, people have many choices of cars.

Lesson 49 **Examine the Presentation of Information**

A sedan has a hard top and either two or four doors. A sedan can seat four or more people. A sedan can be plain or fancy. Long ago, sedans looked like the one in the picture. People drove these cars for fun. Of course, they also used them to get from one place to another. Sedans are great for families.

Lesson 49 Examine the Presentation of Information

A sedan has a hard top and either two or four doors. A sedan can seat four or more people. A sedan can be plain or fancy. Long ago, sedans looked like the one in the picture. People drove these cars for fun. Of course, they also used them to get from one place to another. Sedans are great for families.

Sports cars are great for one or two people, but they are not so great for families. Most sports cars do not have backseats. Their trunks are tiny. Sports cars are light and fast.

Lesson 50 Understand Illustrations in a Text

DIRECTIONS Follow along as your teacher reads aloud the title and passage, "Living in the Desert." Look at the illustrations.

Living in the Desert

Deserts are very dry places. The Sonoran Desert in the United States can get very hot during the day. But it can become very cold at night.

Deserts are very hard places to live. Water is hard to find. Some plants such as cactuses can store water, or hold it to use later. Animals get water from their food. For example, kangaroo rats never need to drink water. They get all the water they need from the seeds they find on the desert floor.

Kangaroo rats and pocket mice build homes underground. This helps keep them cool during the hot days. It also protects them from snakes. At night, these little animals come out of their homes to look for food.

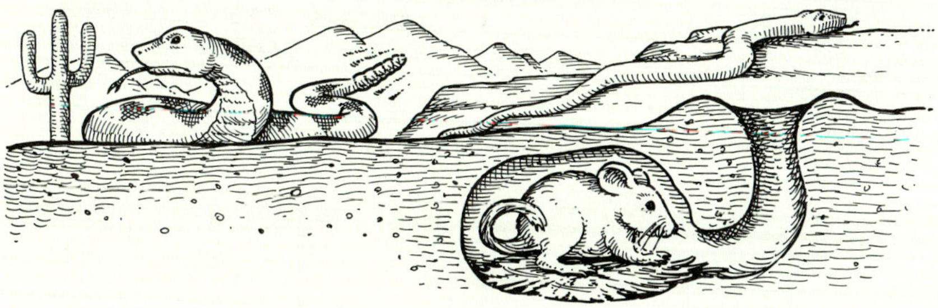

Lesson 50 Understand Illustrations in a Text

Living in the Desert, *continued*

The diamondback rattlesnake spends much of the day resting. It lives under rocks or other places to get out of the sun. Sometimes it even steals the underground nests of other animals! The rattlesnake will eat a mouse if it catches one.

Rattlesnakes can also sense the heat of other animals. This helps the snakes find food. It also helps them slither away from animals that want to attack them.

The gray fox is another animal that lives in the desert. Like other desert animals, the gray fox does most of its hunting at night.

Lesson 50 Understand Illustrations in a Text

INTRODUCE Say: You know that authors write words. Many texts you see also have pictures. Sometimes, the author makes the pictures. Other times, an illustrator draws pictures to go with the author's text.

MODEL Display or distribute Student Page S305. Have students study the illustration as you read aloud the text.

Kangaroo rats and pocket mice build homes underground. This helps keep them cool during the hot days. It also protects them from snakes. At night, these little animals come out of their homes to look for food.

TEACH Ask: What do you see in this picture? Encourage students to point out every detail, including the texture of the earth, the background, and the appearance of the animals. Where is the mouse? Point to the words *homes underground* and say: You can see that the illustration shows the mouse's underground home. Point to the words *mice* and *snakes* as you read each one. Where do you see snakes in the picture? Point out that the illustration shows animals mentioned in the text.

Say: The text says the underground home protects mice from snakes. What details in the illustration help show you that the mouse's home helps protect it from snakes? Guide students to suggest that the snakes might be looking for a mouse to eat, but the mouse is hidden in its underground home. The picture helps you understand that a snake hunts other animals for food, so the mouse needs a home that hides and protects it.

OBJECTIVES:

- Describe illustrations.
- Link illustrations to a text.
- Explain how illustrations clarify a text.

BUILD VOCABULARY

Use Antonyms

Say: Words that mean the opposite of each other are antonyms. What is the antonym of *up*? (*down*)

Direct students to look at the first paragraph. Read aloud sentences containing antonyms. "The Sonoran Desert in the United States can get very hot during the day. But it can become very cold at night." What pair of antonyms do you hear? (*hot, cold*)

Have students discuss antonym pairs that they know or find antonyms for words in the passage.

Lesson 50 Understand Illustrations in a Text

REMIND STUDENTS THAT...

- sometimes an author prepares text and illustrations at the same time.
- sometimes a separate person draws pictures to go with a text.

PRACTICE 1: Describe Illustrations Display or distribute Student Page S306. Read the text aloud.

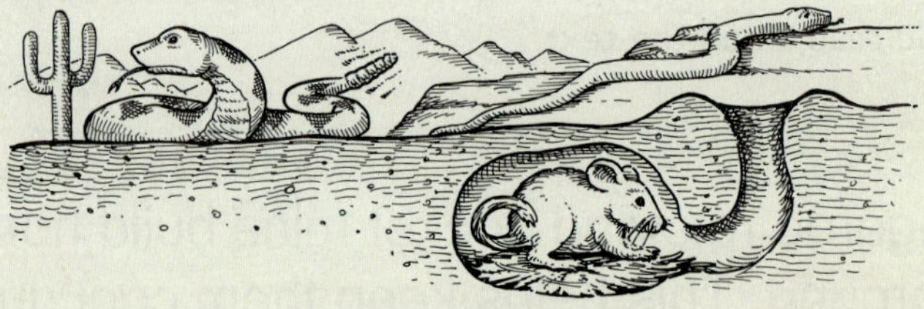

The diamondback rattlesnake spends much of the day resting. It lives under rocks or other places to get out of the sun.

Ask students to describe the snakes in the picture. What do they look like? Where are they? What are they doing? Help them note key details such as the diamonds on the left-hand snake's back and the rattle at the end of its tail.

☑ **MONITOR PROGRESS** Have students study the same illustration on Student Page S306 as you read the following sentence about the diamondback rattlesnake from Teacher Page T304: *Sometimes it even steals the underground nests of other animals!*

Say: Describe the nest in the illustration. Use your own words and also words from the passage.

IF... students do not use relevant words to explain that the nest is an underground home of a desert rat or mouse,
THEN... direct students to look only at the bottom right corner of the illustration and have them examine it more closely.

Lesson 50 Understand Illustrations in a Text

PRACTICE 2: Link Illustrations to Text Display or distribute Student Page S307. Read aloud the sentence about plants. Have students point to the plants in the illustration.

Some plants such as cactuses can store water, or hold it to use later.

The gray fox is another animal that lives in the desert.

Ask: What information do you learn about the plants from the text? What information do you learn from the illustration?

REMIND STUDENTS THAT...

- they can describe illustrations in detail.

MONITOR PROGRESS Display or distribute Student Page S307. Read aloud the sentence about the fox. Ask: How does the illustration connect to this sentence?

IF... students cannot recognize the fox in the illustration,
THEN... remind them that a fox is an animal, and guide them to find the only animal in the illustration.

Lesson 50 Understand Illustrations in a Text

REMIND STUDENTS THAT...

- illustrations show in pictures what is described in a text.
- sometimes, illustrations show more than what the text describes.

PRACTICE 3: Explain How Illustrations Clarify Text Explain that usually an illustration matches what an author writes. Therefore, an illustration can help make the text clear.

Direct students to look closely at the illustration on Teacher Page T304. Read this sentence aloud, emphasizing the word *most: Like other desert animals, the gray fox does most of its hunting at night.*

Ask: Does *most* mean *all?* (no) Does the fox do some of its hunting during the day? (yes) What part of the illustration makes this clear? (the sun)

INDEPENDENT PRACTICE Display or distribute Student Page S308. Read the sentence aloud. Have students examine the illustration independently. Say: Look at the snake on the right. How does the illustration help you understand what it means to "slither away"?

It also helps them slither away from animals that want to attack them.

IF... students cannot explain how the illustration of the snake relates to the verb *slither,*
THEN... guide students to connect prior knowledge about how snakes move with what is shown in the illustration, using the phrase *slither away.*

Lesson 50 Understand Illustrations in a Text

Kangaroo rats and pocket mice build homes underground. This helps keep them cool during the hot days. It also protects them from snakes. At night, these little animals come out of their homes to look for food.

Lesson 50 Understand Illustrations in a Text

The diamondback rattlesnake spends much of the day resting. It lives under rocks or other places to get out of the sun.

Lesson 50 Understand Illustrations in a Text

Some plants such as cactuses can store water, or hold it to use later.

The gray fox is another animal that lives in the desert.

Lesson 50 **Understand Illustrations in a Text**

It also helps them slither away from animals that want to attack them.

Lesson 51 Author's Purpose

DIRECTIONS Follow along as your teacher reads aloud the title and the passage, "From Seed to Strawberry." Look at the picture and the diagram.

From Seed to Strawberry

Strawberries are delicious fruit. They are bright red, sweet, and juicy. People eat strawberries in different ways. They may use strawberries to make jam, ice cream, or pie. Or they may eat strawberries plain.

Have you ever thought about how strawberries grow? Here's how. It starts with a strawberry seed planted in the soil. Once the seed sprouts, it sends roots down into the soil. The roots are like the feet of the plant. They keep it anchored in the ground. The roots also gather water and nutrients from the soil to help the plant grow.

As the roots grow down, the young plant grows up. It sends out runners. These runners are stems that run along the ground. New plants may spring up from the runners.

Lesson 51 Author's Purpose

From Seed to Strawberry, *continued*

The strawberry plant gets bigger and leaves start to grow. Each bright green leaf has three parts. The leaves pull in light to help the plant grow.

The roots and the leaves are important parts of the strawberry plant. They work together. They turn water, nutrients, and light into food for the growing plant.

The strawberry plant keeps growing. Soon, it has flowers. The flowers are tiny. They have white petals and yellow centers.

A berry then forms at the base of each flower. The strawberries are small and green at first. They keep growing and turn bright red. That means they are ripe and ready to be picked.

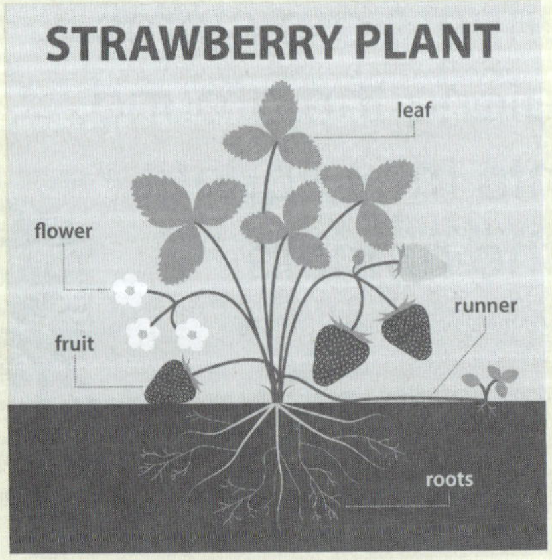

Lesson 51 Author's Purpose

INTRODUCE Say: A purpose is a reason for doing something. Every author has a purpose, or reason, for writing. An author who writes a nonfiction text is writing to give facts and information.

MODEL Display and read aloud Student Page S311.

From Seed to Strawberry

Strawberries are delicious fruit. They are bright red, sweet, and juicy. People eat strawberries in different ways. They may use strawberries to make jam, ice cream, or pie. Or they may eat strawberries plain.

TEACH Say: In this article, the author wants you to know about strawberries. What are strawberries? (delicious fruit) How do people eat strawberries? (in jam, ice cream, pie, or just plain) The author's purpose in this part of the article is to explain what strawberries are and how people eat them.

Help students use words to visualize. Say: Notice the words the author uses to describe strawberries. Point out the words *bright red, sweet, juicy.* The author uses these words to help you visualize, or make a picture in your mind. How do strawberries look? How do they taste? What picture did you make in your mind?

Develop students' understanding of graphic features. Say: Sometimes an author includes a picture, photo, diagram, or map to help you understand more about the text. What can you learn about strawberries from the picture? Elicit that strawberry jam can come in a jar and can be spread on toast. The author included this picture to show one example of how people use strawberry jam.

OBJECTIVES:

- Identify the author's purpose for writing.
- Recognize how the text structure supports the author's purpose.
- Understand the purpose of print and graphic features.
- Understand how the author uses words to help readers visualize.

Lesson 51 Author's Purpose

REMIND STUDENTS THAT…

- an author's purpose is the reason the author writes.
- an author's purpose for writing a nonfiction text is to give facts and information.

PRACTICE 1: Identify the Author's Purpose Often, the title of an article can help you figure out the author's purpose.

Display or distribute Student Page S312. Remind students that the title of the passage is "From Seed to Strawberry." Then read the paragraph aloud.

> Have you ever thought about how strawberries grow? Here's how. It starts with a strawberry seed planted in the soil. Once the seed sprouts, it sends roots down into the soil. The roots are like the feet of the plant. They keep it anchored in the ground. The roots also gather water and nutrients from the soil to help the plant grow.

Say: Think about the title and the question the author asks. What does the author want you to learn about in this article? (how strawberries grow from seeds) The author's purpose for writing this article is to explain how strawberries grow.

☑ MONITOR PROGRESS Read aloud the last paragraph on Teacher Page T309. What is the author's purpose for writing this part of the article? (to explain what runners are)

IF… students have difficulty identifying the author's purpose,
THEN… ask questions to help them focus on the information the author gives. Ask: What part of the plant does the author tell about? What does the author want you to know about runners?

Lesson 51 Author's Purpose

PRACTICE 2: Use Print and Graphic Features Remind students that an author may include pictures, photos, diagrams, or maps in a text. Say: A picture or a photo may have a caption—words that tell what the picture or photo shows. A diagram usually has labels to name parts or to explain how something works. A map usually has labels to name places.

Display or distribute Student Page S313. Read the text aloud and have students study the diagram.

The strawberry plant gets bigger and leaves start to grow. Each bright green leaf has three parts. The leaves pull in light to help the plant grow.

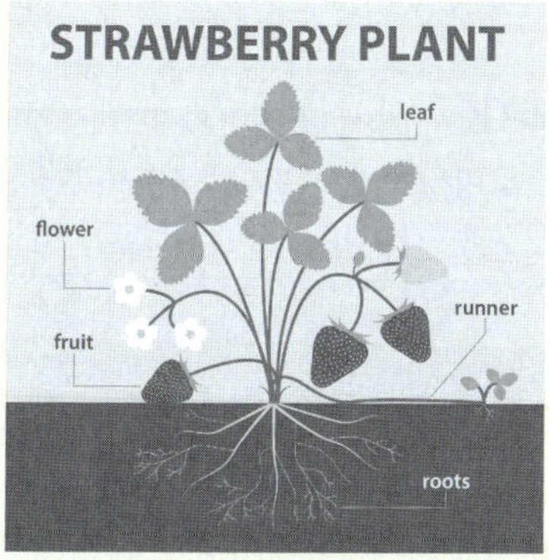

Call attention to the diagram and read the title and labels. What does the diagram show? (a strawberry plant) What information do the labels give? (the names of each part of the plant) How does the diagram help you learn more about a strawberry plant? (It shows what the parts of the strawberry plant look like and where they are located on the plant.)

REMIND STUDENTS THAT...

- an author may include pictures, photos, diagrams, or maps in a text.
- they can study pictures, photos, diagrams, or maps to understand information in the text.

MONITOR PROGRESS Have students look at the diagram on Student Page S313 again as you reread the page. Say: The author tells about the leaves in the text and includes a label for a leaf in the diagram. Based on the diagram, what does the author want you to know about the leaf?

IF... students need help explaining the purpose of the diagram,
THEN... point to the labeled leaf in the diagram and have students describe what it looks like and where it is located on the plant.

Lesson 51 Author's Purpose

REMIND STUDENTS THAT...

- authors use describing words to help readers visualize.

PRACTICE 3: Visualize Say: When you listen to or read a text, pay attention to describing words the author uses. This can help you visualize, or make pictures in your mind.

Display or distribute Student Page S314. Read it aloud.

> The strawberry plant keeps growing. Soon, it has flowers. The flowers are tiny. They have white petals and yellow centers.

Ask: What words does the author use to help you visualize the strawberry flowers? (tiny, white petals, yellow centers) Describe the picture of the flowers you make in your mind.

☑ **INDEPENDENT PRACTICE** Ask students to listen for describing words as you read aloud the last paragraph on Teacher Page T310. Have individual students draw a young strawberry and a ripe strawberry, based on what they visualized from the text.

IF... students have difficulty visualizing,
THEN... reread these sentences, one at a time, and have students describe what the strawberry looks like at each stage before they draw: *The strawberries are small and green at first. They keep growing and turn bright red.*

From Seed to Strawberry

Strawberries are delicious fruit. They are bright red, sweet, and juicy. People eat strawberries in different ways. They may use strawberries to make jam, ice cream, or pie. Or they may eat strawberries plain.

Lesson 51 Author's Purpose

Have you ever thought about how strawberries grow? Here's how. It starts with a strawberry seed planted in the soil. Once the seed sprouts, it sends roots down into the soil. The roots are like the feet of the plant. They keep it anchored in the ground. The roots also gather water and nutrients from the soil to help the plant grow.

Lesson 51 Author's Purpose

The strawberry plant gets bigger and leaves start to grow. Each bright green leaf has three parts. The leaves pull in light to help the plant grow.

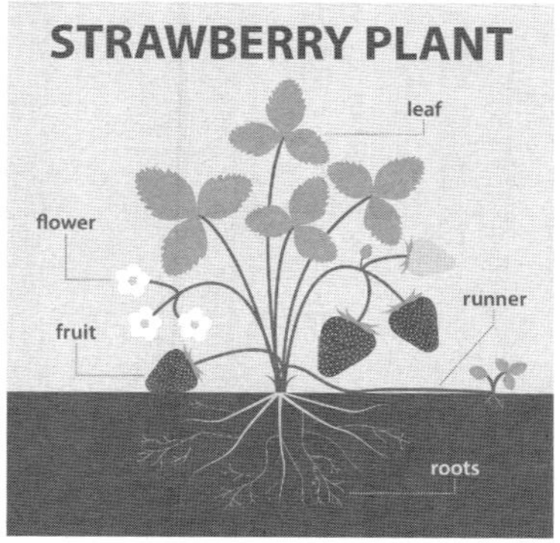

Lesson 51 **Author's Purpose**

The strawberry plant keeps growing. Soon, it has flowers. The flowers are tiny. They have white petals and yellow centers.

Lesson 52 Compare Texts

PRACTICE 2: Identify Text Similarities Display or distribute Student Pages S319 and S320. Read them aloud.

New York Is the Place for Pizza!

New York-style pizza is the most delicate, delicious dining you'll ever have. Its crust is so thin that you can fold it like paper. Its toppings are so gooey that you can almost drink them. Grab a slice. Have a bite, and then have another. You'll love New York pizza!

Chicago Is the Place for Pizza!

Nothing, *nothing,* satisfies your hunger like a deep-dish Chicago-style pizza. Imagine a slice of pie so thick you need a knife and fork to eat it. The filling is cheesy rich. It is tomato tasty. Mmmmmm . . . dive in to a Chicago pizza today!

Ask: What do these texts have in common? (They describe a kind of pizza in an appetizing way.) How do both authors try to make you hungry for their kind of pizza? Guide students to recognize that both authors describe what it will feel like to eat a slice of their pizza. If you are using a Venn diagram, add quotations to the New York and Chicago cells. These authors like different kinds of pizza, but they use a similar writing style to describe them.

REMIND STUDENTS THAT...

- they will hear and read more than one text about a topic.
- two texts on the same topic will be the same in some ways.

✔ **MONITOR PROGRESS** Reread Student Pages S319 and S320 with students. Then ask: How are the two texts alike?

IF... students do not recognize that each text uses detailed sensory descriptions,
THEN... have them act out each description of eating, and then ask what is similar about their responses to two experiences.

Lesson 52 Compare Texts

REMIND STUDENTS THAT...

- they will hear and read more than one text about a topic.
- two texts on the same topic will be different in some ways.

PRACTICE 3: Identify Text Differences Display or distribute Student Pages S319 and S320. Reread the texts aloud for students.

New York Is the Place for Pizza!

New York-style pizza is the most delicate, delicious dining you'll ever have. Its crust is so thin that you can fold it like paper. Its toppings are so gooey that you can almost drink them. Grab a slice. Have a bite, and then have another. You'll love New York pizza!

Chicago Is the Place for Pizza!

Nothing, *nothing,* satisfies your hunger like a deep-dish Chicago-style pizza. Imagine a slice of pie so thick you need a knife and fork to eat it. The filling is cheesy rich. It is tomato tasty. Mmmmmm . . . dive in to a Chicago pizza today!

Say: These texts are both about pizza. What is different about these two texts? Have students focus on the final sentence in each text, and guide them to state that one text persuades readers to eat New York-style pizza and the other persuades readers to eat Chicago-style pizza. If you are using a Venn diagram, quote the final sentences in the New York and Chicago cells.

☑ **INDEPENDENT PRACTICE** Reread Teacher Pages T315–T317 aloud. Have individual students answer these questions to identify differences between the three texts: *Which text talks about both New York- and Chicago-style pizza? Which one only talks about a [thin/thick] slice of pizza? What does it say about the [thin/thick] slice of pizza?*

IF... students have difficulty answering the questions,
THEN... reread the texts and help them identify key details that are unique to each text.

Lesson 52 Compare Texts

New York-style pizza is the most delicate, delicious dining you'll ever have.

Nothing, *nothing,* satisfies your hunger like a deep-dish Chicago-style pizza.

Paragon Pizza is *the* place to eat.

Lesson 52 Compare Texts

T-Chart

New York-style	Chicago-style

New York Is the Place for Pizza!

New York-style pizza is the most delicate, delicious dining you'll ever have. Its crust is so thin that you can fold it like paper. Its toppings are so gooey that you can almost drink them. Grab a slice. Have a bite, and then have another. You'll love New York pizza!

Chicago Is the Place for Pizza!

Nothing, *nothing,* satisfies your hunger like a deep-dish Chicago-style pizza. Imagine a slice of pie so thick you need a knife and fork to eat it. The filling is cheesy rich. It is tomato tasty. Mmmmmm . . . dive in to a Chicago pizza today!

ASSESSMENT
LESSONS 49–52

Reading Informational Text

ASSESS MASTERY Use this Checkpoint to assess students' mastery of the Level A reading skills listed in the chart.

ADMINISTER THE TEST Administer the Checkpoint orally to each student. Distribute copies of the following page. Read aloud the passages as students follow along. Then read aloud questions 1–5 below and have students respond. Check their answers using the scoring chart.

1. Who is the author of the text about tomatoes? What reason does the author give for starting tomato plants indoors?
2. Which text does the illustration go with? How can you tell?
3. What words does the author use so you know what tomato plants look like?
4. Which topic is in both texts: planting seeds, beans, or tomatoes?
5. What is different about the planting time in the two texts?

SCORING

SKILL/LESSON	ANSWER	SCORE
1. Examine the Presentation of Information (Lesson 49)	Indra Seth; In spring, it is still too cold for gardening outdoors.	_____ / 2
2. Understand Illustrations in a Text (Lesson 50)	the text about beans; it shows plants in rows of soil outdoors	_____ / 2
3. Author's Purpose (Lesson 51)	tall plants, pointy and green leaves, bright red tomatoes	_____ / 1
4. Compare Texts (Lesson 52)	planting seeds	_____ / 1
5. Compare Texts (Lesson 52)	Beans: when ground is warm; Tomatoes: when ground is still too cold for a garden	_____ / 1

An overall score of 80% is typically considered mastery. Use your judgment and your individual students' needs as well to determine skill mastery.

IF... you determine that students have not demonstrated sufficient mastery of one or more skills,
THEN... review needed skills, going back to the lessons to reteach and scaffold as needed.

ASSESSMENT
LESSONS 49–52

Reading Informational Text

Planting Beans

by Rob Gould

Have you ever opened a green bean and seen the seeds? You can plant those seeds outside. In about eight weeks, you will have beans to eat. Make sure the ground is warm before you plant. That way, your beans will grow quickly and be strong.

Starting Tomatoes Indoors

by Indra Seth

It is spring, but the ground is too cold for a garden. So begin your garden indoors! Plant some tiny tomato seeds in a sunny spot. The seeds will begin to sprout.

When the weather is warm, move the plants to the soil. Start by putting the plants outside for a few hours a day. Increase the time outdoors a bit each day for a week. Finally, add the tall plants to your garden. The leaves will be pointy and green. Soon the branches will have bright red tomatoes. You can add them to salads. Yum!

Lesson 53 Ask and Answer Questions About a Prompt

OBJECTIVES:

- Ask questions to identify the topic in a prompt.
- Ask questions to understand the type of writing requested in a prompt.
- Use a chart to record all aspects of a writing prompt.

INTRODUCE Explain to students that people often write about a topic to show that they know something about that topic. Say: In school, you will have assignments to draw or write about a topic.

MODEL Distribute Student Page S323 for students. Read aloud the prompt and complete the chart together.

Prompt: Give information about an animal you know about. Draw and describe the animal.

What is the topic?	What kind of writing is it?	What details do I include?
animal I know about	Does it give an opinion? no Does it give information? yes Does it tell a story? no	details that describe the animal (words and pictures)

TEACH Say: When you get an assignment, you must figure out exactly what you have to do. Asking and answering questions about the assignment will help you figure it out. First, find the topic. Read the prompt again. What are you supposed to draw and describe? Pause for responses. The topic in this assignment is an animal you know about. Write *animal I know about* in the left column.

Say: Sometimes an assignment will tell you the kind of writing you are supposed to do. You might give an opinion, give information or explain how something works, or tell a story. Reread the prompt and have students answer the questions in the middle column of the chart to determine the kind of writing.

Circle *describe* in the prompt. Say: This word tells you how to give information. Circle *Draw*. You can draw to help describe the animal. These words tell you how to give information. Explain that in the right column, students can state that they must describe, or tell about, the animal through both drawing pictures and writing words.

Lesson 53 Ask and Answer Questions About a Prompt

REMIND STUDENTS THAT. . .

- they can figure out the topic of an assignment.
- they can ask and answer questions to figure out the kind of writing an assignment is asking them to do.
- they can use a chart to make sure they understand every part of an assignment.

PRACTICE 1: Opinion Writing Say: Some assignments may ask you for your opinion. An opinion is what you think about a topic. For example, an assignment might ask you to answer a question, such as *Which juice do you think is best?* The topic of the assignment is "the best juice." You have to decide what you think about it and why you have that opinion. Help students understand that an opinion is not right or wrong, but it can be supported by reasons.

Distribute or display Student Page S324. Read the prompt aloud for students.

Opinion Writing

Prompt: Draw and write an opinion about which art supplies are the best for coloring: colored pencils, crayons, paints, or markers.

What is the topic?	What kind of writing is it?	What details do I include?

Say: To find the topic, you can ask *What is this assignment about?* Guide students to identify the topic of the prompt as "art supplies for coloring."

Say: You can ask *What is the assignment asking me to do?* to find out what kind of writing you need to do. Make sure students understand that the assignment asks students to give an opinion. What other details must your drawing and writing include? (the choice of pencils, crayons, paints, or markers)

Finally, reread the prompt aloud, emphasizing the word *best*. Conclude by asking: Which art supply do you think is the best?

☑ **MONITOR PROGRESS** Using the prompt above, have students tell you what should go in each column of the chart on Student Page S324. Encourage them to pay extra attention to the *What kind of writing is it?* column.

IF… students cannot identify the topic,
THEN… rephrase the prompt as a question and ask students what they would draw in response.

Lesson 53 Ask and Answer Questions About a Prompt

PRACTICE 2: Informative/Explanatory Writing Say: When you know the basic topic of an assignment, ask questions to learn more about what you are supposed to do. The assignment may have details about the kind of writing as well as the topic. Pay close attention when an assignment says "be sure to" or "include." Those words are clues to details.

Distribute or display Student Page S325 and read it aloud.

Informative/Explanatory Writing

Prompt: Draw and describe what the weather is like where you live. Be sure to include descriptions about how the weather is different during different times of the year.

What is the topic?	What kind of writing is it?	What details do I include?

Ask: What is the topic? (weather) What questions does the assignment want you to answer about the topic? (*What is the weather like where I live? How is the weather here different during different times of the year?*)

Read the prompt aloud again. Ask: What kind of writing should you do? (describe the weather) Is this an opinion, an explanation or information, or a story? (information)

MONITOR PROGRESS Using the prompt above, have students tell you what should go in each column of the chart on Student Page S325. Encourage them to pay extra attention to the *What details do I include?* column.

IF... students misunderstand the prompt,
THEN... read the prompt several times, posing questions about several words at a time (*Draw and describe, what the weather is like, where you live,* etc.) to make sure students understand each component of the prompt.

REMIND STUDENTS THAT. . .

- they can figure out the topic of an assignment.
- they can ask and answer questions to figure out the kind of writing an assignment is asking them to do.
- they can use a chart to make sure they understand every part of an assignment.

Lesson 53 Ask and Answer Questions About a Prompt

REMIND STUDENTS THAT. . .

- they can figure out the topic of an assignment.
- they can ask and answer questions to figure out the kind of writing an assignment is asking them to do.
- they can use a chart to make sure they understand every part of an assignment.

PRACTICE 3: Narrative Writing Say: Assignments usually list some details about what you must do or include. Point out that in narrative writing, students should include details about their characters, the action or events, and the place where the action happens. Distribute or display Student Page S326 and read it aloud.

Narrative Writing

Prompt: Draw and tell a story about an unexpected hero who saves the school. The hero can be any person, animal, or creature.

What is the topic?	What kind of writing is it?	What details do I include?

Explain that a *narrative* tells a story. Say: The topic of this assignment is a hero. What kind of hero? Read the prompt aloud again if necessary. Make sure students understand what *unexpected* means. Use questions to help them give you as many details about the hero as they can. What is the hero supposed to do? (save the school) What kind of writing does the assignment ask you to do? (tell a story) What are the other details in the assignment? (The hero can be a person, animal, or creature.)

☑ **INDEPENDENT PRACTICE** Using the prompt above, have students tell you what should go in each column of the chart on Student Page S326. Encourage them to pay extra attention to the *What is the topic?* and *What details do I include?* columns.

IF... students cannot separate details from the basic topic,
THEN... help them generate questions they should or could ask about the topic of a hero, such as these: *What kind of hero is in my story? When does my hero save the school? Where does my hero live? What can my hero do?*

Lesson 54 Use a Topic to Recall and Gather Information

INTRODUCE Explain that often writing assignments ask for students to draw on information they already know or gather information before they start drawing or writing their responses. Say: Your experiences and what you already know can help you complete an assignment. Knowing where to find information can also help you. Point out that students can use the topic of a writing assignment or prompt to help them complete this step.

MODEL Distribute or display Student Page S327 and read it aloud.

Informative/Explanatory Writing

Prompt: Give information about an animal you know about. Draw and describe the animal.

TEACH Point out that an important step in writing is to remember or gather information about a topic. Ask: What is the topic of this assignment? (an animal I know about) What are you supposed to do? (draw and describe it) Tell students that they must organize their information. Ask: What is the most important thing you want to show about your animal? What do you want to tell people about it?

Point out that some writing assignments will ask students to explain a topic that they do not already know about. As an example, ask: What if the assignment said that you should describe an animal you wish you knew more about? Where could you find information? Guide students to name several print or digital resources, such as books, magazines, or websites. Offer additional suggestions, such as asking an expert or visiting a zoo, pet store, farm, or museum.

OBJECTIVES:

- Recall relevant information to respond to a prompt.
- Gather information from sources to respond to a prompt.
- Develop drafts in oral, pictorial, or written form by organizing ideas.

Lesson 54 Use a Topic to Recall and Gather Information

REMIND STUDENTS THAT...

- they can read a prompt and figure out the topic of an assignment.
- they may have had experiences that will help them answer questions.
- sources may contain information they can use to answer a question.
- they must organize their ideas when they draw or write about a topic.

PRACTICE 1: Opinion Writing Remind students that an opinion is what they think about a topic. Explain that writers have to organize information about a topic to support their opinion about that topic. Distribute or display Student Page S328 and read it aloud.

> **Opinion Writing**
>
> **Prompt:** Draw and write an opinion about which art supplies are the best for coloring: colored pencils, crayons, paints, or markers.

Ask: What is this assignment asking you to do? Make sure students understand the topic, what an opinion is, and their choices. Tell me about your experiences with each kind of art supply. Draw out details of how easy or difficult each art supply is to use, asking questions such as: What other materials do you need to use with this supply? For example, you might need a sharpener to use colored pencils. Are there enough colors, or too few or too many? Can you mix the colors?

Guide students to organize their opinions and reasons. Ask: Which kind of supply is your favorite for coloring? As students respond, ask: Why? Have them provide details from the discussion to support their opinions.

☑ **MONITOR PROGRESS** Display or distribute Student Page S328 and reread it aloud. Provide and read aloud the following sentence frames: *In my opinion, ________ are the best for coloring. This is because ________.*

Help students complete the frames. Ask: What would you draw to show this opinion?

IF... students cannot choose which medium is best,
THEN... review with them the reasons they said they liked one of the materials the most. Point out that this is information from their experiences. Then help students use that information to complete the sentence frames.

Lesson 54 Use a Topic to Recall and Gather Information

PRACTICE 2: Informative/Explanatory Writing Point out that in informational writing, an assignment will ask for students to explain information about a topic. Make available several books about weather or pictures of the local area along with a recent weather page from a website or a newspaper. Display or distribute Student Page S329 and read the prompt aloud.

Informative/Explanatory Writing

Prompt: Draw and describe what the weather is like where you live. Be sure to include descriptions about how the weather is different during different times of the year.

Ask: What is the topic of this assignment? (weather where I live) What do you already know about this topic? Pause for responses. You can use what you know to complete the assignment.

Then say: You can also use information from sources. Look at these sources. Discuss each source with students, asking questions such as: What does the website or the newspaper tell about weather?

Reread the prompt. Guide students to organize information and ideas. Say: The prompt tells us to say how the weather is different during different times of the year. We can organize information by time order and tell what the weather is like during different times or months. What do the sources tell us about the weather at different times of the year?

REMIND STUDENTS THAT. . .

- they can read a prompt and figure out the topic of an assignment.
- they may have had experiences that will help them answer questions.
- sources may contain information they can use to answer a question.
- they must organize their ideas when they draw or write about a topic.

☑ **MONITOR PROGRESS** Display or distribute Student Page S329. Reread the prompt, and then read aloud the following sentence frames for student responses.

In January, the weather where I live is _______.
In May, the weather is _______.
In October, the weather is _______.

IF... students cannot find useful information in the sources,
THEN... guide them to describe the pictures you have provided and ask them to describe how it would feel to be in the weather shown. Allow students to recall information from their personal knowledge and experience with the weather.

Lesson 54 Use a Topic to Recall and Gather Information

REMIND STUDENTS THAT. . .

- they can read a prompt and figure out the topic of an assignment.
- they may have had experiences that will help them answer questions.
- sources may contain information they can use to answer a question.
- they must organize their ideas when they draw and tell a story.

PRACTICE 3: Narrative Writing Explain to students that many writers use information to help them write stories, even if those stories are fictional, or not about real-life events. Say: When you get a narrative or story assignment, think about the information you already have about the topic. You can use your experiences as part of that information.

Distribute or display Student Page S330 and read the prompt aloud.

Narrative Writing

Prompt: Draw and tell a story about an unexpected hero who saves the school. The hero can be any person, animal, or creature.

Say: Think of what you already know about heroes. Use questions to guide student responses, such as: What stories have you already heard about heroes? What person, animal, or creature would be an *unexpected* hero? Why might the school need to be saved? How could your unexpected hero save the school? Point out that experiences students have had in school or books that they remember will help them make up a story.

Guide students to organize story ideas. Say: When you draw or write a story, think about what you want to tell. A story has a person who must do something. What will the person do? How will he or she do it? What comes first? Second? Last?

☑ **INDEPENDENT PRACTICE** Display or distribute Student Page S330. Reread the prompt, and then read aloud the sentence frames for student responses.

My unexpected hero will be _______.
The school will need to be saved from _______.
The hero will save the school by _______.

IF. . . students struggle to think of a plot,
THEN. . . provide a sample hero and problem, such as saving a dog in a dangerous storm. Guide students to draft and organize their ideas about dogs and storms by drawing a picture and completing the sentence frames.

Lesson 54 Use a Topic to Recall and Gather Information

Informative/Explanatory Writing

Prompt: Give information about an animal you know about. Draw and describe the animal.

Lesson 54 **Use a Topic to Recall and Gather Information**

Opinion Writing

Prompt: Draw and write an opinion about which art supplies are the best for coloring: colored pencils, crayons, paints, or markers.

Lesson 54 Use a Topic to Recall and Gather Information

Informative/Explanatory Writing

Prompt: Draw and describe what the weather is like where you live. Be sure to include descriptions about how the weather is different during different times of the year.

In January, the weather where I live is ______________.

In May, the weather is ______________.

In October, the weather is ______________.

Lesson 54 Use a Topic to Recall and Gather Information

Narrative Writing

Prompt: Draw and tell a story about an unexpected hero who saves the school. The hero can be any person, animal, or creature.

My unexpected hero will be ______________________.

The school will need to be saved from ____________

____.

The hero will save the school by _________________

____.

Lesson 55 Revise and Edit

INTRODUCE Show students an illustration in a picture book. Say: Tell me everything you see in this picture. Point to various parts of the picture as you encourage students to identify every detail in the illustration. You have just told me all of the details you see in this picture. You can add details to your drawings and writing to make them stronger.

MODEL Display Student Page S331 and read it aloud.

Informative/Explanatory Writing

Prompt: Give information about an animal you know about. Draw and describe the animal.

Draft: My cat is gray. It has green eyes.

TEACH Ask: What was the assignment? Reread the prompt if necessary. Then read the draft response. Do you think the writer knows a lot about the cat? Has the writer told everything he or she knows? After students reply, ask: What questions could we ask the writer to find out more about the cat? Guide students to mention questions about the cat's name, age, and behavior.

Say: Imagine asking the writer those questions. What other details could the writer add to the draft? After students respond, say: When you do an assignment, other people can ask you questions about it. Answering their questions will help you add details to make your work stronger. You can help others, too. Ask them questions to learn more details about their topic.

Introduce the concepts of revising and editing. Say: Changing writing and drawings to make them better is called revising. Adding details is a good way to revise a draft. Fixing mistakes in a draft is called editing. When we edit, we fix mistakes in words, letters, and end marks. In this lesson, we will practice revising and editing some drafts.

OBJECTIVES:

- Answer questions about a draft.
- Revise drafts by adding details in pictures or words.
- Edit drafts with adult assistance using standard English conventions.

Lesson 55 Revise and Edit

REMIND STUDENTS THAT. . .

- they can ask questions about other students' drawings and writing.
- answering questions will help them think of details to add to their own drafts.

PRACTICE 1: Opinion Writing Display and read aloud the prompt and first draft on Student Page S332.

Opinion Writing

Prompt: Draw and write an opinion about which art supplies are the best for coloring: colored pencils, crayons, paints, or markers.

Draft: Colored pencils are best for coloring.

Ask students if they think the draft response is interesting. Point out that the writer hasn't given a reason for his or her opinion. Ask: What questions could you ask the writer to make this answer better and more interesting? Guide students to ask questions such as these: *Why are colored pencils best? Why are colored pencils better than crayons, paints, and markers? Why do you like to use colored pencils?*

MONITOR PROGRESS Display or distribute Student Page S332. Reread the prompt, and then read aloud the second draft.

Draft: I think markers are the best for coloring. I like them best.

Say: Imagine that this is your draft. So that you can add details, I will ask: What makes you like markers better than crayons? After students respond, ask how they would add that detail to their draft and drawing.

IF... students do not understand how details strengthen a draft,
THEN... reread the sample draft and ask: Would this make you want to try markers? What details would make you want to try markers?

Lesson 55 Revise and Edit

PRACTICE 2: Informative/Explanatory Writing Display Student Page S333. Read the prompt and draft aloud. Tell students that the writer has already added details to this draft. Say: Now it is time to edit the sentences. When we edit, we fix mistakes in words, letters, and end marks. Explain that a correct sentence begins with a capital letter and ends with an end mark.

Informative/Explanatory Writing

Prompt: Draw and describe what the weather is like where you live. Be sure to include descriptions about how the weather is different during different times of the year.

Revised Draft: the weather where I live is warm. Spring is pretty and green. summer is sunny and hot. Sometimes it is rainy in winter

Reread the draft, pointing out where each sentence begins and ends. Say: I see a mistake in the first sentence. It needs to begin with a capital letter. Model correcting the sentence. Then guide students to check and edit the remaining sentences. Point out the corrections in the edited draft. (capital "S" in "Summer")

REMIND STUDENTS THAT. . .

- they can answer questions to add details to a draft.
- they can edit a draft to fix mistakes.
- writers must begin each sentence with a capital letter and end each sentence with punctuation.

MONITOR PROGRESS Display or distribute Student Page S333. Reread the prompt, and then read aloud the second draft on the page.

Draft: The weather is nice here. it snows sometimes in winter

Ask: What details would make these descriptions stronger? What do you think the writer means by "the weather is nice"? What questions can you ask to find out? (When is the weather nice? Is it warm or cold? Is it sunny or cloudy?) Ask: What mistakes should the writer correct in the second sentence?

IF... students cannot add details or correct mistakes,
THEN... ask them to use their senses—sight, hearing, smell, taste, and feeling—to think of questions to ask about the draft. Guide students to correct capitalization and end punctuation. Write the edited draft on the board.

Lesson 55 Revise and Edit

REMIND STUDENTS THAT. . .

- they can ask questions about other students' drawings and writing.
- answering questions will help them think of details to add to their own drafts.
- they can edit a draft to fix mistakes.

PRACTICE 3: Narrative Writing Display and read aloud the prompt and first draft on Student Page S334.

Narrative Writing

Prompt: Draw and tell a story about an unexpected hero who saves the school. The hero can be any person, animal, or creature.

Draft: One day a storm came. I was at school. A dog saved everyone.

Ask: What else could this writer tell you that would make the story better? On the board, write *who, what, when, where, why,* and *how.* Point to each word and say: Think of a [who] question to ask about the story. Have students offer answers to the questions they pose. Finally, ask: How could you use those answers to make the story and drawing stronger?

INDEPENDENT PRACTICE Display or distribute Student Page S334. Reread the prompt, and then read aloud the second draft on the page.

Draft: It rained really hard. The school basement filled with water. A dog saved the school.

Ask: What details would make this story better? Pose questions to help students agree on three details to add, such as where the dog was, what the dog did, and how the problem was solved. Use student responses to write a revised draft, and guide students to find mistakes. Model editing the draft to fix errors in capitalization, punctuation, or spelling.

IF... students struggle to imagine an unexpected hero,
THEN... have students explain how an adult would solve the problem, and then have them change the adult in the story to an animal. Ask them to retell the story using the animal hero. Remind students to check sentences for capital letters and end marks.

Lesson 55 **Revise and Edit**

Informative/Explanatory Writing

Prompt: Give information about an animal you know about. Draw and describe the animal.

Draft: My cat is brown. It has green eyes.

Opinion Writing

Prompt: Draw and write an opinion about which art supplies are the best for coloring: colored pencils, crayons, paints, or markers.

Draft: Colored pencils are best for coloring.

Draft: I think markers are the best for coloring. I like them best.

Informative/Explanatory Writing

Prompt: Draw and describe what the weather is like where you live. Be sure to include descriptions about how the weather is different during different times of the year.

Revised Draft: the weather where I live is warm. Spring is pretty and green. summer is sunny and hot. Sometimes it is rainy in winter

Edited Draft: The weather where I live is warm. Spring is pretty and green. Summer is sunny and hot. Sometimes it is rainy in winter.

Draft: The weather is nice here. it snows sometimes in winter

Narrative Writing

Prompt: Draw and tell a story about an unexpected hero who saves the school. The hero can be any person, animal, or creature.

Draft: One day a storm came. I was at school. A dog saved everyone.

Draft: It rained really hard. The school basement filled with water. A dog saved the school.

ASSESSMENT
LESSONS 53–55

Writing

ASSESS MASTERY Use this Checkpoint to assess students' mastery of the Level A writing skills listed here.

ADMINISTER THE TEST Administer the Checkpoint orally to each student.

1. Read aloud the prompt on the following page.
2. Read questions 1 and 2. Write or display the relevant text as necessary, and have students respond. Check their answers using the scoring chart.
3. Read aloud and display the draft on the following page and have students respond to questions 3 and 4. Check their answers using the scoring chart.

SCORING

SKILL/LESSON	ANSWER	SCORE
1. Ask and Answer Questions about a Prompt (Lesson 53)	Topic: a place in my home town or city that I know well Kind of Writing: informative Details: how it is used, the people who visit or work there	_____ / 3
2. Use a Topic to Recall and Gather Information (Lesson 54)	Responses will vary; students should complete all the sentence frames.	_____ / 4
3. Revise and Edit (Lesson 55)	Responses will vary; students should complete all the questions.	_____ / 3
4. Revise and Edit (Lesson 55)	Draft corrections: Capitalize *The*; add a period after *skate*.	_____ / 2

An overall score of 80% is typically considered mastery. Use your judgment and your individual students' needs as well to determine skill mastery.

IF... you determine that students have not demonstrated sufficient mastery of one or more skills,
THEN... review needed skills, going back to the lessons to reteach and scaffold as needed.

ASSESSMENT
LESSONS 53–55

Writing

Prompt: Draw and describe a place in your home town or city that you know well. Be sure to include information about how the place is used and information about the people who visit or work there.

Draft: the ice rink is a place I Know well. It is open all year. People go there to skate

1. What should go in each column of this chart?

What is the topic?	What kind of writing is it?	What details do I include?

2. Complete the following sentence frames:
   _______ is a place I know well. The place is used _______. The people there _______. My experiences there include _______.
3. What questions could you ask to help the writer add details to strengthen the draft? Complete these frames:
   - Who _______?
   - What happens _______?
   - How does the ice rink _______?
4. What two mistakes in the draft could you fix?

Lesson 56 Write Text: Narrative and Informational

INTRODUCE Tell students that they can learn to write many kinds of texts. Say: One kind of text you can write is called narrative. Narrative text is often a made-up story. Another kind of text is informational. Informational text gives you facts about something in real life.

Display Lesson 39 Teacher Pages T229–T230 and read the story "A Good Catch" aloud. Then display Lesson 46 Teacher Page T277 and read the informational text "A Good Home for a Cat" aloud.

MODEL Display or distribute Student Page S337. Explain that students will use the chart as you discuss the two kinds of text.

Narrative	Informational
A Good Catch	**A Good Home for a Cat**
• a made-up story • has characters and setting • tells events in order	• informational • includes facts • can tell how to do or make something

TEACH Say: First let's look at "A Good Catch." This is a made-up story. Point out that some stories have characters that are like real people, places, and events from real life. But, other stories are not like real life at all. Say: Chad, Mom, and Captain Joe are the characters. The setting is when and where the story takes place. This story takes place one morning on a fishing boat. Story events are the things that happen. Most stories tell about events in order. Point out the first sentence on Teacher Page T229. The words *early one morning* lets us know what happened first.

Explain that narrative text can also tell a *true* story. Say: Writers can tell a true story about a real person. The story would include facts about the person, about when and where the person lived, and about events that took place.

Say: Now let's look at "A Good Home for a Cat." This is informational text. It includes facts about a topic. It tells how to make a good home for a cat. Point out the three steps on Teacher Page T277. The steps give information that tells readers what to do.

Tell students that they can use what they learn about different kinds of texts when they think about what they want to write.

OBJECTIVES:

- Write narrative and informational texts.
- Write narrative texts with characters, setting, and events.
- Tell story events in order.
- Write informational texts that give facts about a topic.

Lesson 56 Write Text: Narrative and Informational

REMIND STUDENTS THAT. . .

- a fiction text is a type of narrative that is made up.
- writers make up the characters, setting, and events.
- story events happen in an order that makes sense.

PRACTICE 1: Write Narrative Text: Fiction Say: When you are asked to write a narrative text that is fiction, you can make up the story. Make up the characters, the setting, and what happens, or the events, in the story.

Display or distribute Student Page S338. Read the prompt and example aloud.

Prompt: Draw and tell a story about a boy who runs a race.

Jan's Narrative Text:

One day on the playground, Tim and his friends ran a race. At first, Tim tripped. Then he ran so fast. He crossed the finish line first. His friends cheered and cheered for him!

Say: First, let's look at Jan's example. Who are the characters in Jan's story? (Tim and his friends) When and where does it take place? ("One day"; on the playground) What are some events that happen? (The children run a race; Tim trips, then runs fast; he wins the race.)

Now work as a class to respond to the prompt to write a class narrative. Ask: Who will be our character or characters in this story? Say: The prompt doesn't tell us the setting. When and where do we want our story to take place? Pause for students to respond, then offer some examples, such as *in the summer* or *at the park*. Finally, have students brainstorm some ideas for story events. Offer guidance by writing *Beginning, Middle,* and *End* on the board. Prompt students with questions: What should happen at the beginning? What happens next? What should happen at the end of the story? Point out that story events happen in an order that makes sense. Explain to students that the conclusion is at the end of a story. It tells the last thing that happens.

☑ **MONITOR PROGRESS** Have students draw or write about something that happens at the end of the class narrative.

IF... students have difficulty drawing or writing an ending,
THEN... model brainstorming some ideas by asking questions such as, *What usually happens at the end of a race? What happens if you win? What happens if you lose?*

Lesson 56 Write Text: Narrative and Informational

PRACTICE 2: Write Narrative Text: Nonfiction Say: When you are asked to write a narrative text that is nonfiction, you tell facts about a real person. That person might be you; you might write about something that happened to you. Or, it might be any other person. Everything in nonfiction narrative is true; there is nothing made up.

Display or distribute Student Page S339. Read the prompt aloud.

Prompt: Draw and tell about a time when you learned how to do something new.

Dan's Nonfiction Narrative:

Last year I learned to ride a bike. My mom helped me. She held my bike and said I was doing a great job. Finally, I could ride by myself. I was so excited!

I learned how to . . .	
It made me feel . . .	

Examine the example text with students. Lead them to understand who the characters are, what the setting is, and what happens.

Now work as a class to respond to the prompt. Ask: What are some new things we have learned to do? Did someone teach us or help us? How did it make us feel? Say: When we write about something from our own lives, we give facts about what happened and we tell what we learned and how we felt about it. Have students draw or write the agreed-upon responses on Student Page S339.

REMIND STUDENTS THAT. . .

- a nonfiction narrative tells about something or someone that is true.
- one kind of nonfiction narrative tells a true story from the writer's own life.

☑ **MONITOR PROGRESS** On their copies of Student Page S339, have students draw circles around the words or pictures that show what they learned to do. Have them draw a box around the words or pictures that show how it made them feel.

IF... students are not able to identify the parts of the class nonfiction narrative, THEN... use Dan's example as a model and circle "I learned to ride a bike" and draw a box around "I was so excited."

Lesson 56 Write Text: Narrative and Informational

REMIND STUDENTS THAT. . .

- informational text includes facts.
- informational text may tell how to make or do something.
- informational text that tells how to make or do something includes steps in order.

PRACTICE 3: Write Informational Text About How to Do Something Say: All informational text provides facts. One kind of informational text we can write is how to do or make something.

Display or distribute Student Page S340. Read the prompt aloud.

Prompt: Draw and write about how to make something or do something. Tell the steps in the right order.

Sam's Informational Text:

Making s'mores is easy. There are just three steps. The first step is to ask an adult to help you toast a marshmallow. The next step is to put the marshmallow and a piece of chocolate on a graham cracker. The last step is to enjoy your s'more!

How to . . .

The first step is . . .
The next step is . . .
The last step is . . .

Say: Let's first look at Sam's example. What does Sam know how to make? What are the steps?

Now work as a class to respond to the prompt as a class. Ask: What do we know how to do or make? What are the steps? Model writing or sketching agreed-upon ideas in the chart on Student Page S340. Say: When we write to tell how to do or make something, we give information or facts. We write the facts in order so that someone else can make or do it too.

☑ **INDEPENDENT PRACTICE** Have students use the notes from the class brainstorming to respond to the prompt on Student Page S340 by drawing and/or writing.

IF... students need support drawing or writing about how to do something, THEN... review the example. Guide students to notice how Sam began his nonfiction text. Point out what he wrote about first, next, and last.

Lesson 56 Write Text: Narrative and Informational

Narrative	Informational
A Good Catch	**A Good Home for a Cat**
• a made-up story • has characters and setting • tells events in order	• informational • includes facts • can tell how to do or make something

Lesson 56 **Write Text: Narrative and Informational**

Prompt: Draw and tell a story about a boy who runs a race.

Jan's Narrative Text:

One day on the playground, Tim and his friends ran a race. At first, Tim tripped. Then he ran so fast. He crossed the finish line first. His friends cheered and cheered for him!

Lesson 56 **Write Text: Narrative and Informational**

Prompt: Draw and tell about a time when you learned how to do something new.

Dan's Nonfiction Narrative:

Last year I learned to ride a bike. My mom helped me. She held my bike and said I was doing a great job. Finally, I could ride by myself. I was so excited!

I learned how to . . .	
It made me feel . . .	

Lesson 56 **Write Text: Narrative and Informational**

Prompt: Draw and write about how to make something or do something. Tell the steps in the right order.

Sam's Informational Text:

Making s'mores is easy. There are just three steps. The first step is to ask an adult to help you toast a marshmallow. The next step is to put the marshmallow and a piece of chocolate on a graham cracker. The last step is to enjoy your s'more!

How to . . .

The first step is . . .
The next step is . . .
The last step is . . .

ASSESSMENT
LESSON 56

Writing

ASSESS MASTERY Use this Checkpoint to assess students' mastery of writing narrative text and informational text.

ADMINISTER THE TEST Administer the Checkpoint orally to each student. Give each student a copy of Teacher Page T342. Read aloud the passages as students follow along. Then read aloud questions 1–5 and have students respond. Reread relevant text as necessary. Check their answers using the scoring chart.

1. Which draft is narrative text? How do you know?
2. What could the author add about how she felt when she learned how to swim?
3. Which draft is informational text? How do you know?
4. What would happen if the writer switched the first and last steps in "How to Braid Hair"?
5. How could a picture help you understand the information in "How to Braid Hair"? What would you draw?

SCORING

SKILL/LESSON	ANSWER	SCORE
1. Write Text: Narrative and Informational (Lesson 56)	1. It is narrative text. It has characters, setting, and a story.	_____ / 2
	2. Answers will vary. Sample Answer: I was proud that I learned how to swim.	_____ / 1
	3. "How to Braid Hair" is informational text. It tells how to do something.	_____ / 2
	4. Sample Answer: The directions would be out of order and wouldn't make sense.	_____ / 1
	5. Answers will vary. Sample Answer: A picture would help me see what to do. I would draw a braid.	_____ / 2

An overall score of 80% correct is typically considered mastery. Use your judgment and your individual students' needs as well to determine skill mastery.

IF... you determine that students have not demonstrated sufficient mastery of one or more skills,
THEN... review the skill(s), going back to the lessons to reteach and scaffold as needed.

ASSESSMENT
LESSON 56

Writing

Draft: Learning to Swim

My whole family was at the lake. My cousins were swimming. I wanted to swim, but I did not know how. Grandma said she would teach me. She held me up in the water. She showed me how to move my arms and kick my feet. When I was ready, she let me go. I swam for the first time!

Draft: How to Braid Hair

Did you ever wonder how to braid hair? It is easy with a little practice. Just follow these steps.

First, part your hair into three sections.

Next, cross the right section of hair over the middle section of hair. Then cross the left section of hair over the middle. Keep criss-crossing hair sections. You will see a braid form.

Last, finish off your braid with a hair tie. This will keep the braid in place.

Lesson 57 Understand Nouns, Verbs, and Prepositions

INTRODUCE Say: When you talk, you use different kinds of words. Point to a desk and ask: What is this? (a desk) The word *desk* is a noun. A noun is one kind of word. It names a person, place, or thing. Today you will learn about nouns and other kinds of words called verbs and prepositions.

MODEL Display or distribute Student Page S343.

OBJECTIVES:

- Use common nouns, verbs, and prepositions.
- Form regular plural nouns.

Henrik hid under the desk.

Drake built a boat.

The boy sees six concerts.

TEACH Read the first sentence aloud. Say: There are two nouns in this sentence. One of them is *desk*. The other noun is the name of a person. Can you tell me that noun? (*Henrik*)

Next, ask: What did Henrik do? (He hid under the desk.) The word *hid* is a verb. Verbs are also called action words. Verbs tell what happens. Reread the sentence. The word *under* is a preposition. Prepositions show how words are related. *Under* tells where Henrik is in relation to the desk.

Read aloud the second sentence. Say: This sentence has two nouns and a verb. What are the two nouns? (*Drake, boat*) What is the verb? (*built*)

Read aloud the third sentence. Say: The words *boy* and *concerts* are nouns. There is more than one concert, so the word has an s on the end: *concerts*. Adding s to a noun makes it mean "more than one." The word *sees* is a verb; it tells what is happening.

Lesson 57 Understand Nouns, Verbs, and Prepositions

REMIND STUDENTS THAT. . .

- nouns are words that name people, places, and things.
- verbs are action words; they tell what happens.

PRACTICE 1: Use Common Nouns and Verbs Explain that a sentence always has a noun and a verb. Say: *Rosa sits* is a sentence. The noun in this sentence is *Rosa.* It names the person doing the action. The verb is *sits.* It tells the action.

Clap your hands and say the sentence *The people clap.* Ask: What is the noun? (*people*) What is the verb, or the action word? (*clap*) Repeat with the sentences *Dogs bark, Planes fly,* and *Doors open.*

Extend the activity by having students tell you several two-word sentences of their own. Ask students to identify the noun and verb in each sentence. Offer the following sentence frames from Student Page S344, if needed.

Fish ________________. ________________ walk.

Cars ________________. ________________ run.

☑ **MONITOR PROGRESS** Display or distribute Student Page S344 and read each column aloud. Have students make sentences by combining a noun on the left and a verb on the right.

Children	sing.
Cats	play.
Birds	jump.

IF... students cannot distinguish nouns and verbs,
THEN... act out the three verbs above and have students imitate you. Emphasize that verbs tell about actions or about what happens.

Lesson 57 Understand Nouns, Verbs, and Prepositions

PRACTICE 2: Form Regular Plural Nouns Say: To make most nouns mean "more than one," add *s* or *es* to the end of the noun. For example, if I want to say that I have more than one hat, I add *s* to *hat*. I have many *hats*.

Display or distribute Student Page S345.

Bill has one shirt. Jim has two shirts. shirts, *s*
Leah has nine boxes. Kim has one box. boxes, *es*
The family has one car. The police department has ten cars. cars, *s*
Tuesday is one day. A week has seven days. days, *s*

Reread aloud the first pair of sentences. Have students clap when they hear a noun that means "more than one." (They should clap for *shirts*.) *Shirts* means more than one shirt. Notice that an *s* was added to the end of the noun *shirt* to make it *shirts*.

Repeat the activity with the remaining sentence pairs. Have students clap when they hear the noun that means "more than one." Have them say what the plural noun is and whether an *s* or *es* was added to the noun to make it plural.

REMIND STUDENTS THAT. . .

- nouns are words that name people, places, and things.
- verbs are action words; they tell what happens.
- adding *s* or *es* to a noun makes it mean "more than one."

☑ **MONITOR PROGRESS** Display or distribute Student Page S345. Read each word aloud and ask: How can you change the noun so it means "more than one" of this item?

desk desks	bus buses	dish dishes
window windows	pen pens	wall walls

IF... students cannot form these regular plural nouns,
THEN... place two desks together, draw two buses, and hold up two pens. In each case, have students tell you what they see.

Lesson 57 Understand Nouns, Verbs, and Prepositions

REMIND STUDENTS THAT. . .

- nouns are words that name people, places, and things.
- prepositions show how nouns are related.

PRACTICE 3: Use Common Prepositions Remind students that prepositions show how nouns are related. Then ask students to explain what they do when they walk from the classroom to outside the school building. As they respond, point out any common prepositions that they use. For example, if they say "The children walk to the door," point out that *to* tells where the noun *children* goes in relation to the noun *door.*

Display or distribute Student Page S346 and read the words aloud.

in	into	under	over
on	to	before	after
with	off	from	for

Say: I am going to choose a preposition and then use it in a sentence. Point to *over.* I know *over* means "across something." I can make a sentence with *over,* such as *I jumped over the puddle.*

Define any unfamiliar words for students. Then encourage them to choose two prepositions and use those prepositions in short sentences. If needed, offer sentence frames, such as *I ate* _______ *the party* or *Casey is* _______ *Tennessee.*

☑ **INDEPENDENT PRACTICE** Display or distribute Student Page S346, and read aloud the following sentence frames for students. Then have them choose a preposition to complete each sentence. Answers may vary, but make sure students use appropriate prepositions.

Some children go _______ the playground.
The kitten jumped _______ the couch.
I eat breakfast _______ my family _______ I leave the house.

IF... students cannot choose an appropriate preposition,
THEN... review the list on Student Page S346 and have students practice making a sentence for each preposition.

Lesson 57 **Understand Nouns, Verbs, and Prepositions**

Henrik hid under the desk.

Drake built a boat.

The boy sees six concerts.

Lesson 57 **Understand Nouns, Verbs, and Prepositions**

Fish ________________.   ________________ walk.

Cars ________________.   ________________ run.

Children   sing.

Cats   play.

Birds   jump.

Lesson 57 Understand Nouns, Verbs, and Prepositions

Bill has one shirt. Jim has two shirts.

Leah has nine boxes. Kim has one box.

The family has one car. The police department has ten cars.

Tuesday is one day. A week has seven days.

desk ________ bus ________ dish ________

window ________ pen ________ wall ________

Lesson 57 Understand Nouns, Verbs, and Prepositions

in	into	under	over
on	to	before	after
with	off	from	for

Some children go ______ the playground.

The kitten jumped ______ the couch.

I eat breakfast ______ my family ______ I leave the house.

Lesson 58 Understand Pronouns and Adjectives

INTRODUCE Tell students that nouns are words that name people, places, or things. Say: Now you will learn about some words that help to tell more about nouns. Adjectives are words that describe nouns. Pronouns are words that we sometimes use to take the place of nouns in sentences.

MODEL Display or distribute Student Page S347 and read it aloud.

Tom has a big box.
He puts toys in the box.
Now it is heavy!
The toys are his.
He will keep them in the box.

TEACH Say: Adjectives are words that tell about nouns. I will reread the first sentence. Listen for the word that tells "what kind of" box. Read aloud "Tom has a big box," emphasizing the word *big*. Ask: What kind of box is it? (*big*) Yes, *big* tells about the noun *box*. *Big* is an adjective.

Reread the second sentence. Ask: Who is this second sentence talking about? (Tom) That's right. The author is talking about Tom. But the author did not use the word Tom in this sentence. What word did the author use instead? Point out the word *He*. Explain: *He* is a pronoun. Pronouns are words that take the place of nouns. The word *he* replaces Tom's name.

Tell students that there is a pronoun and an adjective in the third sentence. Then read the sentence aloud. Guide students to find the pronoun and adjective *it* and *heavy*. Say: I see the word *it*. *It* is a pronoun. What noun do you think *it* stands for in this sentence? (*box*) Yes, *it* stands for *box*. What word in this sentence describes what *it* (the box) is like? (*heavy*) Yes, *heavy* describes the noun *box*. *Heavy* is an adjective.

Point out the words *a* and *the* in the first and second sentences. Explain that these are special adjectives called articles. Say: You will learn more about articles, adjectives, and pronouns in the rest of this lesson.

OBJECTIVES:

- Understand that adjectives are words that describe nouns.
- With assistance, identify and use adjectives and articles to describe nouns.
- Understand that pronouns are words that replace nouns.
- With assistance, use pronouns correctly, including subjective, objective, and possessive cases.

Lesson 58 Understand Pronouns and Adjectives

REMIND STUDENTS THAT. . .

- a noun is a word that names a person, place, or thing.
- an adjective is a word that tells about a noun.
- *a, an,* and *the* are special words that come before a noun.
- the article *the* comes before a specific noun or a noun that is more than one.
- the article *a* comes before a word beginning with a consonant.
- the article *an* comes before a word beginning with a vowel.

PRACTICE 1: Adjectives and Articles Explain: Adjectives are words that tell about nouns. They tell size, color, shape, or how many. Display or distribute Student Page S348.

red ball	nice girl	tiny bug
tall man	five stars	hot pan
_____ rabbit	_____ car	_____ day

Read the first item aloud. Point to the word *ball*. Say: A ball is a thing, so *ball* is a noun. What word tells about the ball? (*red*) Yes. *Red* is the adjective that describes *ball*. It tells the color of the ball. Repeat the process for the remaining items in the first and second rows.

Read the nouns in the third row and guide students to suggest an adjective for each (for example: *soft, fast, sunny*). List the adjectives on the board. Sort them into categories, such as color, shape, size, number, or how something feels (texture).

Display the chart at the bottom of Student Page S348. Say: The little words *a, an,* and *the* are special words that come before a noun. They are called articles.

a	***an***	***the***
a bee	**an apple**	**the boy, the boys**

1. I see _____ birds. (the)
2. One bird has _____ worm. (a)
3. That bird has _____ egg. (an)
4. _____ little bird sings. (The)

Read the articles and the examples in the top row of the chart. Say: Use *a* before a word that begins with a consonant sound. Use *an* before a word that begins with a vowel sound. Use *the* to name a specific noun or a noun that names more than one person, place, or thing. Read aloud each sentence and guide students to use the correct article in each sentence.

☑ **MONITOR PROGRESS** Display and read aloud the following sentences: *I see the cat. It is a fat cat.* Have students identify the articles (*the, a*) and the adjective (*fat*).

IF... students need support identifying articles and adjectives,
THEN... remind students that articles are the little words *a, an,* and *the*. Guide them to identify the noun. (*cat*) Ask: What word tells about the cat? (*fat*)

Lesson 58 Understand Pronouns and Adjectives

PRACTICE 2: Subject and Object Pronouns Explain that pronouns are words that take the place of nouns. Display or distribute Student Page S349.

Subject Pronouns		Object Pronouns	
I	I see Max.	me	Max sees me.
you	You see Max.	you	Max sees you.
he	He sees Max.	him	Max sees him.
she	She sees Max.	her	Max sees her.
it	It sees Max.	it	Max sees it.
we	We see Max.	us	Max sees us.
they	They see Max.	them	Max sees them.

Explain that the subject of a sentence is the person, animal, or thing that does the action. Read aloud the subject pronouns. As you read, point to yourself, students, and objects to demonstrate meaning. Say: We use these words when the pronoun is doing the action. Read aloud the first sentence. Point to see. See is the action word. Point to *I*. In this sentence, *I* does the action (I see), so *I* is the subject pronoun. Repeat for the remaining subject pronouns.

Explain that the object of a sentence is the person, animal, or thing that the action is happening to. Read the object pronouns aloud, following the same procedure as above. Display the sentences on Student Page S349.

1. The girl jumps. (She Him)
2. Mom hugged Ben. (her him)
3. Dogs run. (They It)
4. Max likes Sam and Jen. (he them)

Model replacing a noun with a pronoun. Read aloud sentence 1. Ask: Is "The girl" doing the action in this sentence? (Yes. The girl *jumps*.) We need a subject pronoun that fits with *girl*. Yes, we can replace *The girl* with *She*. *She* jumps. Repeat for sentence 2.

REMIND STUDENTS THAT. . .

- pronouns take the place of nouns.
- some pronouns act as the subject in a sentence.
- some pronouns act as the object in a sentence.

MONITOR PROGRESS Have students complete sentences 3 and 4.

IF... students have difficulty choosing the correct pronoun,
THEN... guide students to determine who or what is doing the action.

Lesson 58 Understand Pronouns and Adjectives

REMIND STUDENTS THAT. . .

- pronouns take the place of nouns.
- some pronouns show who or what owns or has something.

PRACTICE 3: Possessive Pronouns Review that pronouns take the place of nouns. Say: Some pronouns show who or what owns or has something. These words are called possessive pronouns. Display or distribute Student Page S350.

Who has or owns the hat?	
I own the hat.	The hat is **mine**.
You own the hat.	The hat is **yours**.
He owns the hat.	The hat is **his**.
She owns the hat.	The hat is **hers**.
It has the hat.	The dog has **its** hat.
They own the hat.	The hat is **theirs**.
We own the hat.	The hat is **ours**.

Say: We can tell who has or owns something by the possessive pronoun that is used. Read the first example. Point to the boldfaced pronoun *mine*. Point to yourself. Say: If *I* own the hat, the hat is *mine*. I use the possessive pronoun *mine*. Read the second example and continue explaining in the same manner. Then display the second half of Student Page S350.

1. The man has a bag. The bag is ____. (his hers)
2. The boys eat apples. The apples are ____. (his theirs)
3. I wear boots. The boots are ____. (yours mine)
4. The girl sat in a seat. The seat is ____. (hers ours)

Model using possessive pronouns in sentences. Read aloud sentence 1. Point to the words *man* and *bag*. Ask: Who has the bag? (the man) Point to the two possessive pronouns in parentheses. If it is the man's bag, should we use the pronoun *his* or *hers*? (*his*) Guide students to complete sentences 2 and 3.

☑ **INDEPENDENT PRACTICE** Have students complete sentence 4.

IF… students have difficulty choosing the correct possessive pronoun,
THEN… point to the subject *The girl*. Ask: Whose seat is it? Is the seat hers? Is the seat ours?

Lesson 58 Understand Pronouns and Adjectives

Tom has a big box.
He puts toys in the box.
Now it is heavy!
The toys are his.
He will keep them in the box.

Lesson 58 Understand Pronouns and Adjectives

red ball	**nice girl**	**tiny bug**
tall man	**five stars**	**hot pan**
______ rabbit	**______ car**	**______ day**

a	***an***	***the***
a bee	**an apple**	**the boy, the boys**

1. I see __________ birds.
2. One bird has __________ worm.
3. That bird has __________ egg.
4. __________ little bird sings.

Lesson 58 Understand Pronouns and Adjectives

Subject Pronouns		Object Pronouns	
I	I see Max.	**me**	Max sees me.
you	You see Max.	**you**	Max sees you.
he	He sees Max.	**him**	Max sees him.
she	She sees Max.	**her**	Max sees her.
it	It sees Max.	**it**	Max sees it.
we	We see Max.	**us**	Max sees us.
they	They see Max.	**them**	Max sees them.

1. The girl jumps. (She Him)
2. Mom hugged Ben. (her him)
3. Dogs run. (They It)
4. Max likes Sam and Jen. (he them)

Lesson 58 Understand Pronouns and Adjectives

Who has or owns the hat?

I own the hat.	The hat is **mine**.
You own the hat.	The hat is **yours**.
He owns the hat.	The hat is **his**.
She owns the hat.	The hat is **hers**.
It has the hat.	The dog has **its** hat.
They own the hat.	The hat is **theirs**.
We own the hat.	The hat is **ours**.

1. The man has a bag. The bag is ______. (his hers)
2. The boys eat apples. The apples are ______. (his theirs)
3. I wear boots. The boots are ______. (yours mine)
4. The girl sat in a seat. The seat is ______. (hers ours)

Lesson 59 Capitalize and Punctuate Sentences

INTRODUCE Remind students that a noun is a word that names a person, place, or thing, and that a verb is an action word. Say: A sentence usually has a noun (or pronoun) and a verb. So a sentence tells about an action and a person, place, or thing. A sentence always starts with a capital letter and ends with a punctuation mark.

MODEL Display or distribute Student Page S351. You may wish to point out that the art includes Spanish punctuation marks (the inverted question mark and inverted exclamation point) that are placed in front of sentences in Spanish. In English, sentence punctuation appears only at the end of sentences. Read aloud each sentence for students.

OBJECTIVES:

- Recognize sentences.
- Begin a sentence with a capital letter.
- End a sentence with a punctuation mark.
- Capitalize the pronoun *I*.

Whales swim.	Birds fly.	Bugs crawl.
Dogs eat food.	Where is Kat?	Now I will eat.

TEACH Reread the top row of sentences for students. Each of these groups of words is a sentence. Each sentence has a noun: *Whales, Birds, Bugs*. Each sentence has a verb: *swim, fly, crawl*. These sentences are two words long. The first word starts with a capital letter. Write *W* and *B* on the board. There is a period at the end of each sentence. Make a dot on the board.

Next, read aloud the sentence *Dogs eat food*. This is also a sentence. It has more than one noun. Write *Dogs* and *food* on the board. This sentence has at least one noun and one verb (*eat*). Read aloud *Where is Kat?* This sentence is a question. It ends with a question mark, not a period. Write a question mark on the board. Read aloud and write *Now I will eat*. This sentence has a capital letter for the first word, *Now*, as well as a capital *I*. *I* is a word for a person. It is always capitalized. When you write about yourself, capitalize the word *I*.

Lesson 59 Capitalize and Punctuate Sentences

REMIND STUDENTS THAT...

- a sentence begins with a capital letter and ends with a punctuation mark.
- the word *I* is always capitalized.

PRACTICE 1: Capitalization in Sentences Remind students that a sentence tells about an action and a person, place, or thing. Then say: A sentence always begins with a capital letter. Some words inside a sentence can also have a capital letter. The word *I* is always capitalized.

Next, display or distribute Student Page S352.

You have rice.
I have noodles.
What game can I play?

Read the first sentence aloud and ask: Which word has a capital letter? (*You*) Next, read the second sentence aloud and ask: Which word has a capital letter? (*I*) Say: In this sentence, *I* is the first word so it is capitalized, but remember that the word *I* is always capitalized. Finally, read the third sentence aloud and ask: How many words should be capitalized in this sentence? (two) Which word or words should be capitalized? (*What* and *I*)

MONITOR PROGRESS Display Student Page S352 and read the sentences aloud.

lions roar.
yet i am not afraid.
are you afraid?

Have students identify which letters should be capitals in the sentence and the question. (the *l* in *lions*, the *y* in *yet*, the word *I*, and the *a* in *are*)

IF... students do not correctly name the capital letters,
THEN... review the definition of a sentence and capitalization of the word *I*.

Lesson 59 Capitalize and Punctuate Sentences

PRACTICE 2: Identify and Use End Punctuation Say: A sentence always ends with punctuation, or a mark that tells you the sentence has ended. These sentences show three different punctuation marks.

Display or distribute Student Page S353.

Our power is out.
This is an emergency!
Who can we call to get it fixed?

Reread the first sentence and circle the period. One mark is the period. It tells you that you have come to the end of a thought. Read aloud the second sentence and circle the exclamation mark. Another type of mark is the exclamation mark. It tells you that the sentence says something loudly or with strong feeling. Finally, read aloud the third sentence and circle the question mark. The question mark tells you that the sentence asks a question. Explain that punctuation helps readers understand the meaning of a sentence.

Extend the activity by writing *Have a good day* on the board. Write a period and then say: This sentence is a simple thought. Erase the period and write an exclamation mark. Now this sentence shows excitement. Erase the exclamation point and write a question mark. Now this sentence is asking a question. Explain that by changing the mark, writers can make the same words either a statement, an exclamation, or a question. You may want to point out, though, that usually a question has several different words or a different order of words than a statement does. "Have a good day" as a question would probably be asked, "Will you have a good day?"

REMIND STUDENTS THAT...

- a sentence begins with a capital letter, and the word *I* is always capitalized.
- a sentence ends with punctuation.
- a question ends with a question mark.

☑ **MONITOR PROGRESS** On the board, draw a question mark, an exclamation mark, and a period. Have students make up a sentence for each of the marks.

IF... students confuse the exclamation mark and the period,
THEN... explain that exclamation marks are only for sentences that have a lot of feeling or excitement, and have students give a new sample exclamation.

Lesson 59 Capitalize and Punctuate Sentences

REMIND STUDENTS THAT…

- a sentence begins with a capital letter, and the word *I* is always capitalized.
- a sentence ends with a punctuation mark.
- a period shows the end of a thought, an exclamation point shows loudness or a strong feeling, and a question mark shows that the writer is asking a question.

PRACTICE 3: Form and Punctuate Questions Say: People ask questions all the time, such as *Which book is the best?* or *May I have some water, please?* You know how to ask questions, too. Questions begin with a capital letter and end with a question mark.

Display Student Page S354 and read aloud the first two sentences.

Who wants a cheese sandwich?
Where can I buy some cheese?
I wish I knew why we are out of bread.

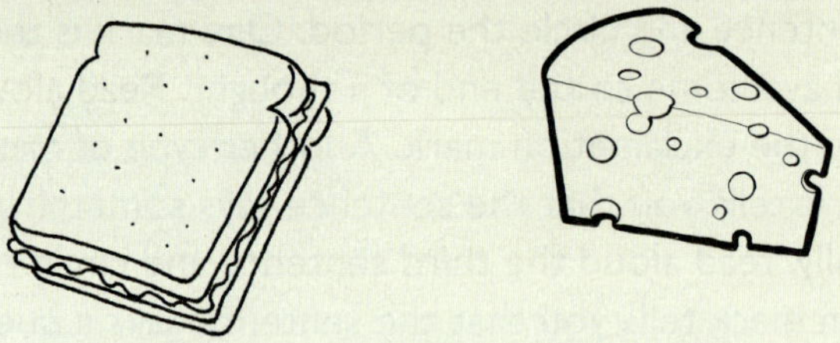

Have students identify the capital letters in each question. Ask: What punctuation mark always comes at the end of a question? (question mark) Read aloud the third sentence. How can you turn this sentence into a question? Guide students to form the question. Say: If I remove the first four words and move the word *are*, then I create the question *Why are we out of bread?*

Extend the activity by helping students form questions using statements such as *I want to know what your name is* or *I want to know if you have any brothers or sisters.*

☑ **INDEPENDENT PRACTICE** Display Student Page S354. Read each line aloud.

when will we get home
i'd like to know which sport you want to play

Ask: Which letters should be capitalized? What mark should be at the end of each line? How could you change the second line into a question?

IF… students cannot form a question from a statement,
THEN… explain that to turn a statement into a question, some words are moved and removed. Suggest that students listen for a word that begins with the /w/ sound and use it to begin the question.

Lesson 59 Capitalize and Punctuate Sentences

Whales swim. Birds fly. Bugs crawl.

Dogs eat food. Where is Kat? Now I will eat.

Lesson 59

Capitalize and Punctuate Sentences

You have rice.

I have noodles.

What game can I play?

lions roar.

yet i am not afraid.

are you afraid?

Lesson 59 Capitalize and Punctuate Sentences

Our power is out.

This is an emergency!

Who can we call to get it fixed?

Lesson 59 Capitalize and Punctuate Sentences

Who wants a cheese sandwich?

Where can I buy some cheese?

I wish I knew why we are out of bread.

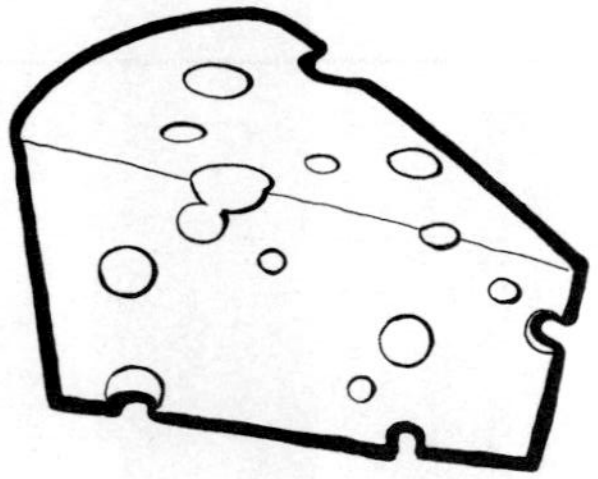

when will we get home

i'd like to know which sport you want to play

ASSESSMENT
LESSONS 57–59

Language and Conventions

ASSESS MASTERY Use this Checkpoint to assess students' mastery of the Level A language and conventions skills listed here.

ADMINISTER THE TEST Administer the Checkpoint orally to each student.

1. Read aloud the passage on the following page.
2. Read questions 1–5, reread the relevant text as necessary, and have students respond. Check their answers using the scoring chart.

SCORING

SKILL/LESSON	ANSWER	SCORE
1. Understand Nouns, Verbs, and Prepositions (Lesson 57)	Nouns: *dog, cat* Verb: *ran* Preposition: *after*	_____ / 4
2. Understand Pronouns and Adjectives (Lesson 58)	Adjectives: *happy, sleepy* Article: *the*	_____ / 3
3. Understand Pronouns and Adjectives (Lesson 58)	Pronouns: *I, them*	_____ / 2
4. Capitalize and Punctuate Sentences (Lesson 59)	Why did it do that?	_____ / 1
5. Capitalize and Punctuate Sentences (Lesson 59)	the first letter	_____ / 1

An overall score of 80% is typically considered mastery. Use your judgment and your individual students' needs as well to determine skill mastery.

IF... you determine that students have not demonstrated sufficient mastery of one or more skills,
THEN... review needed skills, going back to the lessons to reteach and scaffold as needed.

ASSESSMENT
LESSONS 57–59

Language and Conventions

A Good Game

by Becky Garcia

The dog ran after the cat. Why did it do that? The dog was sleeping. The happy cat scratched the sleepy dog's nose. The dog was mad! However, chasing was a good game. The animals had a fun run. I saw them go fast!

1. In the first sentence, what are the nouns? What is the verb? What is the preposition?
2. In the fourth sentence, which words are adjectives? Which word is an article?
3. In the last sentence, what are the pronouns?
4. Which sentence in the story ends with a question mark?
5. Which letter is capitalized in each sentence?

Lesson 60 Inquiry and Research

INTRODUCE Tell students that to learn about a topic, they can do research. Say: Sometimes you are asked to write about something you know. But sometimes you may be asked to write, draw, or tell about something you do not know as much about. You can do research to get the information you need. Begin your research by asking questions. This helps you figure out what you need to know.

MODEL Display Student Page S357 and read it aloud.

Prompt: Give information about whales. Draw and describe a whale.

Whales	
What I Know	**What I Want to Know**
Whales are big. Whales live in water. Whales have a spout. 	What do whales eat? How big do whales get? Why do whales have a spout?

TEACH Point out that an important step in doing research is asking questions. A chart helps you figure out what you know and what you don't know about your topic. Ask: What is the topic? (whales) You can ask yourself what you already know about whales. This students knows that whales are big, live in water, and have a spout. Point out the second column. Say: This student has thought of three questions about whales. Explain that the student will have to do research to find the answers to these questions. Say: After you make a list of questions, you can form a research plan. A plan will help guide you to find the answers.

Guide students to name some print or digital sources of information, such as books, magazines, or websites. Offer additional suggestions, such as asking an expert or visiting a marine center. Share examples of classroom books and resources on different topics.

OBJECTIVES:

- Generate questions for inquiry and develop and follow a research plan.
- Identify and gather sources to answer questions about a topic.
- Understand and use information from sources to write, tell, or draw about a topic.

Lesson 60 Inquiry and Research

REMIND STUDENTS THAT. . .

- they can ask questions to help them narrow a research topic.
- making a research plan helps guide their research and keeps them focused on the topic.

PRACTICE 1: Ask Questions and Develop a Research Plan Say: To learn about a topic, first ask questions and then use your questions to help you make a plan to find the answers. Let's find out how Kim asked questions and made a plan to write about bees. Display Student Page S358 and read it aloud.

Prompt: Draw and write about honey bees.

What I Know	What I Want to Know
Bees are small. Bees make honey. Bees like flowers.	1. Where do bees live? 2. How do bees make honey? 3. What does a bee look like up close?

Kim's Research Plan:

1. Find a book that tells where honey bees live.
2. Ask my uncle, the beekeeper, how bees make honey.
3. Find a picture that shows a honey bee.

Point to the chart. Say: Kim already knows several things about bees. She can ask questions to figure out what she wants to know about bees. For example, she knows that bees make honey, but she doesn't know how they make honey. Explain that thinking about what you know and what you want to know helps you have a focus when you make your research plan.

Then say: Now let's talk about Kim's research plan. To find out where bees live, she will find a book that will answer her question. Point out that to learn how bees make honey, she will ask her uncle. Say: We can often find answers in books, but we may also get answers from experts, or people who know about a topic. Read Kim's third question. Why do you think Kim wants to know what a bee looks like up close? (She wants to draw a picture of a bee.)

MONITOR PROGRESS Have students think of a question they might ask about honey bees or another insect.

IF... students cannot come up with a question,
THEN... review a few things they know about honey bees and then model asking a related question. For example: How far can a bee fly?

Lesson 60 Inquiry and Research

PRACTICE 2: Identify and Gather Information Explain that part of research is figuring out what information you need and then finding it. Say: You can find information, such as words and pictures that tell about your topic, in sources. Sources can be books, magazines, newspapers, websites, and people who know a lot about a topic.

Display or distribute Student Page S359. Explain that Kim has several sources of information about bees.

Kim's Sources		
Read Books	**Look at Websites**	**Talk to Experts**
Bees Around the World Life in the Hive	"Let's Look at Honey Bees"	Beekeeper, Uncle Cal

Remind students of Kim's prompt: *Draw and write about honey bees.* Read aloud the chart and point out each type of source.

Say: Kim found two picture books about bees. She wants to learn more about where bees live. Point out the website and ask: How will a website help Kim learn about honey bees? (She can see pictures and videos of bees to help her when she draws a bee.)

Explain that Kim's uncle is an expert because he keeps bees. When Kim talks to her uncle, she will ask him questions. What kinds of questions do you think Kim should ask? Guide students with questions, such as: Why do bees like flowers? How do they make honey?

REMIND STUDENTS THAT. . .

- research means gathering or bringing information together.
- information comes from sources.
- a chart can be helpful in organizing sources and information that you need.

✓ **MONITOR PROGRESS** Reread the sources on Student Page S359 and ask: Which source will help Kim find out what bees do in a hive? (Book: Life in the Hive)

IF... students cannot identify the source,
THEN... point out each source, reading aloud the title of each. Ask guiding questions to help students understand what kind of information they could expect to find in each source.

Lesson 60 Inquiry and Research

REMIND STUDENTS THAT. . .

- they can use information from their sources to answer questions about their topic.
- they can write down or draw pictures of what they learn from each source.

PRACTICE 3: Understand and Use Information Remind students how Kim asked questions, made a research plan, and chose sources. Explain that the next step is to understand and use the information.

Display or distribute Student Page S360 and read it aloud.

Kim's Sources	Information
Books: Bees Around the World; Life in the Hive	Bees live and work in a hive. A hive has lots of small holes. A queen bee lays eggs in the hive.
Website: "Let's Look at Honey Bees"	Bees have wings and big eyes. They have a long tongue for getting nectar.
Expert: Beekeeper, Uncle Cal	Bees fly to flowers to get nectar. They take it back to the hive. They store nectar in the holes. The nectar turns to honey.

Tell students that Kim found different words and pictures about her topic in each source. Say: When you look at sources, you can write down or draw what you learn. Ask: What did Kim learn from the books? Reread the information in the first row and pause for a response. Ask: How do you think Kim will use the information from the website? (She can draw a picture of a bee.) Ask students to discuss how Uncle Cal's information will be useful to Kim. Emphasize that Kim can use what she learned from her sources to draw and write about bees.

☑ **INDEPENDENT PRACTICE** Have students tell, write, or draw one thing they learned about bees from the information in Kim's sources.

IF... students have difficulty identifying what they learned,
THEN... review the sources and the information in the chart. Give students sentence frames such as: *I learned that bees live in ____. I found out that a bee has ____.*

Lesson 60 Inquiry and Research

Whales	
What I Know	**What I Want to Know**
Whales are big. Whales live in water. Whales have a spout. 	What do whales eat? How big do whales get? Why do whales have a spout?

Prompt: Draw and write about bees.

What I Know	What I Want to Know
Bees are small. Bees make honey. Bees like flowers.	1. Where do bees live? 2. How do bees make honey? 3. What does a bee look like up close?

Kim's Research Plan:

1. Find a book that tells where honey bees live.
2. Ask my uncle, the beekeeper, how bees make honey.
3. Find a picture that shows a honey bee.

Lesson 60 Inquiry and Research

Kim's Sources

Read Books	Look at Websites	Talk to Experts
Bees Around the World Life in the Hive	"Let's Look at Honey Bees"	Beekeeper, Uncle Cal

Kim's Sources	Information
Books: Bees Around the World Life in the Hive	Bees live and work in a hive. A hive has lots of small holes. A queen bee lays eggs in the hive. 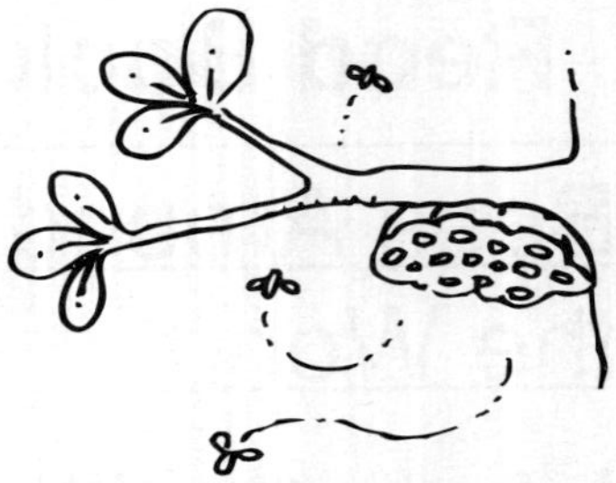
Website: "Let's Look at Honey Bees"	Bees have wings and big eyes. They have a long tongue for getting nectar. 
Expert: Beekeeper, Uncle Cal	Bees fly to flowers to get nectar. They take it back to the hive. They store nectar in the holes. The nectar turns to honey. 

ASSESSMENT LESSON 60 — Inquiry and Research

ASSESS MASTERY Use this Checkpoint to assess students' mastery of inquiry and research skills.

ADMINISTER THE TEST Administer the Checkpoint orally to each student. Distribute copies of Teacher Page T362. Read aloud the prompt and sources. Then read aloud questions 1–5 and have students respond. Check their answers using the scoring chart.

1. What are two things you already know about airplanes?
2. What do you want to know about airplanes?
3. What is a question you could ask about airplanes?
4. Which would be the best source to help you draw a picture of an airplane?
5. Which would be the best source to help you learn what it is like to fly an airplane?

SCORING

SKILL/LESSON	ANSWER	SCORE
1. Inquiry and Research (Lesson 60)	Answers will vary. Sample Answers: Airplanes are machines. Airplanes have wings. Airplanes can fly.	____ / 2
2. Inquiry and Research (Lesson 60)	Accept any relevant answers. Sample Answers: I want to know how airplanes fly. I want to know about different kinds of airplanes. I want to know how to draw an airplane.	____ / 1
3. Inquiry and Research (Lesson 60)	Accept any relevant answers. Sample Answers: How does an airplane fly? What are some different kinds of airplanes? What does an airplane look like?	____ / 1
4. Inquiry and Research (Lesson 60)	Picture book: <u>Kinds of Airplanes</u>	____ / 1
5. Inquiry and Research (Lesson 60)	Expert: Talk to an airplane pilot.	____ / 1

An overall score of 80% correct is typically considered mastery. Use your judgment and your individual students' needs as well to determine skill mastery.

IF... you determine that students have not demonstrated sufficient mastery of one or more skills,
THEN... review the skill(s), going back to the lessons to reteach and scaffold as needed.

ASSESSMENT
LESSON 60

Inquiry and Research

Prompt: Draw and write about airplanes.

Sources

Picture Book:	Kinds of Airplanes 
Website:	"Things that Fly"
Expert:	Talk to an airplane pilot.